GREAT WESTERN
RAILWAY
STATIONS
1947

A PHOTOGRAPHIC & TRACK DIAGRAM SURVEY

PART TWO

(NUMBERS 721 - 1612)

THE WIRRAL, WELSH BORDERS AND WALES

A PHOTOGRAPHIC & TRACK DIAGRAM SURVEY
OF STATIONS UNDER GREAT WESTERN OR
GREAT WESTERN JOINT OWNERSHIP

R. J. SMITH

PORT SUNLIGHT   N. 1957
Facing Down (Birkenhead)   H.B.Priestley

NANTYDERRY   N. c.1958
Facing Up (Hereford)   J.Beardsmore

LLANYMYNECH   S. 1962
Facing Up (Newtown)   M.M.Lloyd

Issue A
31st July 2015

First published in 2015 by Robin Smith

ISBN 978-0-9567317-1-5

Printed in Great Britain by
Amadeus Press
Cleckheaton

CONTENTS

CONDOVER
North showing some detail of the Up shelter.

ACKNOWLEDGEMENTS

I am extremely grateful to everyone who has helped me, no matter how little, in producing this book.
I include in this, all the books and publications I have sourced. All the photographers whose photographs I have either used, or studied to assist in the details of the track diagrams. The collectors who have kindly allowed me to use their photographs. Finally, all those who have given assistance with information to ensure, I hope, an historically accurate account of the stations during 1947.

I acknowledge the assistance, in alphabetical order, of ;
Austin Attewell, Audie Baker, Mike Bentley, Rod Blencowe, Stewart Blencowe, Paul Bolger, W. R. Burton,
C. L. Caddy, Roger Carpenter, R. M. Casserley, Terry Cole, R. A. Cooke, P. Coutanche, Hugh Davies,
Edward Dorricott, John Gale, The Great Western Trust, Keith Greenwood, The Historical Model Railway Society,
Barry Hoper, Industrial Railway Society, D. K. Jones, Tony Jones, Patrick Kingston, Jon Maden, Milepost 92½,
David Postle, Michael Quick, R.G.Simmonds, Signalling Record Society, The Stephenson Locomotive Society,
Jeremy Suter, Garth Tilt, Terry Walsh, Laurence Waters, Welsh Railways Research Circle, M. Whitehouse,
S. Wolstenholme and Alan Wycherley.
I also acknowledge the photographs I have used where I have sought unsuccessfully to find the photographer.
Many of these I have had for a number of years before photographs normally had information on the back.
Although I suspect a number are from the Lens of Sutton Collection.

ONIBURY
An impression of a view South East, Down towards Hereford

INTRODUCTION

This Book is the second part of a Photographic and Track Diagram survey of Great Western Railway Stations which were open for passengers in 1947. Also included are several former passenger stations still open for goods traffic. It is designed to give an overview of all Great Western and Great Western Joint stations of that period.

The order of the survey follows that of Great Western Railway Stations (and Great Western Joint Stations) 1941-1947, Published in 2005. Due to the large number of stations, the series is divided in two parts. Part One, published in 2011 covers all stations in the South, South West and Midlands. It covers numbers 1 to 720. This part covers all stations in the Wirral, Welsh Borders and Wales. It covers numbers 721 to 1612.

The survey is designed to give an overview of each station, for the historian, railway modeller, or general public. It can be used to give a quick reference to the architecture used on certain lines, or by certain railway companies. Anyone wishing to find a more detailed analysis of most stations can refer to the numerous branch line, or main line books or articles which have been published. Even the internet can be a good source for detailed analysis of some stations.

It would be virtually impossible to obtain photographs of each station in 1947. So most station photographs show the station similar to its appearance in 1947. Most stations did not change significantly, and many were photographed in the late 1950's and early 1960's. An analysis of any significant variation of the photograph shown and the station in 1947, can be found in Appendix B.

Unfortunately it has not been possible to obtain a photograph of every station for Part Two. There are several stations for which there is no known photograph. I have taken the liberty in some cases, to make a sketch based on known photographs, resembling how the station may have looked based on the limited data available.

For the track diagrams I gratefully acknowledge the use of R.A.Cooke's Track Diagrams of the GWR. I have used many other sources to ensure the track diagrams are correct for 1947. That includes many photographs to assist in this respect, resulting in some interesting anomalies to the previously printed diagrams. An example being at Treherbert. Sometimes the track layout has changed regularly so it has been difficult to establish the actual layout in 1947. Minor discrepancies like single or double slips are not shown, but there is a list of more major discrepancies in Appendix B.

I appreciate the help too, from various sources which have assisted me with the historic data and track diagrams.

I have set out the data as accurately as I can and in good faith. My main concern is the data supplied is accurate for historical reasons. In some cases I have had to make a decision as to the most accurate data. This has not always been easy as no one particular source of information has been found to be totally accurate, even official publications have discrepancies. Those who have my first book Great Western Railway Stations (and Great Western Joint Stations) 1941 – 1947, ISBN 0953 4775 5X, will notice changes on some station dates and many gaps filled in. These I have been collating over the years and more recently I acknowledge the help of Michael Quick's book Railway Passenger Stations in Great Britain A Chronology.

If anyone can provide information on any anomalies or missing dates then I would be very grateful to hear from them.

I am extremely grateful to all the photographers who had the foresight to photograph all the stations. Many of these stations are no longer in existence, or look very different today. I also appreciate all the numerous photographers and collectors for allowing me to use their photographs. A full list can be found in Appendix E.

To complete this survey I have used much of the railway literature in my possession. I acknowledge all those authors' whose publications I have used. I hope it is appreciated that it is not possible to give a list.

I would also like to thank those at Kidderminster Railway Museum who have been so supportive of my efforts. I also appreciate the assistance from members of the Welsh Railways Research Circle.

Finally, I hope those who use this book find it a useful source of information, for whichever purpose they intend. I know of no other publication where all Great Western Railway Stations can be found in one publication series.

Robin Smith
Kidderminster Railway Museum
January 2015

JORDANSTON HALT   S. 1959
Facing Up (Clarbeston Road)   F.A.Blencowe

STATION TYPES IN THE SURVEY

This survey contains Great Western and Great Western Joint Stations which were open for passengers in 1947. Also included are several former passenger stations still open for goods traffic.

Shown are; Passenger stations open to the public, privately, or untimetabled. This includes several stations and halts open for workmens trains, or for special occasions only.

Some stations shown in Great Western Railway Stations (and Great Western Joint Stations) 1941-1947, but which were closed entirely prior to 1947, are listed within the survey, but without a photograph or track diagram. This is to continue the numerical sequence started in this book. Details are not given as some were demolished by 1947. Birkenhead Town, Little Drayton Halt, Wern Hir, Milkwall, Cwmrhyd-y-gau Halt, Port Talbot (Central), Cilfach Goch Colliers Platform, Wainfelin Halt, Cwmffrwdoer Halt, Pentrepiod Halt and Pentwyn Halt.

Stations opened by British Railways on former Great Western lines are not shown.

Also shown are some former passenger stations, still open for goods traffic, where the station building is known to have survived in to 1947. An example being Pont Lliw on the Swansea District Line. This list is however not comprehensive.

FORMAT NOTES

The stations appear in the order defined in the book Great Western Railway Stations (and Great Western Joint Stations) 1941 – 1947. Stations are in sequence on the line they were built.

Each line is defined by the stations it starts and ends at, or in some cases the junction (in lower case).
The official name for the line is given, in some cases there were several when the line continues on to another line. For example Llanelly to Llandilo Line, and Vale of Towy Line.
There then follows the companies associated with the line. The Act of Incorporation date for the line. A brief outline of the various opening and closure dates of the line. However intermediate closure and openings are not always shown. The closure dates generally refer to the last scheduled passengers service, and public goods services. In some cases the line may still have remained open for a specific type of private freight. The survey only refers to the general status of the line. (Note that closure dates normally follow the survey order of the line, hence some closure dates will not be in chronological order).

A map showing the general location of the lines which start on the two open pages in view is also given.

Nearly every station has a track diagram and photograph or sketch (except 9) associated with it.

Some stations have more than one photograph. This is not related to the size of station, but generally occurs where room permits, or the station is not covered well in other literature.

The photographs show the station number, station name (as used at 6th October 1947, or the last name used where stations have been closed earlier.), and the company whose Act of Incorporation authorised the line on which the station lies. (This is not necessarily the company responsible for opening the station).

Underneath this information is the passenger opening date for the station shown. (This is normally public opening, but in some cases this is the initial opening date for private, workmen's trains, or special events). The date shown may not necessarily be the for the original station on that site, if the station has been substantially rebuilt. I have taken the view that if the platforms are in different locations then the later date is shown. Where stations were enlarged with an extra platform or more, the original opening date is shown in the case of Newport (High Street), and Cardiff (General). Some stations are difficult to assess, Magor and Llanwern have the original opening date, not the 1941-1942 rebuilding. Treforest opened in 12/1846, but it was rebuilt in a slightly different location c.1885, so this date is used. Also for Wellington (Salop.), the date of the last major rebuilding is used. Although Greens Siding may have been opened in 1901, the opening date given is 1903, since this is when the platform was built. Foley Park Halt opened in 1905, but was moved to the north side in 1925. Glascoed Halt is shown as 1938, since this is when the replacement timber platform was built on the up side.

The closure date to passengers is shown, generally for the last scheduled public passenger use. The last day of service is shown, or where there is uncertainty, the official closure date. (Although some stations were used after the date shown, such as Kirby Park. However these were on irregular dates only, or in this case, for school trains).
Some stations are shown closed earlier than the recognised date due to being completely rebuilt. These include Jackfield Halt, Crumlin Valleys Colliery Platform for which the rebuilt island platform closed on 06/11/1961, South Pit Halt for which the platform shown closed on 30/10/1964.

The direction the photograph faces is shown, using an eight compass point system. Followed by the year the photograph was taken.

Each photograph has the photographer or collection acknowledged, if known. A full list is shown in Appendix E.

Each station has a track diagram associated with it. This is identified with the station name and its number.
The diagrams follow the line in diagrammatic orientation. So the line will start from left to right, or right to left depending on the lines general orientation (generally with north towards the top of the page) and continue as such. This means that if the line curves significantly then the north compass point, shown on all track diagrams, may face down the page. This compass point should be taken as a general orientation of the station, since many station layouts were on a curve. (Details of the track diagram symbols are given on page xi)

For a more detailed history of each line and the stations associated with it, refer to Great Western Railway Stations (and Great Western Joint Stations) 1941 – 1947, ISBN 0953 4775 5X. It will be noted that some dates shown have been amended here in Part Two as more information has become available. An example being Buttington, which is now shown as closing to passengers in 1960.

ABBREVIATIONS

ABBREVIATION	EXPLANATION
c.	Circa.
CG:	Closed to Goods Traffic (generally public goods).
CMin:	Closed to Mineral Traffic.
CP.	Closed to Passengers (generally public closure date and date of last train).
CPG:	Closed to Passengers and Goods.
E	East.
Exc.	Excluded.
H.L.	High Level.
Jc.	Junction.
Junc.	Junction.
L.L.	Low Level.
N	North.
NE	North East.
NW	North West.
OG:	Opened to Goods Traffic.
OMin:	Opened for Mineral Traffic.
OP:	Opened to Passengers (generally public opening date).
OPG:	Opened to Passengers and Goods (public opening).
ReOP:	Reopened to Passengers.
ReOPG:	Reopened to Passengers and Goods.
R.O.F.	Royal Ordnance Factory
S B.	Signal box
S	South
SE	South East.
SW	South West.
W	West.

TRACK DIAGRAM EXPLANATIONS

The survey shows the Track Diagram of the station as it was in 1947. In some cases there is uncertainty and it is likely to show a later rather than earlier arrangement. This is because most photographs sourced are of a later date.

The Track Diagrams are drawn to give a simple overview of the station layout around the platforms. This often, but not always, includes the goods yard for stations. They show platforms, main and secondary buildings for passenger use, signal boxes, goods sheds, carriage sheds and engine sheds. Other non passenger buildings are shown, but this is not comprehensive. The diagrams are designed to show similarity of layout, so all crossovers etc. are shown the same on all diagrams. In reality of course crossover lengths will vary. Also many stations were on a curve, the diagrams are shown with the main line straight through, and extending either side in a straight line. Since the diagrams are not to scale the track separation is distorted. This requires compromises in showing the layout accurately, for example at Cardiff General and Queen Street.

Note that references to bridges (except where railways cross each other), viaducts, roads etc. are not shown. However, as a change to Part One, diagrammatic representation of footbridges are shown, but not always the direction of the steps. In the case of large stations (Newport (High Street)), or where information is not available, the footbridges are not shown.

Each station has reference to the stations at each end of the line, for that particular survey. At each location where the next station (in capitals) is on another line, the page reference is given. Where there are junctions then the station reference is to a major station on the line referred to, or the end station on that line. It is not normally the next station along that line. Lower case is used to refer to station locations via a goods only line (Ninian Park Halt, although this is an anomaly as the line was used for Football Specials). Non station locations (Butts Branch), or where the line continues to join a non Great Western line, (Whitchurch).

The tracks running off the edge of the diagrams are distinguished by the passenger lines extending further. Where there are junctions with passenger lines, the branch line is indented. The goods loops, sidings, or private lines are all indented from the passenger or running lines.

TRACK DIAGRAM KEY

ABBREVIATION   EXPLANATION

GW&L.M.S.R.Jt.   Great Western & London Midland & Scottish Joint Railway
L.N.E.R.   London & North Eastern Railway
L.M.S.R.   London Midland & Scottish Railway
S.& M.R.   Shropshire & Montgomeryshire Railway

The following symbols have been used. In all cases they are not to scale, but a representation of the location.

SYMBOL   EXPLANATION

Track. In this case, the end of a siding on the right. Lines which continue beyond the extent of the diagram do so as that on the left. Great Western lines only.

Track. Thinner, denoting a non Great Western line. These are other companies, private or military lines or sidings.

Passenger Platforms. They are a representation of length, with minor stations and halts having a progressively shorter length. Curved platforms are always shown straight on the diagrams.
It will be noted that some platforms are shown very short (from Nantgarw Halt). This is because these halts were ground level and only a sleeper or so in length.

Passenger Platforms. Where the dashed line shows there is no platform edge for the line passing beside it. This is only shown where there is likely to be ambiguity.

Main building. In some cases this may not be trackside (Magor). Also shown are main buildings which crossed the line on a road overbridge (Rock Ferry).

Building or shelter, on halts or platforms. Shown smaller, as generally this was just a pagoda.

Secondary building or shelter, generally on a second platform. The buildings shown are for passenger use.

Canopy protection only, with no sides (Tynycwm Halt). To distinguish platforms which have no protective shelter at all (Marine Colliery Platform).

Other buildings, not for passenger use. Not all are shown , especially those in the goods yards. Pagodas and other metal sheds are not shown.

Former passenger buildings, no longer in use, or on lines closed to passengers (Llanycefn).

Signal box. The line denotes the line of levers, the signalman standing behind.
Only covered conventional signal boxes are shown. Signal boxes demoted to ground frames are not shown with this symbol, but are shown with the 'other building' symbol (Rogerstone).

Carriage Shed.

Engine Shed.

Goods Shed.

Tunnel. In this case double track. The track inside the tunnel is hatched.

Turntable. There are two sizes, the larger for engines, and the smaller for wagons.

North symbol. This should be taken as a general indication, since most stations were on a curved layout. For diagrammatic reasons the layouts are all in a straight line.

Footbridge, across two tracks. In this case the step direction is shown. More complex step arrangements (as at Onibury), or where step arrangements are uncertain, are not shown.

NORTH WALES

KEY

1038 PWLLHELI — Station Number and Name

367 — Page Number for Stations along this Section of Line

———— Passenger Lines

———— Goods Only Lines

———— Goods Lines (not in survey), Lines (shown in Part One)

740 BIRKENHEAD (WOODSIDE)
268
271
270
725 HELSBY
747 HOOTON
752 CHESTER
279
739 WEST KIRBY
273
277
287
758 WREXHAM
1117 WREXHAM CENTRAL
777 BRYMBO
288
761 RUABON
392
393
1104 ELLESMERE
284
308
846 WESTBURY (SALOP.)
1097 LLANYMYNECH
309
1093 BUTTINGTON
851 MINSTERLEY
298
388
1034 LLANGOLLEN
768 GOBOWEN
1100 OSWESTRY
289
1029 CORWEN
367
1128 LLANGYNOG
1133 LLANFYLLIN
398
400
387
1089 ABERMULE
1134 KERRY
1088 NEWTOWN
997 BALA
365
358
1011 BLAENAU FFESTINIOG
373
361
1014 DOLGELLEY
379
1070 DINAS MAWDDWY
1079 CEMMES ROAD
1078 MACHYNLLETH
1086 MOAT LANE JUNCTION
384
1137 LLANIDLOES
402
404
1147 BUILTH WELLS
1057 BARMOUTH
1050 HARLECH
371
1038 PWLLHELI
377
1064 ABERDOVEY
381
1071 ABERYSTWYTH
445
1276 ABERAYRON
446
443
1256 LAMPETER
295
313
318
321
885 BEWDLEY
934 WORCESTER (FOREGATE STREET)
917 BROMYARD
292
794 MARKET DRAYTON
291
802 WELLINGTON (SALOP.)
873 BUILDWAS
863 MUCH WENLOCK
314
323
893 TENBURY WELLS
330
776 SHREWSBURY
316
819 CRAVEN ARMS & STOKESAY
823 WOOFFERTON
825 LEOMINSTER
302
824
326
898 TITLEY
902 NEW RADNOR

SOUTH WALES

318
321
314
323
298
885 BEWDLEY
863 MUCH WENLOCK
819 CRAVEN ARMS & STOKESAY
934 WORCESTER (FOREGATE STREET)
893 TENBURY WELLS
917 BROMYARD
330
332
334
924 LEDBURY
337
939
946 ROSS-ON-WYE
339
408
348
982 BERKELEY ROAD
351
1159 GRANGE COURT
972 CINDER-FORD
977 LYDNEY TOWN
355
344
342
956 MONMOUTH (TROY)
304
835 ABERGAVENNY JUNCTION
962 USK
1166 CHEPSTOW
412
1169 SEVERN TUNNEL JUNCTION
823 WOOFFERTON
825 LEOMINSTER
824
302
829 HEREFORD (BARRS COURT)
328
832 PONTRILAS
904 PRESTEIGN
326
898 TITLEY
902 NEW RADNOR
406
1154 THREE COCKS JUNCTION
1564 TALYLLYN JUNCTION
550
1607 BLAENAVON
1594 EBBW VALE
545
1173 NEWPORT (HIGH STREET)
1175 CARDIFF (GENERAL)
501
1498 CAERPHILLY
1134 KERRY
1089 ABERMULE
1088 NEWTOWN
1086 MOAT LANE JUNCTION
384
1137 LLANIDLOES
402
1147 BUILTH WELLS
1566 BRECON
541
1568 DOWLAIS (CENTRAL)
464
479
482
1417 COWBRIDGE
493
1428 BARRY
498
495
1384 PORTHCAWL
483
1078 MACHYNLLETH
1064 ABERDOVEY
377
381
1071 ABERYSTWYTH
445
443
1256 LAMPETER
446
1302 LLANDOVERY
455
475
476
1307 BRYNAMMAN
458
1187 NEATH (GENERAL)
1191 SWANSEA (HIGH STREET)
440
1276 ABERAYRON
1247 PENCADER
449
1287 CWMMAWR
1199 KIDWELLY
1230 CARDIGAN
1251 NEWCASTLE EMLYN
439
1243 CARMARTHEN
424
1203 WHITLAND
435
433
430
1204 CLYNDERWEN
1208 NEYLAND
1215 FISHGUARD HARBOUR
1205 CLARBESTON ROAD
428
1209 MILFORD HAVEN
426
1242 PEMBROKE DOCK

THE VALLEYS

835 ABERGAVENNY JUNCTION
305
962 USK
346
839 PONTYPOOL ROAD
1595 CWMBRAN
307
1173 NEWPORT (HIGH STREET)
1607 BLAENAVON
556
470
557
551
1584 ABERBEEG
1589 NANTYGLO
550
1582 CRUMLIN (L.L.)
553
547
1575 RISCA
545
413
504
1448
1447 CARDIFF (CLARENCE ROAD)
CARDIFF (BUTE ROAD)
1175 CARDIFF (GENERAL)
534
520
528
519
1442 PENARTH
501
1594 EBBW VALE
1550 NEW TREDEGAR
537
1506 BARGOED
468
1337 HENGOED (H.L.)
1539 MACHEN
1510 RHYMNEY
526
539
1535 DOWLAIS (CAE HARRIS)
532
523
1458 ABERCYNON
1525 SENGHENYDD
529
527
1498 CAERPHILLY
1494 CORYTON HALT
1453 RADYR
506
500
1430 CADOXTON
1426 BARRY PIER
541
1559 PONTSTICILL JUNCTION
509
531
1480 OLD YNYSYBWL HALT
1465 PORTH
1457 PONTYPRIDD
492
1428 BARRY
498
496
544
1568 DOWLAIS (CENTRAL)
1463 MERTHYR
470
1475 MAERDY
514
415
1327 HIRWAUN
518
1487 ABERDARE (L.L.)
512
490
1179 LLANTRISANT
493
1417 COWBRIDGE
464
1471 TREHERBERT
1404 NANTYMOEL
1409 PENYGRAIG
490
489
1421 LLANTWIT MAJOR
474
1357 COLBREN JUNCTION
479
1394 ABERGWYNFI
1398 BLAENGARW
487
1387 TONDU
484
1183 BRIDGEND
494
476
481
1390 MAESTEG (CASTLE STREET)
1184 PYLE
482
471
462
1187 NEATH (GENERAL)
1368 ABERAVON (TOWN)
418
483
1384 PORTHCAWL
1307 BRYNAMMAN
477
1185 PORT TALBOT (GENERAL)
1291 PANTYFFYNNON
457
458
460
1191 SWANSEA (HIGH STREET)
421
1287 CWMMAWR
452

GREAT WESTERN RAILWAY STATIONS 1947

A PHOTOGRAPHIC & TRACK DIAGRAM SURVEY

PART TWO

(NUMBERS 721 - 1612)

ISSUE A

31ST JULY 2015

Great Western Railway — Map of the Company's System

Birkenhead Lancashire & Cheshire Junction Railway -
Name changed to Birkenhead Railway (01/08/1859) -
Great Western & LNW Joint Railway (20/11/1860)
ACT: 26/06/1846 (Walton Junction to Chester No.1 Junction)
OP: 18/12/1850
OG: 18/12/1850
CP: OPEN
CG: OPEN

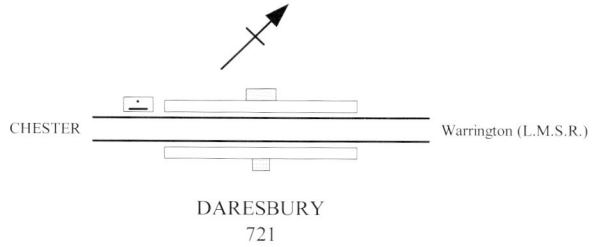

CHESTER — Warrington (L.M.S.R.)

DARESBURY
721

721	**DARESBURY**	[BL&CJR]
OP: 18/12/1850		Photo: NE. 1959
CP: 07/07/1952		Stations U.K.

CHESTER — Warrington (L.M.S.R.)

NORTON (CHES.)
722

722	**NORTON (CHES.)**	[BL&CJR]
OP: 03/1852		Photo: NE. c.1910
CP: 30/08/1952		Stations U.K.

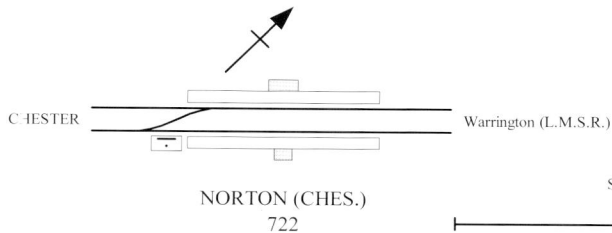

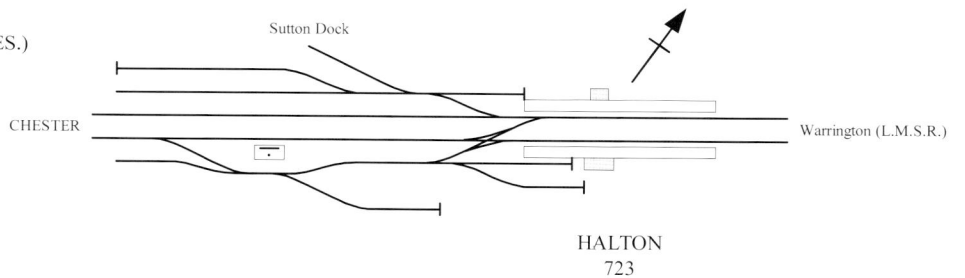

Sutton Dock

CHESTER — Warrington (L.M.S.R.)

HALTON
723

723	**HALTON**	[BL&CJR]
OP: 08/1851		Photo: NE. 1949
CP: 07/07/1952		Stations U.K.

723	**HALTON**	[BL&CJR]
		Photo: SW. 1949
		Stations U.K.

724   **FRODSHAM**   **[BL&CJR]**
OP: 18/12/1850   Photo: NE. 1958
CP: OPEN   R.Carpenter

724   **FRODSHAM**   **[BL&CJR]**
Photo: SW. c.1960
M.J.Lewis

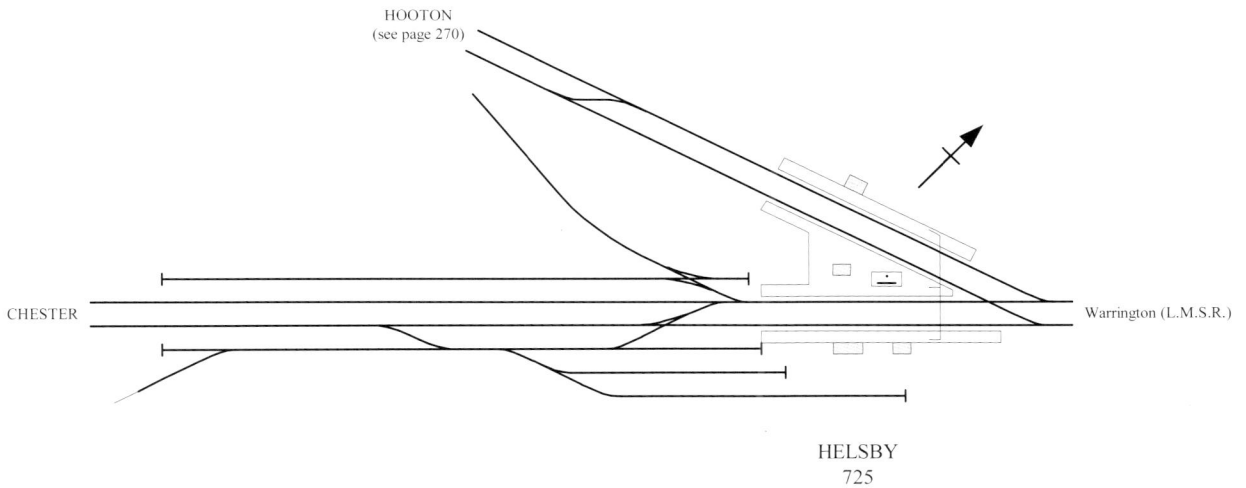

CHESTER

Warrington (L.M.S.R.)

GS

FRODSHAM
724

HOOTON
(see page 270)

CHESTER

Warrington (L.M.S.R.)

HELSBY
725

725   **HELSBY**   **[BL&CJR]**
OP: 09/1852   Photo: SW. c.1910
CP: OPEN   R.Carpenter

725   **HELSBY**   **[BL&CJR]**
Photo: N. c.1960
M.J.Lewis

DUNHAM HILL
726

726   **DUNHAM HILL**   **[BL&CJR]**
OP 18/12/1850   Photo: SW. 1949
CP: 07/04/1952   Stations U.K.

727   **MICKLE TRAFFORD**   **[BL&CJR]**
OP: 02/12/1889   Photo: SW. 1949
CP: 31/03/1951   Stations U.K.

MICKLE TRAFFORD
727

HELSBY (Exc) TO HOOTON
(Exc)
HOOTON & HELSBY LINE
Birkenhead Railway -
Great Western & LNW Joint Railway (20/11/1860)
ACT: 01/08/1859
OP: 01/07/1863
OG: 01/07/1863
CP: OPEN

728   **INCE & ELTON**   **[BirkRly]**
OP: 01/07/1863   Photo: E. c.1910
CP: OPEN   R.Carpenter

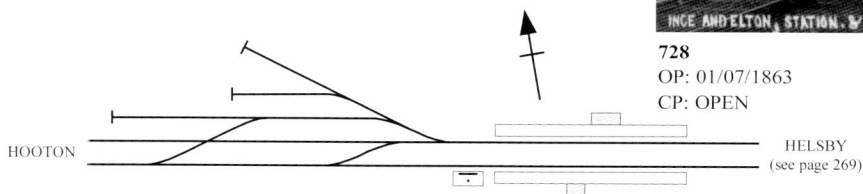

INCE & ELTON
728

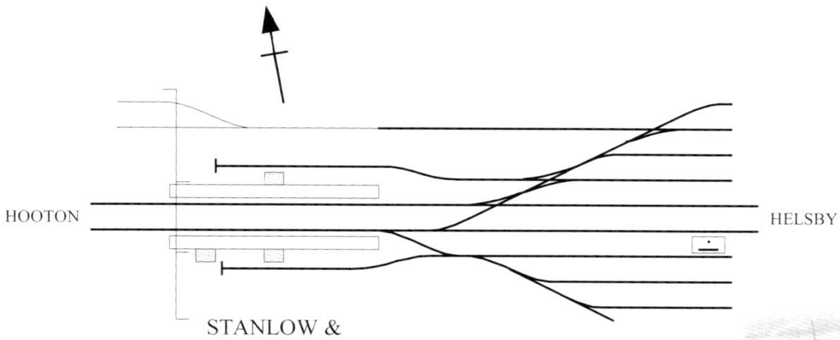

STANLOW &
THORNTON
729

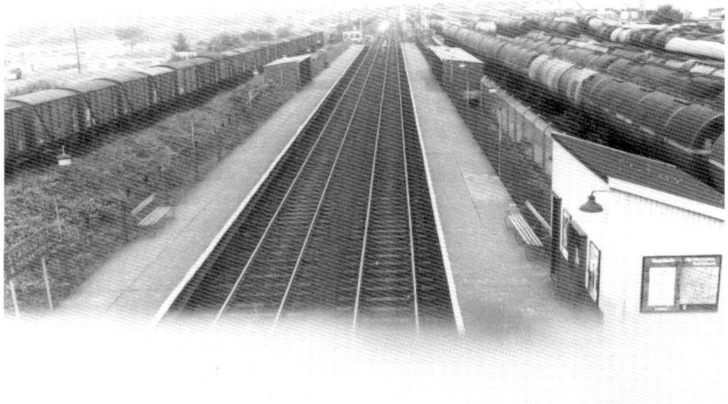

729   **STANLOW & THORNTON**   **[BirkRly]**
OP: 23/12/1940   Photo: E. 1971
CP: OPEN   Stations U.K.

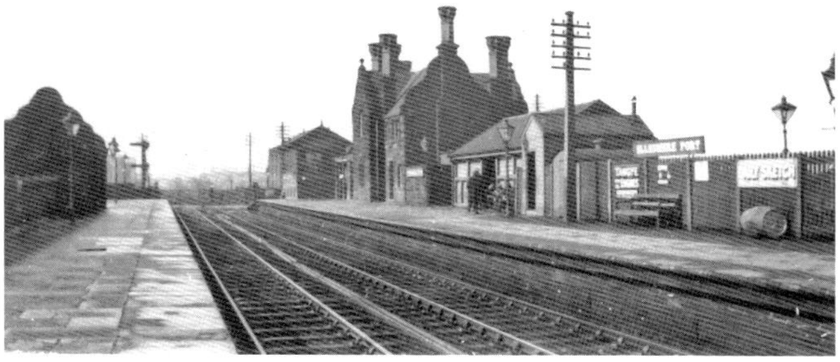

730   **ELLESMERE PORT**   **[BirkRly]**
OP: 01/07/1863   Photo: W. c.1930
CP: OPEN   Stations U.K.

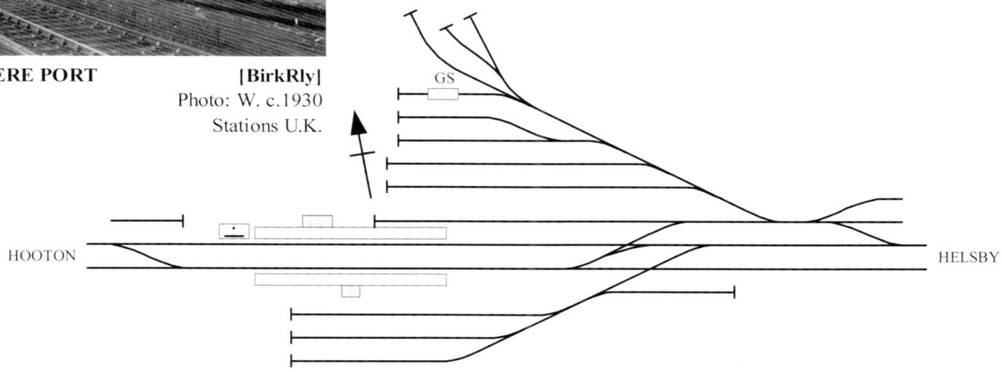

ELLESMERE PORT
730

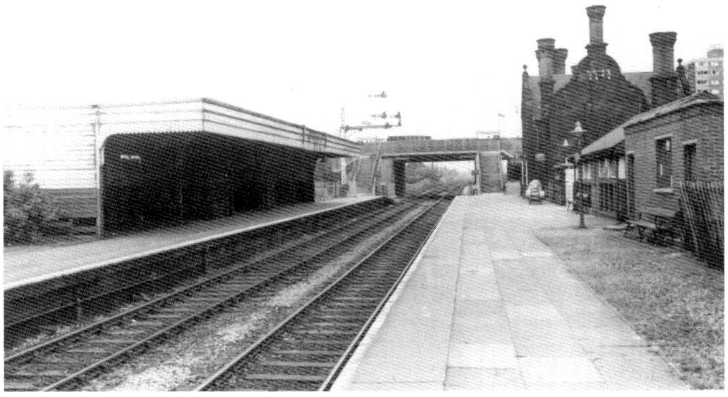

730   **ELLESMERE PORT**   **[BirkRly]**
Photo: W. 1971
Stations U.K.

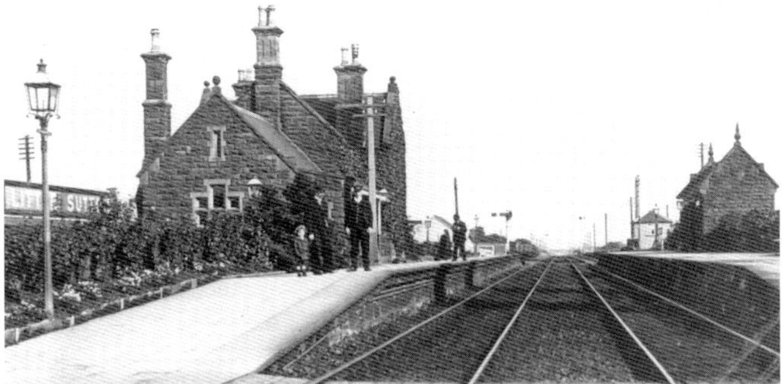

731   **LITTLE SUTTON**   **[BirkRly]**
OP: 01/07/1863   Photo: E. c.1907
CP: OPEN   Stations U.K.

HOOTON
(see page 276)

HELSBY

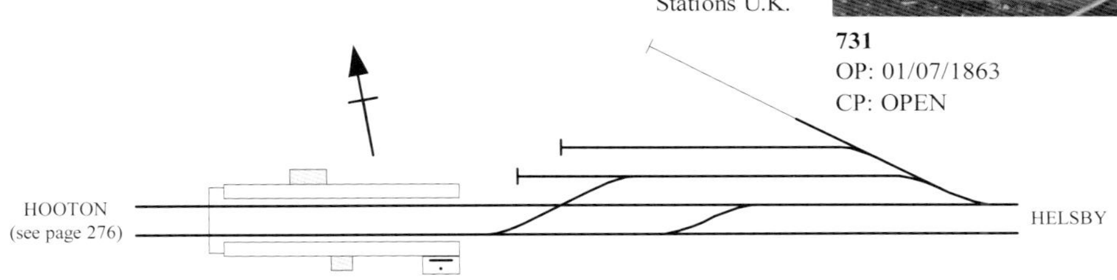

LITTLE SUTTON
731

GREAT WESTERN
RAILWAY
MAP OF THE COMPANY'S SYSTEM

HOOTON (Exc) TO WEST KIRBY
HOOTON & WEST KIRBY LINE
Great Western & LNW Joint Railway
ACT: 17/07/1862 (Hooton to Parkgate)
ACT: 12/07/1882 (Parkgate to West Kirby)
OPG: 01/10/1866 (Hooton to Parkgate)
OPG: 19/04/1886 (Parkgate to West Kirby)
CP: 15/09/1956
CG: 07/05/1962

WEST KIRBY   HOOTON
(see page 276)

HADLOW ROAD
732

732	**HADLOW ROAD**	**[GW&LNWJ]**
OP: 01/10/1866		Photo: E. c.1950
CP: 15/09/1956		Stations U.K.

WEST KIRBY   HOOTON

NESTON
733

733	**NESTON**	**[GW&LNWJ]**
OP: 01/10/1866		Photo: E. 1961
CP: 15/09/1956		Stations U.K.

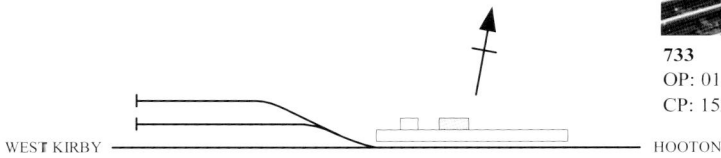

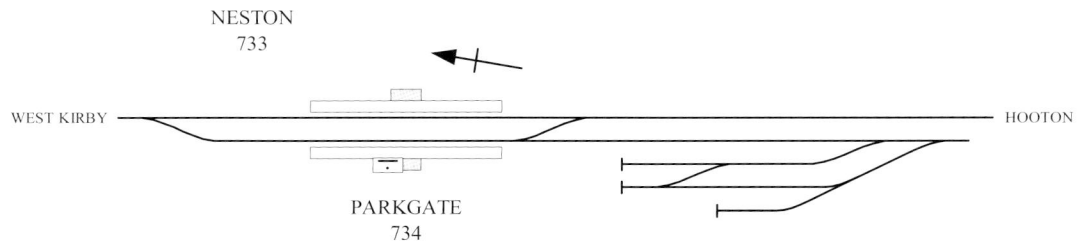

WEST KIRBY   HOOTON

PARKGATE
734

734	**PARKGATE**	**[GW&LNWJ]**
OP: 19/04/1886		Photo: S. 1961
CP: 15/09/1956		Stations U.K.

735	**HESWALL**	**[GW&LNWJ]**
OP: 19/04/1886		Photo: NW. 1960
CP: 15/09/1956		Stations U.K.

HESWALL
735

WEST KIRBY — GS — HOOTON

736
OP: 19/04/1886
CP: 30/01/1954

THURSTASTON [GW&LNWJ]
Photo: SE. 1946
Stations U.K.

736
THURSTASTON [GW&LNWJ]
Photo: SW. 1963
M.M.Lloyd

WEST KIRBY — HOOTON

THURSTASTON
736

WEST KIRBY — HOOTON

CALDY
737

737
OP: 01/05/1909
CP: 30/01/1954

CALDY [GW&LNWJ]
Photo: SE. 1953
Stations U.K.

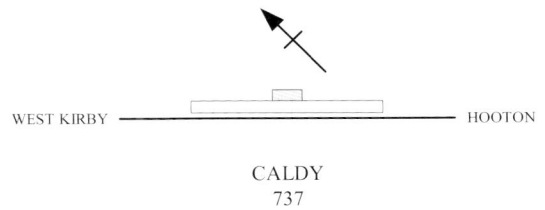

738
OP: 01/10/1894
CP: 05/07/1954

KIRBY PARK [GW&LNWJ]
Photo: N. 1954
Stations U.K.

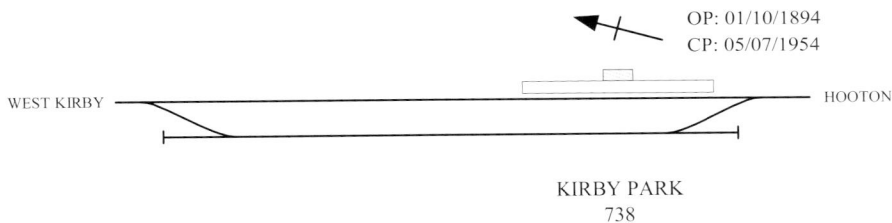

WEST KIRBY — HOOTON

KIRBY PARK
738

(Bidston L.M.S.R.)

HOOTON

(West Kirby L.M.S.R.)   WEST KIRBY
739

739   **WEST KIRBY**   **[GW&LNWJ]**
OP: 19/04/1886   Photo: NW. 1954
CP: 15/09/1956   Stations U.K.

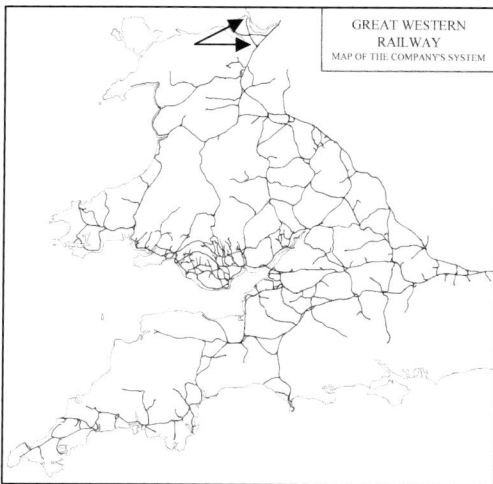

BIRKENHEAD (WOODSIDE) TO CHESTER (GENERAL)
CHESTER & BIRKENHEAD LINE
Great Western & LNW Joint Railway
(Birkenhead (Woodside) to Birkenhead Green Lane Junction)
Chester & Birkenhead Railway -
Birkenhead Lancashire & Cheshire Junction Railway (22/07/1847) -
Name changed to Birkenhead Railway (01/08/1859) -
Great Western & LNW Joint Railway (20/11/1860)
(Birkenhead Green Lane Junction to Chester)
ACT: 31/07/1871 (Birkenhead (Woodside) to Green Lane Junction)
ACT: 12/07/1837 (Birkenhead Green Lane Junction to Chester)
OP: 31/03/1878 (Birkenhead (Woodside) to Green Lane Junction)
OP: 23/09/1840 (Grange Lane to Chester)
OG: 23/09/1840 (Grange Lane to Chester)
CPG: 04/11/1967 (Birkenhead (Woodside) to Green Lane Junction)
CG: OPEN

GREAT WESTERN
RAILWAY
MAP OF THE COMPANY'S SYSTEM

CHESTER

BIRKENHEAD (WOODSIDE)
740

740   **BIRKENHEAD (WOODSIDE)**   **[GW&LNWJ]**
OP: 31/03/1878   Photo: NE. 1948
CP: 04/11/1967   R.G.Nelson

740   **BIRKENHEAD (WOODSIDE)**   **[GW&LNWJ]**
                                                Photo: W. 1960
                                                Stations U.K.

741   **BIRKENHEAD TOWN**   **[C&BR]**
NO INFORMATION AS CLOSED BY 1947
CP: 07/05/1945

ROCK FERRY
742

BIRKENHEAD
(WOODSIDE)

BIRKENHEAD
(WOODSIDE)

(Liverpool
Mersey Railway)

GS

CHESTER

CHESTER

742   **ROCK FERRY**   **[C&BR]**
Photo: N. 1956
Stations U.K.

742   **ROCK FERRY**   **[C&BR]**
OP: 15/06/1891   Photo: S. 1961
CP: OPEN   R.M.Casserley

BIRKENHEAD
(WOODSIDE)

BIRKENHEAD
(WOODSIDE)

CHESTER

CHESTER

BEBINGTON &
NEW FERRY
743

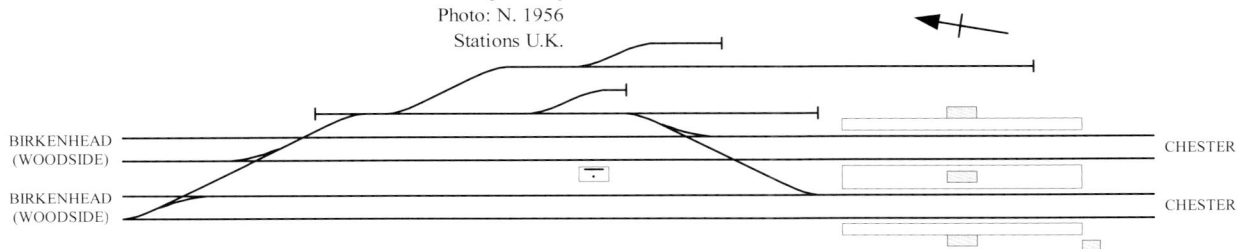

743   **BEBINGTON & NEW FERRY**   **[C&BR]**
OP: 23/09/1840   Photo: S. 1960
CP: OPEN   Stations U.K.

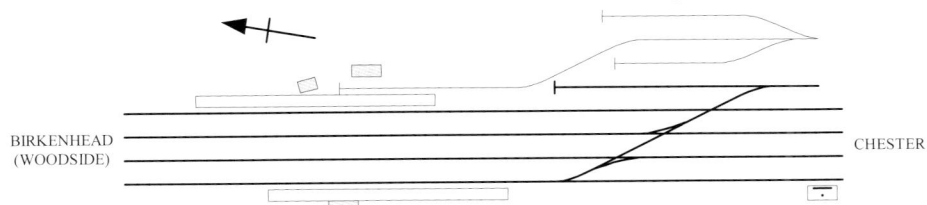

744   **PORT SUNLIGHT**   **[C&BR]**
OP: 04/05/1914   Photo: N. 1960
CP: OPEN   Stations U.K.

BIRKENHEAD
(WOODSIDE)

CHESTER

PORT SUNLIGHT
744

BIRKENHEAD
(WOODSIDE)   CHESTER

BIRKENHEAD
(WOODSIDE)   CHESTER

SPITAL
745

745   **SPITAL**   **[C&BR]**
OP: 30/05/1846   Photo: S. 1960
CP: OPEN   Stations U.K.

BIRKENHEAD
(WOODSIDE)   CHESTER

BIRKENHEAD
(WOODSIDE)   CHESTER

BROMBOROUGH
GS

746 **BROMBOROUGH** **[C&BR]**
OP: 30/05/1846   Photo: N. c.1910
CP: OPEN   Stations U.K.

746 **BROMBOROUGH** **[C&BR]**
        Photo: S. 1961
        R.M.Casserley

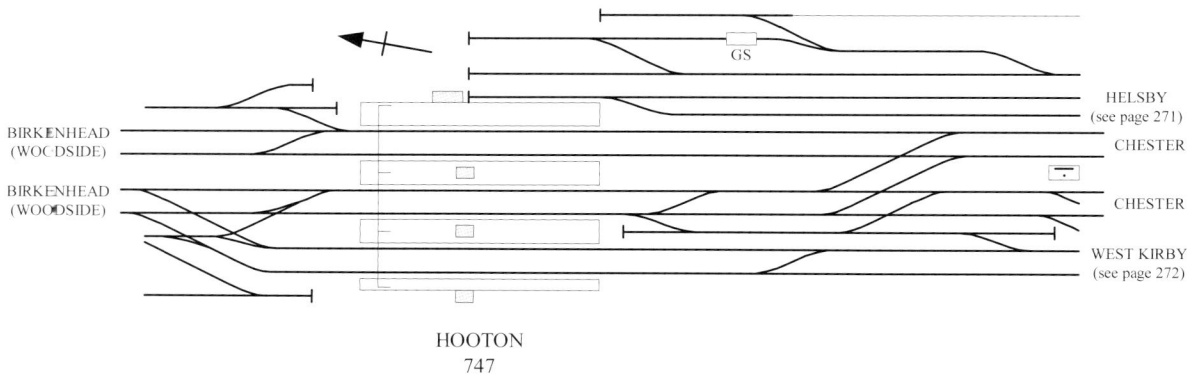

GS

HELSBY
(see page 271)

BIRKENHEAD
(WOODSIDE)   CHESTER

BIRKENHEAD
(WOODSIDE)   CHESTER

WEST KIRBY
(see page 272)

HOOTON
747

747   **HOOTON**   **[C&BR]**
OP: 23/09/1840
CP: OPEN

Photo: N. c.1910
Stations U.K.

747   **HOOTON**   **[C&BR]**
Photo: N. 1956
Stations U.K.

BIRKENHEAD (WOODSIDE) — CHESTER
BIRKENHEAD (WOODSIDE) — CHESTER

LEDSHAM
748

748   **LEDSHAM**   **[C&BR]**
OP: 23/09/1840
CP: 18/07/1959

SE. 1947
Stations U.K.

BIRKENHEAD (WOODSIDE) — CHESTER

CAPENHURST
749

749   **CAPENHURST**   **[C&BR]**
OP: 01/08/1870
CP: OPEN

SE. 1961
R.M.Casserley

749   **CAPENHURST**   **[C&BR]**
NW. c.1960
LOSA

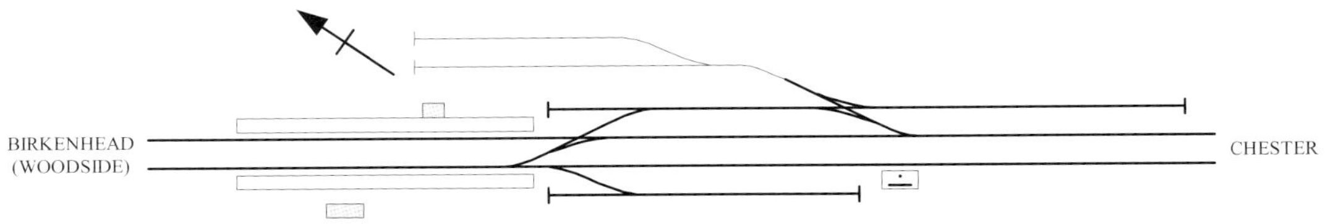

MOLLINGTON
750

750   **MOLLINGTON**   **[C&BR]**
OP: 23/09/1840   NW. 1960
CP: 03/03/1960   Stations U.K.

751   **UPTON-BY-CHESTER HALT**   **[C&BR]**
OP: 17/07/1939   N. c.1965
CP: 09/01/1984   S.Wolstenholme

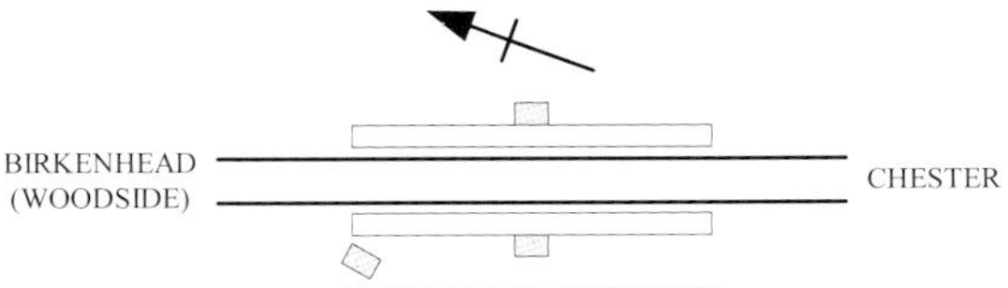

UPTON-BY-CHESTER
HALT
751

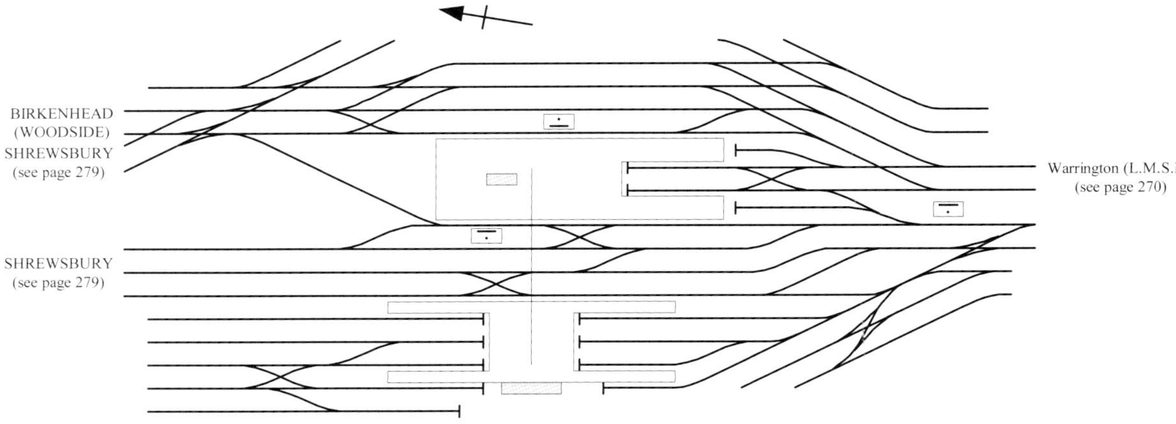

CHESTER (GENERAL)
752

752   **CHESTER**   **[C&BR]**
OP: 01/08/1848   W. 1955
CP: OPEN   Stations U.K.

752   **CHESTER**   **[C&BR]**
E. 1963
I.Travers

GREAT WESTERN
RAILWAY
MAP OF THE COMPANY'S SYSTEM

CHESTER (Exc) TO SHREWSBURY
DIDCOT & CHESTER LINE
North Wales Mineral Railway -
Shrewsbury & Chester Railway (28/08/1846) -
Great Western Railway (01/09/1854)
(Chester to Ruabon)
Shrewsbury Oswestry & Chester Junction Railway -
Shrewsbury & Chester Railway (28/08/1846) -
Great Western Railway (01/09/1854)
(Ruabon to Shrewsbury)
ACT: 06/08/1844 (Saltney Junction to Wrexham)
ACT: 21/07/1845 (Wrexham to Ruabon)
ACT: 30/06/1845 (Ruabon to Shrewsbury)
OPG: 04/11/1846 (Chester to Ruabon)
OPG: 16/10/1848 (Ruabon to Shrewsbury)
CP: OPEN
CG: OPEN

SHREWSBURY — CHESTER (see page 278)

SALTNEY
753

753	**SALTNEY**	[NWMR]
OP: 04/07/1932		N. 1951
CP: 10/09/1960		Stations U.K.

754	**BALDERTON**	[NWMR]
OP: 01/07/1901		N. 1954
CP: 03/03/1952		Stations U.K.

SHREWSBURY — CHESTER

BALDERTON
754

SHREWSBURY — CHESTER

GS

ROSSETT
755

In his early days my father was Station Foreman at Rossett. Later he was at Rossett Signal Box.

755	**ROSSETT**	[NWMR]
OP: 04/11/1846		N. 1960
CP: 26/10/1964		R.G.Nelson

GRESFORD
756

756   **GRESFORD**   **[NWMR]**
OP 04/11/1846   Photo: NE. c.1920
CP: 15/10/1962   LOSA

My father began as a Lad Porter at Gresford.

756   **GRESFORD**   **[NWMR]**
Photo: SW. 1954
Stations U.K.

RHOSROBIN HALT
757

757   **RHOSROBIN HALT**   **[NWMR]**
OP: 01/09/1932   Photo: S. c.1963
CP: 06/10/1947   J.M.Bentley

758   **WREXHAM**   **[NWMR]**
OP: 04/11/1846   Photo: S. 1954
CP: OPEN   Stations U.K.

WREXHAM
758

758 **WREXHAM** **[NWMR]**
Photo: N. 1960
R.G.Nelson

759 **JOHNSTOWN & HAFOD** **[NWMR]**
OP: 01/06/1896
CP: 10/09/1960
Photo: N. 1961
Stations U.K.

My father was a signalman here. The heavy traffic from the Hafod Colliery made it a very busy box

JOHNSTOWN & HAFOD
759

WYNNVILLE
HALT
760

760 **WYNNVILLE HALT** **[NWMR]**
OP: 01/02/1934
CP: 10/09/1960
Photo: S. 1960
M.Hale

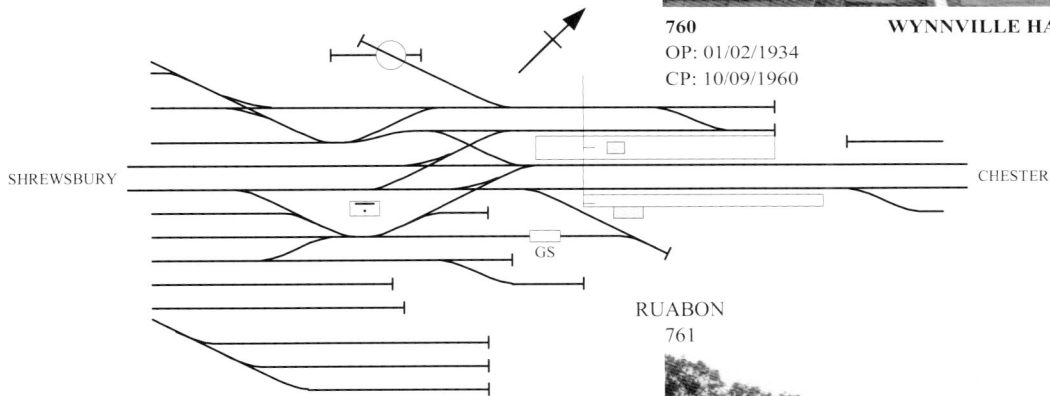

RUABON
761

761 **RUABON** **[NWMR]**
OP: 04/11/1846
CP: OPEN
Photo: SW. 1960
M.Hale

762   **RHOSYMEDRE HALT**   **[SO&CJR]**
OP: 01/09/1906   Photo: NE. 1906
CP: 28/02/1959   Stations U.K.

RHOSYMEDRE
HALT
762

CEFN
763

763   **CEFN**   **[SO&CJR]**
OP: 16/10/1848   Photo: N. 1950
CP: 11/09/1960   Stations U.K.

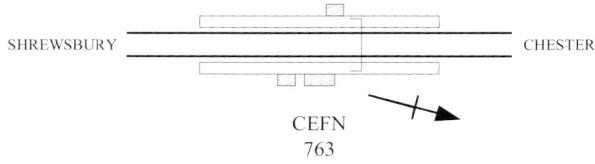

WHITEHURST
764

764   **WHITEHURST**   **[SO&CJR]**
OP: 01/10/1905   Photo: N. 1950
CP: 10/09/1960   Stations U.K.

CHIRK
765

765   **CHIRK**   **[SO&CJR]**
OP: 16/10/1848   Photo: S. 1960
CP: OPEN   R.G.Nelson

765   **CHIRK**   **[SO&CJR]**
       Photo: N. 1937
       R.Carpenter

SHREWSBURY ———————— CHESTER

TREHOWELL
HALT
766

PHOTOGRAPH UNAVAILABLE

766
OP: 27/07/1935
CP: 27/10/1951

TREHOWELL HALT

[SO&CJR]
Photo: None
Available

767
OP: 16/10/1848
CP: 10/09/1960

WESTON RHYN

[SO&CJR]
Photo: N. 1960
R.G.Nelson

SHREWSBURY

WESTON RHYN
767

CHESTER

Ifton Colliery

OSWESTRY
(see page 289)

GS

SHREWSBURY

CHESTER

GOBOWEN
768

768
OP: 16/10/1848
CP: OPEN

GOBOWEN

[SO&CJR]
Photo: SE. 1950
Stations U.K.

768

GOBOWEN

[SO&CJR]
Photo: NW. 1950
Stations U.K.

SHREWSBURY ──────────────────────── CHESTER

WHITTINGTON (L.L.)
769

769 **WHITTINGTON (L.L.)** **[SO&CJR]**
OP: 16/10/1848 Photo: NW. 1956
CP: 11/09/1960 R.G.Nelson

770 **REDNAL & WEST FELTON** **[SO&CJR]**
OP: 16/10/1848 Photo: SE. 1959
CP: 10/09/1960 Stations U.K.

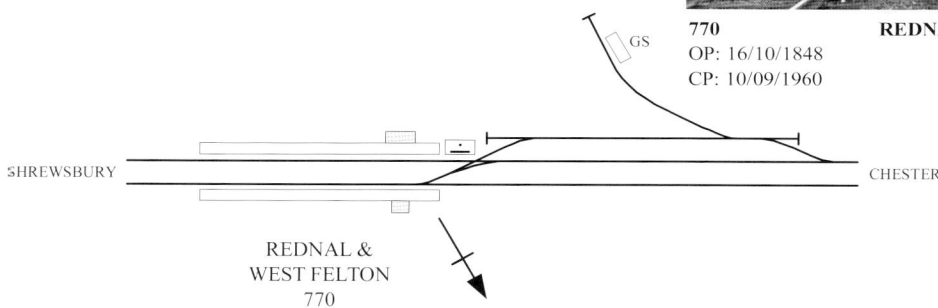

GS

SHREWSBURY ──────────────────────── CHESTER

REDNAL &
WEST FELTON
770

SHREWSBURY ──────────────────────── CHESTER

HAUGHTON
HALT
771

771 **HAUGHTON HALT** **[SO&CJR]**
CP: 22/09/1934 Photo: NW. 1960
CP: 10/09/1960 M.Hale

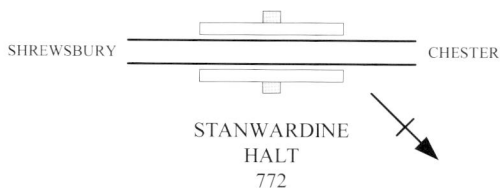

SHREWSBURY ──────────────────────── CHESTER

STANWARDINE
HALT
772

772 **STANWARDINE HALT** **[SO&CJR]**
OP: 27/02/1933 Photo: NW. 1960
CP: 10/09/1960 M.Hale

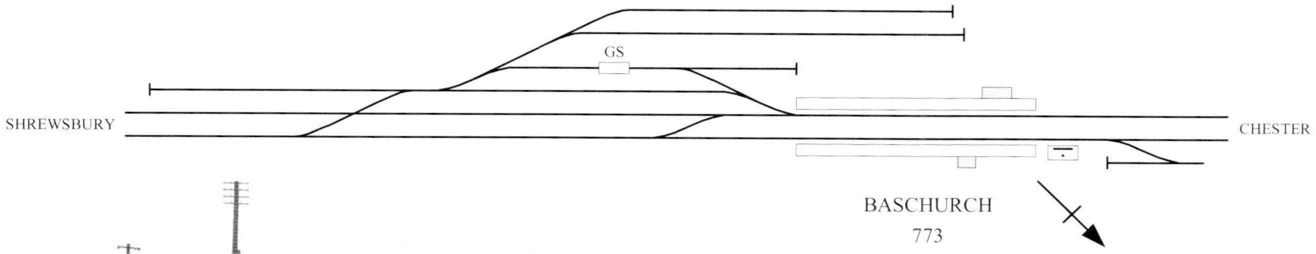

BASCHURCH
773

SHREWSBURY — GS — CHESTER

773   **BASCHURCH**   **[SO&CJR]**
OP: 16/10/1848   Photo: NW. 1960
CP: 10/09/1960   R.G.Nelson

774   **OLDWOODS HALT**   **[SO&CJR]**
OP: 03/07/1933   Photo: SE. 1960
CP: 10/09/1960   M.Hale

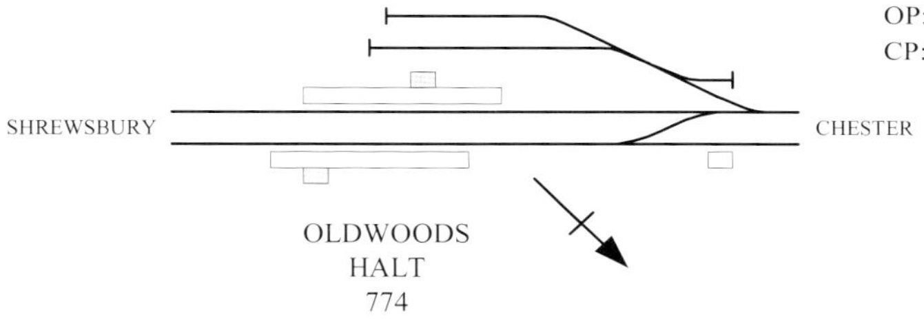

SHREWSBURY — CHESTER

OLDWOODS
HALT
774

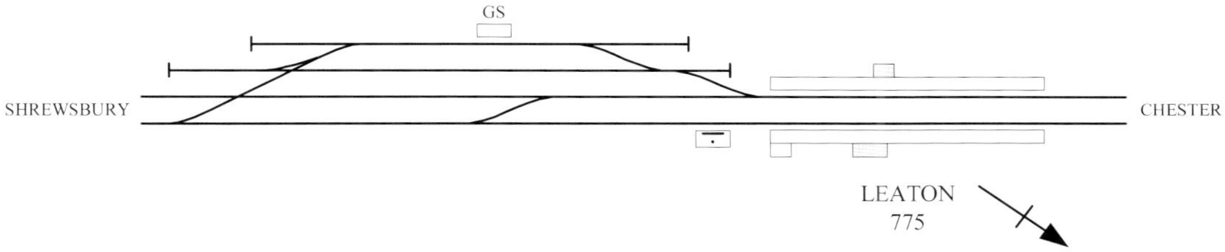

SHREWSBURY — GS — CHESTER

LEATON
775

775   **LEATON**   **[SO&CJR]**
OP: 16/10/1848   Photo: SE. 1950
CP: 10/09/1960   Stations U.K.

775   **LEATON**   **[SO&CJR]**
       Photo: NW. 1963
       P.Garland

HEREFORD
(see page 297)

WOLVERHAMPTON
(see page 293)

WOLVERHAMPTON
(see page 293)

CHESTER

GS

(L.M.S.R. Goods Yard)

(Whitchurch L.M.S.R.)

SHREWSBURY
776

776   **SHREWSBURY**   **[SO&CJR,S&HR]**
OP: 01/06/1849   Photo: SE. 1957
CP: OPEN   F.G.Wood

776   **SHREWSBURY**   **[SO&CJR,S&HR]**
Photo: NW. 1958
F.G.Wood

GREAT WESTERN
RAILWAY
MAP OF THE COMPANY'S SYSTEM

WREXHAM (Exc) TO Minera (Exc)
WREXHAM & MINERA BRANCH
Wrexham & Minera Railway -
Great Western Railway (31/07/1871)
(Wrexham to Brymbo)
North Wales Mineral Railway -
Shrewsbury & Chester Railway (28/08/1846) -
Great Western Railway (01/09/1854)
(Brymbo to Minera)
ACT: 17/05/1861 (Croes Newydd Junction to Brymbo)
ACT: 21/07/1845 (Brymbo to Minera)
OP: 24/04/1882 (Wrexham to Brymbo)
OP: 15/11/1897 (Brymbo to Coed Poeth)
OG: 22/05/1862 (Wrexham to Brymbo)
OG: 07/1847 (Brymbo to Minera)
CP: 31/12/1931 (Wrexham to Coed Poeth)
CP: 27/03/1950 (Brymbo station, trains from Mold)
CG: 01/01/1972 (Brymbo to Minera)
CG: 29/09/1982 (Croes Newydd to Brymbo)

Minera Mineral
Branch

WREXHAM
(see page 280)

BRYMBO
777

777   **BRYMBO**   **[W&MR]**
OP: 24/04/1882   Photo: SE. 1948
CP: 27/03/1950   R.G.Nelson

COED POETH
778
[CLOSED]

778   **COED POETH**   **[NWMR]**
OP: 15/11/1897   Photo: NE. 1959
CP: 31/12/1930   P.Garland

BRYMBO (Exc) TO COED TALON (Exc)
WREXHAM & MINERA EXTENSION LINE
Wrexham & Minera Railway -
Great Western Railway & LNW Joint Railway (11/06/1866)
ACT: 05/07/1865
OP: 15/11/1897
OG: 27/01/1872
CP: 27/03/1950 (Public Services)
CG: 01/05/1952 (Public Goods only)

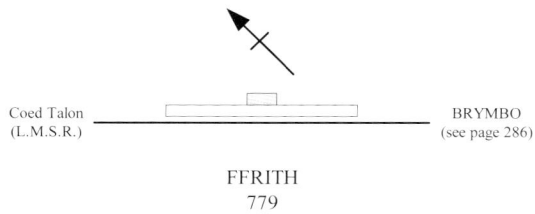

FFRITH
779

779   **FFRITH**   **[W&MR]**
OP: 02/05/1898   Photo: SE. 1953
CP: 27/03/1950   LOSA

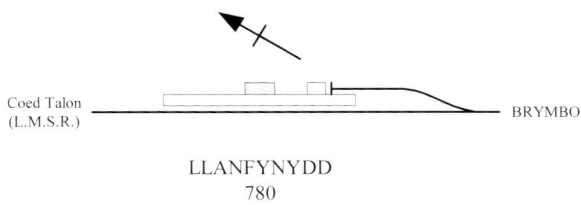

LLANFYNYDD
780

780   **LLANFYNYDD**   **[W&MR]**
OP: 02/05/1898   Photo: SE. c.1910
CP: 27/03/1950   LOSA

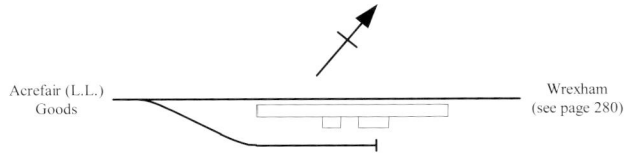

GREAT WESTERN
RAILWAY
MAP OF THE COMPANY'S SYSTEM

WREXHAM (Exc) TO Acrefair
RHOS BRANCH,
PONTCYSYLLTE BRANCH
Great Western Railway
(Rhos Junction to Legacy Junction)
Shropshire Union Railway & Canal Company -
Great Western Railway (01/02/1896)
(Legacy Junction to Acrefair L.L. Goods)
ACT: 20/07/1896 (Rhos Junction to Legacy Junction)
OP: 01/10/1901
OG: 01/10/1901 (Wrexham to Legacy)
OG: 30/01/1867 (Legacy to Pontcysyllte Basin)
CP: 31/12/1930
CG: 14/01/1963 (Rhos Junction to Pant)
CG: 1953 (Pant to Hughes & Lancaster Siding)

Acrefair (L.L.)
Goods

Wrexham
(see page 280)

RHOSTYLLEN
781
[CLOSED]

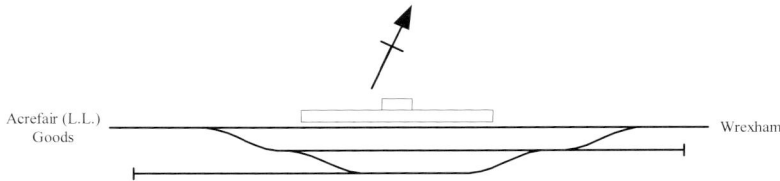

781	**RHOSTYLLEN**	[GWR]
OP: 01/10/1901		Photo: NE. 1949
CP: 31/12/1930		R.Carpenter

Acrefair (L.L.)
Goods

Wrexham

LEGACY
782
[CLOSED]

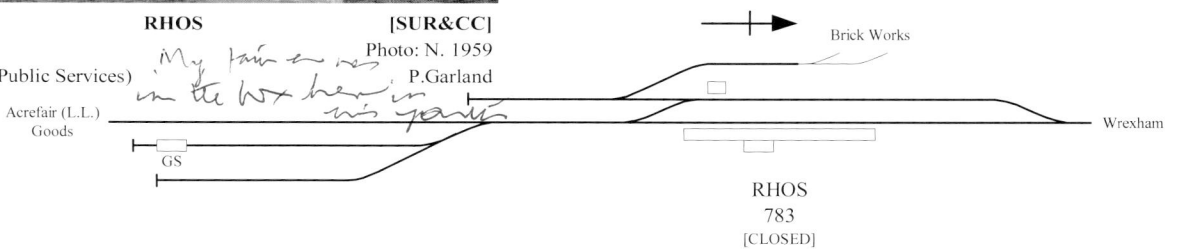

782	**LEGACY**	[GWR]
OP: 01/10/1901		Photo: E. 1957
CP: 31/12/1930		Hugh Davies

783	**RHOS**	[SUR&CC]
OP: 01/10/1901		Photo: N. 1959
CP: 3 /12/1930 (Public Services)		P.Garland

*My fair ... ...
in the box ... in
... ...*

Brick Works

Acrefair (L.L.)
Goods

GS

Wrexham

RHOS
783
[CLOSED]

GOBOWEN (Exc) TO OSWESTRY (Exc)
OSWESTRY BRANCH,
Shrewsbury & Chester Railway -
Great Western Railway (01/09/1854)
ACT: 27/07/1846
OP: 01/01/1849
OG: 01/01/1849
CP: 07/11/1966
CG: 06/12/1971 (Public Goods)

OSWESTRY ————————————————— GOBOWEN
(see page 390)   (see page 283)

PARK HALL
HALT
784

784   **PARK HALL HALT**   **[S&CR]**
OP: 05/07/1926   Photo: NE. c.1959
CP: 07/11/1966   unknown

WELLINGTON (Exc) TO NANTWICH (Exc)
MARKET DRAYTON BRANCH
Wellington & Drayton Railway -
Great Western Railway (30/07/1866)
(Wellington to Market Drayton)
Nsntwich & Market Drayton Railway -
Great Western Railway (01/07/1897)
(Market Drayton to Nantwich)
ACT: 07/08/1862 (Market Drayton Junc. (Wellington) to Market Drayton)
ACT: 07/06/1861 (Market Drayton to Market Drayton Junc. (Nantwich))
OPG: 16/10/1867 (Wellington to Market Drayton)
OPG: 20/10/1863 (Market Drayton to Nantwich)
CP: 07/09/1963
CG: 01/05/1967

WELLINGTON ——————————————— Crewe (L.M.S.R.)
(see page 294)

LONGDON
HALT
785

785   **LONGDON HALT**   **[W&DR]**
OP: 20/10/1934   Photo: N. 1950
CP: 07/09/1963   Stations U.K.

786   **CRUDGINGTON**   **[W&DR]**
OP: 16/10/1867   Photo: S. 1960
CP: 07/09/1963   R.G.Nelson

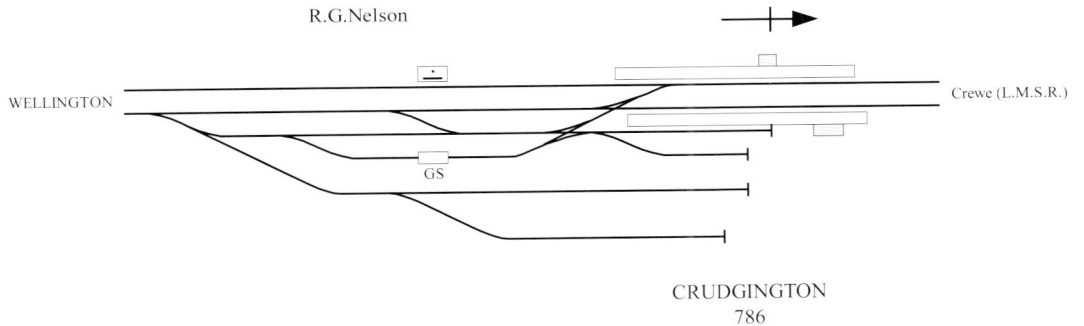

WELLINGTON ——————————————— Crewe (L.M.S.R.)

GS

CRUDGINGTON
786

787   **ROWTON HALT**   **[W&DR]**
OP: 29/06/1935
CP: 07/09/1963   Photo: S. 1957
      H.C.Casserley

WELLINGTON   Crewe (L.M.S.R.)

ROWTON
HALT
787

WELLINGTON   Crewe
(L.M.S.R.)

ELLERDINE
HALT
788

788   **ELLERDINE HALT**   **[W&DR]**
OP: 07/07/1930
CP: 07/09/1963   Photo: S. 1957
      R.M.Casserley

788   **ELLERDINE HALT**   **[W&DR]**
      Photo: N. c.1960
      M.Hale

WELLINGTON   Crewe (L.M.S.R.)

GS

PEPLOW
789

789   **PEPLOW**   **[W&DR]**
OP: 06/1870
CP: 07/09/1963   Photo: N. 1963
      P.Garland

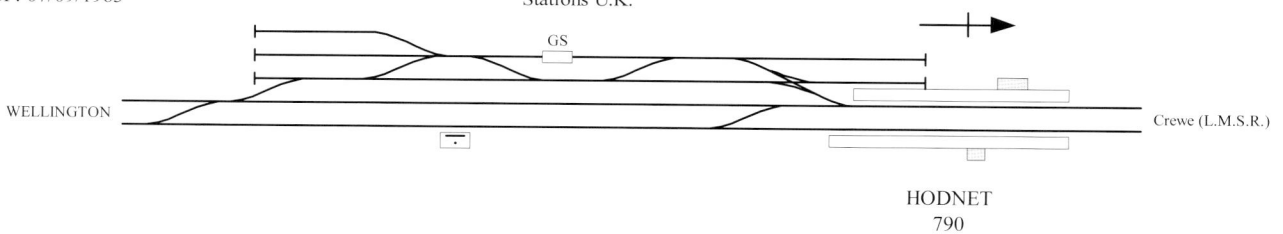

790   **HODNET**   **[W&DR]**
OP: 16/10/1867
CP: 07/09/1963   Photo: S. 1958
      Stations U.K.

GS

WELLINGTON   Crewe (L.M.S.R.)

HODNET
790

WELLINGTON ——————————— Crewe (L.M.S.R.)

WOLLERTON
HALT
791

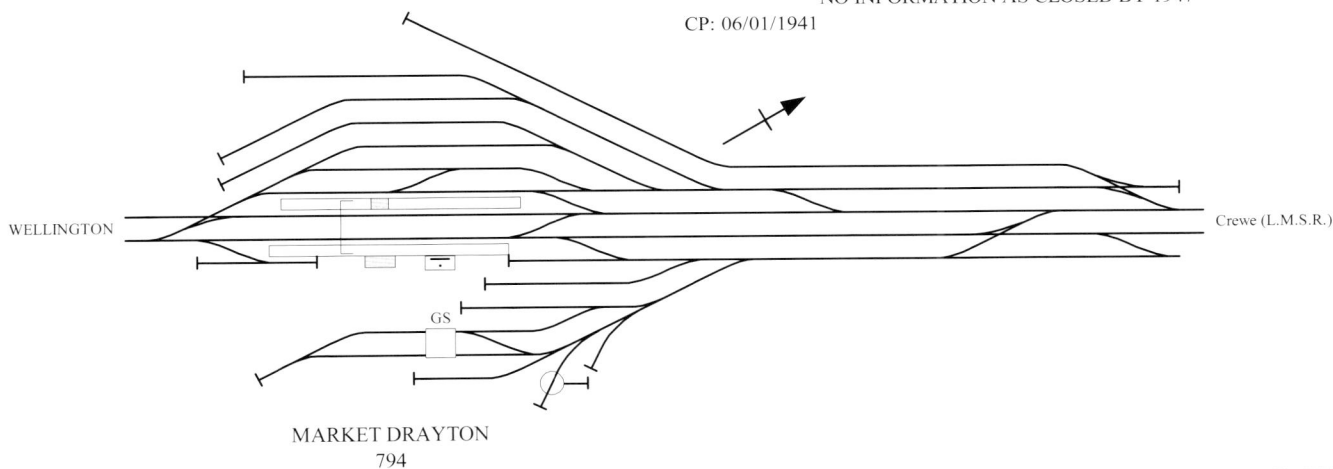

791
OP: 02/11/1931
CP: 07/09/1963

WOLLERTON HALT   **[W&DR]**
Photo: N. c.1964
LOSA

792
OP: 03/04/1899
CP: 08/09/1963

TERN HILL   **[W&DR]**
Photo: S. 1958
Stations U.K.

WELLINGTON ——————————— Crewe (L.M.S.R.)

TERN HILL
792

793   **LITTLE DRAYTON HALT**   **[W&DR]**
NO INFORMATION AS CLOSED BY 1947
CP: 06/01/1941

WELLINGTON ——————————— Crewe (L.M.S.R.)

GS

MARKET DRAYTON
794

794
OP: 20/10/1863
CP: 08/09/1963

MARKET DRAYTON   **[N&MDR]**
Photo: NE. c.1960
A.W.Mace

794
MARKET DRAYTON   **[N&MDR]**
Photo: SW. c.1960
J.Maden Collection

ADDERLEY
795

COXBANK
HALT
796

795   **ADDERLEY**   **[N&MDR]**
OP: 20/10/1863   Photo: S. 1953
CP: 07/09/1963   Stations U.K.

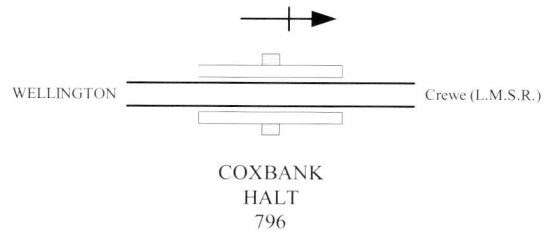

796   **COXBANK HALT**   **[N&MDR]**
OP: 23/06/1934   Photo: S. 1957
CP: 07/09/1963   R.M.Casserley

797   **AUDLEM**   **[N&MDR]**
OP: 20/10/1863   Photo: S. 1957
CP: 07/09/1963   H.C.Casserley

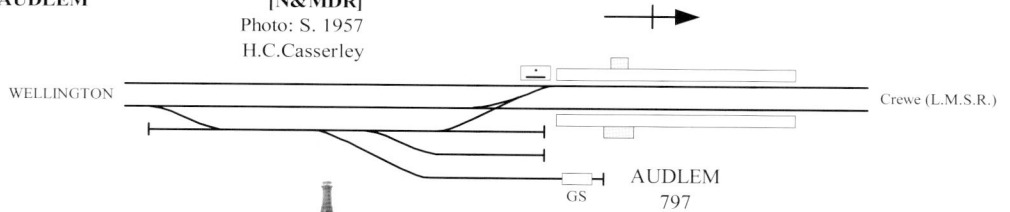

GS

AUDLEM
797

797   **AUDLEM**   **[N&MDR]**
Photo: N. c.1960
M.Hale

COOLE PILATE
HALT
798

798   **COOLE PILATE HALT**   **[N&MDR]**
OP: 17/08/1935   Photo: S. c.1960
CP: 07/09/1963   R.G.Nelson

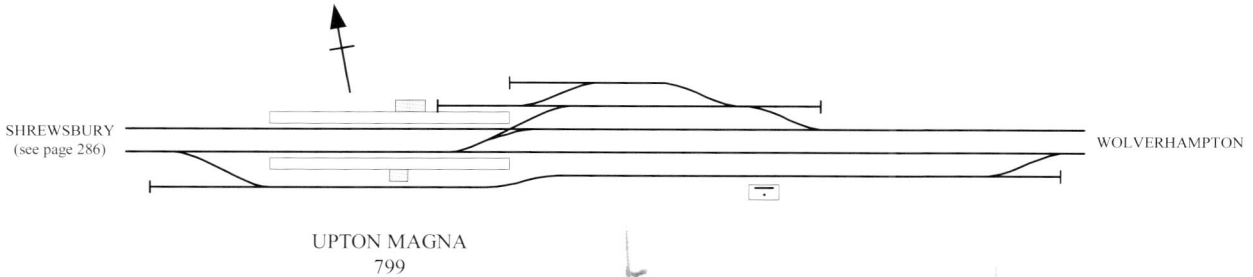

SHREWSBURY (Exc) TO WOLVERHAMPTON (Exc)
SHREWSBURY & WELLINGTON LINE,
DIDCOT & CHESTER LINE
Shrewsbury & Birmingham Railway -
Great Western & LNW Joint Railway (01/09/1854)
(Shrewsbury to Wellington)
Shrewsbury & Birmingham Railway -
Great Western Railway (01/09/1854)
(Wellington to Wolverhampton (Stafford Road Junc.))
Great Western Railway
(Stafford Road Junction to Cannock Road Junction)
ACT: 03/08/1846 (Shrewsbury to Wolverhampton (Stafford Road Junc.))
ACT: 03/06/1852 (Stafford Road Junction to Cannock Road Junction)
OPG: 01/06/1849 (Shrewsbury to Oakengates)
OPG: 12/11/1849 (Oakengates to Stafford Road Junction)
OPG: 11/11/1854 (Stafford Road Junction to Wolverhampton (L.L.))
CP: OPEN
CG: OPEN

SHREWSBURY
(see page 286)

WOLVERHAMPTON

UPTON MAGNA
799

799   **UPTON MAGNA**   **[S&BR]**
OP: 01/06/1849   Photo: W. 1962
CP: 05/09/1964   R.M.Casserley

800   **WALCOT**   **[S&BR]**
OP: 01/06/1849   Photo: W. 1950
CP: 05/09/1964   Stations U.K.

SHREWSBURY

WOLVERHAMPTON

WALCOT
800

SHREWSBURY

WOLVERHAMPTON

ADMASTON
801

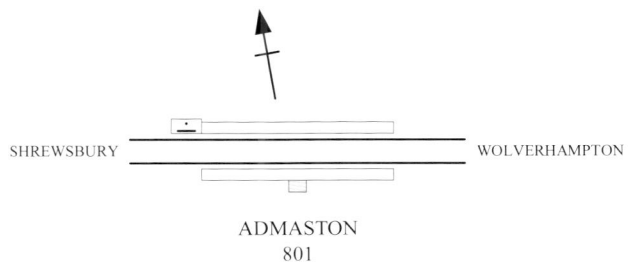

801   **ADMASTON**   **[S&BR]**
OP: by 09/1849   Photo: W. 1950
CP: 05/09/1964   Stations U.K.

293 Issue A 31/07/2015

WELLINGTON (SALOP.)
802

802   **WELLINGTON (SALOP.)**   **[S&BR]**
OP: 1881   Photo: W. 1951
CP: OPEN   T.C.Cole

803   **NEW HADLEY HALT**   **[S&BR]**
OP: 03/11/1934   Photo: E. c.1960
CP: 1985   unknown

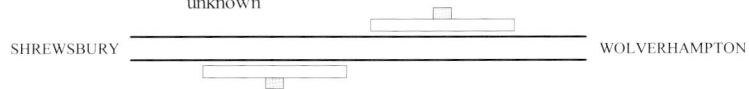

SHREWSBURY   WOLVERHAMPTON

NEW HADLEY
HALT
803

OAKENGATES
804

SHREWSBURY   WOLVERHAMPTON

804   **OAKENGATES**   **[S&BR]**
OP: 01/06/1849   Photo: NW. 1932
CP: OPEN   L&GRP

804   **OAKENGATES**   **[S&BR]**
                                   Photo: SE. 1950
                                   Stations U.K.

SHREWSBURY ← → WOLVERHAMPTON

SHIFNAL
805

805
OP: 13/11/1849
CP: OPEN

SHIFNAL [S&BR]

Photo: E. 1963
P.Garland

805
SHIFNAL [S&BR]

Photo: E. 1963
P.Garland

SHREWSBURY ← → WOLVERHAMPTON

COSFORD
806

806
OP: 31/03/1938
CP: OPEN

COSFORD [S&BR]

Photo: E. 1950
Stations U.K.

806
COSFORD [S&BR]

Photo: W. 1991
R.J.Smith

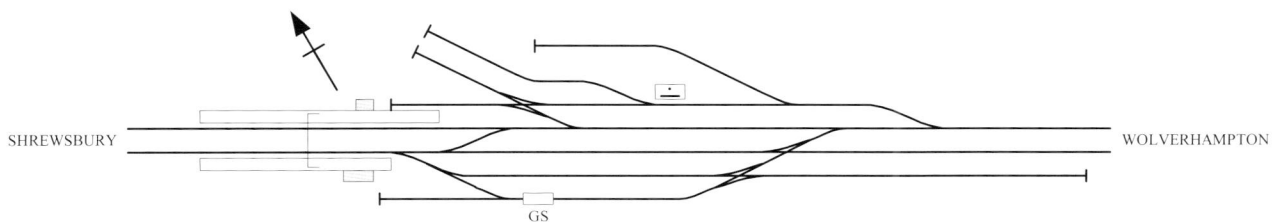

SHREWSBURY ← → WOLVERHAMPTON

GS

ALBRIGHTON
807

807   **ALBRIGHTON**   **[S&BR]**
OP: 13/11/1849   Photo: W. 1963
CP: OPEN   P.Garland

808   **CODSALL**   **[S&BR]**
OP: 13/11/1849   Photo: W. 1950
CP: OPEN   Stations U.K.

SHREWSBURY   WOLVERHAMPTON

CODSALL
808

SHREWSBURY   WOLVER-HAMPTON

BIRCHES & BILBROOK
HALT
809

809   **BIRCHES & BILBROOK HALT**   **[S&BR]**
OP: 30/04/1934   Photo: E. 1950
CP: OPEN   Stations U.K.

809   **BIRCHES & BILBROOK HALT**   **[S&BR]**
Photo: W. c.1960
M.Hale

810   **DUNSTALL PARK**   **[GWR]**
OP: 01/12/1896   Photo: E. c.1950
CP: 04/03/1968   W.A.Camwell

Gas Works

(Stafford L.M.S.R.)

SHREWSBURY   WOLVERHAMPTON
(see Part 1 page 213)

DUNSTALL PARK   Engine Shed
810   (Wolverhampton (H.L.)
L.M.S.R.)

SHREWSBURY (Exc) TO HEREFORD
SHREWSBURY & HEREFORD LINE
Shrewsbury & Hereford Railway -
Great Western & LNW Joint Railway (04/07/1870)
ACT: 03/08/1846
OP: 21/04/1852 (Shrewsbury to Ludlow)
OP: 06/12/1853 (Ludlow to Hereford)
OG: 30/07/1852
CP: OPEN
CG: OPEN

GREAT WESTERN
RAILWAY
MAP OF THE COMPANY'S SYSTEM

811   **CONDOVER**   **[S&HR]**
OP: 21/04/1852   Photo: N. 1955
CP: 07/06/1958   Stations U.K.

HEREFORD

SHREWSBURY
(see page 286)

CONDOVER
811

HEREFORD   SHREWSBURY

GS

DORRINGTON
812

812   **DORRINGTON**   **[S&HR]**
OP: 21/04/1852   Photo: N. 1955
CP: 08/06/1958   Stations U.K.

812   **DORRINGTON**   **[S&HR]**
Photo: S. 1955
Stations U.K.

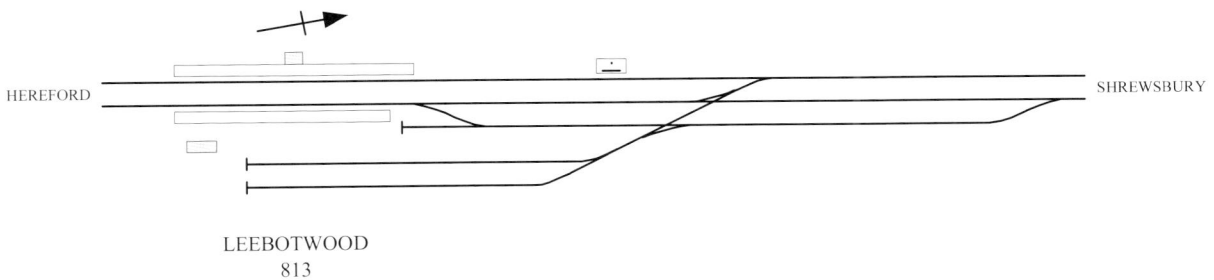

HEREFORD   SHREWSBURY

LEEBOTWOOD
813

813   **LEEBOTWOOD**   **[S&HR]**
OP: 21/04/1852   Photo: N. 1955
CP: 07/06/1958   Stations U.K.

HEREFORD   SHREWSBURY

ALL STRETTON
HALT
814

814   **ALL STRETTON HALT**   **[S&HR]**
OP: 21/02/1936   Photo: N. 1948
CP: 07/06/1958   J.D.Darby

814   **ALL STRETTON HALT**   **[S&HR]**
Photo: N. c.1960
M.Hale

GS

HEREFORD   SHREWSBURY

CHURCH STRETTON
815

815   **CHURCH STRETTON**   **[S&HR]**
OP: 23/05/1914   Photo: N. 1961
CP: OPEN   R.G.Nelson

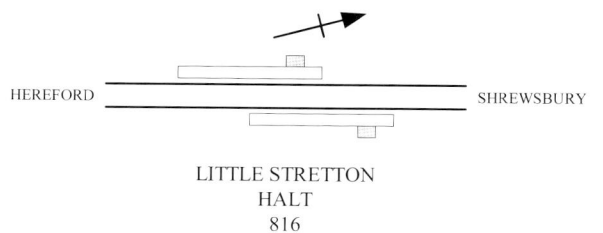

HEREFORD   SHREWSBURY

LITTLE STRETTON
HALT
816

816   **LITTLE STRETTON HALT**   **[S&HR]**
OP: 18/04/1935   Photo: N. c.1935
CP: 07/06/1958   unknown

MARSHBROOK
817

817   **MARSHBROOK**   **[S&HR]**
OP: 21/04/1852   Photo: N. c.1955
CP: 08/06/1958   R.Carpenter

WISTANSTOW
HALT
818

818   **WISTANSTOW HALT**   **[S&HR]**
OP: 07/05/1934   Photo: N. c.1955
CP: 11/06/1956   LOSA

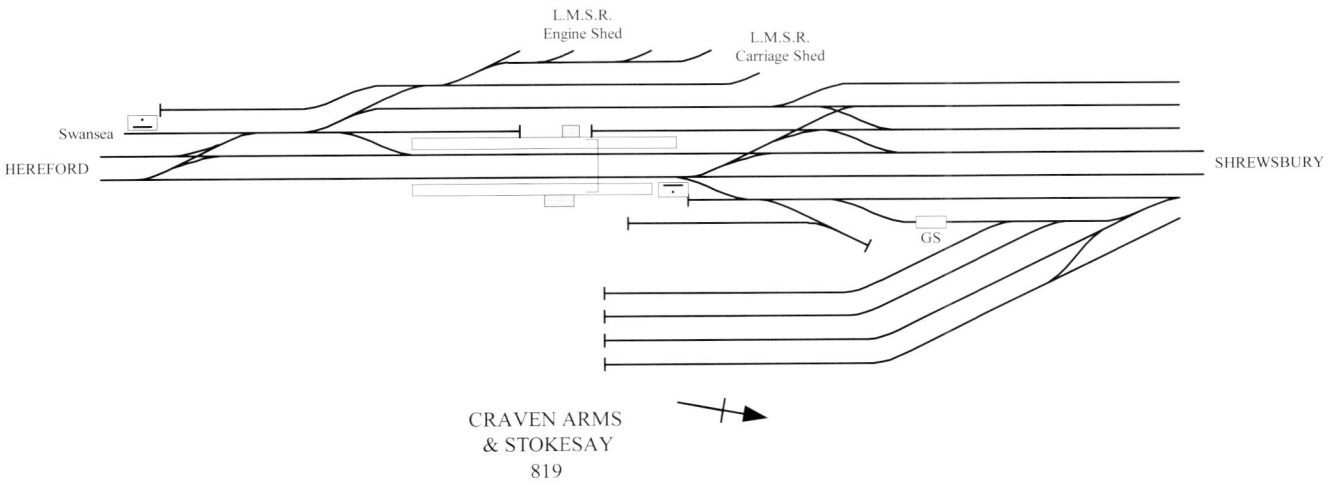

CRAVEN ARMS
& STOKESAY
819

819   **CRAVEN ARMS & STOKESAY**   **[S&HR]**
OP: 21/04/1852   Photo: N. c.1960
CP: OPEN   LOSA

819   **CRAVEN ARMS & STOKESAY**   **[S&HR]**
Photo: S. c.1960
J.Tarrant

HEREFORD ——————————— SHREWSBURY

ONIBURY
820

820   **ONIBURY**   **[S&HR]**
OP: 21/04/1852
CP: 08/06/1958   Photo: NW. 1958
     Stations U.K.

821   **BROMFIELD**   **[S&HR]**
OP: 21/04/1852   Photo: NW. c.1963
CP: 29/04/1965 (Races)   R.G.Nelson

HEREFORD ——————————— SHREWSBURY

BROMFIELD
821

HEREFORD ——————————— SHREWSBURY
     GS
     Clee Hill

LUDLOW
822

822   **LUDLOW**   **[S&HR]**
OP: 21/04/1852
CP: OPEN   Photo: SE. 1965
     P.Garland

823   **WOOFFERTON**   **[S&HR]**
OP: 06/12/1853   Photo: NE. c.1953
CP: 29/07/1961   P.Garland

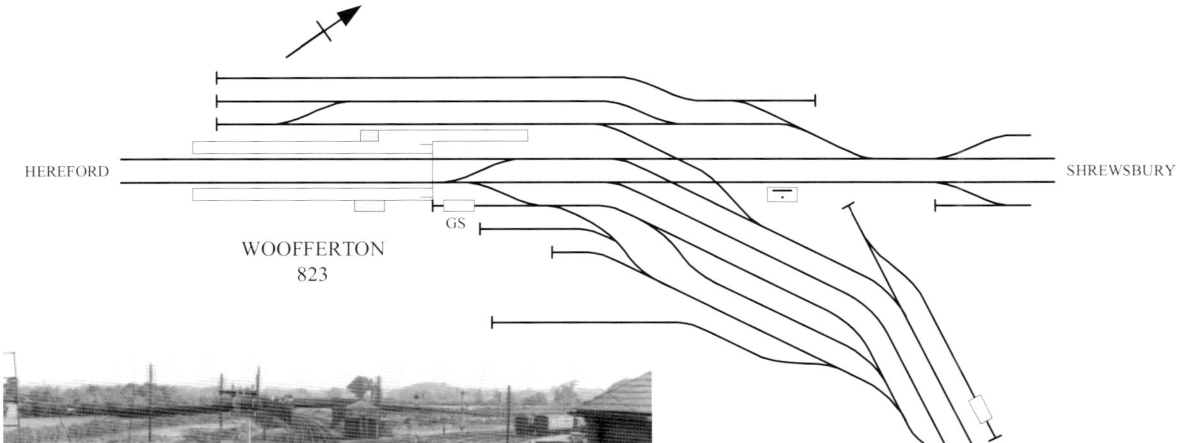

WOOFFERTON
823

HEREFORD

SHREWSBURY

GS

TENBURY WELLS
(see page 323)

823   **WOOFFERTON**   **[S&HR]**
Photo: NE. 1949
Joe Moss

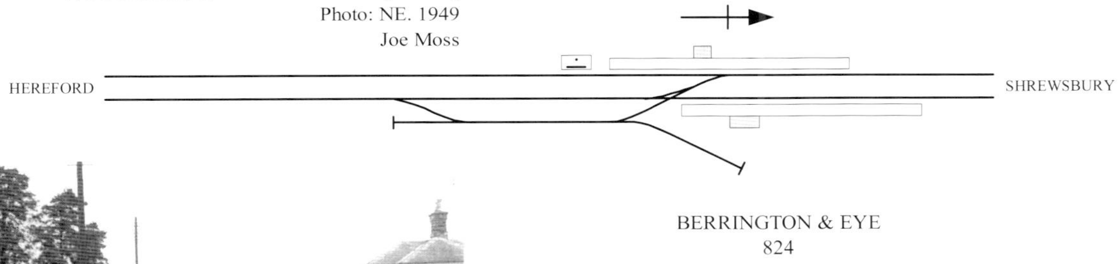

HEREFORD

SHREWSBURY

BERRINGTON & EYE
824

824   **BERRINGTON & EYE**   **[S&HR]**
OP: 06/12/1853   Photo: N. c.1935
CP: 07/06/1958   Stations U.K.

825   **LEOMINSTER**   **[S&HR]**
OP: 06/12/1853   Photo: S. c.1960
CP: OPEN   LOSA

GS

HEREFORD

SHREWSBURY

BROMYARD
(see page 329)

LEOMINSTER
825

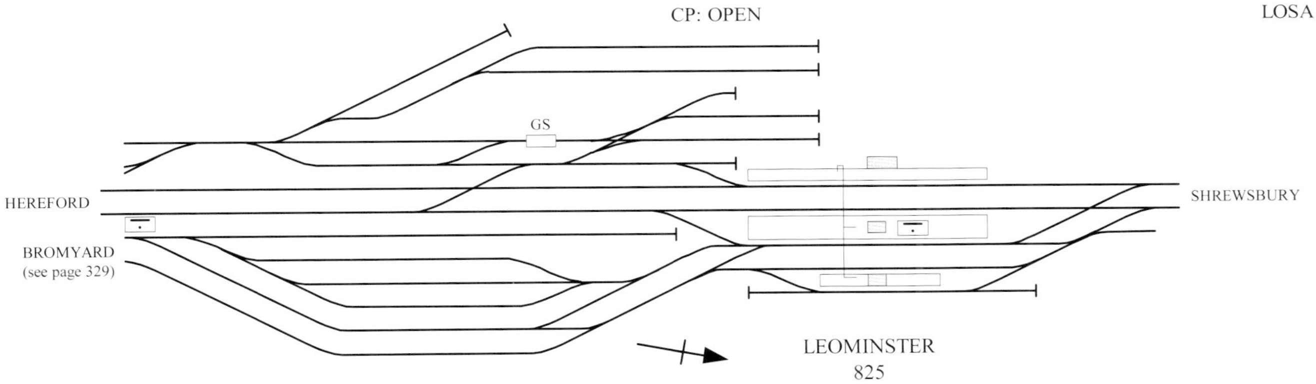

HEREFORD   SHREWSBURY

FORD BRIDGE
826

826   **FORD BRIDGE**   **[S&HR]**
OP: 06/12/1853   Photo: S. c.1930
CP: 05/04/1954   Stations U.K.

826   **FORD BRIDGE**   **[S&HR]**
                            Photo: N. c.1930
                                  LOSA

HEREFORD   SHREWSBURY

DINMORE
827

827   **DINMORE**   **[S&HR]**
OP: 06/12/1853   Photo: N. c.1910
CP: 07/06/1958   R.Carpenter

HEREFORD   SHREWSBURY

MORETON-ON-LUGG
828

828   **MORETON-ON-LUGG**   **[S&HR]**
OP: 06/12/1853   Photo: NW. 1958
CP: 07/06/1958   R.M.Casserley

828   **MORETON-ON-LUGG**   **[S&HR]**
                            Photo: SE. 1954
                            H.C.Casserley

HEREFORD
(BARRS COURT)
829

829   **HEREFORD (BARRS COURT)**   **[S&HR]**
OP: 06/12/1853   Photo: SE. 1964
CP: OPEN   S.V.Blencowe

GREAT WESTERN
RAILWAY
MAP OF THE COMPANY'S SYSTEM

HEREFORD (Exc) TO NEWPORT (Exc)
HEREFORD AND NEWPORT LINE
Newport Abergavenny & Hereford Railway -
West Midland Railway (01/07/1860) -
Great Western Railway (01/08/1863)
(Hereford (Barton) to Coedygric Junction)
Pontypool Caerleon & Newport Railway -
Great Western Railway (13/07/1876)
(Pontypool Road to Maindee Junction)
ACT: 03/08/1846 (Hereford (Barton) to Coedygric Junction)
ACT: 05/07/1865 (Pontypool Road to Maindee Junction)
OPG: 02/01/1854 (Hereford to Pontypool Road)
OPG: 21/12/1874 (Pontypool Road to Newport)
CP: OPEN
CG: OPEN

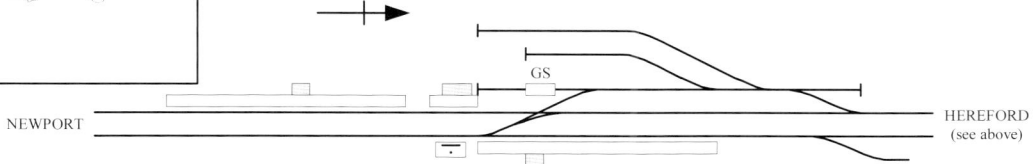

TRAM INN
830

830   **TRAM INN**   **[NA&HR]**   **830**   **TRAM INN**   **[NA&HR]**
OP: 02/01/1854   Photo: N. c.1935   Photo: N. c.1958
CP: 07/06/1958   Stations U.K.   M.Hale

ST. DEVEREUX
831

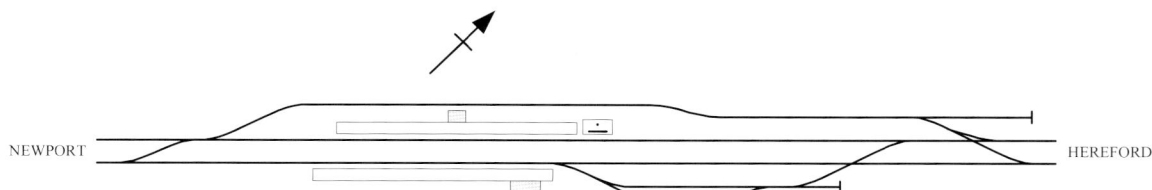

831   **ST. DEVEREUX**   **[NA&HR]**
OP: 02/01/1854   Photo: SW. c.1935
CP: 07/06/1958   Stations U.K.

832   **PONTRILAS**   **[NA&HR]**
OP: 02/01/1854   Photo: NE. 1950
CP: 07/06/1958   R.G.Nelson

HAY-ON-WYE
(see page 327)

PONTRILAS
832

PANDY
833

833   **PANDY**   **[NA&HR]**
OP: 02/01/1854   Photo: NE. 1958
CP: 07/06/1958   M.Hale

834   **LLANVIHANGEL (MON.)**   **[NA&HR]**
OP: 02/01/1854   Photo: NE. 1962
CP: 07/06/1958   R.G.Nelson

LLANVIHANGEL (MON.)
834

NEWPORT

HEREFORD

834 **LLANVIHANGEL (MON.)** **[NA&HR]**
Photo: NE. 1962
R.G.Nelson

834 **LLANVIHANGEL (MON.)** **[NA&HR]**
Photo: NE. 1964
M.Hale

(Merthyr Tydfil
L.M.S.R.)

NEWPORT

HEREFORD

ABERGAVENNY
JUNCTION
835

835 **ABERGAVENNY JUNCTION** **[NA&HR]**
OP: 20/06/1870
CP: 08/06/1958
Photo: N. 1958
Stations U.K.

836 **ABERGAVENNY** **[NA&HR]**
OP: 02/01/1854
CP: OPEN
Photo: S. c.1960
LOSA

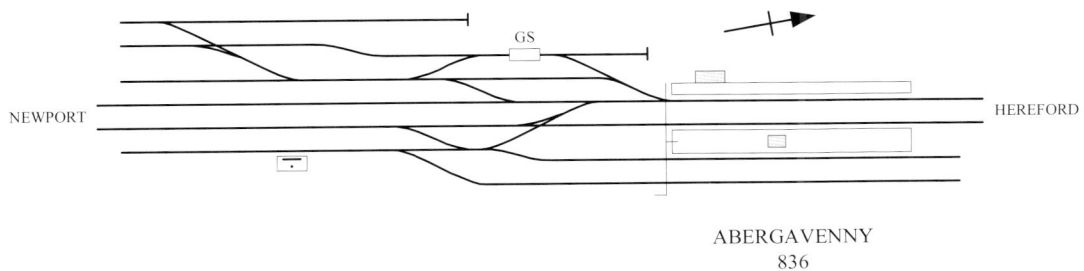

NEWPORT

GS

HEREFORD

ABERGAVENNY
836

NEWPORT   HEREFORD

GS

PENPERGWM
837

837   **PENPERGWM**   **[NA&HR]**
OP: 02/01/1854   Photo: SE. 1961
CP: 08/06/1958   M.Hale

838   **NANTYDERRY**   **[NA&HR]**
OP: 02/01/1854   Photo: S. c.1958
CP: 08/06/1958   J.Beardsmore

NEWPORT   HEREFORD

NANTYDERRY
838

838   **NANTYDERRY**   **[NA&HR]**
                                     Photo: N. 1961
                                          M.Hale

839   **PONTYPOOL ROAD**   **[NA&HR]**
OP: 01/03/1909   Photo: NE. c.1962
CP: OPEN   LOSA

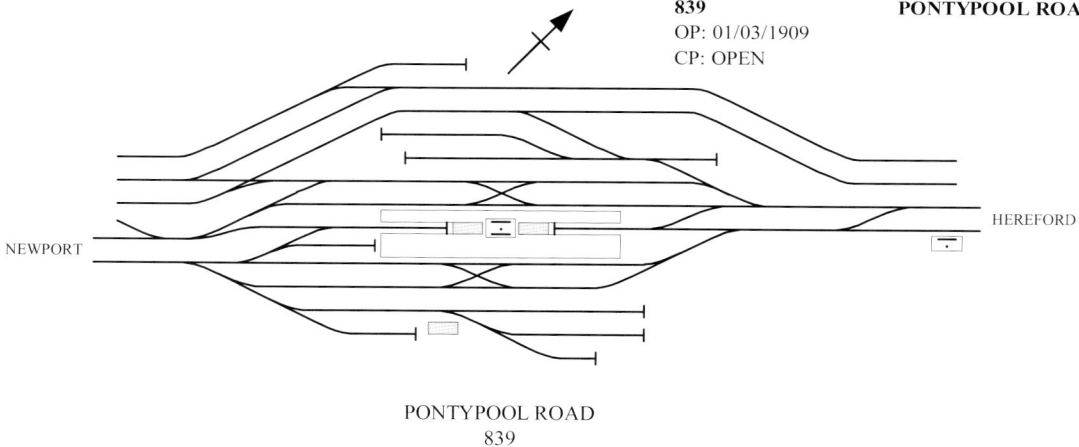

NEWPORT   HEREFORD

PONTYPOOL ROAD
839

LOWER PONTNEWYDD
840

840　　　　　**LOWER PONTNEWYDD**　　　　　[PC&NR]
OP: 21/12/1874　　　　　　　　　　　　　　　Photo: N. 1961
CP: 08/06/1958　　　　　　　　　　　　　　　　　　M.Hale

841　　　　　**LLANTARNAM**　　　　　[PC&NR]
OP: by 08/1878　　　　　　　　　　　Photo: NW. c.1960
CP: 30/04/1962　　　　　　　　　　　　　　　　unknown

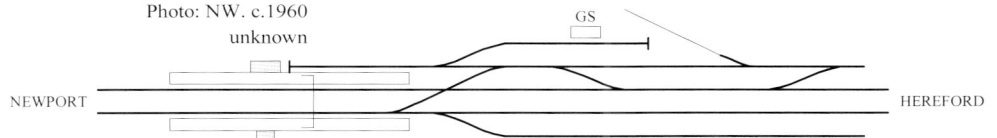

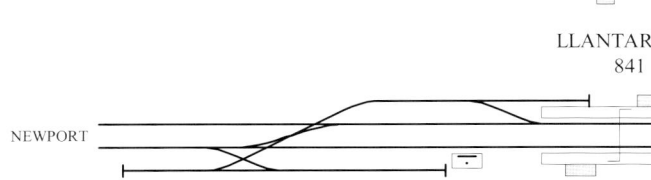

LLANTARNAM
841

PONTHIR
842

842　　　　　**PONTHIR**　　　　　[PC&NR]
OP: 01/06/1878　　　　　　　　　　Photo: SE. 1962
CP: 30/04/1962　　　　　　　　　　　　Stations U.K.

843　　　　　**CAERLEON**　　　　　[PC&NR]
OP: 21/12/1874　　　　　　　　　　Photo: NE. c.1935
CP: 30/04/1962　　　　　　　　　　　　Stations U.K.

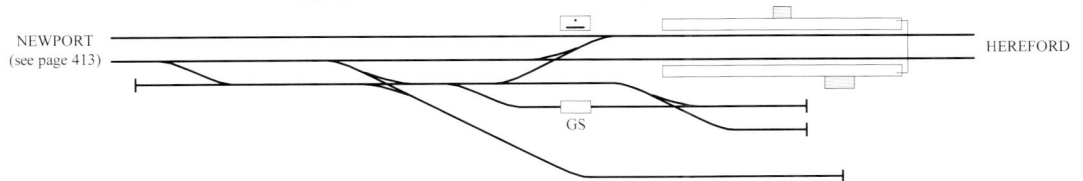

CAERLEON
843

SHREWSBURY (Exc) TO BUTTINGTON (Exc)
SHREWSBURY & WELSHPOOL BRANCH
Shrewsbury & Welshpool Railway -
Great Western & LNW Joint Railway (05/07/1865)
ACT: 29/07/1856
OP: 27/01/1862
OG: 27/01/1862
CP: 10/09/1960 (Local Services only)
CG: OPEN

844   **HANWOOD**   **[S&WPoolJ]**
OP: 14/02/1861   Photo: NE. 1961
CP: 10/09/1960   Stations U.K.

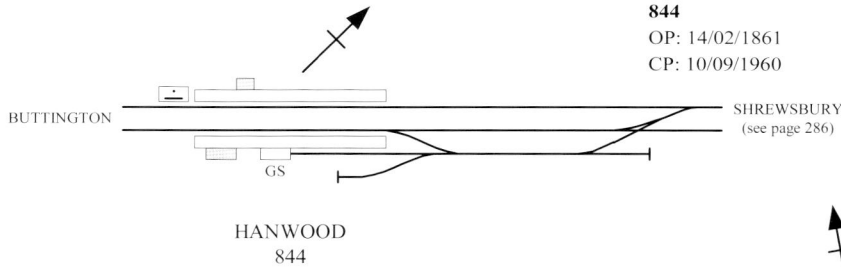

BUTTINGTON   SHREWSBURY
(see page 286)
GS

HANWOOD
844

BUTTINGTON   SHREWSBURY

YOCKLETON
845

845   **YOCKLETON**   **[S&WPoolJ]**
OP: 27/01/1862   Photo: E. 1961
CP: 10/09/1960   Stations U.K.

846   **WESTBURY (SALOP.)**   **[S&WPoolJ]**
OP: 27/01/1862   Photo: E. 1961
CP: 10/09/1960   Stations U.K.

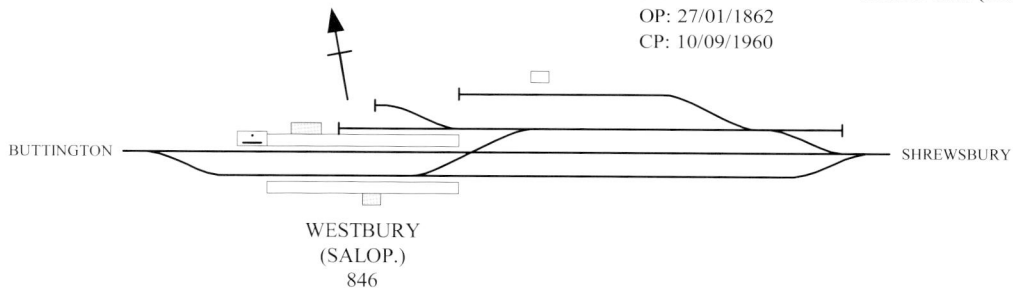

BUTTINGTON   SHREWSBURY

WESTBURY
(SALOP.)
846

BUTTINGTON ———————————— SHREWSBURY

PLAS-Y-COURT
HALT
847

847　　　　　**PLAS-Y-COURT HALT**　　　　**[S&WPoolJ]**
OP: 03/11/1934　　　　　　　　　　　　Photo: E. 1961
CP: 10/09/1960　　　　　　　　　　　　R.G.Nelson

BUTTINGTON
(see page 388)　　　　　　　　　　　　　　　　SHREWSBURY

BREIDDEN
848

848　　　　**BREIDDEN**　　　**[S&WPoolJ]**
OP: 27/01/1862　　　　　　Photo: W. c.1960
CP: 10/09/1960　　　　　　　　M.Hale

848　　　　**BREIDDEN**　　　**[S&WPoolJ]**
　　　　　　　　　　　　Photo: E. 1961
　　　　　　　　　　　　R.G.Nelson

HANWOOD (Exc) TO MINSTERLEY
MINSTERLEY BRANCH
Shrewsbury & Welshpool Railway -
Great Western & LNW Joint Railway (05/07/1865)
ACT: 29/07/1856
OP: 01/02/1862
OG: 01/02/1862
CP: 03/02/1951
CG: 01/05/1967

849　　　　**PLEALEY ROAD**　　　**[S&WPoolJ]**
OP: 14/02/1861　　　　　　　Photo: SW. 1958
CP: 03/02/1951　　　　　　　R.M.Casserley

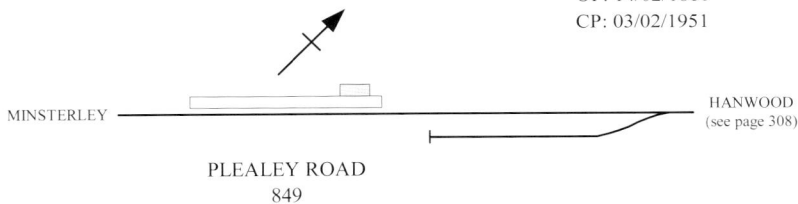

MINSTERLEY ———————————— HANWOOD
　　　　　　　　　　　　　　　　　(see page 308)

PLEALEY ROAD
849

PONTESBURY
850

850   **PONTESBURY**   [S&WPoolJ]
OP: 14/02/1861   Photo: E. 1958
CP: 03/02/1951   H.C.Casserley

851   **MINSTERLEY**   [S&WPoolJ]
OP: 14/02/1861   Photo: NE. 1955
CP: 03/02/1951   Stations U.K.

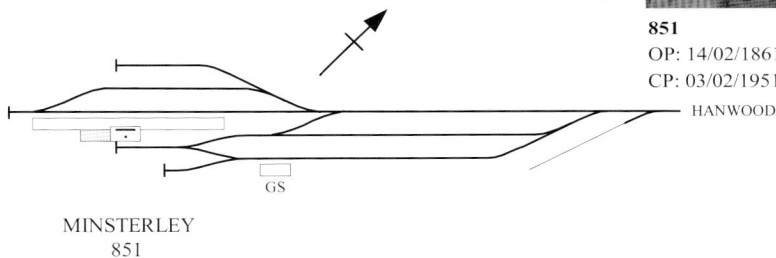

MINSTERLEY
851

GREAT WESTERN
RAILWAY
MAP OF THE COMPANY'S SYSTEM

WELLINGTON (Exc) TO LIGHTMOOR PLATFORM (Exc)
KETLEY BRANCH
Wellington & Severn Junction Railway -
Great Western Railway (01/07/1892)
ACT: 28/08/1853
OP: 02/05/1859
OG: 01/05/1857 (Ketley Junction to Horsehay)
OG: by 05/1859 (Horsehay to Lightmoor Junction)
CP: 21/07/1962
CG: 06/07/1964 (Ketley Junction to Horsehay Ironworks)
CG: 05/1979 (Horsehay Ironworks to Lightmoor Junction)

852   **KETLEY**   [W&SJR]
OP: 02/05/1859   Photo: N. 1962
CP: 21/07/1962   G.H.Tilt

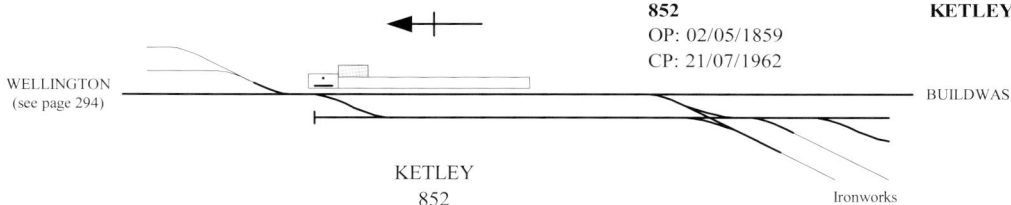

WELLINGTON
(see page 294)

BUILDWAS

KETLEY
852

Ironworks

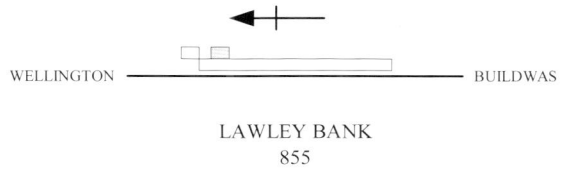

853   **KETLEY TOWN HALT**   **[W&SJR]**
OP: 06/03/1936   Photo: S. 1962
CP: 21/07/1962   G.H.Tilt

WELLINGTON ——————————— BUILDWAS

NEW DALE
HALT
854

KETLEY TOWN
HALT
853

854   **NEW DALE HALT**   **[W&SJR]**
OP: 29/01/1934   Photo: N. 1962
CP: 21/07/1962   G.H.Tilt

855   **LAWLEY BANK**   **[W&SJR]**
OP: 02/05/1859   Photo: N. 1962
CP: 21/07/1962   G.H.Tilt

WELLINGTON ——————————— BUILDWAS

LAWLEY BANK
855

WELLINGTON ——————————— BUILDWAS

Horsehay
Iron Works

HORSEHAY
& DAWLEY
856

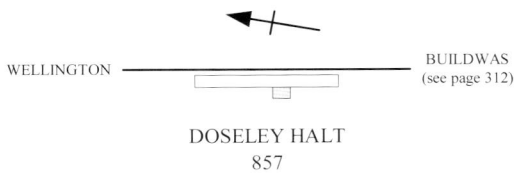

856   **HORSEHAY & DAWLEY**   **[W&SJR]**
OP: 02/05/1859   Photo: S. 1961
CP: 21/07/1962   R.G.Nelson

WELLINGTON ——————————— BUILDWAS
(see page 312)

DOSELEY HALT
857

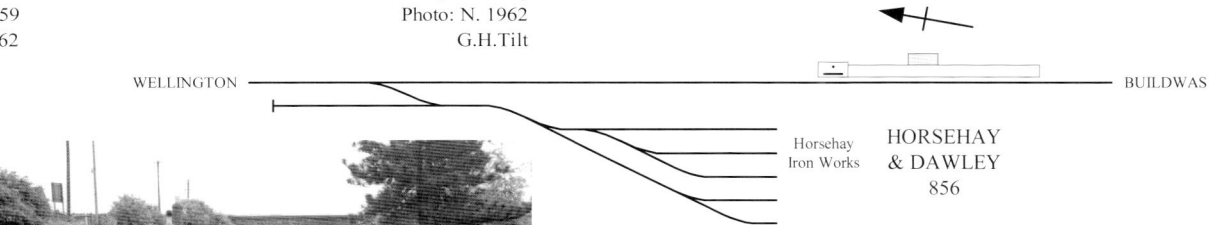

857   **DOSELEY HALT**   **[W&SJR]**
OP: 01/12/1932   Photo: S. c.1960
CP: 21/07/1962   M.Hale

GREAT WESTERN
RAILWAY
MAP OF THE COMPANY'S SYSTEM

SHIFNAL (Exc) TO BUILDWAS (Exc)
MADELEY BRANCH, KETLEY BRANCH
Shrewsbury & Birmingham Railway -
Great Western Railway (01/09/1854)
(Madeley Junction to Lightmoor)
Great Western Railway
(Lightmoor to Upper Forge)
Much Wenlock Craven Arms & Coalbrookdale Railway -
Great Western Railway (01/07/1896)
(Upper Forge to Buildwas Junction)
ACT: 03/08/1846 (Madeley Junction to Lightmoor)
ACT: 01/08/1861 (Lightmoor to Upper Forge)
ACT: 22/07/1861 (Upper Forge to Buildwas Junction)
OP: 01/10/1855 (Madeley Junction to Lightmoor)
OG: 11/1854 (Madeley Junction to Madeley)
OG: 01/10/1855 (Madeley to Lightmoor)
OPG: 01/11/1864 (Lightmoor to Buildwas)
CP: 21/09/1925 (Madeley Junction to Lightmoor)
CP: 21/07/1962 (Lightmoor to Buildwas)
CG: 06/07/1964 (Public Goods only)

(Oakengates L.M.S.R.)

Buildwas

GS

Shifnal
(see page 295)

(Coalport L.M.S.R.)

MADELEY
(SALOP.)
858
[CLOSED]

858   **MADELEY (SALOP.)**   **[S&BR]**
OP: 01/10/1855   Photo: E. 1950
CP: 21/09/1925   W.A.Camwell

WELLINGTON
(see page 311)

BUILDWAS

Shifnal

LIGHTMOOR
PLATFORM
859

859   **LIGHTMOOR PLATFORM**   **[GWR]**
OP: 12/08/1907   Photo: E. 1932
CP: 21/07/1962   C.Mowat

859   **LIGHTMOOR PLATFORM**   **[GWR]**
Photo: W. 1963
P.Garland

GREEN BANK
HALT
860

860   **GREEN BANK HALT**   **[GWR]**
OP: 12/03/1934   Photo: NE. c.1960
CP: 21/07/1962   M.Hale

861   **COALBROOKDALE**   **[MWCA&CR]**
OP: 01/11/1864   Photo: N. 1959
CP: 21/07/1962   Stations U.K.

COALBROOKDALE
861

BUILDWAS (Exc) TO CRAVEN ARMS (Exc)
MUCH WENLOCK BRANCH

Much Wenlock & Severn Junction Railway -
Great Western Railway (01/07/1896)
(Buildwas to Much Wenlock)
Much Wenlock Craven Arms & Coalbrookdale Railway -
Great Western Railway (01/07/1896)
(Much Wenlock to Marsh Farm Junction)
ACT: 21/07/1859 (Buildwas to Much Wenlock)
ACT: 22/07/1861 (Much Wenlock to Marsh Farm Junction)
OPG: 01/02/1862 (Buildwas to Much Wenlock)
OP: 16/12/1867 (Much Wenlock to Marsh Farm Junction)
OG: 05/12/1864 (Buildwas to Presthope)
OG: 16/12/1867 (Presthope to Marsh Farm Junction)
CP: 21/07/1962 (Buildwas to Much Wenlock)
CP: 29/12/1951 (Much Wenlock to Marsh Farm Junction)
CG: 19/01/1964 (Buildwas to Much Wenlcok)
CG: 02/12/1963 (Much Wenlock to Longville)
CG: 29/12/1951 (Longville to Marsh Farm Junction)

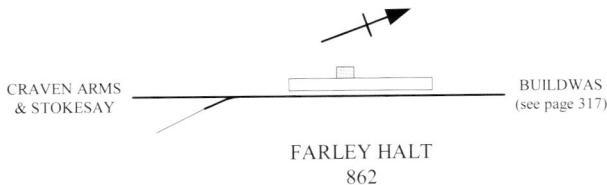

FARLEY HALT
862

862   **FARLEY HALT**   **[MW&SJR]**
OP: 27/10/1934   Photo: S. c.1960
CP: 21/07/1962   LOSA

CRAVEN ARMS

ES

GS

BUILDWAS

MUCH WENLOCK
863

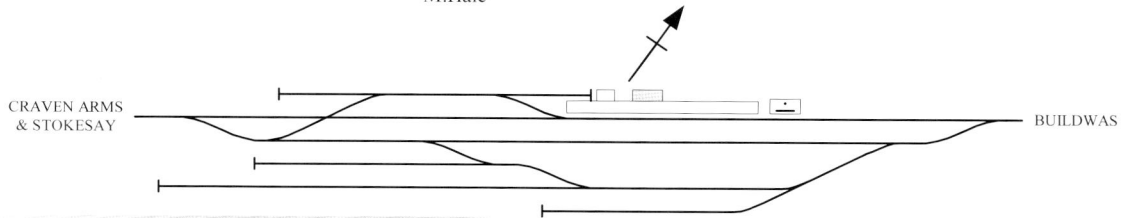

863
OP: 05/12/1864
CP: 21/07/1962

MUCH WENLOCK

[MW&SJR]
Photo: NE. 1961
R.G.Nelson

864
OP: 07/12/1935
CP: 29/12/1951

WESTWOOD HALT

[MWCA&CR]
SW. c.1960
M.Hale

CRAVEN ARMS
& STOKESAY

BUILDWAS

WESTWOOD
HALT
864

CRAVEN ARMS
& STOKESAY

BUILDWAS

PRESTHOPE
865

865
OP: 16/12/1867
CP: 29/12/1951

PRESTHOPE

[MWCA&CR]
Photo: NE. 1951
W.A.Camwell

CRAVEN ARMS
& STOKESAY

BUILDWAS

EASTHOPE
HALT
866

866
OP: 04/04/1936
CP: 29/12/1951

EASTHOPE HALT

[MWCA&CR]
SW. c.1955
J.Marshall

CRAVEN ARMS
& STOKESAY

BUILDWAS

LONGVILLE
867

867
OP: 16/12/1867
CP: 29/12/1951

LONGVILLE

[MWCA&CR]
Photo: NE. 1951
W.A.Camwell

867

LONGVILLE

[MWCA&CR]
Photo: SW. 1960
N.Forrest

CRAVEN ARMS
& STOKESAY

BUILDWAS

RUSHBURY
868

868
OP: 16/12/1867
CP: 29/12/1951

RUSHBURY

[MWCA&CR]
Photo: NE. 1953
P.Garland

CRAVEN ARMS & STOKESAY
(see page 299)

BUILDWAS

HARTON ROAD
869

869
OP: 16/12/1867
CP: 29/12/1951

HARTON ROAD

[MWCA&CR]
Photo: W. 1953
P.Garland

ACT: 20/08/1853
OP: 01/02/1862
OG: 01/02/1862
CP: 08/09/1963 (Shrewsbury (exc) to Bewdley)
CP: 03/01/1970 (Bewdley to Hartlebury)
CG: 02/12/1963 (Shrewsbury (exc) to Bewdley) (Public Goods)
CG: 01/02/1965 (Bewdley to Hartlebury) (Public Goods)

SHREWSBURY
(see page 286)

HARTLEBURY

BERRINGTON
870

870	**BERRINGTON**	[SVR]
OP: 01/02/1862		Photo: SE. c.1962
CP: 08/09/1963		Joe Moss

SHREWSBURY ———————— HARTLEBURY

COUND HALT
871

871	**COUND HALT**	[SVR]
OP: 04/08/1934		Photo: W. c.1960
CP: 08/09/1963		J.Tarrant

SHREWSBURY ———————— HARTLEBURY

CRESSAGE
872

872	**CRESSAGE**	[SVR]
OP: 01/02/1862		Photo: SE. c.1952
CP: 08/09/1963		Joe Moss

My father was Station Master here from 1948 to his death in 1951. He delayed his promotion for many years to allow me to complete my time at Ruabon Grammar School & Abergavenny.

Ironbridge
Power Station

SHREWSBURY

HARTLEBURY

MUCH WENLOCK
(see page 313)

BUILDWAS
873

873	**BUILDWAS**	[SVR]
OP: 01/02/1862		Photo: W. c.1960
CP: 08/09/1963		LOSA

873	**BUILDWAS**	[SVR]
		Photo: W. 1959
		V.R.Webster

SHREWSBURY

HARTLEBURY

GS

IRONBRIDGE
& BROSELEY
874

874	**IRONBRIDGE & BROSELEY**	[SVR]
OP: 01/02/1862		Photo: E. c.1959
CP: 08/09/1963		M.Hale

874	**IRONBRIDGE & BROSELEY**	[SVR]
		Photo: W. 1959
		R.M.Casserley

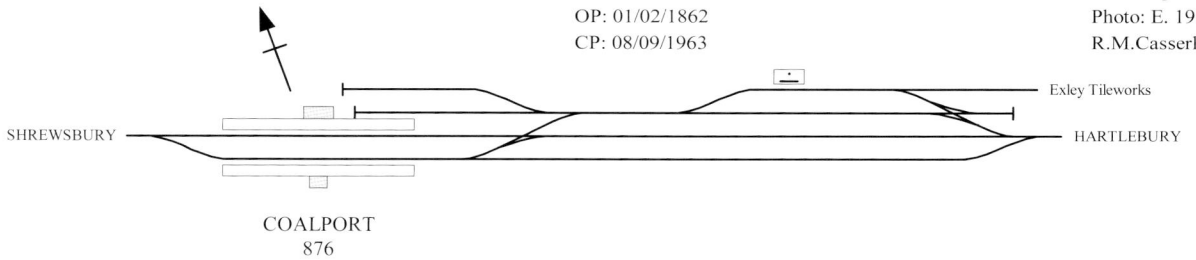

JACKFIELD
HALT
875

875   **JACKFIELD HALT**   **[SVR]**
OP: 03/12/1934   Photo: E. c.1952
CP: 01/03/1954   LOSA

SHREWSBURY ———————————— HARTLEBURY

JACKFIELD
HALT
875

876   **COALPORT**   **[SVR]**
OP: 01/02/1862   Photo: E. 1959
CP: 08/09/1963   R.M.Casserley

SHREWSBURY   Exley Tileworks   HARTLEBURY

COALPORT
876

SHREWSBURY ———————————— HARTLEBURY

LINLEY
877

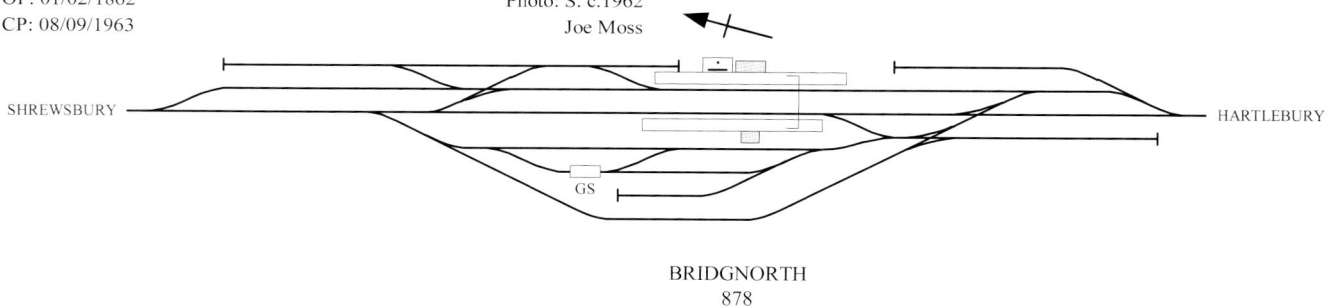

877   **LINLEY**   **[SVR]**
OP: 01/02/1862   Photo: N. 1961
CP: 08/09/1963   P.Coutanche

878   **BRIDGNORTH**   **[SVR]**
OP: 01/02/1862   Photo: S. c.1962
CP: 08/09/1963   Joe Moss

SHREWSBURY   GS   HARTLEBURY

BRIDGNORTH
878

EARDINGTON
879

879   **EARDINGTON**   **[SVR]**
OP: 01/06/1868   Photo: S. c.1960
CP: 08/09/1963   J.Tarrant

880   **HAMPTON LOADE**   **[SVR]**
OP: 01/02/1862   Photo: S. 1959
CP: 08/09/1963   R.M.Casserley

HAMPTON LOADE
880

ALVELEY
COLLIERY HALT
881

881   **ALVELEY COLLIERY HALT**   **[SVR]**
OP: 1940   Photo: N. c.1958
CP: 07/09/1963 (Workmens trains)   B.Johnson

882   **HIGHLEY**   **[SVR]**
OP: 01/02/1862   Photo: N. c.1963
CP: 08/09/1963   G.Parker

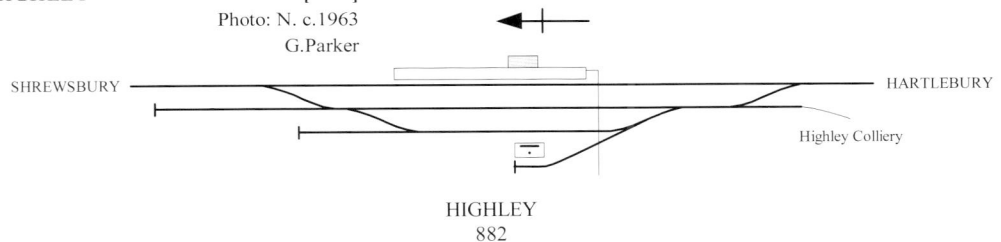

Highley Colliery

HIGHLEY
882

ARLEY
883

SHREWSBURY —————————————— HARTLEBURY

883   **ARLEY**   **[SVR]**
OP: 01/02/1862   Photo: NW. c.1958
CP: 08/09/1963   Joe Moss

SHREWSBURY —————————————— HARTLEBURY

NORTHWOOD
HALT
884

884   **NORTHWOOD HALT**   **[SVR]**
OP: 17/06/1935   Photo: SE. c.1960
CP: 08/09/1963   M.Hale

SHREWSBURY —————————————— KIDDERMINSTER
(see page 321)
—————————————— HARTLEBURY

WOOFFERTON
(see page 322)

GS

BEWDLEY
885

885   **BEWDLEY**   **[SVR]**
OP: 01/02/1862   Photo: NW. 1961
CP: 03/01/1970   Joe Moss

SHREWSBURY —————————————— HARTLEBURY

BURLISH
HALT
886

886   **BURLISH HALT**   **[SVR]**
OP: 31/03/1930   Photo: SE. 1958
CP: 03/01/1970   Stations U.K.

STOURPORT
887

SHREWSBURY

HARTLEBURY
(see Part 1 page 208)

GS

887
OP: 01/02/1862
CP: 03/01/1970

STOURPORT-ON-SEVERN   [SVR]

Photo: E. 1957
P.Garland

887   **STOURPORT-ON-SEVERN**   [SVR]

Photo: W. 1958
Joe Moss

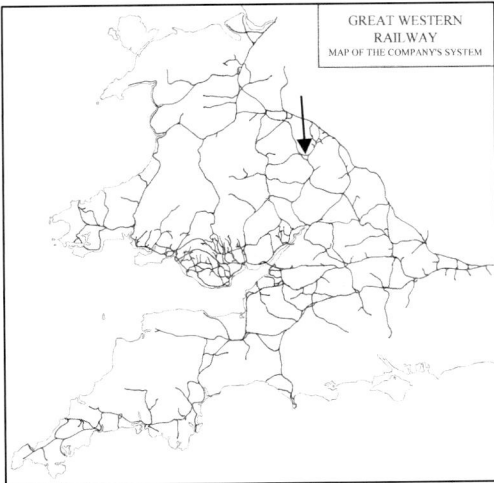

GREAT WESTERN
RAILWAY
MAP OF THE COMPANY'S SYSTEM

BEWDLEY (Exc) TO KIDDERMINSTER (Exc)
KIDDERMINSTER LOOP
West Midland & Severn Valley Railways -
Great Western Railway (18/07/1872)
ACT: 01/08/1861
OP: 01/06/1878
OG: 01/06/1878
CP: 03/01/1970
CG: 01/02/1965 (Public Goods only)

BEWDLEY
(see page 320)

KIDDERMINSTER
(see Part 1 page 208)

FOLEY PARK
HALT
888

888   **FOLEY PARK HALT**   [WMR,SVR]
OP: 1925   Photo: E. 1958
CP: 03/01/1970   Stations U.K.

GREAT WESTERN
RAILWAY
MAP OF THE COMPANY'S SYSTEM

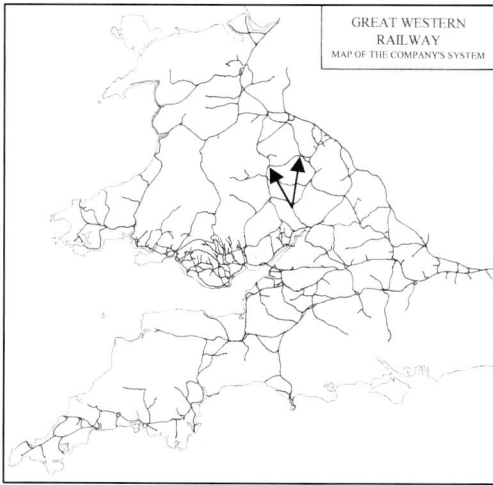

BEWDLEY (Exc) TO WOOFFERTON (Exc)
TENBURY BRANCH,
WOOFFERTON AND TENBURY WELLS BRANCH
Tenbury & Bewdley Railway -
Great Western Railway (12/07/1869)
(Bewdley to Tenbury Wells)
Tenbury Railway -
Great Western & LNW Joint Railway (01/01/1869)
(Tenbury Wells to Woofferton)
ACT: 03/07/1860 (Bewdley to 4 chains East of Tenbury Wells)
ACT: 21/07/1859 (Tenbury Wells to Woofferton)
OPG: 13/08/1864 (Bewdley to Tenbury Wells)
OPG: 01/08/1861 (Tenbury Wells to Woofferton)
CP: 31/07/1962 (Bewdley to Tenbury Wells)
CP: 29/07/1961 (Tenbury Wells to Woofferton)
CG: 04/01/1964 (Bewdley to Tenbury Wells) (Public Goods only)
CG: 29/07/1961 (Tenbury Wells to Woofferton)

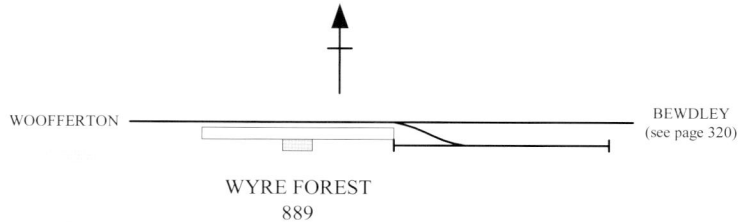

WOOFFERTON ———————————————————————— BEWDLEY
(see page 320)

WYRE FOREST
889

889   **WYRE FOREST**   [T&BR]
OP: 01/06/1869   Photo: E. 1959
CP: 31/07/1962   R.M.Casserley

890   **CLEOBURY MORTIMER**   [T&BR]
OP: 13/08/1864   Photo: S. 1938
CP: 31/07/1962   F.A.Wycherley

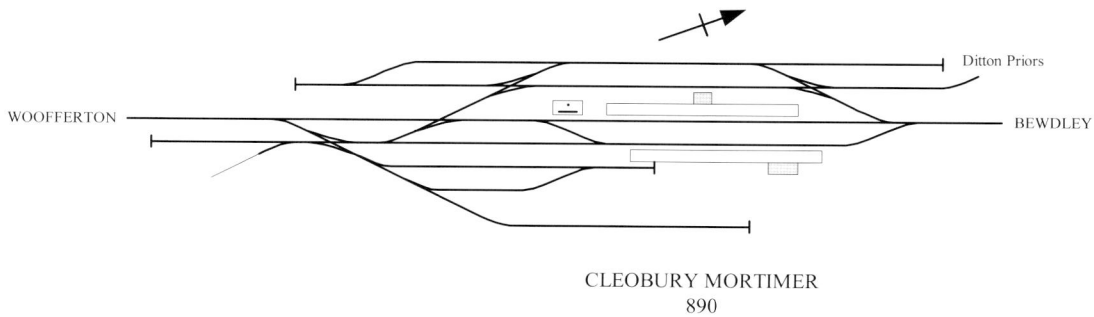

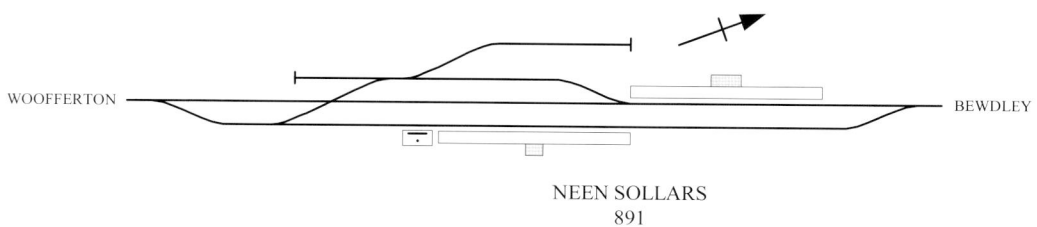

Ditton Priors

WOOFFERTON ———————————————————————— BEWDLEY

CLEOBURY MORTIMER
890

WOOFFERTON ———————————————————————— BEWDLEY

NEEN SOLLARS
891

891   **NEEN SOLLARS**   **[T&BR]**
OP: 13/08/1864   Photo: S. 1953
CP: 31/07/1962   unknown

892   **NEWNHAM BRIDGE**   **[T&BR]**
OP: 13/08/1864   Photo: W. c.1962
CP: 31/07/1962   R.G.Nelson

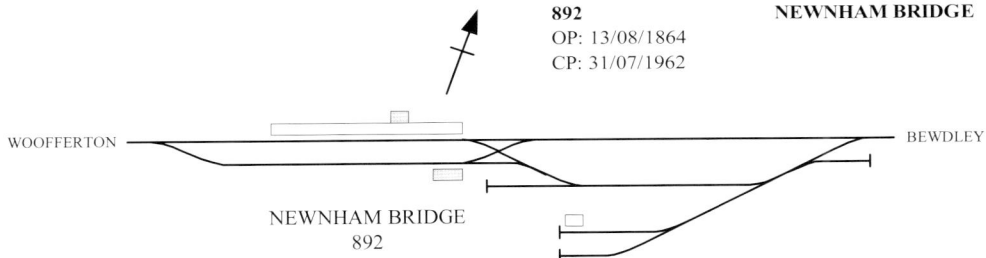

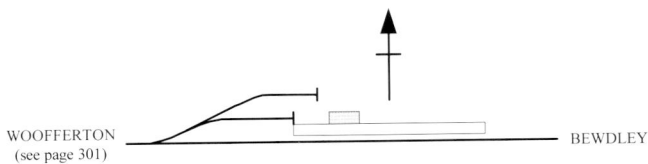

WOOFFERTON   BEWDLEY

NEWNHAM BRIDGE
892

WOOFFERTON   BEWDLEY

GS

TENBURY WELLS
893

893   **TENBURY WELLS**   **[TJ]**
OP: 01/08/1861   Photo: W. c.1962
CP: 31/07/1962   R.G.Nelson

WOOFFERTON   BEWDLEY
(see page 301)

EASTON COURT
894

894   **EASTON COURT**   **[TJ]**
OP: 01/08/1861   Photo: E. c.1961
CP: 29/07/1961   J.Tarrant

GREAT WESTERN
RAILWAY
MAP OF THE COMPANY'S SYSTEM

LEOMINSTER (Exc) TO NEW RADNOR
LEOMINSTER & NEW RADNOR LINE
Leominster & Kington Railway -
Great Western Railway (01/07/1898)
(Leominster to Kington)
Kington & Eardisley Railway -
Great Western Railway (01/07/1897)
(Kington to New Radnor)
ACT: 10/07/1854 (Kington Junction to Kington)
ACT: 16/06/1873 (Kington to New Radnor)
OPG: 20/08/1857 (Leominster to Kington)
OPG: 25/09/1875 (Kington to New Radnor)
CP: 05/02/1955 (Leominster to Kington)
CP: 03/02/1951 (Kington to New Radnor)
CG: 28/09/1964 (Leominster to Kington)
CG: 09/09/1958 (Kington to Dolyhir)
CG: 31/12/1951 (Dolyhir to New Radnor)

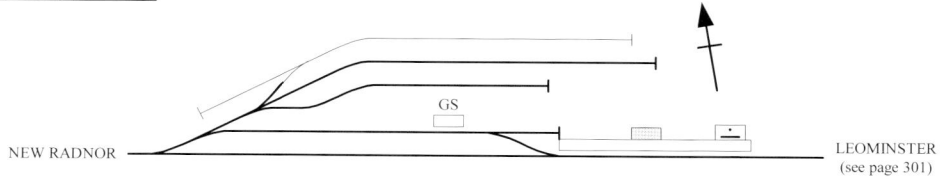

NEW RADNOR — LEOMINSTER (see page 301)

KINGSLAND
895

895
OP: 20/08/1857
CP: 05/02/1955
KINGSLAND
[L&KR]
Photo: W. 1955
Stations U.K.

896
OP: 20/08/1857
CP: 05/02/1955
PEMBRIDGE
[L&KR]
Photo: SW. 1954
Stations U.K.

NEW RADNOR — LEOMINSTER

PEMBRIDGE
896

NEW RADNOR — LEOMINSTER

MARSTON
HALT
897

897
OP: 26/04/1929
CP: 05/02/1955
MARSTON HALT
[L&KR]
Photo: W. 1955
J.E.Norris

TITLEY
898

898   **TITLEY**   **[L&KR]**
OP: 20/08/1857   Photo: W. c.1935
CP: 05/02/1955   Stations U.K.

899   **KINGTON**   **[K&ER]**
OP: 25/09/1875   Photo: W. 1957
CP: 05/02/1955   R.M.Casserley

KINGTON
899

899   **KINGTON**   **[K&ER]**
         Photo: E. 1957
         R.M.Casserley

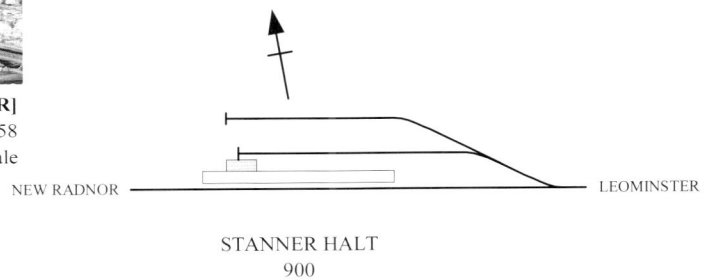

900   **STANNER HALT**   **[K&ER]**
OP: 25/09/1875   Photo: W. c.1958
CP: 03/02/1951   M.Hale

STANNER HALT
900

DOLYHIR
901

NEW RADNOR — LEOMINSTER

901   **DOLYHIR**   **[K&ER]**
OP: 25/09/1875   Photo: E. 1932
CP: 03/02/1951   C.Mowat

902   **NEW RADNOR**   **[K&ER]**
OP: 25/09/1875   Photo: E. 1954
CP: 03/02/1951   Stations U.K.

LEOMINSTER

GS

NEW RADNOR
902

TITLEY (Exc) TO PRESTEIGN
PRESTEIGN BRANCH
Leominster & Kington Railway -
Great Western Railway (01/07/1898)
ACT: 31/07/1871
OP: 10/09/1875
OG: 10/09/1875
CP: 03/02/1951
CG: 28/09/1964

GREAT WESTERN
RAILWAY
MAP OF THE COMPANY'S SYSTEM

TITLEY
(see page 325) — PRESTEIGN

FORGE CROSSING
HALT
903

903   **FORGE CROSSING HALT**   **[L&KR]**
OP: 09/03/1929   Photo: N. c.1950
CP: 03/02/1951   unknown

TITLEY

GS

PRESTEIGN
904

904   **PRESTEIGN**   **|L&KR|**
OP: 10/09/1875   Photo: SE. c.1956
CP: 03/02/1951   Joe Moss

904   **PRESTEIGN**   **|L&KR|**
Photo: NW. c.1952
J.Tarrant

PONTRILAS (Exc) TO HAY-ON-WYE (Exc)
GOLDEN VALLEY BRANCH
Golden Valley Railway -
Great Western Railway (01/07/1899)
ACT: 13/07/1876 (Pontrilas to Hay Junction)
OPG: 01/09/1881 (Pontrilas to Dorstone)
OP: 27/05/1889 (Dorstone to Hay)
OG: 21/04/1889 (Dorstone to Hay)
CP: 06/12/1941
CG: 10/06/1969 (Pontrilas to Elm Bridge R.O.F.)
CG: 03/06/1957 (Elm Bridge to Abbeydore)
CG: 31/01/1953 (Abbeydore to Dorstone)
CG: 31/12/1949 (Dorstone to Hay Junction)

905   **ABBEYDORE**   **|GVR|**
OP: 01/09/1881   Photo: NW. 1956
CP: 06/12/1941   R.J.Leonard

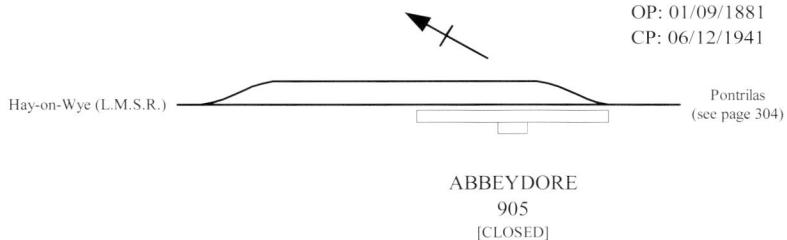

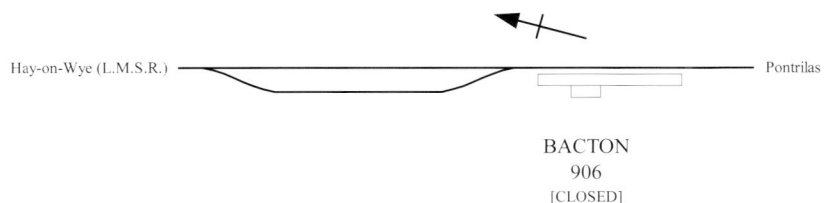

Hay-on-Wye (L.M.S.R.)   Pontrilas
(see page 304)

ABBEYDORE
905
[CLOSED]

Hay-on-Wye (L.M.S.R.)   Pontrilas

BACTON
906
[CLOSED]

906   **BACTON**   **|GVR|**
OP: 01/11/1901   Photo: S. 1953
CP: 06/12/1941   G.Parker

906   **BACTON**   **|GVR|**
Photo: N. 1953
R.G.Nelson

Hay-on-Wye (L.M.S.R.) — Pontrilas

907　　　　　**VOWCHURCH**　　　　　**[GVR]**
OP: 01/09/1881　　　　　Photo: S. 1951
CP: 06/12/1941　　　　　SLS Collection

908　　　　　**PETERCHURCH**　　　　　**[GVR]**
OP: 01/09/1881　　　　　Photo: N. 1950
CP: 06/12/1941　　　　　L&GRP

Hay-on-Wye (L.M.S.R.) — Pontrilas

PETERCHURCH
908
[CLOSED]

Hay-on-Wye (L.M.S.R.) — Pontrilas

DORSTONE
909
[CLOSED]

909　　　　　**DORSTONE**　　　　　**[GVR]**
OP: 01/09/1881　　　　　Photo: SE. c.1939
CP: 06/12/1941　　　　　Bill Smith Collection

Hay-on-Wye (L.M.S.R.) — Pontrilas

WESTBROOK
910
[CLOSED]

910　　　　　**WESTBROOK**　　　　　**[GVR]**
OP: 27/05/1889　　　　　Photo: W. 1948
CP: 06/12/1941　　　　　R.G.Nelson

GREENS SIDING
911
[CLOSED]

911   **GREENS SIDING**   **[GVR]**
OP: 01/07/1903   Photo: SE. 1932
CP: 06/12/1941   C.Mowat

912   **CLIFFORD**   **[GVR]**
OP: 27/05/1889   Photo: NE. 1948
CP: 06/12/1941   R.G.Nelson

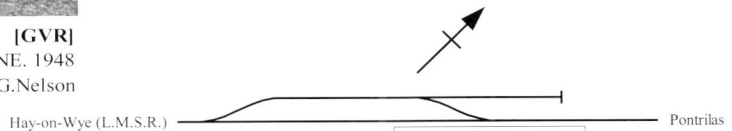

CLIFFORD
912
[CLOSED]

GREAT WESTERN
RAILWAY
MAP OF THE COMPANY'S SYSTEM

LEOMINSTER (Exc) TO WORCESTER (Exc)
BROMYARD BRANCH
Leominster & Bromyard Railway -
Great Western Railway (01/07/1888)
(Leominster to Bromyard)
Worcester Bromyard & Leominster Railway -
Great Western Railway (01/07/1888)
(Bromyard to Leominster Junction)
ACT: 30/07/1874 (Leominster to Bromyard)
ACT: 01/08/1861 (Bromyard to Leominster Junction)
OPG: 01/03/1884 (Leominster to Steens Bridge)
OPG: 01/09/1897 (Steens Bridge to Bromyard)
OPG: 22/10/1877 (Bromyard to Yearsett)
OPG: 02/05/1874 (Yearsett to Leominster Junction)
CP: 13/09/1952 (Leominster to Bromyard)
CP: 05/09/1964 (Bromyard to Leominster Junction)
CG: 13/09/1952 (Leominster to Bromyard)
CG: 04/09/1964 (Bromyard to Leominster Junction)

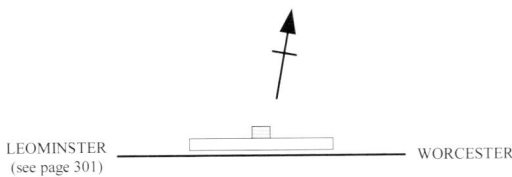

STOKE PRIOR
HALT
913

913   **STOKE PRIOR HALT**   **[L&BR]**
OP: 08/07/1929   Photo: W. 1952
CP: 13/09/1952   H.C.Casserley

STEENS BRIDGE
914

914   **STEENS BRIDGE**   **[L&BR]**
OP: 01/03/1884   Photo: W. c.1939
CP: 13/09/1952   LOSA

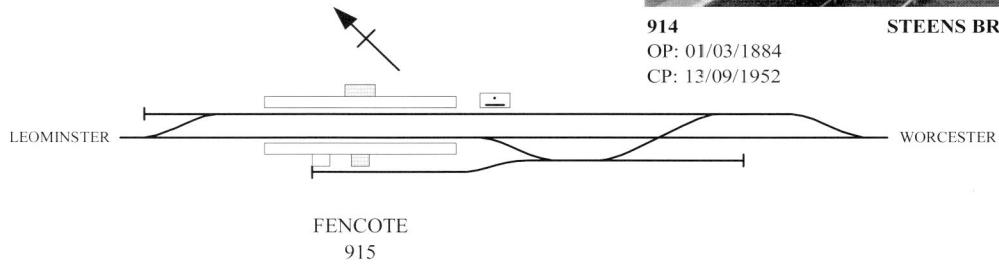

FENCOTE
915

915   **FENCOTE**   **[L&BR]**
OP: 01/09/1897   Photo: SE. 1952
CP: 13/09/1952   H.C.Casserley

915   **FENCOTE**   **[L&BR]**
Photo: NW. 1958
D.K.Jones

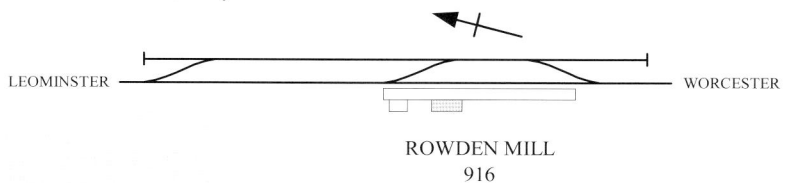

ROWDEN MILL
916

916   **ROWDEN MILL**   **[L&BR]**
OP: 01/09/1897   Photo: N. c.1939
CP: 13/09/1952   LOSA

917   **BROMYARD**   **[WB&LR]**
OP: 22/10/1877   Photo: SE. c.1952
CP: 05/09/1964   Joe Moss

BROMYARD
917

SUCKLEY
918

918   **SUCKLEY**   **[WB&LR]**
OP: 01/02/1878   Photo: E. c.1952
CP: 05/09/1964   Joe Moss

919   **KNIGHTWICK**   **[WB&LR]**
OP: 02/05/1874   Photo: W. 1958
CP: 05/09/1964   H.C.Casserley

KNIGHTWICK
919

LEIGH COURT
920

WORCESTER
(see page 335)

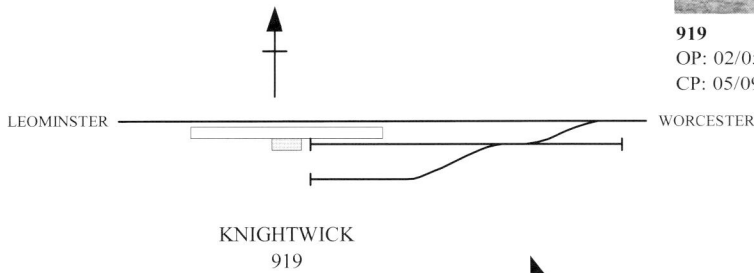

920   **LEIGH COURT**   **[WB&LR]**
OP: 02/05/1874   Photo: NW. c.1962
CP: 05/09/1964   LOSA

HEREFORD (Exc) TO WORCESTER
WORCESTER AND HEREFORD LINE
Worcester & Hereford Railway -
West Midland Railway (01/07/1860) -
Great Western Railway (01/08/1863)

ACT: 15/08/1853
OPG: 13/09/1861 (Shelwick Junction to Malvern Wells)
OPG: 25/05/1860 (Malvern Wells to Malvern Link)
OPG: 25/07/1859 (Malvern Link to Henwick)
OPG: 17/05/1860 (Henwick to Worcester (Shrub Hill) via Tunnel Junc.)
OPG: 25/07/1860 (To Worcester (Shrub Hill) via Rainbow Hill Junc.)
CP: OPEN
CG: OPEN

GS

HEREFORD
(see page 303)

WORCESTER

WITHINGTON
921

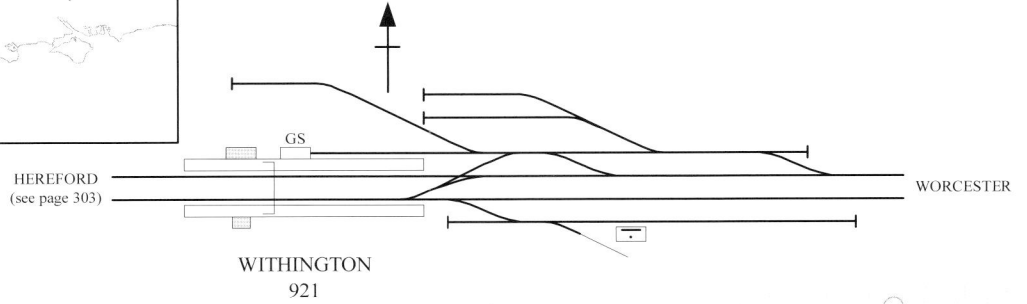

921	WITHINGTON	[W&HR]
OP: 13/09/1861		Photo: E. 1962
CP: 31/12/1960		R.G.Nelson

HEREFORD

WORCESTER

GS

STOKE EDITH
922

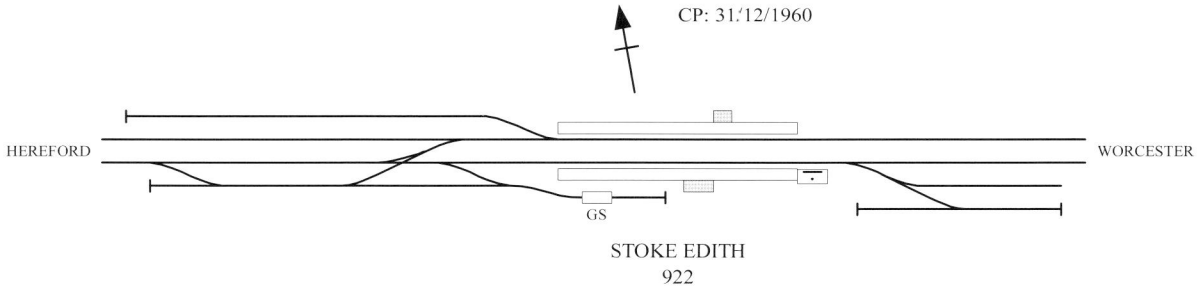

922	STOKE EDITH	[W&HR]	922	STOKE EDITH	[W&HR]
OP: 13/09/1861		Photo: W. 1962			Photo: W. c.1962
CP: 03/04/1965		R.G.Nelson			LOSA

ASHPERTON
923

923   **ASHPERTON**   [W&HR]
OP: 13/09/1861   Photo: W. c.1960
CP: 03/04/1965   LOSA

924   **LEDBURY**   [W&HR]
OP: 13/09/1861   Photo: W. 1954
CP: OPEN   H.C.Casserley

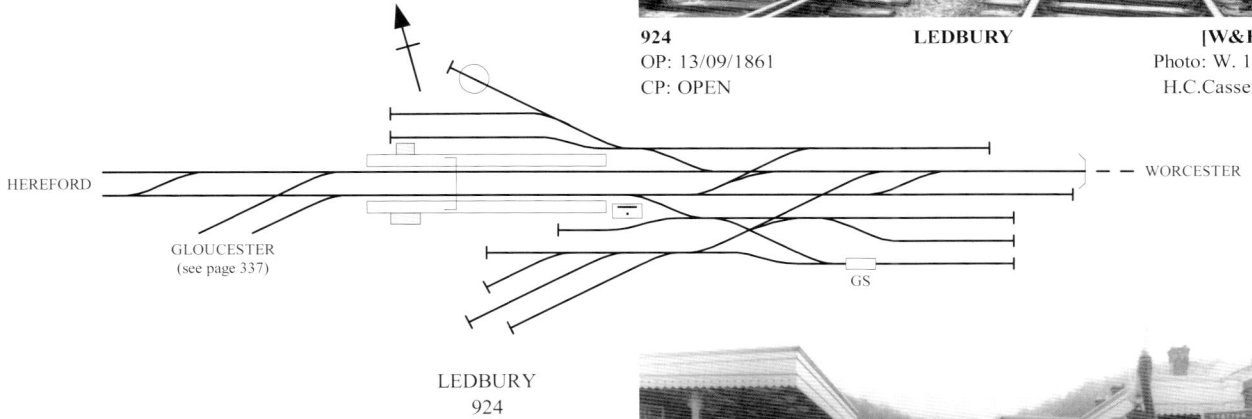

GLOUCESTER
(see page 337)

GS

LEDBURY
924

924   **LEDBURY**   [W&HR]
Photo: E. 1962
R.K.Blencowe

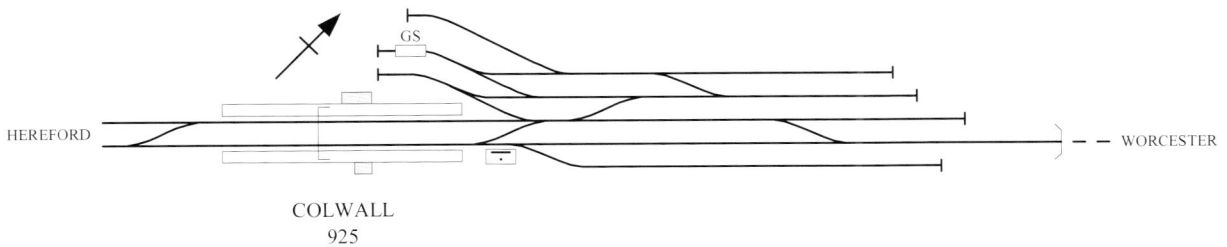

925   **COLWALL**   [W&HR]
OP: 13/09/1861   Photo: NE. c.1920
CP: OPEN   Stations U.K.

GS

COLWALL
925

MALVERN WELLS
926

926
OP: 25/05/1860
CP: 03/04/1965

MALVERN WELLS   **[W&HR]**

Photo: SW. c.1949
Joe Moss

927
OP: 25/05/1860
CP: OPEN

MALVERN (GREAT)   **[W&HR]**

Photo: N. 1949
W.Potter

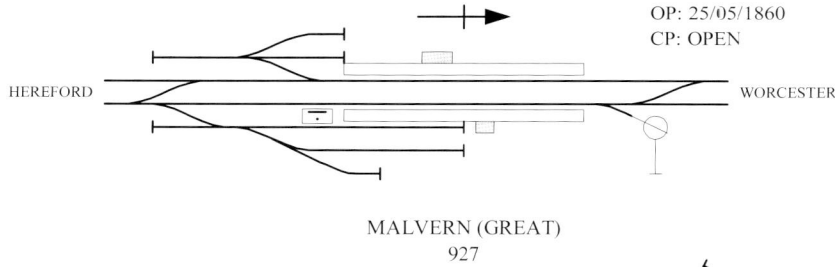

MALVERN (GREAT)
927

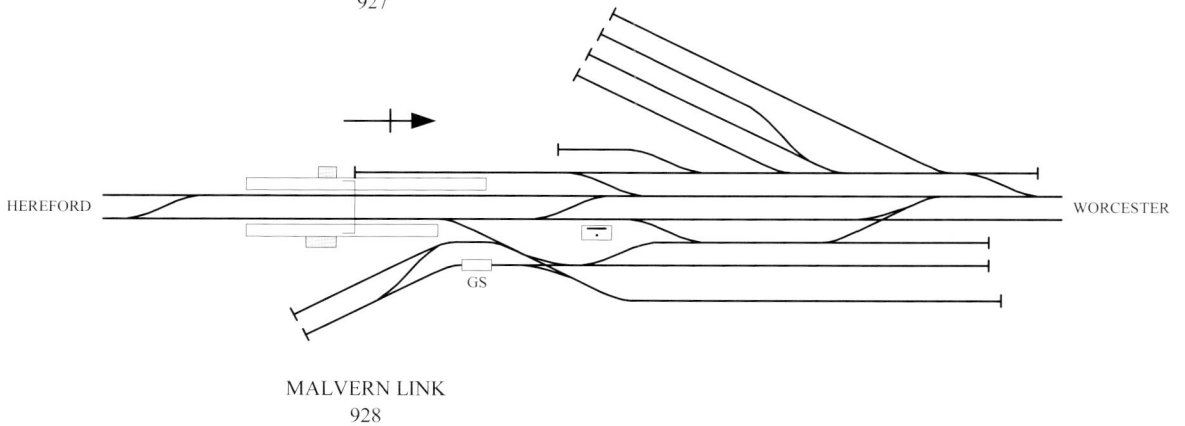

GS

MALVERN LINK
928

928
OP: 25/07/1859
CP: OPEN

MALVERN LINK   **[W&HR]**

Photo: N. 1967
Stations U.K.

928
OP: 25/07/1859
CP: OPEN

MALVERN LINK   **[W&HR]**

Photo: N. c.1965
R.K.Blencowe

NEWLAND HALT
929

929   **NEWLAND HALT**   **[W&HR]**
OP: 18/03/1929   Photo: N. 1939
CP: 03/04/1965   Stations U.K.

929   **NEWLAND HALT**   **[W&HR]**
Photo: S. c.1960
LOSA

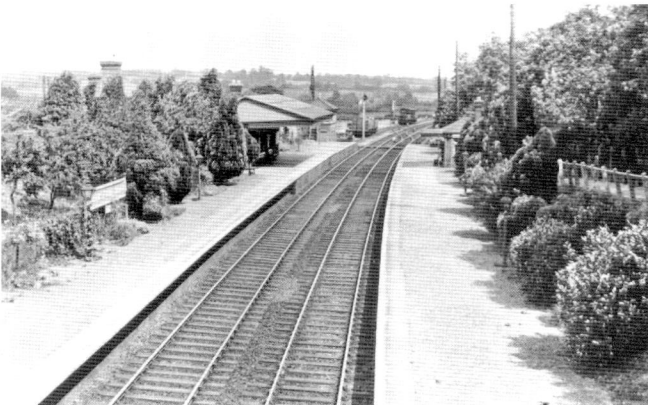

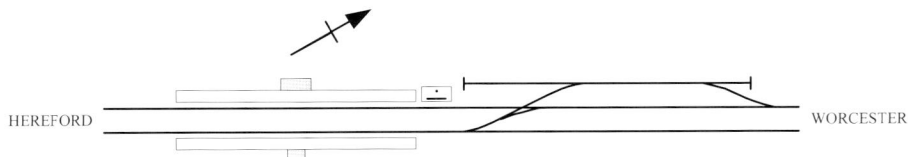

930   **BRANSFORD ROAD**   **[W&HR]**
OP: 01/09/1860   Photo: N. 1934
CP: 04/04/1965   C.Mowat

930   **BRANSFORD ROAD**   **[W&HR]**
Photo: S. c.1960
LOSA

BRANSFORD ROAD
930

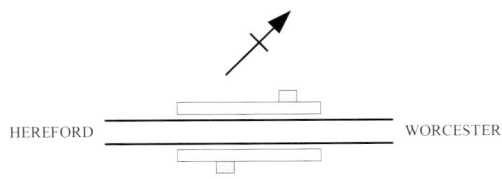

RUSHWICK HALT
931

931   **RUSHWICK HALT**   **[W&HR]**
OP: 31/03/1924   Photo: NE. c.1960
CP: 03/04/1965   R.Carpenter

BOUGHTON HALT
932

932   **BOUGHTON HALT**   **[W&HR]**
OP: 31/03/1924   Photo: SW. c.1960
CP: 03/04/1965   M.Hale

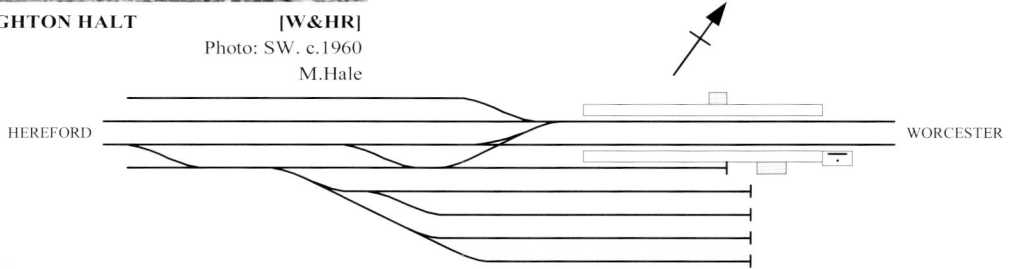

HENWICK
933

933   **HENWICK**   **[W&HR]**
OP: 25/07/1859   Photo: SW. c.1960
CP: 03/04/1965   LOSA

933   **HENWICK**   **[W&HR]**
Photo: NE. c.1960
LOSA

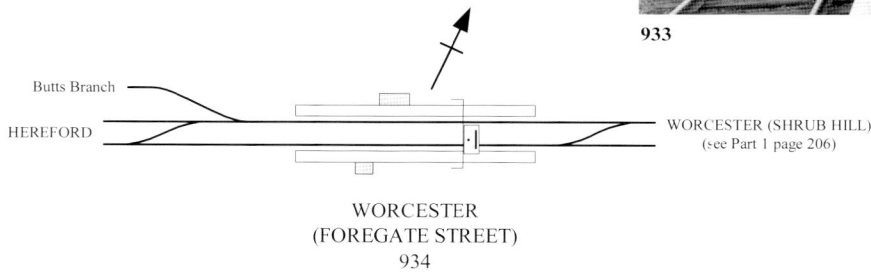

WORCESTER
(FOREGATE STREET)
934

934   **WORCESTER (FOREGATE STREET)**   **[W&HR]**
OP: 17/05/1860   Photo: W. c.1920
CP: OPEN   Stations U.K.

934   **WORCESTER (FOREGATE STREET)**   **[W&HR]**
Photo: E. 1952
LOSA

LEDBURY (Exc) TO GLOUCESTER (Exc)
LEDBURY BRANCH,
Ross & Ledbury Railway -
Great Western Railway (01/07/1892)
(Ledbury to 31 chains north of Dymock)
Newent Railway -
Great Western Railway (01/07/1892)
(31 chains north of Dymock to Over Junction (Gloucester))
ACT: 28/07/1873 (Ledbury to 31 chains north of Dymock)
ACT: 05/08/1873 (31 chains north of Dymock to Over Junction)
OP: 27/07/1885 (Ledbury to Over Junction)
OG: 27/07/1885 (Ledbury to Over Junction)
CP: 11/07/1959
CG: 11/07/1959 (Ledbury to Dymock)
CG: 01/06/1964 (Dymock to Over Junction)

LEDBURY
(see page 333)   GLOUCESTER

LEDBURY TOWN
HALT
935

935	LEDBURY TOWN HALT	[R&LR]
OP: 26/11/1928		Photo: S. 1959
CP: 11/07/1959		P.Garland

LEDBURY   GLOUCESTER

GREENWAY HALT
936

936	GREENWAY HALT	[R&LR]
OP: 01/04/1937		Photo: N. 1959
CP: 11/07/1959		P.Garland

GS

LEDBURY   GLOUCESTER

DYMOCK
937

937	DYMOCK	[NR]
OP: 27/07/1885		Photo: S. 1959
CP: 11/07/1959		Joe Moss

937	DYMOCK	[NR]
		Photo: SW. 1959
		Joe Moss

LEDBURY ——————————— GLOUCESTER

FOUR OAKS
HALT
938

938   **FOUR OAKS HALT**   **[NR]**
OP: 16/10/1937   Photo: SE. 1959
CP: 11/07/1959   P.Garland

LEDBURY ——————————————— GLOUCESTER

GS

NEWENT
939

939   **NEWENT**   **[NR]**
OP: 27/07/1885   Photo: E. 1959
CP: 11/07/1959   P.Garland

LEDBURY ——————————— GLOUCESTER

MALSWICK
HALT
940

940   **MALSWICK HALT**   **[NR]**
OP: 01/02/1938   Photo: NW. 1959
CP: 11/07/1959   P.Garland

941   **BARBERS BRIDGE**   **[NR]**
OP: 27/07/1885   Photo: SE. 1959
CP: 11/07/1959   E.T.Gill

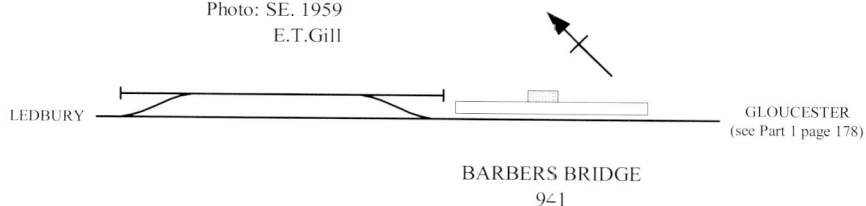

LEDBURY ——————————— GLOUCESTER
(see Part 1 page 178)

BARBERS BRIDGE
941

GREAT WESTERN
RAILWAY
MAP OF THE COMPANY'S SYSTEM

HEREFORD (Exc) TO GRANGE COURT (Exc)
GRANGE COURT AND HEREFORD LINE
Hereford Ross & Gloucester Railway -
Great Western Railway (29/07/1862)
ACT: 05/06/1851
OP: 02/06/1855 (Hereford to Hopesbrook (north of Longhope))
OP: 11/07/1853 (Hopesbrook to Grange Court)
OG: 02/06/1855
CP: 31/10/1964
CG: 12/08/1963 (Rotherwas Junction to Ross-on-Wye)
CG: 01/11/1965 (Ross-on-Wye to Grange Court)

HEREFORD
(see page 303)

GRANGE COURT

HOLME LACY
942

942
OP: 02/06/1855
CP: 31/10/1964
HOLME LACY   [HR&GR]
Photo: NW. 1963
E.T.Gill

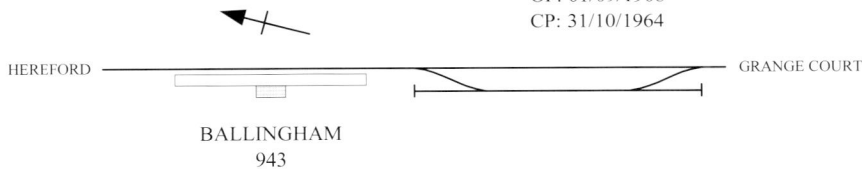

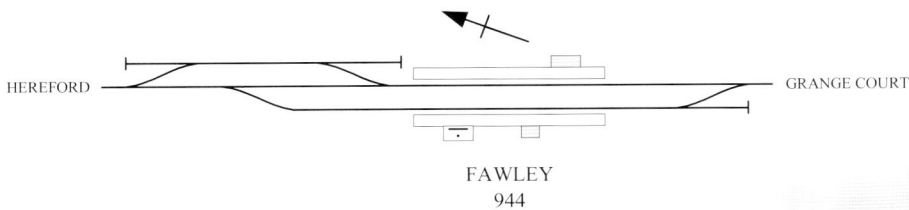

943
OP: 01/09/1908
CP: 31/10/1964
BALLINGHAM   [HR&GR]
Photo: N. 1963
E.T.Gill

HEREFORD

GRANGE COURT

BALLINGHAM
943

HEREFORD

GRANGE COURT

FAWLEY
944

944
OP: 02/06/1855
CP: 31/10/1964
FAWLEY   [HR&GR]
Photo: N. 1962
E.T.Gill

BACKNEY HALT
945

HEREFORD — GRANGE COURT

945   **BACKNEY HALT**   **[HR&GR]**
OP: 17/07/1933   Photo: N. 1962
CP: 10/02/1962   LOSA

946   **ROSS-ON-WYE**   **[HR&GR]**
OP: 02/06/1855   Photo: W. c.1923
CP: 31/10/1964   Stations U.K.

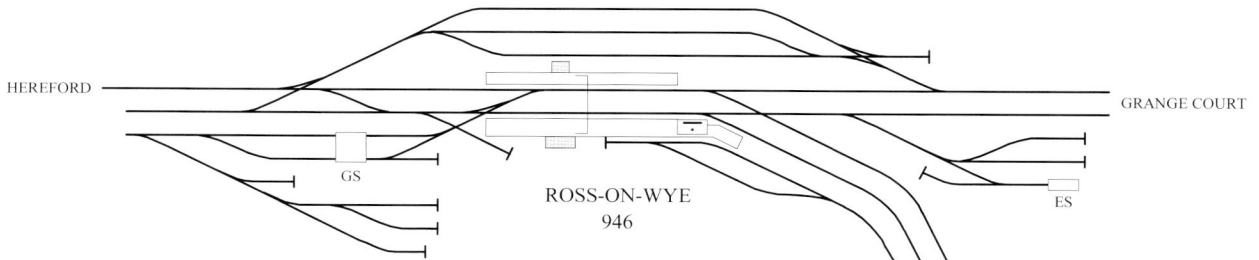

HEREFORD — GRANGE COURT

GS

ES

ROSS-ON-WYE
946

MONMOUTH
(see page 342)

946   **ROSS-ON-WYE**   **[HR&GR]**
Photo: E. c.1962
LOSA

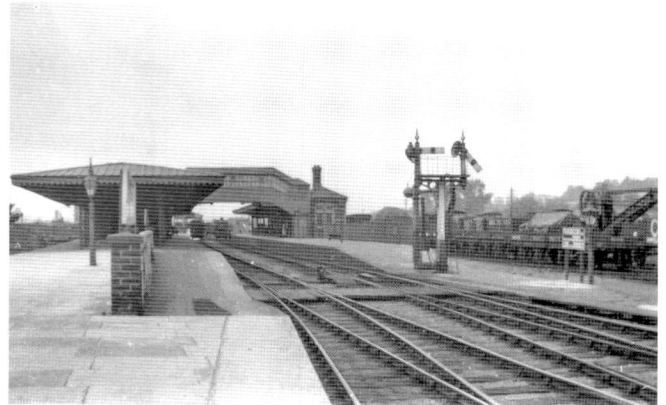

946   **ROSS-ON-WYE**   **[HR&GR]**
Photo: E. 1959
R.Stewartson

HEREFORD — GRANGE COURT

WESTON-
UNDER-PENYARD
HALT
947

947   **WESTON-UNDER-PENYARD HALT**   **[HR&GR]**
OP: 02/12/1929   Photo: W. 1961
CP: 31/10/1964   R.M.Casserley

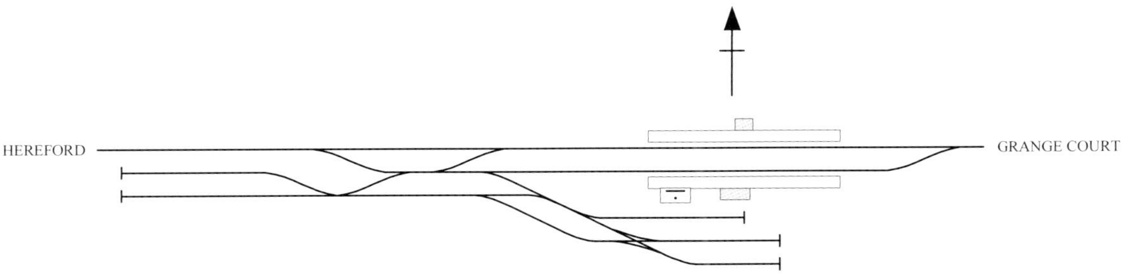
HEREFORD
GRANGE COURT

MITCHELDEAN
ROAD
948

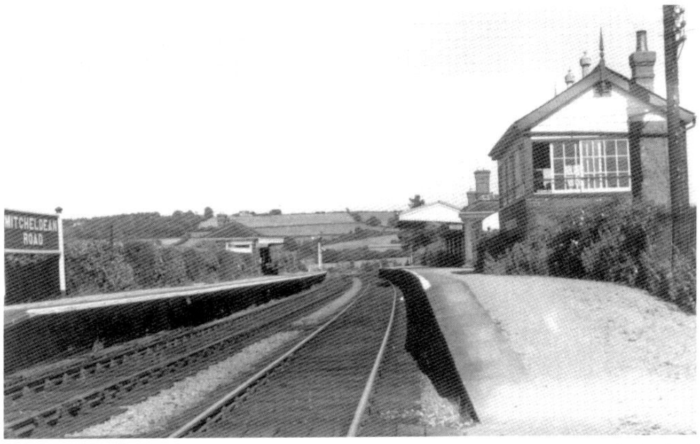
MITCHELDEAN
ROAD

948 **MITCHELDEAN ROAD** **[HR&GR]**
OP: 02/06/1855 Photo: E. 1959
CP: 31/10/1964 P.Garland

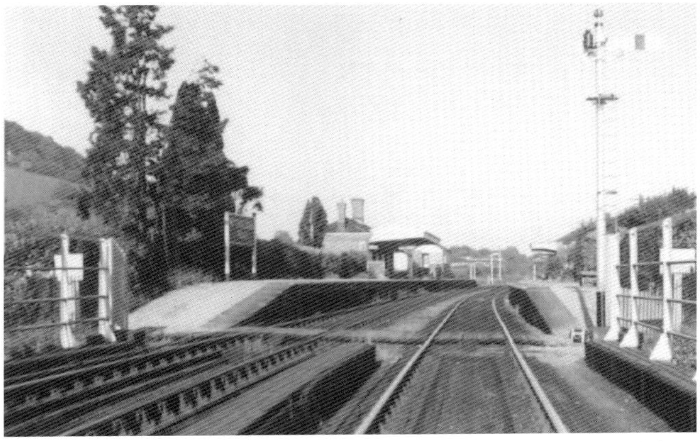

948 **MITCHELDEAN ROAD** **[HR&GR]**
Photo: W. 1961
R.M.Casserley

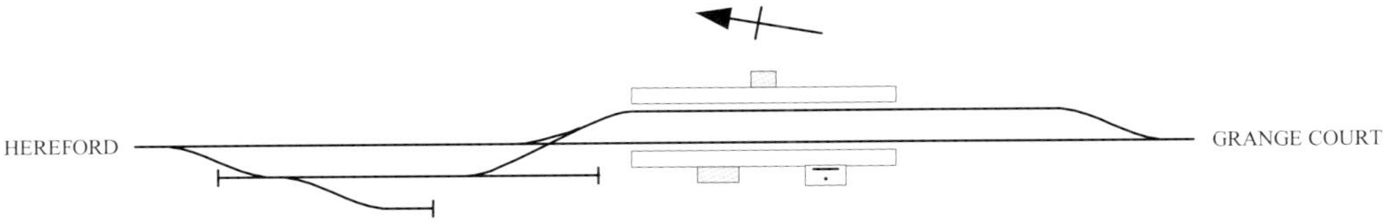
HEREFORD
GRANGE COURT

LONGHOPE
949

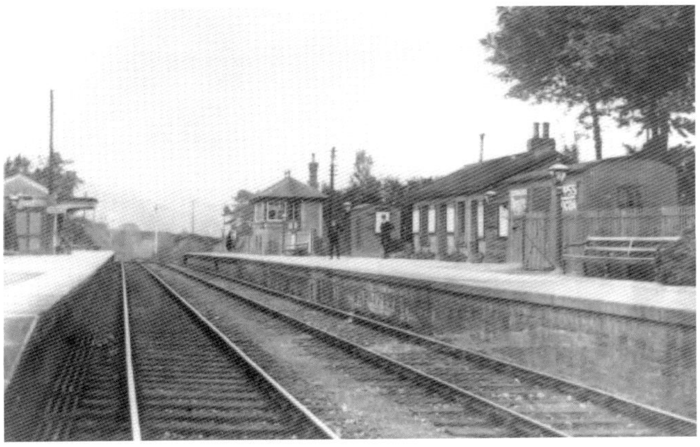

949 **LONGHOPE** **[HR&GR]**
OP: 02/06/1855 Photo: S. c.1920
CP: 31/10/1964 LOSA

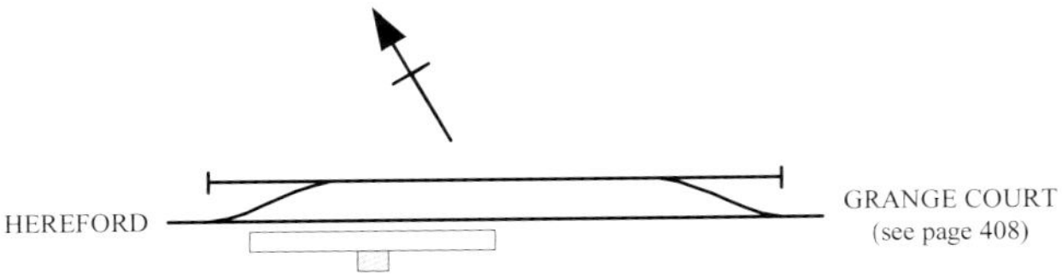
HEREFORD
GRANGE COURT
(see page 408)

BLAISDON HALT
950

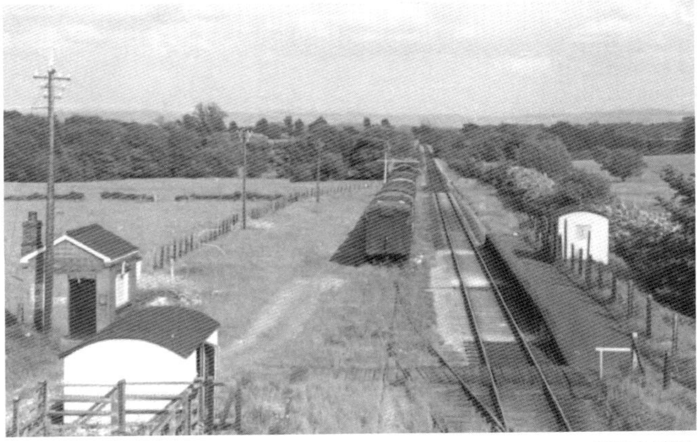

950 **BLAISDON HALT** **[HR&GR]**
OP: 04/11/1929 Photo: SE. 1958
CP: 31/10/1964 Stations U.K.

Ross & Monmouth Railway -
Great Western Railway (01/01/1922)
(Ross-on-Wye to Monmouth (Troy))
Coleford Monmouth Usk & Pontypool Railway -
Great Western Railway (01/01/1887)
(Monmouth (Troy) to Little Mill Junction)
ACT: 05/07/1865 (Ross-on-Wye to Monmouth (Troy))
ACT: 20/08/1853 (Monmouth to Little Mill Junction)
OPG: 03/08/1873 (Ross-on-Wye to Monmouth (May Hill))
OPG: 01/05/1874 (Monmouth (May Hill) to Monmouth (Troy))
OPG: 12/10/1857 (Monmouth (Troy) to Usk)
OPG: 02/06/1856 (Usk to Little Mill Junction)
CP: 03/01/1959 (Ross-on-Wye to Monmouth (Troy))
CP: 28/05/1955 (Monmouth (Troy) to Little Mill Junction)
CG: 31/10/1965 (Ross-on-Wye to Lydbrook Junction)
CG: 03/01/1959 (Lydbrook Junction to Monmouth (May Hill))
CG: 06/01/1964 (Monmouth (May Hill) to Monmouth (Troy))
CG: 13/06/1955 (Monmouth (Troy) to Usk)
CG: 13/09/1965 (Usk to Glascoed (R.O.F.))

951	WALFORD HALT	[R&MR]
OP: 23/02/1931		Photo: S. 1961
CP: 03/01/1959		Stations U.K.

PONTYPOOL ROAD — ROSS-ON-WYE (see page 340)

WALFORD HALT
951

952	KERNE BRIDGE	[R&MR]
OP: 03/08/1873		Photo: N. 1951
CP: 03/01/1959		W.Potter

PONTYPOOL ROAD — ROSS-ON-WYE

KERNE BRIDGE
952

PONTYPOOL ROAD — ROSS-ON-WYE

LYDBROOK JUNCTION
953

CINDERFORD
(see page 352)

953   **LYDBROOK JUNCTION**   **[R&MR]**
OP: 03/08/1873
CP: 03/01/1959

Photo: N. 1961
Stations U.K.

953   **LYDBROOK JUNCTION**   **[R&MR]**

Photo: S. 1961
Stations U.K.

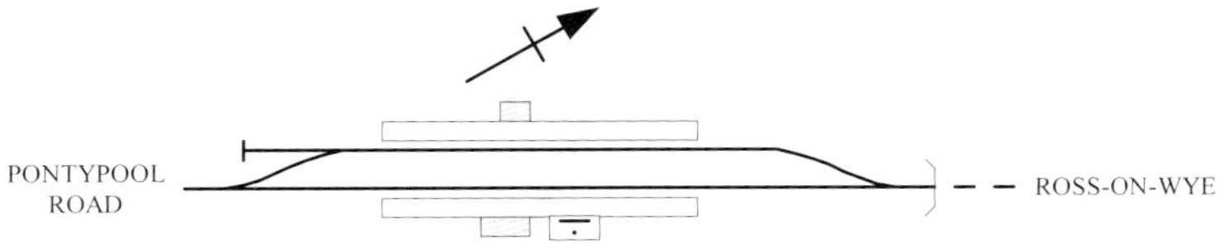

PONTYPOOL
ROAD   ROSS-ON-WYE

SYMONDS YAT
954

954   **SYMONDS YAT**   **[R&MR]**
OP: 03/08/1873
CP: 03/01/1959

Photo: NE. 1922
R.Carpenter

PONTYPOOL
ROAD   ROSS-ON-WYE

MONMOUTH
(MAY HILL)
955

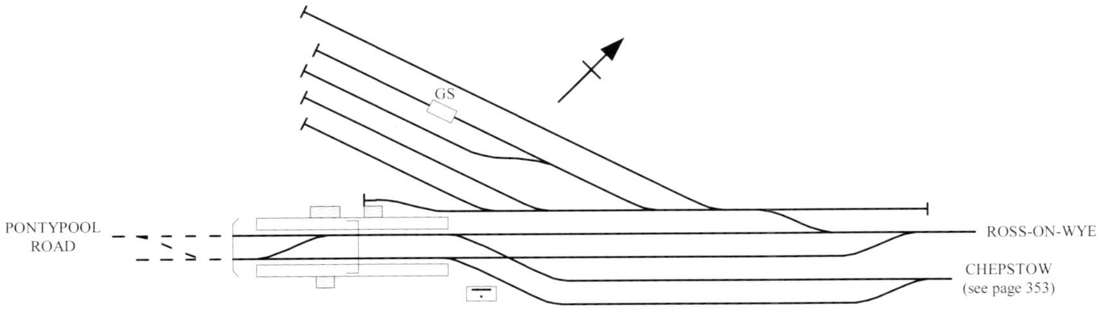

955   **MONMOUTH (MAY HILL)**   **[R&MR]**
OP: 03/08/1873
CP: 03/01/1959

Photo: N. 1948
R.G.Nelson

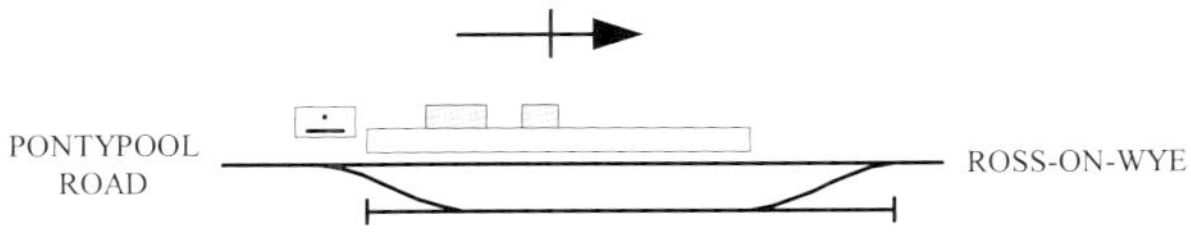

GS

PONTYPOOL
ROAD   ROSS-ON-WYE

CHEPSTOW
(see page 353)

MONMOUTH (TROY)
956

956   **MONMOUTH (TROY)**   **[CMU&PR]**
OP: 12/10/1857   Photo: SW. 1922
CP: 03/01/1959   R.Carpenter

956   **MONMOUTH (TROY)**   **[CMU&PR]**
         Photo: NE. 1948
         R.G.Nelson

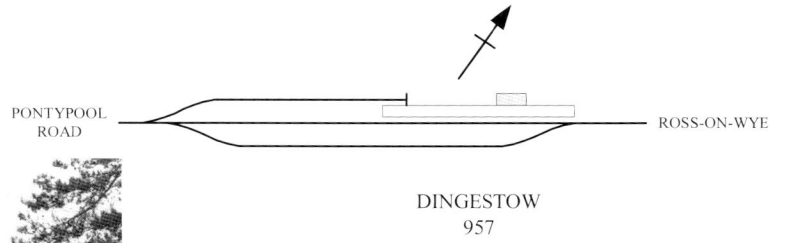

PONTYPOOL ROAD   ROSS-ON-WYE

DINGESTOW
957

957   **DINGESTOW**   **[CMU&PR]**
OP: 12/10/1857   Photo: NE. 1958
CP: 28/05/1955   M.Hale

PONTYPOOL ROAD   ROSS-ON-WYE

ELMS BRIDGE
HALT
958

958   **ELMS BRIDGE HALT**   **[CMU&PR]**
OP: 27/11/1933   Photo: NE. c.1956
CP: 28/05/1955   R.Stewartson

959   **RAGLAN**   **[CMU&PR]**
OP: 01/07/1876   Photo: SW. 1955
CP: 28/05/1955   H.C.Casserley

GS

PONTYPOOL ROAD   ROSS-ON-WYE

RAGLAN
959

PONTYPOOL
ROAD

ROSS-ON-WYE

RAGLAN ROAD
CROSSING HALT
960

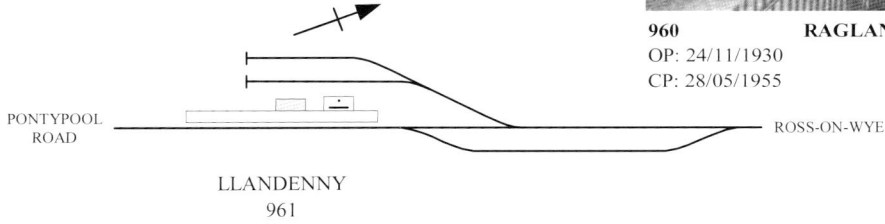

960   **RAGLAN ROAD CROSSING HALT**   **[CMU&PR]**
OP: 24/11/1930   Photo: S. 1955
CP: 28/05/1955   R.M.Casserley

PONTYPOOL
ROAD

ROSS-ON-WYE

LLANDENNY
961

961   **LLANDENNY**   **[CMU&PR]**
OP: 12/10/1857   Photo: S. 1955
CP: 28/05/1955   H.C.Casserley

PONTYPOOL
ROAD

ROSS-ON-WYE

GS

USK
962

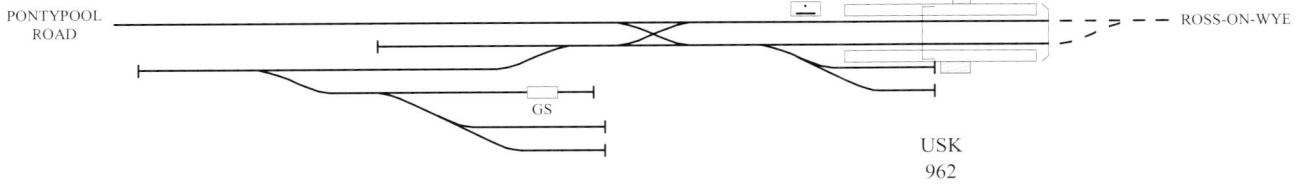

962   **USK**   **[CMU&PR]**
OP: 02/06/1856   Photo: E. c.1939
CP: 28/05/1955   Stations U.K.

962   **USK**   **[CMU&PR]**
    Photo: E. 1955
    H.C.Casserley

963   **WERN HIR**   **[CMU&PR]**
NO INFORMATION AS CLOSED BY 1947
CP: by 05/1941

964   **GLASCOED FACTORY EAST**   **[CMU&PR]**
OP: 03/01/1943   **ACCESS HALT**   Photo: W. 1955
CP: by 08/06/1953 (Workmens trains)   R.M.Casserley

PONTYPOOL   ROSS-ON-WYE
ROAD

GLASCOED FACTORY
EAST ACCESS HALT
964

PONTYPOOL   ROSS-ON-WYE
ROAD

GLASCOED FACTORY
WEST ACCESS HALT
965

965   **GLASCOED FACTORY WEST**   **[CMU&PR]**
OP: 12/06/1941   **ACCESS HALT**   Photo: W. 1955
CP: 28/05/1955 (Workmens trains)   H.C.Casserley

PONTYPOOL   ROSS-ON-WYE
ROAD

GLASCOED
HALT
966

966   **GLASCOED HALT**   **[CMU&PR]**
OP: 22/04/1938   Photo: E. c.1955
CP: 28/05/1955   LOSA

967   **LITTLE MILL JUNCTION**   **[CMU&PR]**
OP: 02/06/1856   Photo: NE. 1961
CP: 28/05/1955   Stations U.K.

HEREFORD
(see page 306)

ROSS-ON-WYE

PONTYPOOL ROAD
(see page 306)

LITTLE MILL
JUNCTION
967

NEWNHAM (Exc) TO CINDERFORD
FOREST OF DEAN BRANCH,
SEVERN & WYE LINE
South Wales Railway -
Great Western Railway (01/08/1863)
(Forest of Dean Junction to Bilson Loop Junction)
Great Western Railway
(Bilson Loop)
Great Western & Midland Joint Railway
(Cinderford Junction to Cinderford)
ACT: 03/07/1851 (Forest of Dean Junc. to Bilson Loop Junc.)
ACT: c.1907 (Bilson Loop)
ACT: 17/08/1893 (Cinderford Junction to Cinderford)
OP: 03/08/1907 (Newnham to Steam Mills Halt)
OP: 06/04/1908 (Bilson Loop)
OP: 02/07/1900 (from Drybrook Road to Cinderford)
OG: 24/07/1854 (Cinderford Junction to Whimsey)
OG: 06/04/1908 (Bilson Loop)
OG: 02/07/1900 (from Laymoor Junction to Cinderford)
CP: 01/11/1958
CG: 03/08/1967

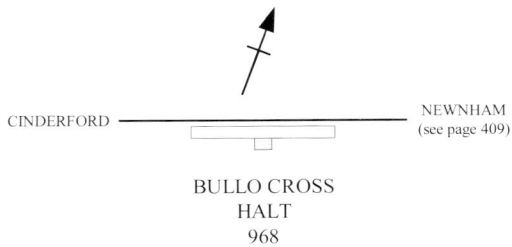

CINDERFORD ———————————— NEWNHAM
(see page 409)

BULLO CROSS
HALT
968

968	BULLO CROSS HALT	[SWR]
OP: 03/08/1907		Photo: E. 1956
CP: 01/11/1958		H.C.Casserley

968	BULLO CROSS HALT	[SWR]
		Photo: W. 1958
		Stations U.K.

969	UPPER SOUDLEY HALT	[SWR]
OP: 03/08/1907		Photo: E. 1956
CP: 01/11/1958		H.C.Casserley

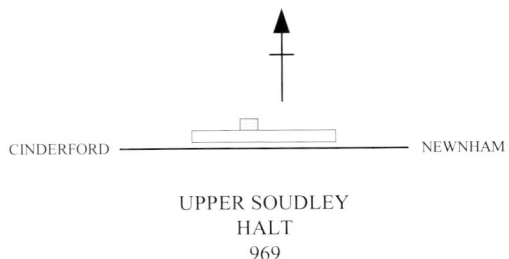

CINDERFORD ———————————— NEWNHAM

UPPER SOUDLEY
HALT
969

CINDERFORD

NEWNHAM

Eastern United
Colliery

STAPLE EDGE
HALT
970

970   **STAPLE EDGE HALT**   **[SWR]**
OP: 03/08/1907   Photo: S. 1958
CP: 01/11/1958   R.Stewartson

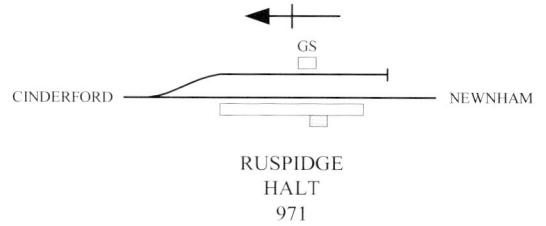

GS

CINDERFORD

NEWNHAM

RUSPIDGE
HALT
971

971   **RUSPIDGE HALT**   **[SWR]**
OP: 03/08/1907   Photo: N. 1922
CP: 01/11/1958   R.Carpenter

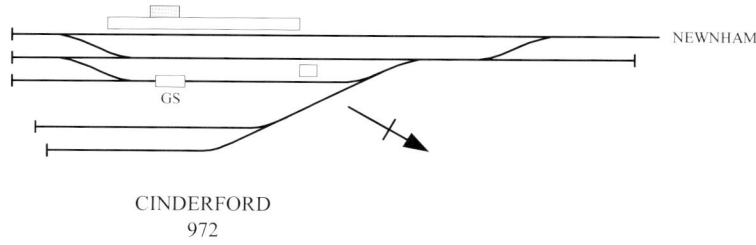

971   **RUSPIDGE HALT**   **[SWR]**
Photo: S. 1956
H.C.Casserley

NEWNHAM

GS

CINDERFORD
972

972   **CINDERFORD**   **[GW&MJ]**
OP: 02/07/1900   Photo: SE. 1949
CP: 01/11/1958   LOSA

972   **CINDERFORD**   **[GW&MJ]**
Photo: NW. 1961
P.Garland

Great Western Railway — Map of the Company's System

CINDERFORD (Exc) TO BERKELEY ROAD
SEVERN & WYE LINE

Severn & Wye Railway -
Severn & Wye and Severn Bridge Railway (21/07/1879) -
Great Western & Midland Joint Railway (01/07/1894)
(Bilson Platform to Lydney Junction (old station))
Severn Bridge Railway -
Severn & Wye and Severn Bridge Railway (21/07/1879) -
Great Western & Midland Joint Railway (01/07/1894)
(Engine Shed Junction to Oldminster Junction)
Midland Railway -
Great Western & Midland Joint Railway (01/07/1894)
(Oldminster Junction to Berkeley Road)

ACT: 26/07/1869 (Bilson Junctions to Lydney Docks)
ACT: 18/07/1872 (Engine Shed Junc. (Lydney) to Oldminster Junc.)
ACT: 25/07/1872 (Oldminster Junction (Sharpness) to Berkeley Road)
OP: 23/09/1879 (Bilson Platform to Lydney Junction (old station))
OP: 17/10/1879 (Lydney Junction to Berkeley)
OP: 01/08/1876 (Berkeley to Berkeley Road)
OG: 1873 (Bilson Junction to Speech House Road)
OG: 19/04/1869 (Speech House Road to Lydney Docks)
OG: 17/10/1879 (Lydney Junction to Oldminster Junction)
OG: 02/08/1875 (Oldminster Junction to Berkeley Road)
CP: 06/07/1929 (Cinderford Junction to Lydney Town)
CP: 25/10/1960 (Lydney Town to Sharpness)
CP: 31/10/1964 (Sharpness to Berkeley Road)
CG: 16/06/1953 (Bilson Junction to Drybrook Road)
CG: 25/07/1949 (Drybrook Road to Serridge Junction)
CG: 21/11/1960 (Serridge Junction to Speech House Road)
CG: 12/08/1963 (Speech House Road to Coleford Junction)
CG: 11/08/1967 (Coleford Junction to Parkend)
CG: 07/05/1976 (Parkend to Lydney Junction)
CG: 25/10/1960 (Lydney Junction to Sharpness)
CG: 02/11/1964 (Sharpness)
CG: 01/11/1966 (Sharpness to Berkeley Road) (Public Goods only)

973   **DRYBROOK ROAD**   **[S&WR]**
OP: 23/09/1875   Photo: E. 1951
CP: 06/07/1929   J.E.Norris

DRYBROOK ROAD
973
[CLOSED]

974   **SPEECH HOUSE ROAD**   **[S&WR]**
OP: 23/09/1875   Photo: N. 1952
CP: 06/07/1929   P.Garland

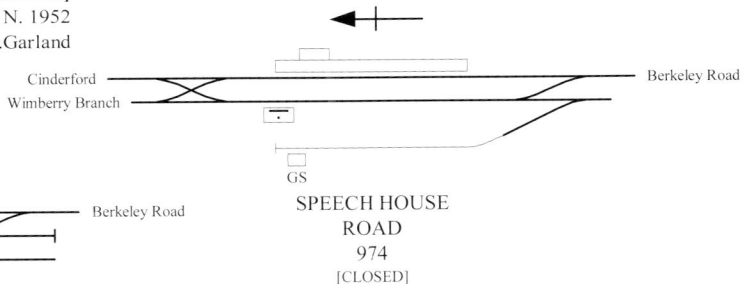

SPEECH HOUSE
ROAD
974
[CLOSED]

PARKEND
975
[CLOSED]

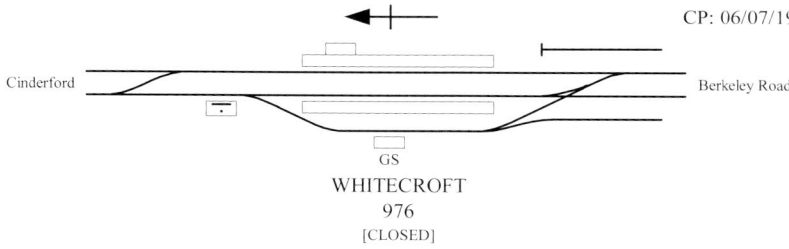

975   **PARKEND**   **[S&WR]**
OP: 23/09/1875   Photo: N. 1959
CP: 06/07/1929   R.M.Casserley

976   **WHITECROFT**   **[S&WR]**
OP: 23/09/1875   Photo: S. 1964
CP: 06/07/1929   R.K.Blencowe

Cinderford   Berkeley Road

GS

WHITECROFT
976
[CLOSED]

Cinderford   BERKELEY ROAD

GS

LYDNEY TOWN
977

977   **LYDNEY TOWN**   **[S&WR]**
OP: 23/09/1875   Photo: N. 1950
CP: 25/10/1960   J.E.Norris

978   **LYDNEY JUNCTION**   **[SBR]**
OP: 17/10/1879   Photo: NW. 1950
CP: 25/10/1960   H.C.Casserley

LYDNEY TOWN   BERKELEY ROAD

LYDNEY JUNCTION
978

SEVERN BRIDGE
979

LYDNEY TOWN

GLOUCESTER
(see page 409)

BERKELEY
ROAD

SWANSEA
(see page 410)

979   **SEVERN BRIDGE**   **[SBR]**
OP: 17/10/1879
CP: 25/10/1960

Photo: W. c.1958
M.Hale

979   **SEVERN BRIDGE**   **[SBR]**

Photo: E. c.1960
R.K.Blencowe

LYDNEY TOWN

BERKELEY
ROAD

SHARPNESS
980

980   **SHARPNESS**   **[SBR]**
OP: 17/10/1879
CP: 31/10/1964

Photo: S. 1950
R.Carpenter

981   **BERKELEY**   **[MR]**
OP: 01/08/1876
CP: 31/10/1964

Photo: W. 1947
Stations U.K.

LYDNEY TOWN

BERKELEY
ROAD

GS

BERKELEY
981

LYDNEY TOWN

Berkeley Road
Junction (L.M.S.R.)

(Gloucester L.M.S.R.)

(Yate L.M.S.R.)

BERKELEY ROAD
982

GREAT WESTERN
RAILWAY
MAP OF THE COMPANY'S SYSTEM

982	BERKELEY ROAD	[MR]
OP: 01/08/1876		Photo: SW. 1947
CP: 31/10/1964		Stations U.K.

Serridge Junction TO LYDBROOK JUNCTION (Exc)
LYDBROOK BRANCH
Severn & Wye Railway -
Severn & Wye and Severn Bridge Railway (21/07/1879) -
Great Western & Midland Joint Railway (01/07/1894)
ACT: 12/05/1870
OP: 23/09/1875
OG: 26/08/1874
CP: 06/07/1929
CG: 21/11/1960 (Serridge Junction to Mierystock)
CG: 30/01/1956 (Mierystock to Upper Lydbrook)
CG: 01/01/1953 (Upper Lydbrook to Lydbrook Junction)

983	UPPER LYDBROOK	[S&WR]
OP: 23/09/1875		Photo: SE. 1922
CP: 06/07/1929		R.Carpenter

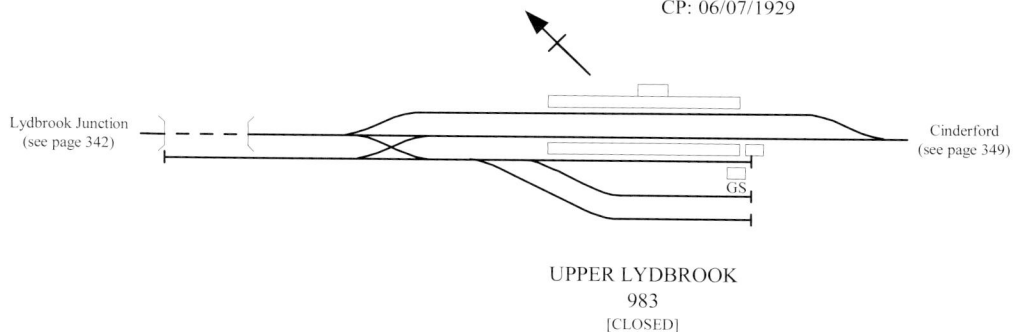

Lydbrook Junction
(see page 342)

Cinderford
(see page 349)

GS

UPPER LYDBROOK
983
[CLOSED]

352 Issue A 31/07/2015

Coleford Junction (Exc) TO COLEFORD (Exc)
COLEFORD BRANCH
Severn & Wye Railway -
Severn & Wye and Severn Bridge Railway (21/07/1879) -
Great Western & Midland Joint Railway (01/07/1894)
(Coleford Junction to Coleford (S&W) station)
Coleford Railway -
Great Western Railway (01/07/1884)
(Coleford to Whitecliffe Quarry)
ACT: 18/07/1872 (Coleford Junction to Coleford)
ACT: 18/07/1872 (Coleford to Wyesham Junction)
OP: 09/12/1875 (Coleford Junction to Coleford (S&W station))
OP: 01/09/1883 (Coleford (GW station) only, from Monmouth)
OG: 19/07/1875 (Coleford Junction to Coleford (S&W station))
OG: 01/09/1883 (Coleford (GW station) only, from Wyesham Junc.)
CP: 06/07/1929 (Coleford Junction to Coleford (S&W station))
CP: 31/12/1916 (Coleford (GW station))
CG: 11/08/1967 (Coleford Junction to Whitecliffe Quarry)

984   **MILKWALL**   **[S&WR]**
NO INFORMATION AS CLOSED BY 1947
CP: 06/07/1929

985   **COLEFORD**   **[S&WR]**
OP: 09/12/1875   Photo: E. 1949
CP: 06/07/1929   LOSA

COLEFORD
985
[CLOSED]

Speech House Road
(see page 349)

GS

GS

Whitecliffe Quarry

COLEFORD
986
[CLOSED]

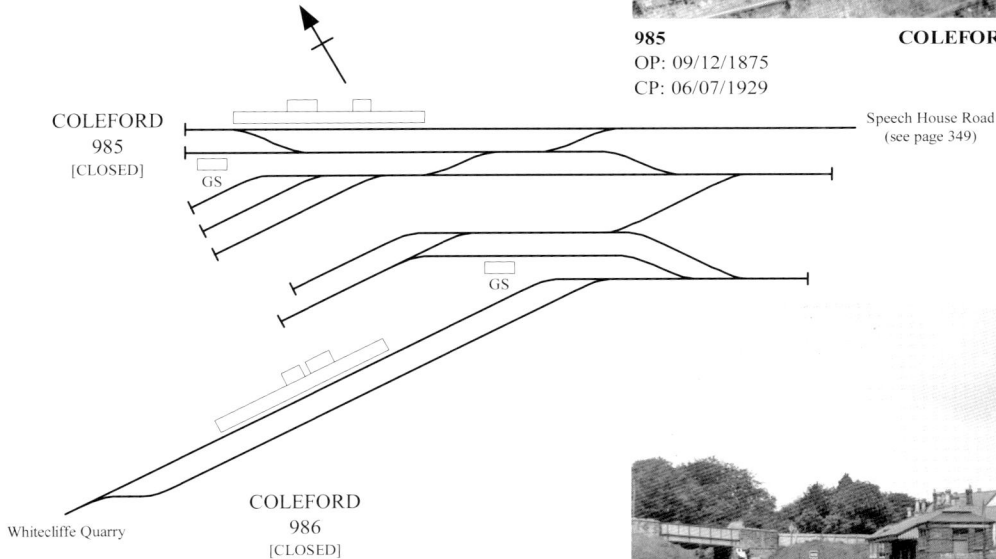

986   **COLEFORD**   **[ColeRly]**
OP: 01/09/1883   Photo: W. 1922
CP: 31/12/1916   R.Carpenter

MONMOUTH (TROY) (Exc) TO CHEPSTOW (Exc)
WYE VALLEY BRANCH
Coleford Monmouth Usk & Pontypool Railway -
Great Western Railway (01/01/1887)
(Monmouth (Troy) to Wyesham Junction)
Wye Valley Railway -
Great Western Railway (01/07/1905)
(Wyesham Junction to Wye Valley Junction)
ACT: 20/08/1853 (Monmouth to Wyesham Junction)
ACT: 10/08/1866 (Wyesham Junction to Wye Valley Junction)
OP: 01/11/1876
OG: 01/07/1861 (Monmouth to Wyesham Junction)
OG: 01/11/1876 (Wyesham Junction to Wye Valley Junction)
CP: 03/01/1959
CG: 06/01/1964

MONMOUTH (TROY)
(see page 343)

CHEPSTOW

WYESHAM
HALT
987

987   **WYESHAM HALT**   **[CMU&PR]**
OP: 12/02/1931   Photo: W. 1959
CP: 03/01/1959   H.C.Casserley

MONMOUTH
(TROY)

GS

CHEPSTOW

REDBROOK
-ON-WYE
988

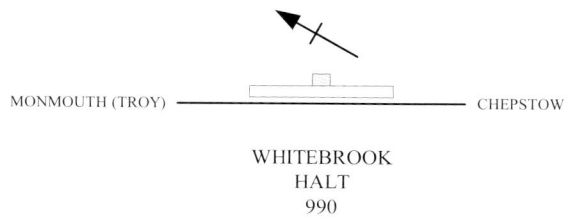

988   **REDBROOK-ON-WYE**   **[WVR]**
OP: 01/11/1876
CP: 03/01/1959   Photo: N. 1955
                       H.C.Casserley

MONMOUTH (TROY) ——————————— CHEPSTOW

PENALLT
HALT
989

989   **PENALLT HALT**   **[WVR]**
OP: 03/08/1931
CP: 03/01/1959   Photo: N. 1958
                      M.Hale

MONMOUTH (TROY) ——————————— CHEPSTOW

WHITEBROOK
HALT
990

990   **WHITEBROOK HALT**   **[WVR]**
OP: 01/02/1927
CP: 03/01/1959   Photo: NW. 1955
                      H.C.Casserley

MONMOUTH
(TROY)

GS

CHEPSTOW

ST. BRIAVELS
991

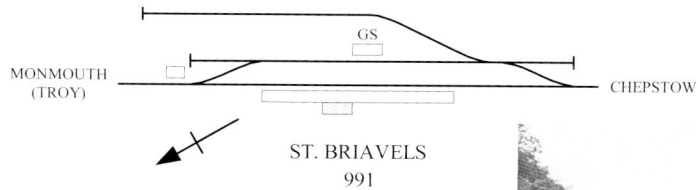

991   **ST. BRIAVELS**   **[WVR]**
OP: 01/11/1876
CP: 03/01/1959   Photo: NW. 1958
                      M.Hale

992   **LLANDOGO HALT**   **[WVR]**
OP: 09/03/1927   Photo: NW. c.1958
CP: 03/01/1959   unknown

MONMOUTH (TROY) ———————————— CHEPSTOW

LLANDOGO
HALT
992

MONMOUTH (TROY) ———————————— CHEPSTOW

BROCKWEIR
HALT
993

993   **BROCKWEIR HALT**   **[WVR]**
OP: 19/08/1929   Photo: NW. 1958
CP: 03/01/1959   M.Hale

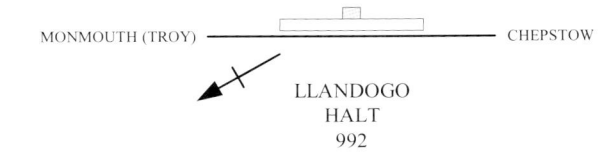

994   **TINTERN**   **[WVR]**
OP: 01/11/1876   Photo: N. 1948
CP: 03/01/1959   R.G.Nelson

MONMOUTH
(TROY) ———————————— CHEPSTOW

TINTERN
994   GS

MONMOUTH (TROY) – – – ———————————— CHEPSTOW

NETHERHOPE
HALT
995

995   **NETHERHOPE HALT**   **[WVR]**
OP: 16/05/1932   Photo: N. 1955
CP: 03/01/1959   H.C.Casserley

MONMOUTH
(TROY) ———————————— CHEPSTOW
(see page 410)
GS
TIDENHAM
996

996   **TIDENHAM**   **[WVR]**
OP: 01/11/1876   Photo: N. c.1949
CP: 03/01/1959   Bill Smith Collection

Bala & Festiniog Railway -
Great Western Railway (01/07/1910)
(Bala Junction to Festiniog)
Festiniog & Blaenau Railway -
Great Western and Bala & Festiniog Railway (13/04/1883) -
Great Western Railway (01/07/1910)
(Festiniog to Blaenau Festiniog)
ACT: 28/07/1873 (Bala Junction to Festiniog)
ACT: 06/08/1882 (Festiniog to Blaenau Festiniog)
OPG: 01/11/1882 (Bala Junction to Festiniog)
OPG: 10/09/1883 (Festiniog to Blaenau Festiniog)
CP: 02/01/1960 (Bala to Blaenau Festiniog)
CP: 16/01/1965 (Bala Junction to Bala)
CG: 27/01/1961 (Bala to Blaenau Festiniog)
CG: 02/11/1964 (Bala Junction to Bala)

GREAT WESTERN
RAILWAY
MAP OF THE COMPANY'S SYSTEM

BLAENAU
FESTINIOG

ES

BALA JUNCTION
(see page 365)

GS

BALA
997

997   **BALA**   **[B&FR]**
OP: 01/11/1882   Photo: NW. c.1960
CP: 16/01/1965   E.T.Gill

997   **BALA**   **[B&FR]**
Photo: SE. 1964
Stations U.K.

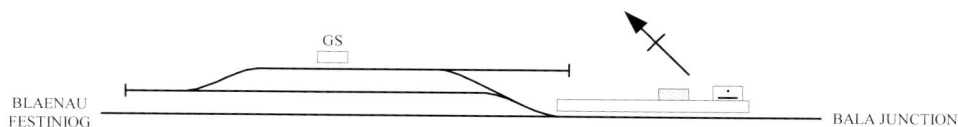

GS

BLAENAU
FESTINIOG

BALA JUNCTION

FRONGOCH
998

998   **FRONGOCH**   **[B&FR]**
OP: 01/11/1882   Photo: NW. c.1960
CP: 02/01/1960   E.T.Gill

999   **TYDDYN BRIDGE HALT**   **[B&FR]**
OP: 01/12/1930   Photo: W. 1961
CP: 02/01/1960   M.M.Lloyd

TYDDYN BRIDGE
HALT
999

BLAENAU
FESTINIOG

BALA JUNCTION

CAPEL CELYN
HALT
1000

BLAENAU
FESTINIOG

BALA JUNCTION

1000
OP: 01/12/1930
CP: 02/01/1960

CAPEL CELYN HALT

[B&FR]
Photo: SW. 1961
M.M.Lloyd

BLAENAU
FESTINIOG

BALA JUNCTION

ARENIG
1001

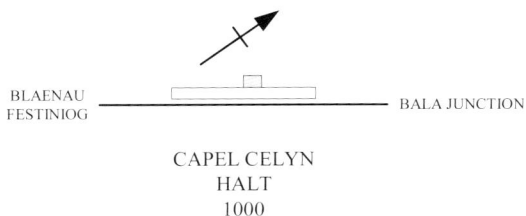

1001
OP: 01/11/1882
CP: 02/01/1960

ARENIG

[B&FR]
Photo: W. 1960
E.T.Gill

1001

ARENIG

[B&FR]
Photo: E. 1960
E.T.Gill

BLAENAU
FESTINIOG

BALA JUNCTION

CWM PRYSOR
1002

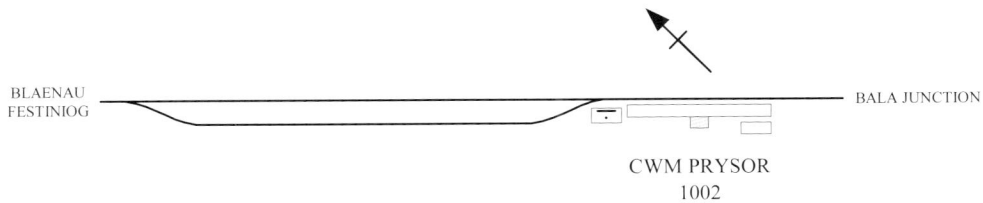

1002
OP: 01/09/1902
CP: 02/01/1960

CWM PRYSOR

[B&FR]
Photo: SE. 1959
M.Hale

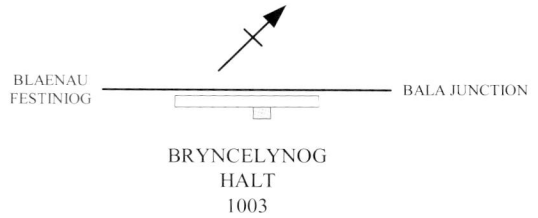

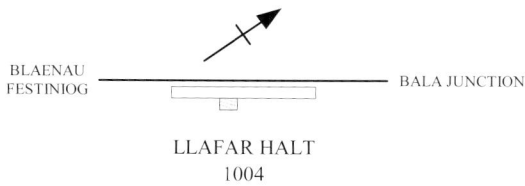

BLAENAU FESTINIOG — BALA JUNCTION

BRYNCELYNOG
HALT
1003

1003   **BRYNCELYNOG HALT**   **[B&FR]**
OP: 13/03/1939
CP: 02/01/1960   Photo: NE. 1959
                                   M.Hale

BLAENAU FESTINIOG — BALA JUNCTION

LLAFAR HALT
1004

1004   **LLAFAR HALT**   **[B&FR]**
OP: 01/03/1932
CP: 02/01/1960   Photo: SW. 1959
                           R.M.Casserley

BLAENAU FESTINIOG — BALA JUNCTION

ES

GS

TRAWSFYNYDD
1005

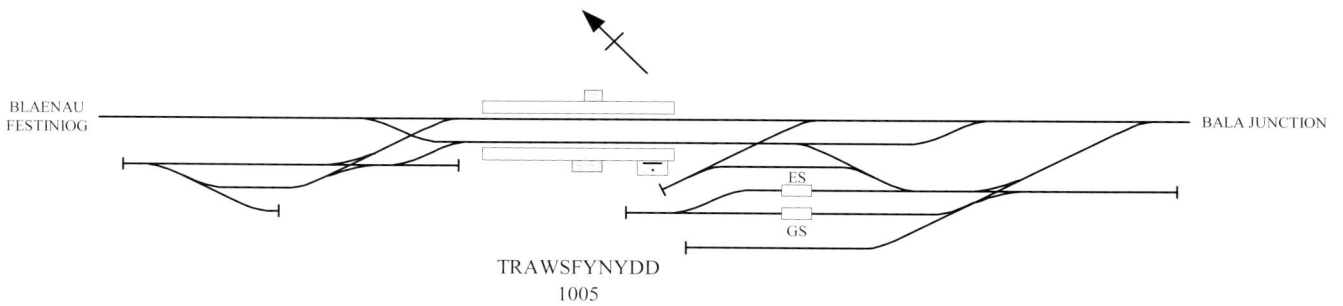

1005   **TRAWSFYNYDD**   **[B&FR]**
OP: 01/11/1882
CP: 02/01/1960   Photo: SE. 1948
               R.G.Nelson

1005   **TRAWSFYNYDD**   **[B&FR]**
              Photo: NW. 1957
              Stations U.K.

TRAWSFYNYDD
LAKE HALT
1006

1006   **TRAWSFYNYDD LAKE HALT**   **[B&FR]**
OP: 14/04/1934   Photo: NW, 1964
CP: 02/01/1960   C.L.Caddy

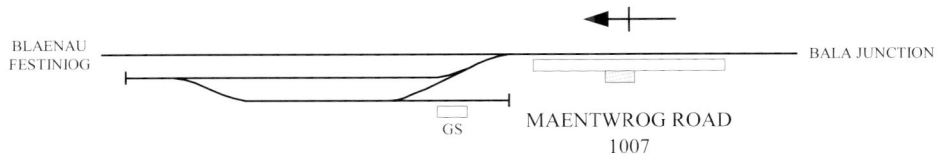

GS   MAENTWROG ROAD
1007

1007   **MAENTWROG ROAD**   **[B&FR]**
OP: 01/11/1882   Photo: N. 1939
CP: 02/01/1960   Stations U.K.

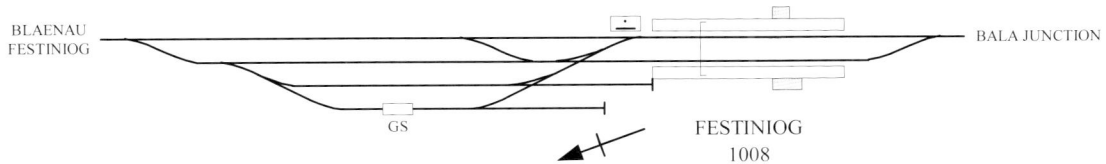

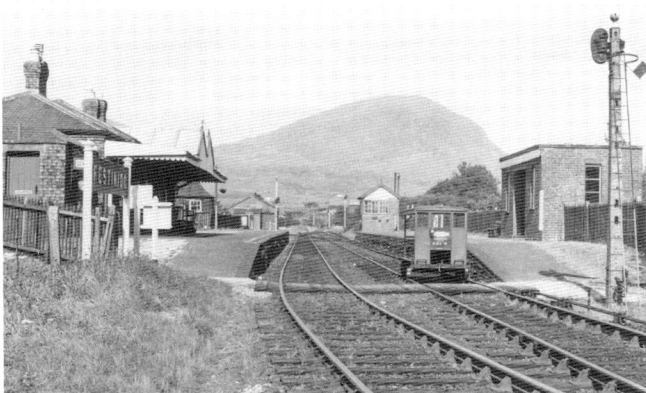

GS   FESTINIOG
1008

1008   **FESTINIOG**   **[B&FR]**
OP: 01/11/1882   Photo: N. 1959
CP: 02/01/1960   M.Hale

1008   **FESTINIOG**   **[B&FR]**
Photo: S. 1948
P.B.Whitehouse

TEIGL HALT
1009

1009   **TEIGL HALT**   **[F&BR]**
OP: 14/09/1931   Photo: SE. 1951
CP: 02/01/1960   R.C.Riley

1010   **MANOD**   **[F&BR]**
OP: 10/09/1883   Photo: N. 1959
CP: 02/01/1960   C.Mowat

MANOD
1010

BLAENAU
FESTINIOG
1011

1011   **BLAENAU FESTINIOG**   **[F&BR]**
OP: 10/09/1883   Photo: E. 1950
CP: 02/01/1960   R.Carpenter

1011   **BLAENAU FESTINIOG**   **[F&BR]**
                                 Photo: W. 1959
                            R.M.Casserley

BARMOUTH JUNCTION (Exc) TO RUABON (Exc)
DOLGELLEY BRANCH,
RUABON AND DOLGELLEY LINE
Aberystwyth & Welsh Coast Railway -
Cambrian Railways (05/07/1865) -
Great Western Railway (01/01/1922)
(Barmouth Junction to Dolgelley)
Bala & Dolgelly Railway -
Great Western Railway (01/08/1877)
(Dolgelley to Bala Lake Halt)
Corwen & Bala Railway -
Great Western Railway (01/07/1896)
(Bala Lake Halt to Corwen)
Llangollen & Corwen Railway -
Great Western Railway (01/07/1896)
(Corwen to Llangollen)
Vale of Llangollen Railway -
Great Western Railway (01/07/1896)
(Llangollen to Llangollen Line Junction)
ACT: 29/07/1862 (Barmouth Junction to Dolgelley)
ACT: 30/06/1862 (Dolgelley to 39 chains west of Bala Junction)
ACT: 30/06/1862 (39 chains west of Bala Junction to Corwen)
ACT: 06/08/1860 (Corwen to Llangollen)
ACT: 01/07/1896 (Llangollen to Llangollen Line Junction)
OPG: 03/07/1865 (Barmouth Junction to Penmaenpool)
OPG: 21/06/1869 (Penmaenpool to Dolgelley)
OP: 04/08/1868 (Dolgelley to Bala old station)
OG: 01/10/1868 (Dolgelley to Bala old station)
OPG: 01/04/1868 (Bala old station to Llandrillo)
OPG: 16/07/1866 (Llandrillo to Corwen)
OPG: 08/05/1865 (Corwen to Llangollen)
OP: 02/06/1862 (Llangollen to Ruabon)
OG: 01/12/1861 (Llangollen to Ruabon)
CP: 16/01/1965 (Barmouth Junction to Bala Junction)
CP: 12/12/1964 (Bala Junction to Llangollen)
CP: 16/01/1965 (Llangollen to Ruabon)
CG: 04/05/1964 (Barmouth Junction to Llangollen)
CG: 01/04/1968 (Llangollen to Ruabon)

1012	**ARTHOG**	[A&WCR]
OP: 28/03/1870		Photo: SW. 1964
CP: 16/01/1965		Stations U.K.

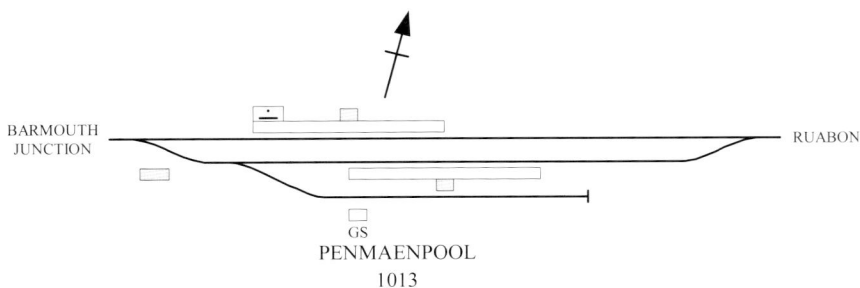

BARMOUTH JUNCTION
(see page 376)

RUABON

ARTHOG
1012

BARMOUTH
JUNCTION

RUABON

GS
PENMAENPOOL
1013

1013	**PENMAENPOOL**	[A&WCR]
OP: 03/07/1865		Photo: E. 1964
CP: 16/01/1965		Stations U.K.

1013	**PENMAENPOOL**	[A&WCR]
		Photo: W. 1962
		P.Garland

DOLGELLEY
1014

1014   **DOLGELLEY**   **[B&DR]**
OP: 04/08/1868   Photo: E. c.1955
CP: 16/01/1965   LOSA

1014   **DOLGELLEY**   **[B&DR]**
     Photo: W. 1963
     Joe Moss

BARMOUTH JUNCTION — RUABON

DOLSERAU
HALT
1015

1015   **DOLSERAU HALT**   **[B&DR]**
OP: 08/02/1935   Photo: NE. 1949
CP: 29/10/1951   L&GRP

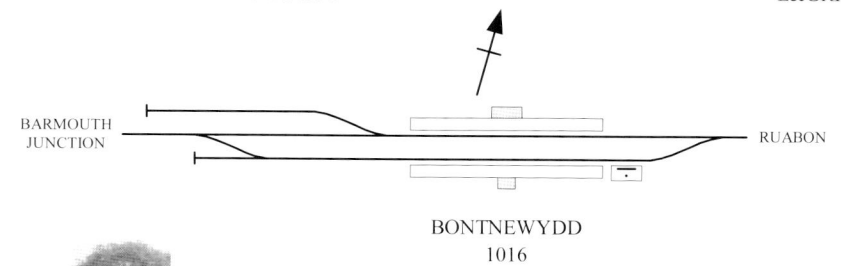

BARMOUTH JUNCTION — RUABON

BONTNEWYDD
1016

1016   **BONTNEWYDD**   **[B&DR]**
OP: 04/08/1868   Photo: E. 1964
CP: 16/01/1965   C.L.Caddy

BARMOUTH
JUNCTION ——————————————— RUABON

WNION HALT
1017

1017   **WNION HALT**   **[B&DR]**
OP: 05/06/1933
CP: 16/01/1965   Photo: SW. 1963
                                                 R.M.Casserley

BARMOUTH
JUNCTION ——————————————— RUABON

DRWS-Y-NANT
1018

1018   **DRWS-Y-NANT**   **[B&DR]**
OP: 04/08/1868   Photo: NE. 1962
CP: 16/01/1965   P.Garland

1018   **DRWS-Y-NANT**   **[B&DR]**
                                  Photo: SW. 1963
                                  R.M.Casserley

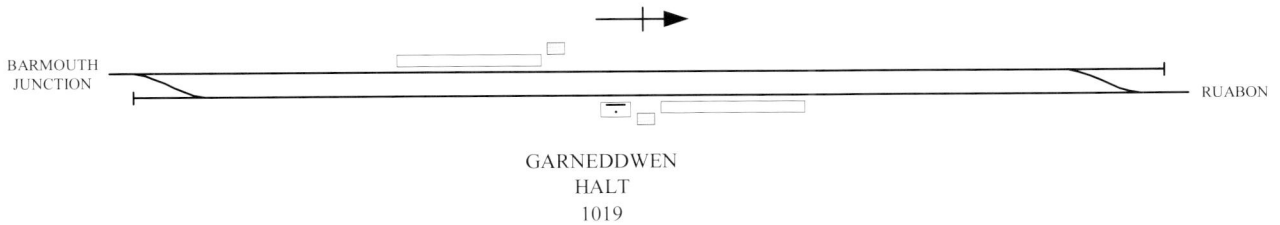

BARMOUTH
JUNCTION ——————————————— RUABON

GARNEDDWEN
HALT
1019

1019   **GARNEDDWEN HALT**   **[B&DR]**
OP: 09/07/1928   Photo: N.1964
CP: 02/11/1963   Stations U.K.

1019   **GARNEDDWEN HALT**   **[B&DR]**
                                    Photo: S. 1964
                                  Stations U.K.

LLYS HALT
1020

1020   **LLYS HALT**   **[B&DR]**
OP: 04/06/1934   Photo: E. 1962
CP: 16/01/1965   P.Garland

LLANUWCHLLYN
1021

1021   **LLANUWCHLLYN**   **[B&DR]**
OP: 04/08/1868   Photo: NE. 1962
CP: 16/01/1965   P.Garland

1021   **LLANUWCHLLYN**   **[B&DR]**
                                       Photo: SW. 1962
                                       P.Garland

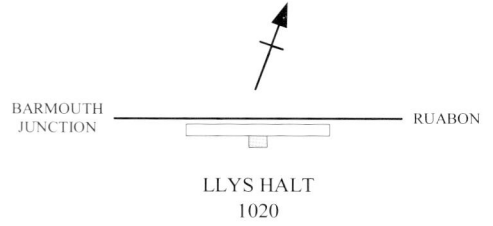

FLAG STATION
HALT
1022

1022   **FLAG STATION HALT**   **[B&DR]**
OP: 04/08/1868   Photo: SW. 1964
CP: 16/01/1965   C.L.Caddy

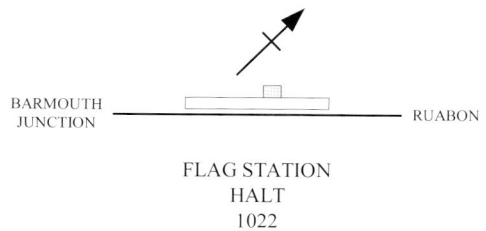

BARMOUTH JUNCTION — RUABON

LLANGOWER
HALT
1023

1023   **LLANGOWER HALT**   **[B&DR]**
OP: 10/06/1929   Photo: NE. 1962
CP: 16/01/1965   P.Garland

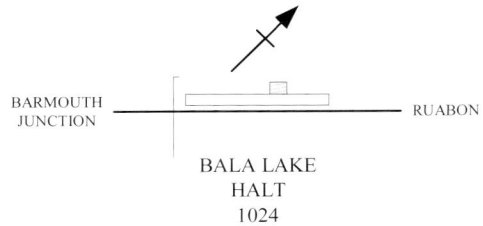

BARMOUTH JUNCTION — RUABON

BALA LAKE
HALT
1024

1024   **BALA LAKE HALT**   **[B&DR]**
OP: 05/02/1934   Photo: NE. c.1960
CP: 04/08/1963 (Excursion train)   LOSA

BALA
(see page 356)

BARMOUTH JUNCTION — RUABON

BALA JUNCTION
1025

1025   **BALA JUNCTION**   **[C&BR]**
OP: 01/11/1882   Photo: W. c.1955
CP: 16/01/1965   P.Garland

1025   **BALA JUNCTION**   **[C&BR]**
                   Photo: E. 1964
                   Stations U.K.

LLANDDERFEL
1026

1026   **LLANDDERFEL**   **[C&BR]**
OP: 01/04/1868
CP: 12/12/1964   Photo: E. c.1939
Stations U.K.

1026   **LLANDDERFEL**   **[C&BR]**
Photo: W. 1962
P.Garland

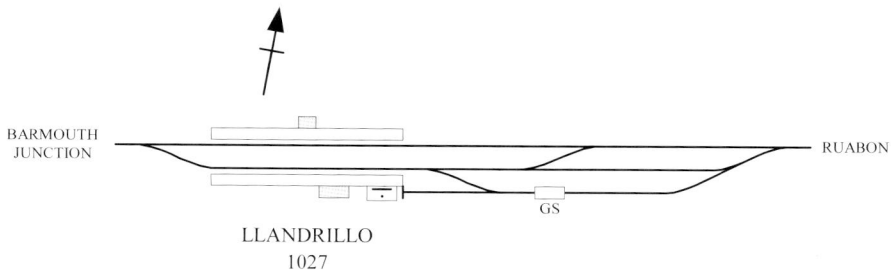

LLANDRILLO
1027

1027   **LLANDRILLO**   **[C&BR]**
OP: 16/07/1866
CP: 12/12/1964   Photo: NE. 1962
P.Garland

1028   **CYNWYD**   **[C&BR]**
OP: 16/07/1866
CP: 12/12/1964   Photo: SW. 1962
P.Garland

CYNWYD
1028

CORWEN
1029

1029   **CORWEN**   **[C&BR]**
OP: 01/09/1865   Photo: E. c.1960
CP: 12/12/1964   R.G.Nelson

1029   **CORWEN**   **[C&BR]**
Photo: W. 1949
P.Garland

BARMOUTH
JUNCTION   RUABON

BONWM HALT
1030

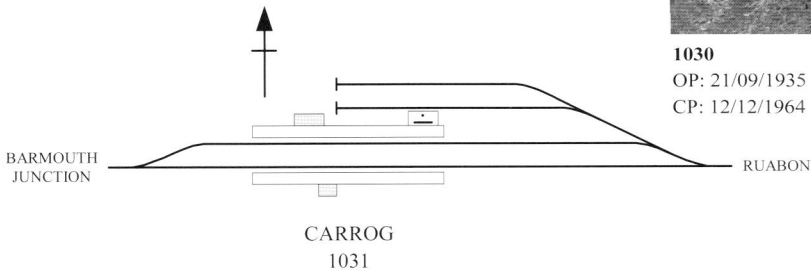

1030   **BONWM HALT**   **[L&CR]**
OP: 21/09/1935   Photo: E. 1964
CP: 12/12/1964   Stations U.K.

BARMOUTH
JUNCTION   RUABON

CARROG
1031

1031   **CARROG**   **[L&CR]**
OP: 08/05/1865   Photo: E. 1959
CP: 12/12/1964   C.Mowat

1031   **CARROG**   **[L&CR]**
Photo: W. 1961
R.K.Blencowe

BARMOUTH
JUNCTION
RUABON

GLYNDYFRDWY
1032

1032   **GLYNDYFRDWY**   **[L&CR]**
OP: 08/05/1865   Photo: W. 1964
CP: 12/12/1964   Stations U.K.

1033   **BERWYN**   **[L&CR]**
OP: 08/05/1865   Photo: W. 1964
CP: 12/12/1964   Stations U.K.

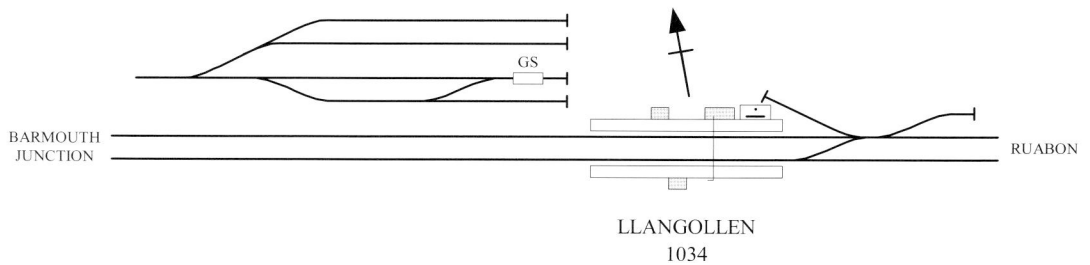

BARMOUTH
JUNCTION
RUABON

BERWYN
1033

GS

BARMOUTH
JUNCTION
RUABON

LLANGOLLEN
1034

1034   **LLANGOLLEN**   **[L&CR]**
OP: 08/05/1865   Photo: W. 1949
CP: 16/01/1965   P.Garland

1034   **LLANGOLLEN**   **[L&CR]**
      Photo: E. 1964
      Stations U.K.

PHOTOGRAPH UNAVAILABLE

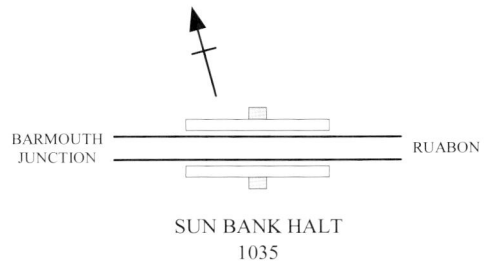

SUN BANK HALT
1035

1035
OP: 24/07/1905
CP: 05/06/1950

SUN BANK HALT

[VLR]
Photo: None
Available

BARMOUTH
JUNCTION

RUABON

Pontcysyllte
Basin Branch

My father was a signalman in Trevor when my mother was Chief Clerk 1916-1921, when they married.

TREVOR
1036

1036
OP: 02/06/1862
CP: 16/01/1965

TREVOR

[VLR]
Photo: SW. c.1955
P.Garland

1036

TREVOR

[VLR]
Photo: NE. 1961
Stations U.K.

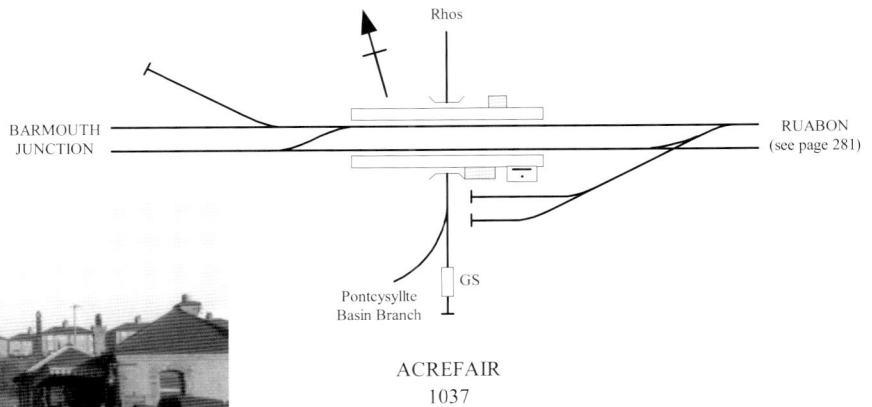

Rhos

BARMOUTH
JUNCTION

RUABON
(see page 281)

Pontcysyllte
Basin Branch

GS

ACREFAIR
1037

1037
OP: 02/06/1862
CP: 16/01/1965

ACREFAIR

[VLR]
Photo: E. 1961
Stations U.K.

GREAT WESTERN
RAILWAY
MAP OF THE COMPANY'S SYSTEM

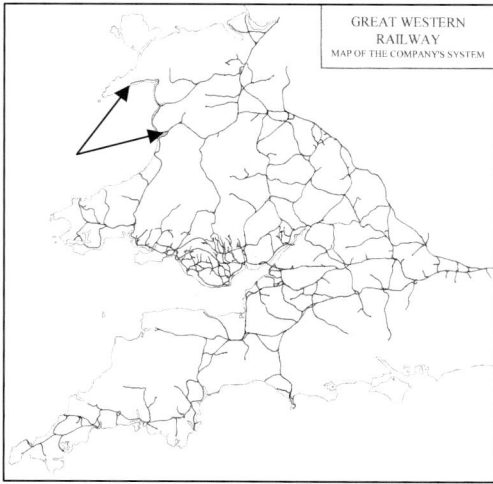

PWLLHELI TO DOVEY JUNCTION (Exc)
DOVEY JUNCTION TO PWLLHELI LINE
Cambrian Railways -
Great Western Railway (01/01/1922)
(Pwllheli to Pwllheli old station)
Aberystwyth & Welsh Coast Railway -
Cambrian Railways (05/07/1865) -
Great Western Railway (01/01/1922)
(Pwllheli old station to Dovey Junction)
ACT: 02/07/1901 (Pwllheli to Pwllheli old station)
ACT: 29/07/1862 (Pwllheli old station to Portmadoc)
ACT: 22/07/1861 (Portmadoc to Aberdovey)
ACT: 05/07/1865 (Aberdovey to Dovey Junction)
OPG: 19/07/1909 (Pwllheli to Pwllheli old station)
OPG: 10/10/1867 (Pwllheli old station to Barmouth)
(OP: 02/09/1867 to 10/10/1867 Afon Wen to
Penrhyndeudraeth for Carnarfonshire Railway trains)
OP: 03/06/1867 (Barmouth to Barmouth Junction)
OG: 10/10/1867 (Barmouth to Barmouth Junction)
OPG: 03/07/1865 (Barmouth Junction to Llwyngwril)
OPG: 24/10/1863 (Llwyngwril to Aberdovey)
OPG: 14/08/1867 (Aberdovey to Dovey Junction)
CP: OPEN
CG: OPEN

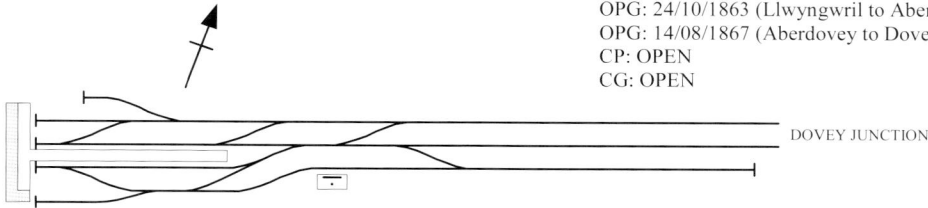

PWLLHELI
1038

1038	**PWLLHELI**	**[CAMRLY]**
OP: 19/07/1909		Photo: W. 1972
CP: OPEN		Audie Baker

1038	**PWLLHELI**	**[CAMRLY]**
		Photo: S. c.1965
		LOSA

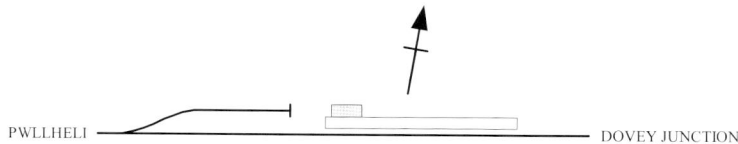

PWLLHELI ——————— DOVEY JUNCTION

ABERERCH
1039

1039	**ABERERCH**	**[A&WCR]**
OP: 07/1884		Photo: E. c.1951
CP: OPEN		Joe Moss

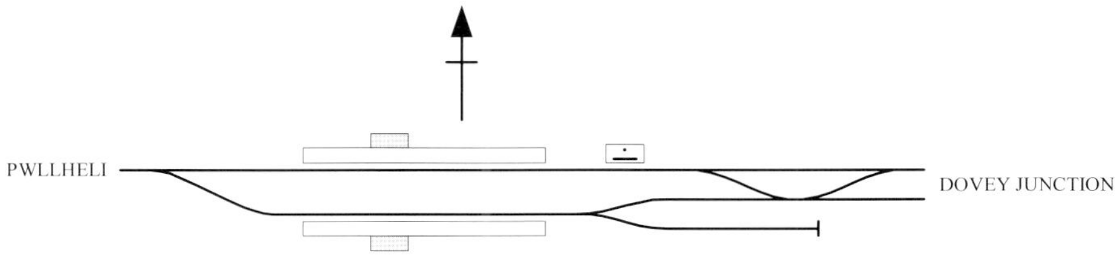

PENYCHAIN
1040

1040   **PENYCHAIN**   **[A&WCR]**
OP: 31/07/1933   Photo: E. 1965
CP: OPEN   C.L.Caddy

1041   **AFON WEN**   **[A&WCR]**
OP: 10/10/1867   Photo: E. 1954
CP: 07/12/1964   R.K.Blencowe

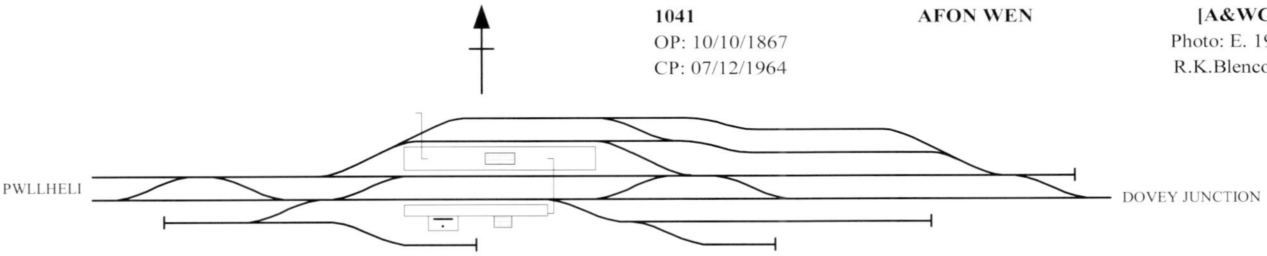

AFON WEN
1041

1041   **AFON WEN**   **[A&WCR]**
Photo: W. c.1960
LOSA

1042   **CRICCIETH**   **[A&WCR]**
OP: 10/10/1867   Photo: E. 1961
CP: OPEN   Stations U.K.

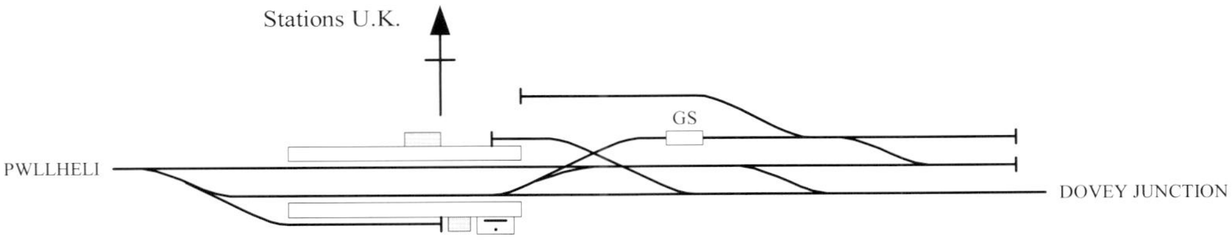

CRICCIETH
1042

PWLLHELI ———————————————— DOVEY JUNCTION

BLACK ROCK
HALT
1043

1043   **BLACK ROCK HALT**   **[A&WCR]**
OP: 09/07/1923   Photo: E. 1954
CP: 13/08/1976   HMRS (ACD731)

1044   **PORTMADOC**   **[A&WCR]**
OP: 10/10/1867   Photo: W. 1939
CP: OPEN   Stations U.K.

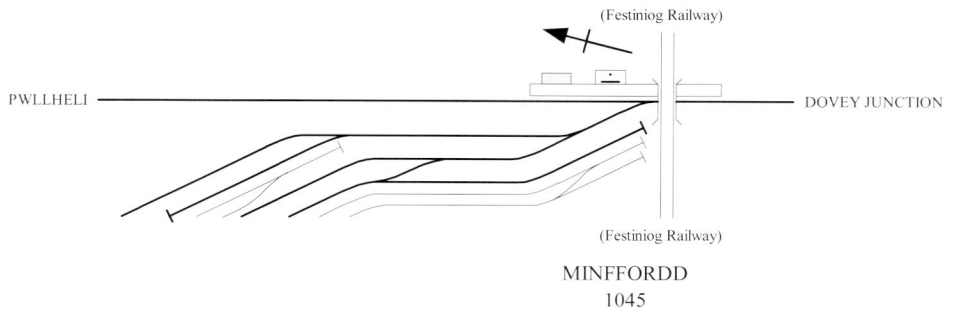

ES
Beddgelert Siding
PWLLHELI ———————————————— DOVEY JUNCTION
GS

PORTMADOC
1044

(Festiniog Railway)
PWLLHELI ———————————————— DOVEY JUNCTION
(Festiniog Railway)

MINFFORDD
1045

1045   **MINFFORDD**   **[A&WCR]**
OP: 01/08/1872   Photo: SE. c.1939
CP: OPEN   Stations U.K.

1046   **PENRHYNDEUDRAETH**   **[A&WCR]**
OP: 10/10/1867   Photo: W. 1959
CP: OPEN   Stations U.K.

PENRHYNDEUDRAETH
1046

LLANDECWYN
HALT
1047

1047   **LLANDECWYN HALT**   **[A&WCR]**
OP: 18/11/1935   Photo: SW. 1964
CP: OPEN   C.L.Caddy

1048   **TALSARNAU**   **[A&WCR]**
OP: 10/10/1867   Photo: SW. 1964
CP: OPEN   Stations U.K.

TALSARNAU
1048

TYGWYN HALT
1049

1049   **TYGWYN HALT**   **[A&WCR]**
OP: 11/07/1927   Photo: SW. 1964
CP: OPEN   Stations U.K.

1050   **HARLECH**   **[A&WCR]**
OP: 10/10/1867   Photo: NE. 1954
CP: OPEN   Stations U.K.

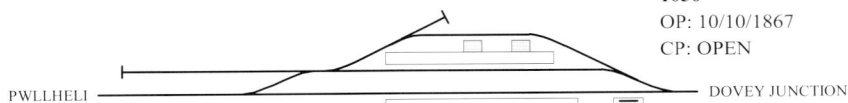

HARLECH
1050

PWLLHELI ———————— DOVEY JUNCTION

LLANDANWG
HALT
1051

1051　　　　**LLANDANWG HALT**　　　　**[A&WCR]**
OP: 08/11/1929　　　　　　　　　　　　Photo: SE. 1964
CP: OPEN　　　　　　　　　　　　　　　Stations U.K.

1052　　　**LLANBEDR & PENSARN**　　　**[A&WCR]**
OP: 10/10/1867　　　　　　　　　　　Photo: NW. c.1939
CP: OPEN　　　　　　　　　　　　　　Stations U.K.

PWLLHELI ———————— DOVEY JUNCTION

LLANBEDR &
PENSARN
1052

PWLLHELI ———————— DOVEY JUNCTION

TALWRN BACH
HALT
1053

1053　　　**TALWRN BACH HALT**　　　**[A&WCR]**
OP: 09/07/1923　　　　　　　　　　　Photo: N. 1964
CP: OPEN　　　　　　　　　　　　　　Stations U.K.

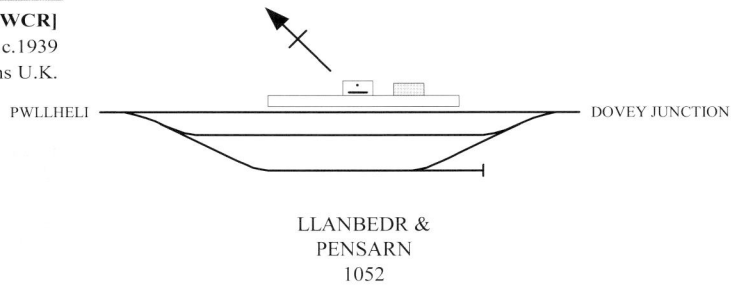

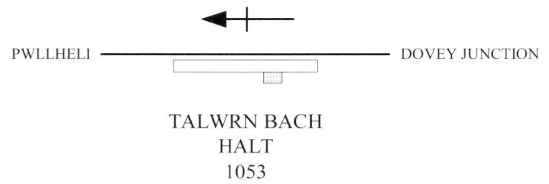

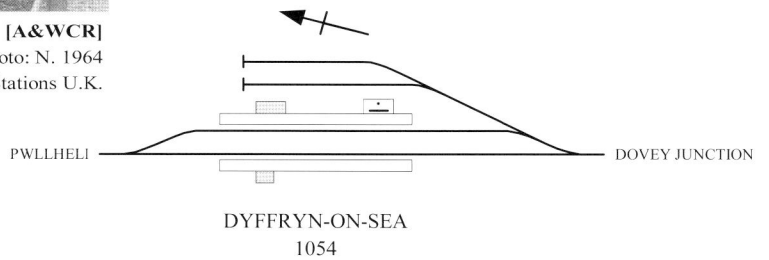

PWLLHELI ———————— DOVEY JUNCTION

DYFFRYN-ON-SEA
1054

1054　　　**DYFFRYN-ON-SEA**　　　**[A&WCR]**
OP: 10/10/1867　　　　　　　　　　Photo: S. 1964
CP: OPEN　　　　　　　　　　　　　Stations U.K.

1054　　　**DYFFRYN-ON-SEA**　　　**[A&WCR]**
　　　　　　　　　　　　　　　　　Photo: N. 1964
　　　　　　　　　　　　　　　　　C.L.Caddy

TALYBONT
HALT
1055

PWLLHELI ──────────── DOVEY JUNCTION

1055   **TALYBONT HALT**   **[A&WCR]**
OP: 07/1914   Photo: N. 1964
CP: OPEN   C.L.Caddy

1056   **LLANABER HALT**   **[A&WCR]**
OP: 07/1914   Photo: N. 1964
CP: OPEN   C.L.Caddy

PWLLHELI ──────────── DOVEY JUNCTION

LLANABER
HALT
1056

GS

PWLLHELI ──────────── DOVEY JUNCTION

BARMOUTH
1057

1057   **BARMOUTH**   **[A&WCR]**
OP: 03/06/1867   Photo: SE. 1939
CP: OPEN   Stations U.K.

1057   **BARMOUTH**   **[A&WCR]**
       Photo: SE. c.1960
       LOSA

DOLGELLEY
(see page 361)

PWLLHELI

DOVEY JUNCTION

BARMOUTH
JUNCTION
1058

1058   **BARMOUTH JUNCTION**   **[A&WCR]**
OP: 03/07/1865   Photo: NW. 1962
CP: OPEN   P.Garland

1058   **BARMOUTH JUNCTION**   **[A&WCR]**
                                 Photo: S. 1964
                                      C.L.Caddy

PWLLHELI   DOVEY JUNCTION

FAIRBOURNE
1059

1059   **FAIRBOURNE**   **[A&WCR]**
OP: 01/07/1897   Photo: NE. 1962
CP: OPEN   P.Garland

1060   **LLWYNGWRIL**   **[A&WCR]**
OP: 24/10/1863   Photo: NE. 1964
CP: OPEN   C.L.Caddy

PWLLHELI

DOVEY JUNCTION

LLWYNGWRIL
1060

PWLLHELI ———————————————— DOVEY JUNCTION

LLANGELYNIN
HALT
1061

1061   **LLANGELYNIN HALT**   **[A&WCR]**
OP: 07/07/1930   Photo: S. 1964
CP: 10/05/1992   C.L.Caddy

Quarry

PWLLHELI ———————————————— DOVEY JUNCTION

TONFANAU
1062

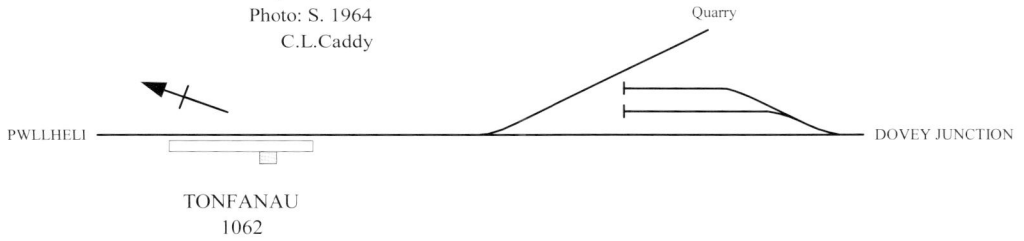

1062   **TONFANAU**   **[A&WCR]**
OP: 18/11/1895   Photo: S. c.1939
CP: OPEN   Stations U.K.

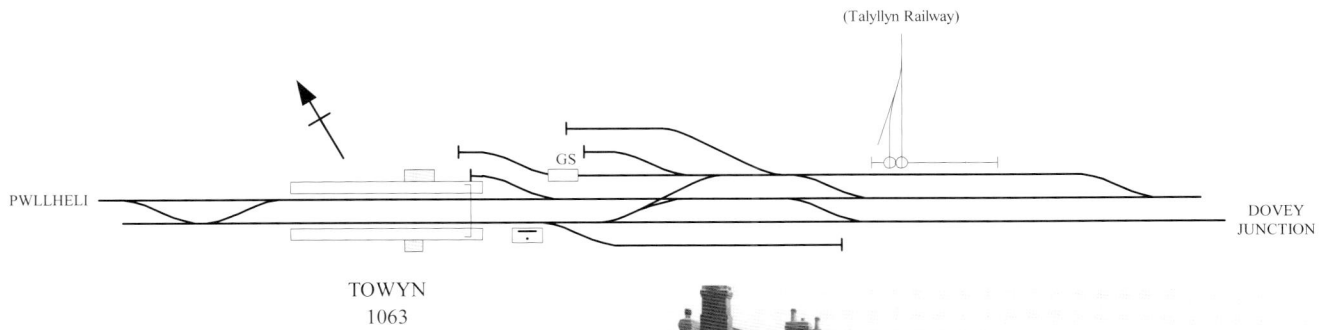

1062   **TONFANAU**   **[A&WCR]**
                          Photo: N. 1972
                          C.L.Caddy

(Talyllyn Railway)

PWLLHELI ———— GS ———————————— DOVEY
                                         JUNCTION

TOWYN
1063

1063   **TOWYN**   **[A&WCR]**
OP: 24/10/1863   Photo: SE. 1959
CP: OPEN   M.Hale

ABERDOVEY
1064

1064   **ABERDOVEY**   **[A&WCR]**
OP: 24/10/1863   Photo: W. c.1960
CP: OPEN   LOSA

1065   **PENHELIG HALT**   **[A&WCR]**
OP: 08/05/1933   Photo: E. 1964
CP: OPEN   Stations U.K.

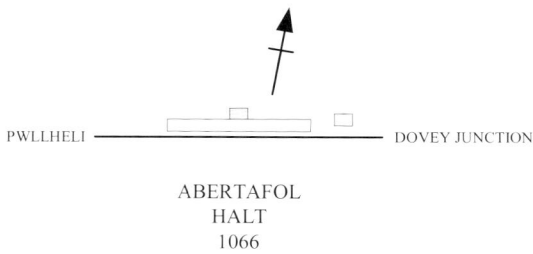

PENHELIG
HALT
1065

ABERTAFOL
HALT
1066

1066   **ABERTAFOL HALT**   **[A&WCR]**
OP: 18/03/1935   Photo: W. 1964
CP: 14/05/1984   Stations U.K.

1067   **GOGARTH HALT**   **[A&WCR]**
OP: 09/07/1923   Photo: NE. 1970
CP: 14/05/1984   C.L.Caddy

(see page 382)

GOGARTH
HALT
1067

GREAT WESTERN
RAILWAY
MAP OF THE COMPANY'S SYSTEM

CEMMES ROAD (Exc) TO DINAS MAWDDWY
MAWDDWY BRANCH
Mawddwy Railway -
Cambrian Railways (31/07/1911) -
Great Western Railway (01/01/1922)
ACT: 05/07/1865
OPG: 01/10/1867
CP: 17/04/1901
CG: 18/04/1908
ReOPG: 29/07/1911
CP: 01/01/1931
CG: 05/09/1950

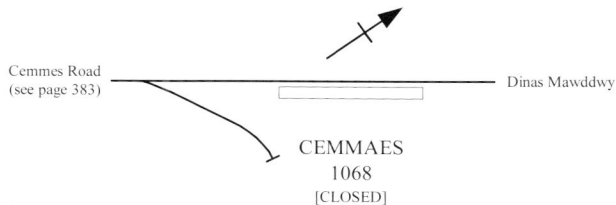

Cemmes Road
(see page 383)   Dinas Mawddwy

CEMMAES
1068
[CLOSED]

1068　　　　　**CEMMAES**　　　　　**[MR]**
OP: 01/10/1867　　　　　　　　　　　　NE. c.1911
CP: 01/01/1931　　　　　　　　　　　　R.Carpenter

Cemmes Road   Dinas Mawddwy

ABERANGELL
1069
[CLOSED]

1069　　　　　**ABERANGELL**　　　　　**[MR]**
OP: 01/10/1867　　　　　　　　　　　　Photo: N. 1950
CP: 01/01/1931　　　　　　　　　　　　W.A.Camwell

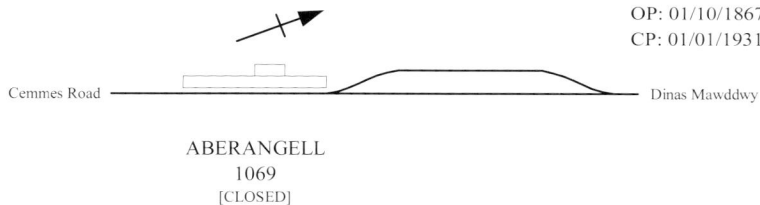

Cemmes Road   GS

DINAS MAWDDWY
1070
[CLOSED]

1070　　　　　**DINAS MAWDDWY**　　　　　**[MR]**
OP: 01/10/1867　　　　　　　　　　　　NE. 1939
CP: 01/01/1931　　　　　　　　　　　　W.A.Camwell

1070　　　　　**DINAS MAWDDWY**　　　　　**[MR]**
　　　　　　　　　　　　　　　　　　　NE. 1948
　　　　　　　　　　　　　　　　　　　R.Carpenter

GREAT WESTERN
RAILWAY
MAP OF THE COMPANY'S SYSTEM

ABERYSTWYTH TO Whitchurch (Exc)
WHITCHURCH AND ABERYSTWYTH LINE

Aberystwyth & Welsh Coast Railway -
Cambrian Railways (05/07/1865) -
Great Western Railway (01/01/1922)
(Aberystwyth to Machynlleth)
Newtown & Machynlleth Railway -
Cambrian Railways (25/07/1864) -
Great Western Railway (01/01/1922)
(Machynlleth to Moat Lane Junction)
Llanidloes & Newtown Railway -
Cambrian Railways (25/07/1864) -
Great Western Railway (01/01/1922)
(Moat Lane Junction to Newtown)
Oswestry & Newtown Railway -
Cambrian Railways (25/07/1864) -
Great Western Railway (01/01/1922)
(Newtown to Oswestry)
Oswestry Ellesmere & Whitchurch Railway -
Cambrian Railways (25/07/1864) -
Great Western Railway (01/01/1922)
(Oswestry to Whitchurch (exc))

ACT: 22/07/1861 (Aberystwyth to Machynlleth)
ACT: 27/07/1857 (Machynlleth to Moat Lane Junction)
ACT: 04/08/1853 (Moat Lane Junction to Newtown)
ACT: 26/06/1855 (Newtown to Oswestry)
ACT: 01/08/1861 (Oswestry to Cambrian Junction Whitchurch)
OPG: 01/07/1863 (Aberystwyth to Machynlleth)
OPG: 05/01/1863 (Machynlleth to Moat Lane Junction)
OP: 31/08/1859 (Moat Lane Junction to Newtown old station)
OG: 30/04/1859 (Moat Lane Junction to Newtown old station)
OPG: 14/08/1860 (Newtown to Abermule)
OPG: 10/06/1861 (Abermule to Welshpool)
OPG: 14/08/1860 (Welshpool to Pool Quay)
OPG: 01/05/1860 (Pool Quay to Oswestry)
OPG: 27/07/1864 (Oswestry to Ellesmere)
OP: 04/05/1863 (Ellesmere to Whitchurch)
OG: 20/04/1863 (Ellesmere to Whitchurch)
CP: 16/01/1965 (Buttington to Whitchurch)
CG: 18/01/1965 (Buttington to Oswestry)
CG: 27/03/1965 (Oswestry to Whitchurch)

1071   **ABERYSTWYTH**   **[A&WCR]**
OP: 23/06/1864   Photo: NW. 1965
CP: OPEN   D.K.Jones

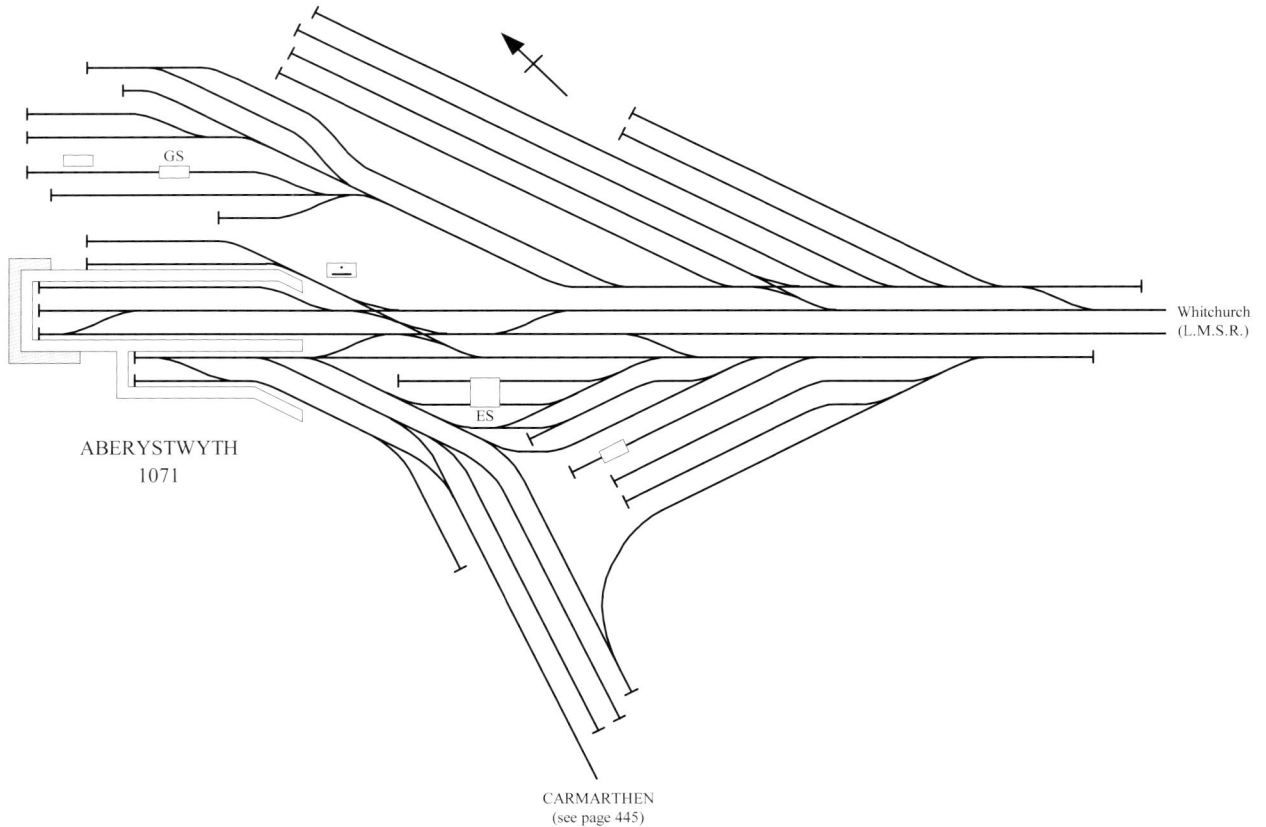

GS

ES

Whitchurch
(L.M.S.R.)

ABERYSTWYTH
1071

CARMARTHEN
(see page 445)

1071   **ABERYSTWYTH**   **[A&WCR]**
Photo: NW. c.1960
LOSA

1072
OP: 23/06/1864
CP: 14/06/1965

BOW STREET   **[A&WCR]**
Photo: S. 1955
Stations U.K.

ABERYSTWYTH — Whitchurch (L.M.S.R.)

BOW STREET
1072

1072   **BOW STREET**   **[A&WCR]**
Photo: N. 1964
C.Mowat

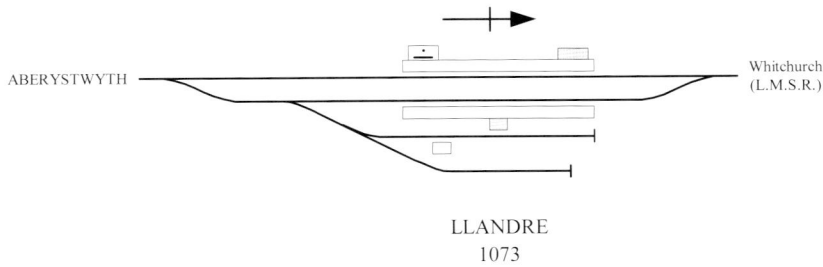

ABERYSTWYTH — Whitchurch (L.M.S.R.)

LLANDRE
1073

1073   **LLANDRE**   **[A&WCR]**
OP: 23/06/1864   Photo: N. 1937
CP: 14/06/1965   Stations U.K.

1073   **LLANDRE**   **[A&WCR]**
Photo: N. 1959
M.Hale

BORTH
1074

1074   **BORTH**   **[A&WCR]**
OP: 01/07/1863   Photo: N. 1956
CP: OPEN   C.Mowat

1075   **YNYSLAS**   **[A&WCR]**
OP: 01/07/1863   Photo: NE. c.1960
CP: 14/06/1965   R.K.Blencowe

YNYSLAS
1075

GLANDYFI
1076

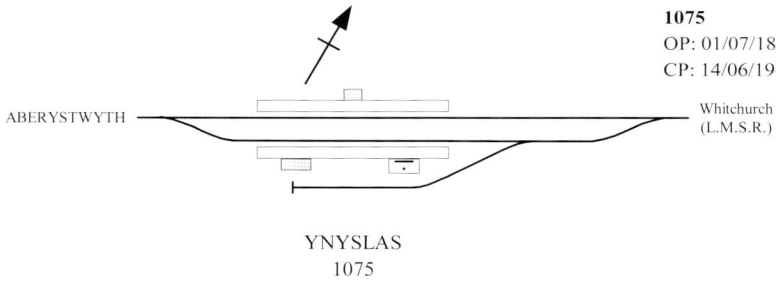

1076   **GLANDYFI**   **[A&WCR]**
OP: 01/07/1863   Photo: NE. 1959
CP: 14/06/1965   M.Hale

1077   **DOVEY JUNCTION**   **[A&WCR]**
OP: 14/08/1867   Photo: S. 1948
CP: OPEN   H.C.Casserley

DOVEY JUNCTION
1077

MACHYNLLETH
1078

1078   **MACHYNLLETH**   **[N&MR]**
OP: 05/01/1863   Photo: NE. c.1960
CP: OPEN   LOSA

1079   **CEMMES ROAD**   **[N&MR]**
OP: 05/01/1863   Photo: E. 1948
CP: 14/06/1965   R.Carpenter

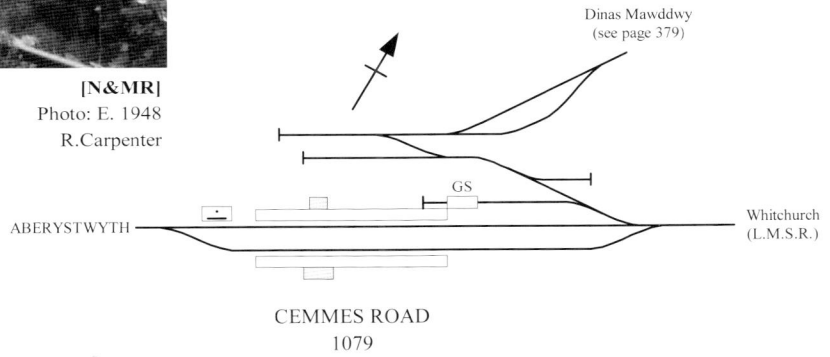

Dinas Mawddwy
(see page 379)

CEMMES ROAD
1079

1079   **CEMMES ROAD**   **[N&MR]**
Photo: SW. 1964
Stations U.K.

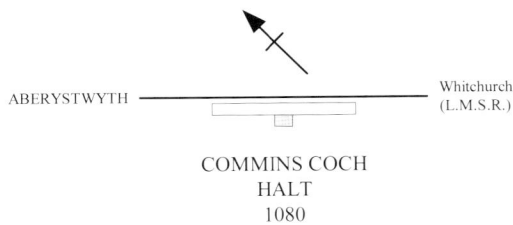

COMMINS COCH
HALT
1080

1080   **COMMINS COCH HALT**   **[N&MR]**
OP: 19/10/1931   Photo: NW. 1964
CP: 14/06/1965   Stations U.K.

ABERYSTWYTH

Whitchurch
(L.M.S.R.)

GS

LLANBRYNMAIR
1081

1081   **LLANBRYNMAIR**   **[N&MR]**
OP: 05/01/1863   Photo: E. 1959
CP: 14/06/1965   M.Hale

1082   **TALERDDIG**   **[N&MR]**
OP: 1896   Photo: N. 1937
CP: 14/06/1965   Stations U.K.

ABERYSTWYTH

Whitchurch
(L.M.S.R.)

TALERDDIG
1082

1082   **TALERDDIG**   **[N&MR]**
                                                            Photo: S. c.1960
                                                                 LOSA

1083   **CARNO**   **[N&MR]**
OP: 05/01/1863   Photo: SE. 1964
CP: 14/06/1965   Stations U.K.

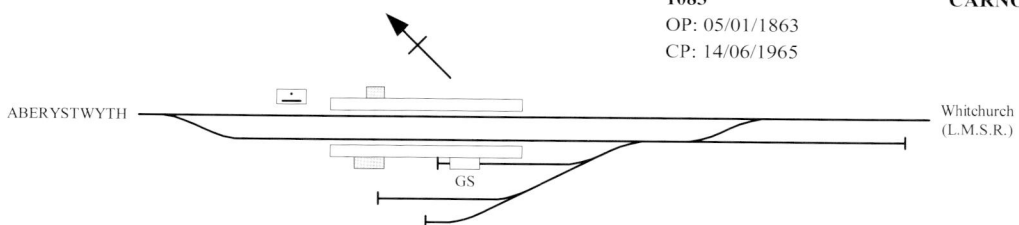

ABERYSTWYTH

Whitchurch
(L.M.S.R.)

GS

CARNO
1083

PONTDOLGOCH
1084

ABERYSTWYTH

Whitchurch
(L.M.S.R.)

1084   **PONTDOLGOCH**   **[N&MR]**
OP: 05/01/1863   Photo: SE. 1964
CP: 14/06/1965   Stations U.K.

1085   **CAERSWS**   **[N&MR]**
OP: 05/01/1863   Photo: NW. 1937
CP: OPEN   Stations U.K.

ABERYSTWYTH

Whitchurch
(L.M.S.R.)

GS

CAERSWS
1085

ABERYSTWYTH

ES

LLANIDLOES
(see page 401)

Whitchurch
(L.M.S.R.)

MOAT LANE
JUNCTION
1086

1086   **MOAT LANE JUNCTION**   **[N&MR]**
OP: 02/09/1859   Photo: W. 1937
CP: 29/12/1962   Stations U.K.

1086   **MOAT LANE JUNCTION**   **[N&MR]**
         Photo: NE. 1937
         Stations U.K.

1087   **SCAFELL**   **[L&NR]**
OP: 05/1863   Photo: E. c.1960
CP: 07/03/1955   LOSA

ABERYSTWYTH   Whitchurch
(L.M.S.R.)

SCAFELL
1087

1088   **NEWTOWN**   **[O&NR]**
OP: 31/05/1869   Photo: NE. 1966
CP: OPEN   G.Parker

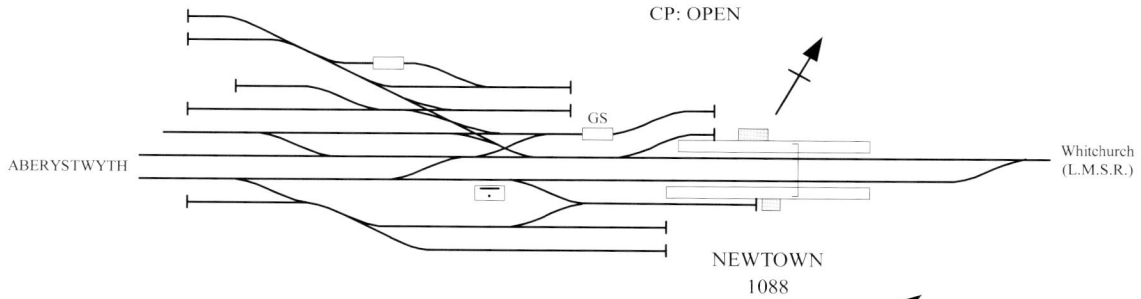

ABERYSTWYTH   GS   Whitchurch
(L.M.S.R.)

NEWTOWN
1088

ABERYSTWYTH   GS   Whitchurch
(L.M.S.R.)

Kerry
(see page 400)

ABERMULE
1089

1089   **ABERMULE**   **[O&NR]**
OP: 14/08/1860   Photo: N. 1959
CP: 14/06/1965   M.M.Lloyd

1089   **ABERMULE**   **[O&NR]**
Photo: SW. 1964
Stations U.K.

MONTGOMERY
1090

1090   **MONTGOMERY**   **[O&NR]**
OP: 10/06/1861
CP: 14/06/1965   Photo: SW. 1961
                             R.G.Nelson

1091   **FORDEN**   **[O&NR]**
OP: 10/06/1861
CP: 14/06/1965   Photo: S. 1964
                           Stations U.K.

FORDEN
1091

WELSHPOOL
1092

1092   **WELSHPOOL**   **[O&NR]**
OP: 14/08/1860
CP: 18/05/1992   Photo: N. c.1960
                           LOSA

1092   **WELSHPOOL**   **[O&NR]**
                           Photo: S. 1961
                           R.G.Nelson

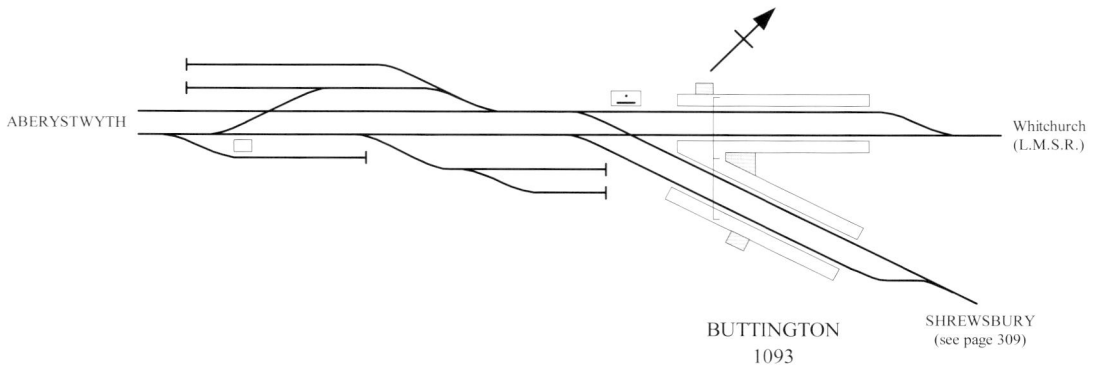

BUTTINGTON
1093

1093 **BUTTINGTON** **[O&NR]**
OP: 11/1860
CP: 12/09/1960 Photo: NE. c.1935
Stations U.K.

1093 **BUTTINGTON** **[O&NR]**
Photo: SW. 1959
R.G.Nelson

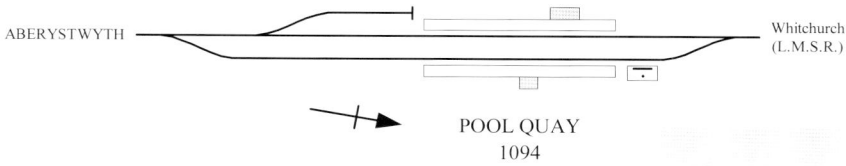

POOL QUAY
1094

1094 **POOL QUAY** **[O&NR]**
OP: 01/05/1860
CP: 18/01/1965 Photo: S. 1963
M.Hale

1095 **ARDDLEEN** **[O&NR]**
OP: 02/1862
CP: 18/01/1965 Photo: N. 1963
P.Garland

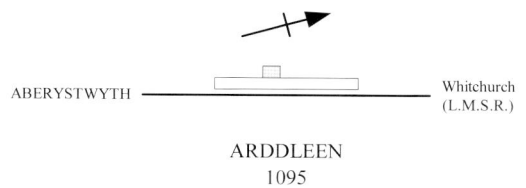

ARDDLEEN
1095

FOUR CROSSES
1096

ABERYSTWYTH

Whitchurch
(L.M.S.R.)

GS

1096   **FOUR CROSSES**   **[O&NR]**
OP: 01/05/1860
CP: 18/01/1965
Photo: S. 1961
Stations U.K.

1097   **LLANYMYNECH**   **[O&NR]**
OP: 01/05/1860
CP: 18/01/1965
Photo: N. 1958
Stations U.K.

LLANFYLLIN
(see page 399)

ABERYSTWYTH

Whitchurch
(L.M.S.R.)

GS

(Shrewsbury
S.& M.R.)

LLANYMYNECH
1097

1098   **PANT (SALOP.)**   **[O&NR]**
OP: 02/1862
CP: 18/01/1965
Photo: S. 1961
Stations U.K.

1097   **LLANYMYNECH**   **[O&NR]**
Photo: S. 1964
Stations U.K.

ABERYSTWYTH

Whitchurch
(L.M.S.R.)

PANT (SALOP.)
1098

ABERYSTWYTH

Whitchurch
(L.M.S.R.)

GS

LLYNCLYS
1099

1099
OP: 01/05/1860
CP: 18/01/1965

LLYNCLYS

[O&NR]

Photo: S. c.1955
R.Carpenter

1100
OP: 01/05/1860
CP: 07/11/1966

OSWESTRY

[O&NR]

Photo: N. c.1960
R.K.Blencowe

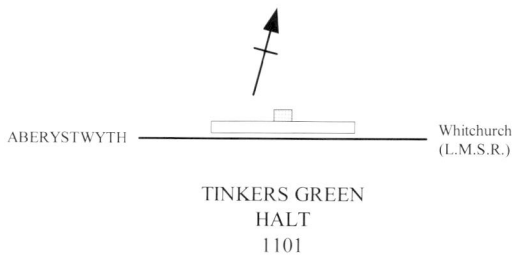

GS

ABERYSTWYTH

GOBOWEN
(see page 289)

Whitchurch
(L.M.S.R.)

Whitchurch
(L.M.S.R.)

Various sidings

OSWESTRY
1100

ABERYSTWYTH

Whitchurch
(L.M.S.R.)

TINKERS GREEN
HALT
1101

1101
OP: 16/10/1939
CP: 18/01/1965

TINKERS GREEN HALT

[OE&WR]

Photo: W. 1961
Stations U.K.

ABERYSTWYTH ———————————————————— Whitchurch
(L.M.S.R.)

WHITTINGTON (H.L.)
1102

1102   **WHITTINGTON (H.L.)**   **[OE&WR]**
OP: 27/07/1864   Photo: NE. c.1935
CP: 04/01/1960   Stations U.K.

1103   **FRANKTON**   **[OE&WR]**
OP: 27/07/1864   Photo: SW. 1958
CP: 18/01/1965   Stations U.K.

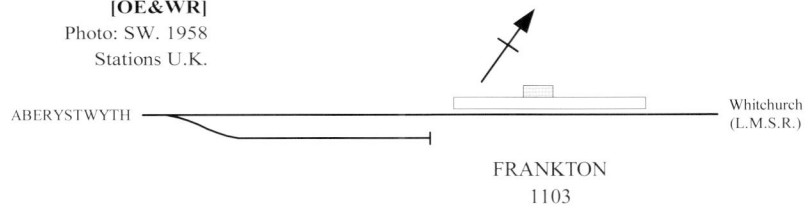

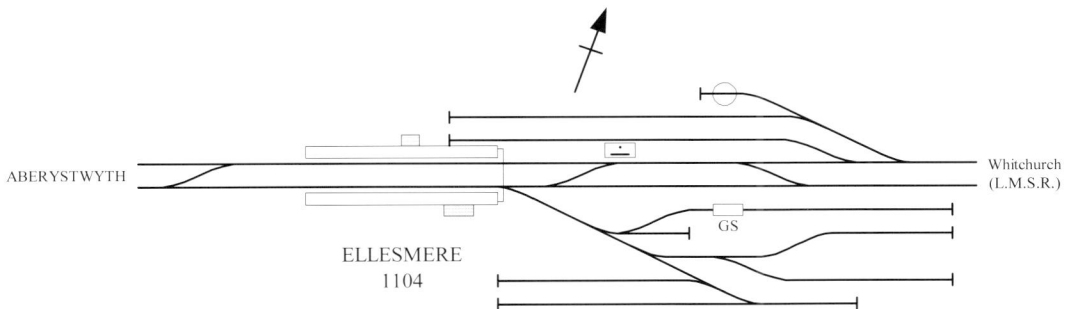

ABERYSTWYTH ———————————————————— Whitchurch
(L.M.S.R.)

FRANKTON
1103

ABERYSTWYTH

ELLESMERE
1104

GS

Whitchurch
(L.M.S.R.)

1104   **ELLESMERE**   **[OE&WR]**
OP: 04/05/1863   Photo: E. 1959
CP: 18/01/1965   P.Garland

1104   **ELLESMERE**   **[OE&WR]**
       Photo: W. 1947
       Stations U.K.

1105   **WELSHAMPTON**   **[OE&WR]**
OP: 04/05/1863   Photo: E. 1959
CP: 18/01/1965   Stations U.K.

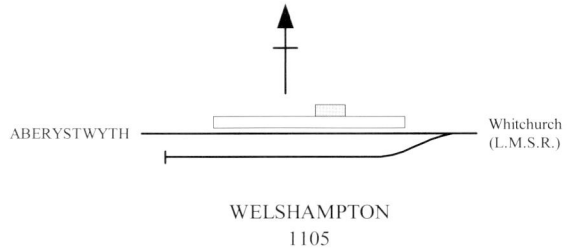

ABERYSTWYTH   Whitchurch (L.M.S.R.)

WELSHAMPTON
1105

1106   **BETTISFIELD**   **[OE&WR]**
OP: 04/05/1863   Photo: W. c.1960
CP: 18/01/1965   LOSA

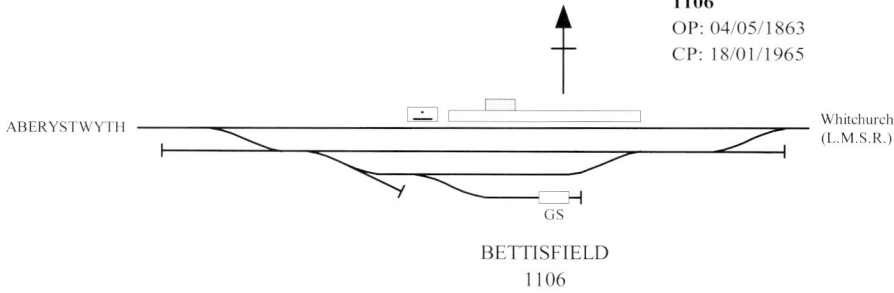

ABERYSTWYTH   Whitchurch (L.M.S.R.)

GS

BETTISFIELD
1106

ABERYSTWYTH   Whitchurch (L.M.S.R.)

GS

FENNS BANK
1107

1107   **FENNS BANK**   **[OE&WR]**
OP: 04/05/1863   Photo: SW. c.1960
CP: 18/01/1965   LOSA

1107   **FENNS BANK**   **[OE&WR]**
Photo: NE. 1960
R.G.Nelson

Wrexham & Ellesmere Railway -
Great Western Railway (01/01/1922)
ACT: 31/07/1885
OP: 02/11/1895
OG: 02/11/1895
CP: 08/09/1962
CG: 08/09/1962 (Ellesmere to Cadbury's siding Pickhill Halt)
CG: 08/09/1962 (Pickhill Halt to Wrexham) (Public Goods only)

ELSON HALT
1108

1109	**TRENCH HALT**	[W&ER]
OP: 08/1914		Photo: N. 1959
CP: 08/09/1962		M.M.Lloyd

1108	**ELSON HALT**	[W&ER]
OP: 08/02/1937		Photo: S. 1958
CP: 08/09/1962		Stations U.K.

TRENCH HALT
1109

OVERTON-ON-DEE
1110

1110	**OVERTON-ON-DEE**	[W&ER]
OP: 02/11/1895		Photo: S. 1954
CP: 08/09/1962		Stations U.K.

1111	**CLOY HALT**	[W&ER]
OP: 30/06/1932		Photo: NE. 1959
CP: 08/09/1962		M.M.Lloyd

CLOY HALT
1111

BANGOR-ON-DEE
1112

WREXHAM CENTRAL — ELLESMERE
GS

1112   **BANGOR-ON-DEE**   **[W&ER]**
OP: 02/11/1895   Photo: S. 1961
CP: 08/09/1962   C.Mowat

PICKHILL HALT
1113

WREXHAM CENTRAL — ELLESMERE
Cadburys Siding

1113   **PICKHILL HALT**   **[W&ER]**
OP: 30/05/1938   Photo: SE. 1962
CP: 08/09/1962   M.Hale

WREXHAM CENTRAL — ELLESMERE

SESSWICK HALT
1114

1114   **SESSWICK HALT**   **[W&ER]**
OP: 10/1913   Photo: SE. c.1962
CP: 08/09/1962   W.A.Camwell

1115   **MARCHWIEL**   **[W&ER]**
OP: 02/11/1895   Photo: W. 1959
CP: 08/09/1962   M.M.Lloyd

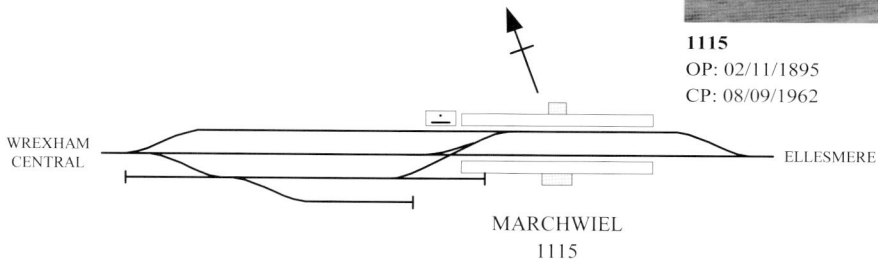

WREXHAM CENTRAL — ELLESMERE

MARCHWIEL
1115

WREXHAM CENTRAL — ELLESMERE

HIGHTOWN HALT
1116

1116   **HIGHTOWN HALT**   **[W&ER]**
OP: 09/07/1923   Photo: NW. 1962
CP: 08/09/1962   M.M.Lloyd

1117   **WREXHAM CENTRAL**   **[W&ER]**
OP: 02/11/1895   Photo: SE. 1958
CP: 08/09/1962   Stations U.K.

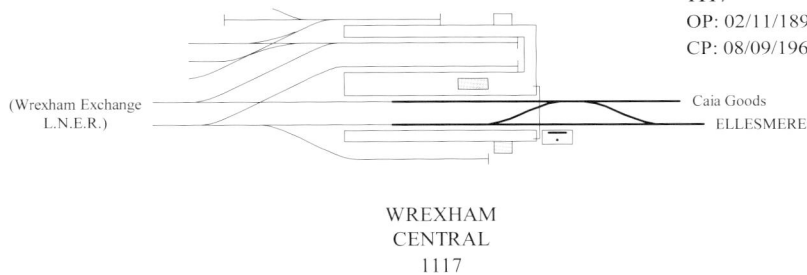

(Wrexham Exchange L.N.E.R.)

Caia Goods
ELLESMERE

WREXHAM
CENTRAL
1117

GREAT WESTERN
RAILWAY
MAP OF THE COMPANY'S SYSTEM

OSWESTRY (Exc) TO LLANGYNOG
TANAT VALLEY BRANCH
Oswestry & Newtown Railway -
Cambrian Railways (25/07/1864) -
Great Western Railway (01/01/1922)
(Llynclys Junction to Porthywaen Branch Junction)
Tanat Valley Light Railway -
Cambrian Railways (12/03/1921) -
Great Western Railway (01/01/1922)
(Porthywaen Branch Junction to Llangynog)
ACT: 03/07/1860 (Llynclys Junction to Porthywaen)
ACT: 04/06/1898 (Porthywaen Branch Junction to Llangynog)
OP: 05/01/1904
OG: 01/05/1861 (Llynclys Junction to Porthywaen Branch Junc.)
OG: 05/01/1904 (Porthywaen Branch Junction to Llangynog)
CP: 13/01/1951
CG: 28/01/1988 (Llynclys Junction to Blodwell Junction)
CG: 05/12/1960 (Blodwell Junction to Llanrhaiadr Mochnant)
CG: 01/07/1952 (Llanrhaiadr Mochnant to Llangynog)

1118   **PORTHYWAEN**   **[TVLR]**
OP: 05/01/1904   Photo: NE. 1948
CP: 13/01/1951   L&GRP

Porthywaen Branch

LLANGYNOG

OSWESTRY
(see page 390)

PORTHYWAEN
1118

BLODWELL
JUNCTION
1119

LLANGYNOG — OSWESTRY

Nantmawr
Branch

1119   **BLODWELL JUNCTION**   **[TVLR]**
OP: 05/01/1904   Photo: NE. 1959
CP: 13/01/1951   R.J.Leonard

LLANGYNOG — OSWESTRY

LLANYBLODWELL
1120

1120   **LLANYBLODWELL**   **[TVLR]**
OP: 05/01/1904   Photo: E. 1947
CP: 13/01/1951   R.J.Leonard

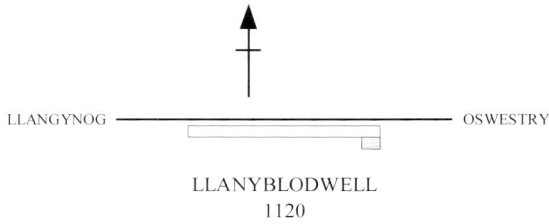

1121   **GLANYRAFON**   **[TVLR]**
OP: 01/09/1904   Sketch: E. c.1950
CP: 13/01/1951

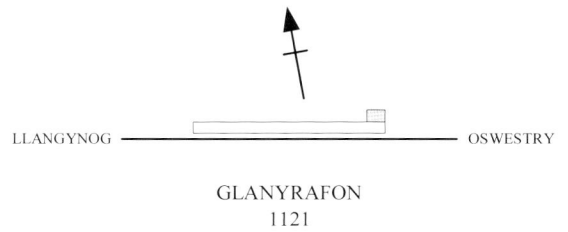

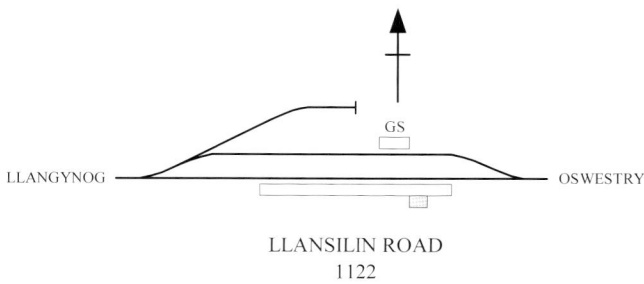

LLANGYNOG — OSWESTRY

GLANYRAFON
1121

LLANGYNOG — OSWESTRY

GS

LLANSILIN ROAD
1122

1122   **LLANSILIN ROAD**   **[TVLR]**
OP: 05/01/1904   Photo: W. 1958
CP: 13/01/1951   Stations U.K.

1123   **LLANGEDWYN**   **[TVLR]**
OP: 05/01/1904   Photo: W. c.1904
CP: 13/01/1951   L&GRP

LLANGEDWYN
1123

1123   **LLANGEDWYN**   **[TVLR]**
Photo: E. 1949
LOSA

1124   **PENTREFELIN**   **[TVLR]**
OP: 05/01/1904   Photo: W. c.1904
CP: 13/01/1951   L&GRP

PENTREFELIN
1124

GS

LLANRHAIADR
MOCHNANT
1125

1125   **LLANRHAIADR MOCHNANT**   **[TVLR]**
OP: 05/01/1904   Photo: W. 1948
CP: 13/01/1951   LOSA

1125   **LLANRHAIADR MOCHNANT**   **[TVLR]**
Photo: E. 1958
R.M.Casserley

1126   **PEDAIR FFORDD**   **[TVLR]**
OP: 05/01/1904   Photo: W. 1904
CP: 13/01/1951   L&GRP

LLANGYNOG ———————————————— OSWESTRY

PEDAIR FFORDD
1126

PENYBONTFAWR
1127

1127   **PENYBONTFAWR**   **[TVLR]**
OP: 05/01/1904   Photo: W. 1958
CP: 13/01/1951   Stations U.K.

GS

———— OSWESTRY

LLANGYNOG
1128

1128   **LLANGYNOG**   **[TVLR]**
OP: 05/01/1904   Photo: E. 1951
CP: 13/01/1951   R.G.Nelson

1128   **LLANGYNOG**   **[TVLR]**
                                      Photo: W. 1958
                                      Stations U.K.

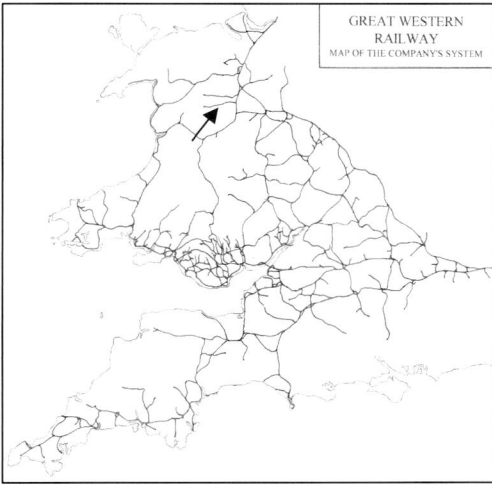

Great Western Railway — Map of the Company's System

LLANYMYNECH (Exc) TO LLANFYLLIN NANTMAWR BRANCH, LLANYMYNECH CURVE, LLANFYLLIN BRANCH

Cambrian Railways -
Great Western Railway (01/01/1922)
(Llanymynech South Junction to Llanfyllin Branch Junction)
Cambrian Railways -
Great Western Railway (01/01/1922)
(Llanfyllin Branch Junction to Wern Junction)
Oswestry & Newtown Railway -
Cambrian Railways (25/07/1864) -
Great Western Railway (01/01/1922)
(Wern Junction to Llanfyllin)
ACT: 1864 (Llanymynech South Jc. to Llanfyllin Branch Jc.)
ACT: c.1895 (Llanfyllin Branch Junction to Wern Junction)
ACT: 17/05/1861 (Wern Junction to Llanfyllin)
OP: 27/01/1896 (Llanymynech South Junction to Wern Junction)
OP: 17/07/1863 (Wern Junction to Llanfyllin)
OG: 01/01/1886 (Llanymynech South Jc. to Llanfyllin Branch Jc.)
OG: 27/01/1896 (Llanymynech South Junction to Wern Junction)
OG: 17/07/1863 (Wern Junction to Llanfyllin)
CP: 16/01/1965
CG: 02/11/1964

LLANFYLLIN ——————————— LLANYMYNECH
(see page 389)

CARREGHOFA HALT
1129

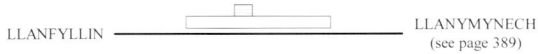

1129   **CARREGHOFA HALT**   **[CAMRLY]**
OP: 11/04/1938   Photo: NW. 1963
CP: 16/01/1965   M.M.Lloyd

1130   **LLANSANTFFRAID**   **[O&NR]**
OP: 17/07/1863   Photo: W. c.1960
CP: 16/01/1965   E.T.Gill

LLANFYLLIN — GS — LLANYMYNECH

LLANSANTFFRAID
1130

1131   **LLANFECHAIN**   **[O&NR]**
OP: 08/1865   Photo: E. 1958
CP: 16/01/1965   Stations U.K.

LLANFYLLIN —————————— LLANYMYNECH

LLANFECHAIN
1131

BRYNGWYN
1132

LLANFYLLIN ——————— LLANYMYNECH

1132   **BRYNGWYN**   **[O&NR]**
OP: 05/1865   Photo: W. 1958
CP: 16/01/1965   Stations U.K.

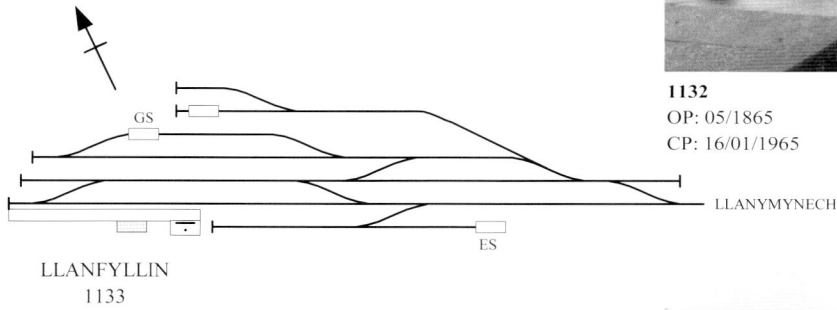

LLANFYLLIN
1133

GS

LLANYMYNECH

ES

1133   **LLANFYLLIN**   **[O&NR]**
OP: 17/07/1863   Photo: E. 1956
CP: 16/01/1965   R.K.Blencowe

ABERMULE (Exc) TO KERRY
KERRY BRANCH
Oswestry & Newtown Railway -
Cambrian Railways (25/07/1864) -
Great Western Railway (01/01/1922)

ACT: 17/05/1861
OP: 01/07/1863
OG: 02/03/1863
CP: 07/02/1931
CG: 01/05/1956

GREAT WESTERN
RAILWAY
MAP OF THE COMPANY'S SYSTEM

Abermule
(see page 386)

KERRY
1134
[CLOSED]

1134   **KERRY**   **[O&NR]**
OP: 01/07/1863   Photo: SW. c.1955
CP: 07/02/1931   R.J.Leonard

MOAT LANE JUNCTION (Exc) TO TALYLLYN JUNCTION (Exc)
MOAT LANE JUNCTION TO TALYLLYN

Llanidloes & Newtown Railway -
Cambrian Railways (25/07/1864) -
Great Western Railway (01/01/1922)
(Moat Lane Junction to Llanidloes)
Mid Wales Railway -
Cambrian Railways (24/06/1904) -
Great Western Railway (01/01/1922)
(Llanidloes to Talyllyn Junction)

ACT: 04/08/1853 (Moat Lane Junction to Llanidloes)
ACT: 01/08/1859 (Llanidloes to Newbridge-on-Wye)
ACT: 03/07/1860 (Newbridge-on-Wye to Talyllyn Junction)
OP: 31/08/1859 (Moat Lane Junction to Llanidloes)
OP: 21/09/1864 (Llanidloes to Talyllyn Junction)
OG: 30/04/1859 (Moat Lane Junction to Llanidloes)
OG: 01/09/1864 (Llanidloes to Talyllyn Junction)
CP: 29/12/1962
CG: 04/05/1964 (Moat Lane Junction to Llanidloes) (Public Goods only)
CG: 29/12/1962 (Llanidloes to Talyllyn Junction)

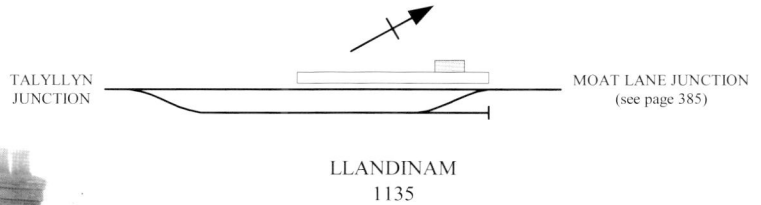

TALYLLYN JUNCTION — MOAT LANE JUNCTION (see page 385)

LLANDINAM
1135

1135   **LLANDINAM**   **[L&NR]**
OP: 31/08/1859   Photo: SW. c.1930
CP: 29/12/1962   LOSA

TALYLLYN JUNCTION — MOAT LANE JUNCTION

DOLWEN
1136

1136   **DOLWEN**   **[L&NR]**
OP: 31/08/1859   Photo: E. c.1939
CP: 29/12/1962   Stations U.K.

TALYLLYN JUNCTION — MOAT LANE JUNCTION

GS

ES

LLANIDLOES
1137

1137   **LLANIDLOES**   **[L&NR]**
OP: 01/1862   Photo: NE. c.1948
CP: 29/12/1962   P.Garland

1137   **LLANIDLOES**   **[L&NR]**
Photo: SW. 1965
C.L.Caddy

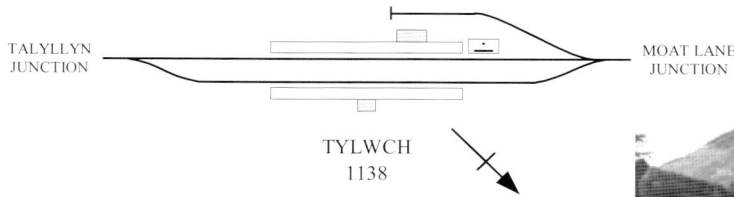

TALYLLYN JUNCTION — MOAT LANE JUNCTION

TYLWCH
1138

1138   **TYLWCH**   **[MWR]**
OP: 21/09/1864   Photo: NW. 1935
CP: 29/12/1962   C.Mowat

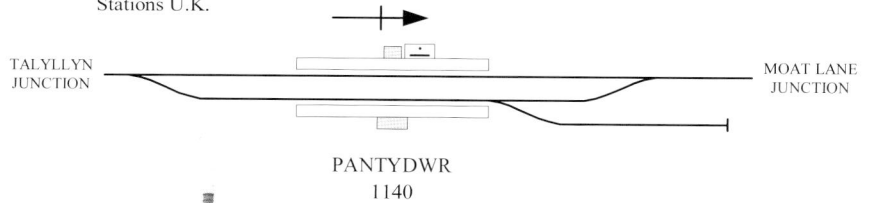

TALYLLYN JUNCTION — MOAT LANE JUNCTION

GLAN-YR-AFON
HALT
1139

1139   **GLAN-YR-AFON HALT**   **[MWR]**
OP: 16/01/1928   Photo: N. 1962
CP: 29/12/1962   Stations U.K.

TALYLLYN JUNCTION — MOAT LANE JUNCTION

PANTYDWR
1140

1140   **PANTYDWR**   **[MWR]**
OP: 21/09/1864   Photo: N. 1939
CP: 29/12/1962   Stations U.K.

ST. HARMONS
1141

1141   **ST. HARMONS**   **[MWR]**
OP: 06/1872   Photo: NE. 1959
CP: 29/12/1962   M.M.Lloyd

MARTEG
HALT
1142

1142   **MARTEG HALT**   **[MWR]**
OP: 18/05/1931   Photo: NE. 1962
CP: 29/12/1962   P.Garland

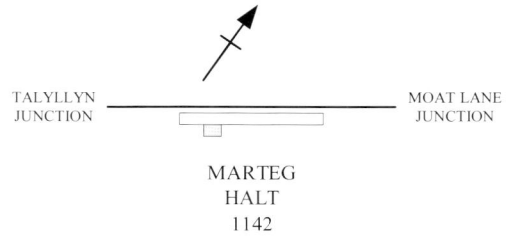

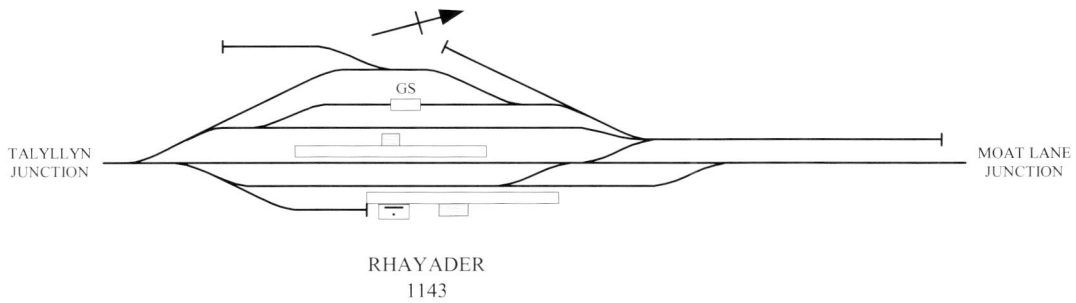

RHAYADER
1143

1143   **RHAYADER**   **[MWR]**
OP: 21/09/1864   Photo: N. 1962
CP: 29/12/1962   P.Garland

1143   **RHAYADER**   **[MWR]**
       Photo: N. 1962
       E.T.Gill

TALYLLYN JUNCTION

MOAT LANE JUNCTION

DOLDOWLOD
1144

1144   **DOLDOWLOD**   **[MWR]**
OP: 21/09/1864   Photo: S. c.1962
CP: 29/12/1962   R.G.Nelson

1144   **DOLDOWLOD**   **[MWR]**
                              Photo: N. 1962
                              J.Tarrant

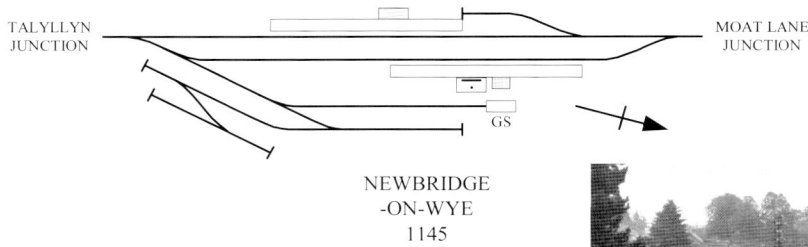

TALYLLYN JUNCTION

MOAT LANE JUNCTION

GS

NEWBRIDGE
-ON-WYE
1145

1145   **NEWBRIDGE-ON-WYE**   **[MWR]**
OP: 21/09/1864   Photo: S. 1962
CP: 29/12/1962   P.Garland

1146   **BUILTH ROAD**   **[MWR]**
OP: 01/11/1866   Photo: NW. c.1960
CP: 29/12/1962   LOSA

(Swansea L.M.S.R.)

TALYLLYN JUNCTION

MOAT LANE JUNCTION

BUILTH ROAD
1146

(Craven Arms & Stokesay L.M.S.R.)

BUILTH WELLS
1147

1147   **BUILTH WELLS**   **[MWR]**
OP: 21/09/1864   Photo: W. 1964
CP: 29/12/1962   Stations U.K.

LLANFAREDD
HALT
1148

1148   **LLANFAREDD HALT**   **[MWR]**
OP: 07/05/1934   Photo: N. c.1960
CP: 29/12/1962   LOSA

ABEREDW
1149

1149   **ABEREDW**   **[MWR]**
OP: 11/1867   Photo: S. 1958
CP: 29/12/1962   Stations U.K.

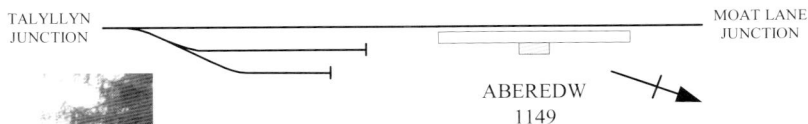

TIRCELYN
HALT
1150

1150   **TIRCELYN HALT**   **[MWR]**
OP: c.1872   Photo: S. 1960
CP: c.1950 (Private)   M.Hale

TALYLLYN
JUNCTION

MOAT LANE
JUNCTION

ERWOOD
1151

1151   **ERWOOD**   **[MWR]**
OP: 21/09/1864
CP: 29/12/1962

Photo: SE. 1958
P.Garland

1151   **ERWOOD**   **[MWR]**
Photo: NW. 1958
Stations U.K.

TALYLLYN
JUNCTION

MOAT LANE
JUNCTION

LLANSTEPHAN
HALT
1152

1152   **LLANSTEPHAN HALT**   **[MWR]**
OP: 06/03/1933
CP: 29/12/1962

Photo: N. 1962
P.Garland

TALYLLYN
JUNCTION

MOAT LANE
JUNCTION

BOUGHROOD &
LLYSWEN
1153

1153   **BOUGHROOD & LLYSWEN**   **[MWR]**
OP: 21/09/1864
CP: 29/12/1962

Photo: NW. 1958
Stations U.K.

1154   **THREE COCKS JUNCTION**   **[MWR]**
OP: 21/09/1864
CP: 29/12/1962

Photo: N. c.1960
J.Tarrant

TALYLLYN
JUNCTION

MOAT LANE
JUNCTION

THREE COCKS
JUNCTION
1154

(Hereford L.M.S.R.)

TALYLLYN
JUNCTION

MOAT LANE
JUNCTION

GS

TALGARTH
1155

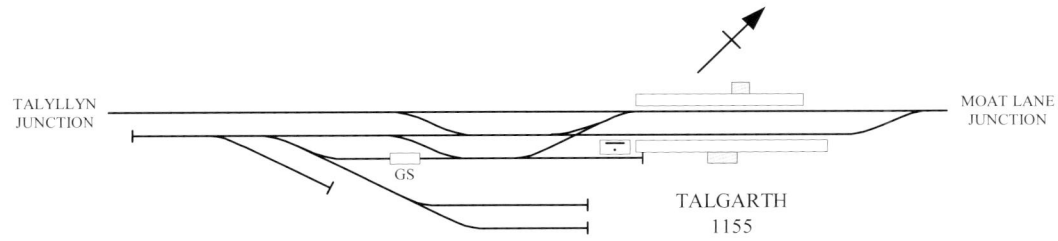

1155   **TALGARTH**   **[MWR]**
OP: 21/09/1864   Photo: SW. 1962
CP: 29/12/1962   E.T.Gill

1156   **TREFEINON**   **[MWR]**
OP: 07/03/1892   Photo: SW. 1959
CP: 29/12/1962   R.M.Casserley

TALYLLYN
JUNCTION

MOAT LANE
JUNCTION

TREFEINON
1156

TALYLLYN JUNCTION
(see page 542)

MOAT LANE
JUNCTION

LLANGORSE
LAKE HALT
1157

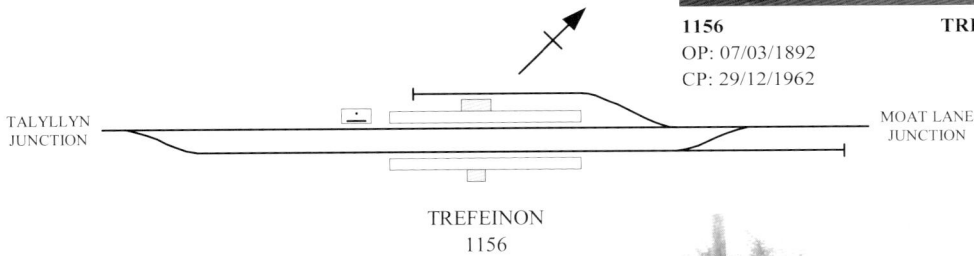

1157   **LLANGORSE LAKE HALT**   **[MWR]**
OP: 09/07/1923   Photo: SW. c.1960
CP: 29/12/1962   R.K.Blencowe

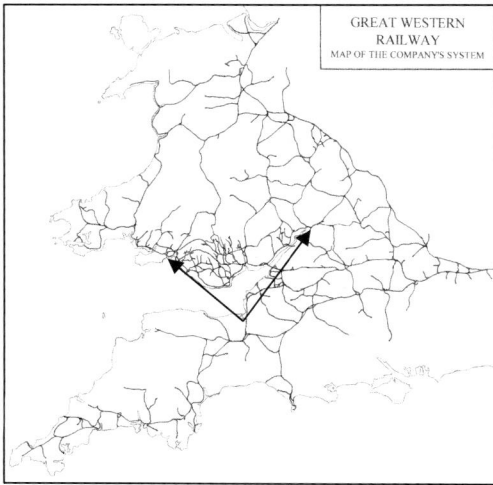

GLOUCESTER (Exc) TO SWANSEA
SOUTH WALES MAIN LINE,
SWANSEA BRANCH
Gloucester & Dean Forest Railway -
Great Western Railway (30/06/1874)
(Gloucester to Grange Court)
South Wales Railway -
Great Western Railway (01/08/1863)
(Grange Court to Swansea)
ACT: 27/07/1846 (Gloucester to Grange Court)
ACT: 27/07/1846 (Grange Court to Chepstow)
ACT: 04/08/1845 (Chepstow to Swansea)
OPG: 19/09/1851 (Gloucester to Chepstow East)
OPG: 19/07/1852 (Chepstow East to Chepstow)
OPG: 19/06/1850 (Chepstow to Swansea)
CP: OPEN
CG: OPEN

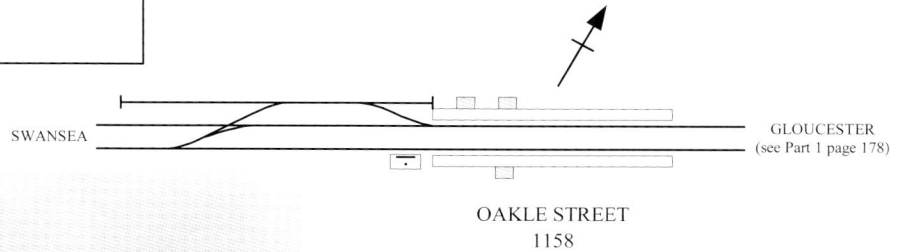

SWANSEA

GLOUCESTER
(see Part 1 page 178)

OAKLE STREET
1158

1158   **OAKLE STREET**   **[G&DFR]**
OP: 19/09/1851   Photo: SW. c.1910
CP: 31/10/1964   LOSA

1159   **GRANGE COURT**   **[G&DFR]**
OP: 19/09/1851   Photo: NE. 1959
CP: 31/10/1964   P.Garland

HEREFORD
(see page 341)

SWANSEA

GLOUCESTER

GRANGE COURT
1159

SWANSEA

GLOUCESTER

WESTBURY-ON-
SEVERN HALT
1160

1160   **WESTBURY-ON-SEVERN HALT**   **[SWR]**
OP: 09/07/1928   Photo: NE. 1958
CP: 08/08/1959   Stations U.K.

NEWNHAM
1161

1161   **NEWNHAM**   **[SWR]**
OP: 19/09/1851
CP: 31/10/1964
Photo: NE. c.1908
LOSA

1161   **NEWNHAM**   **[SWR]**
Photo: NE. 1962
Stations U.K.

AWRE
1162

1163   **LYDNEY**   **[SWR]**
OP: 19/09/1851
CP: OPEN
Photo: W. 1964
R.G.Nelson

1162   **AWRE**   **[SWR]**
OP: 19/09/1851
CP: 08/08/1959
Photo: SW. 1958
C.H.Townley

LYDNEY
1163

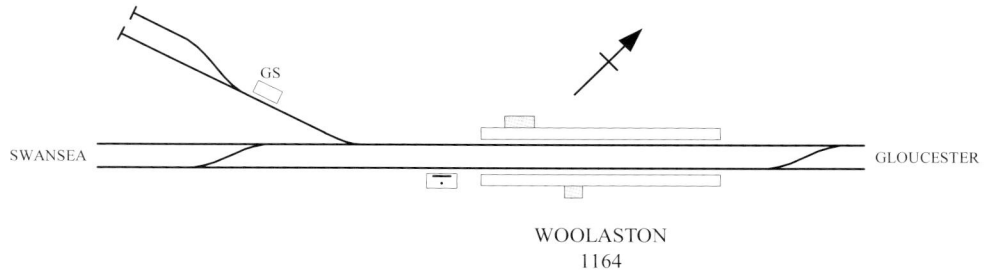

WOOLASTON
1164

SWANSEA GLOUCESTER
GS

1164 **WOOLASTON** **[SWR]**
OP: 01/06/1853
CP: 01/12/1954
Photo: NE. 1958
Stations U.K.

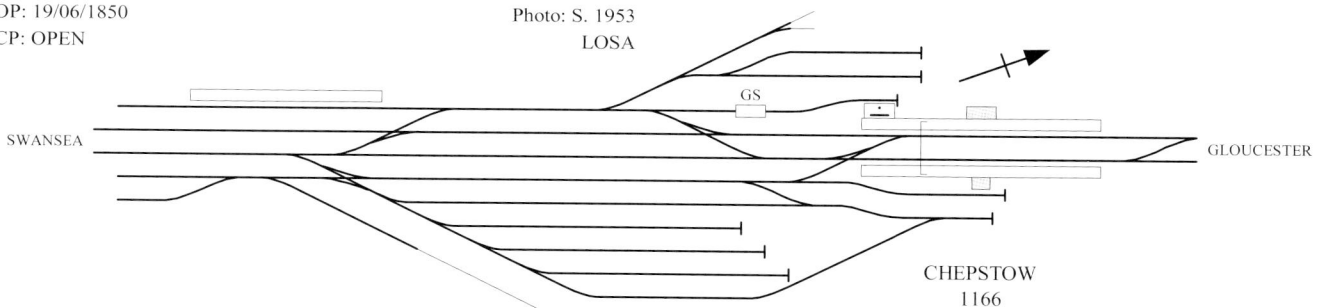

1164 **WOOLASTON** **[SWR]**
Photo: SW. 1958
Stations U.K.

SWANSEA

MONMOUTH
(see page 355)
GLOUCESTER

TUTSHILL HALT
1165

1165 **TUTSHILL HALT** **[SWR]**
OP: 09/07/1934
CP: 03/01/1959
Photo: NE. 1958
Stations U.K.

1166 **CHEPSTOW** **[SWR]**
OP: 19/06/1850
CP: OPEN
Photo: S. 1953
LOSA

SWANSEA GLOUCESTER
GS

CHEPSTOW
1166

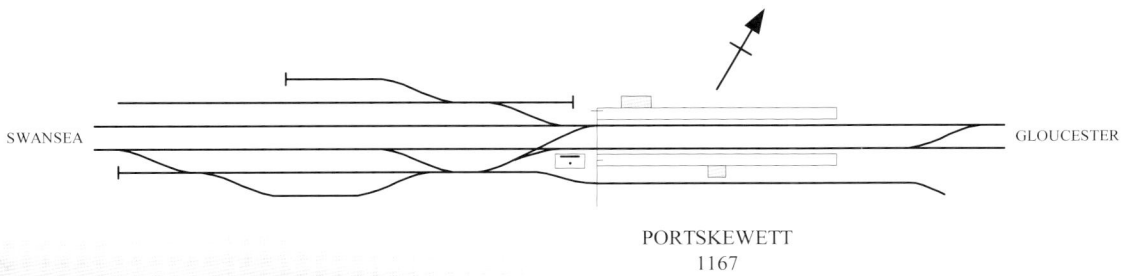

PORTSKEWETT
1167

1167   **PORTSKEWETT**   **[SWR]**
OP: 19/06/1850   Photo: SW. 1961
CP: 31/10/1964   M.Hale

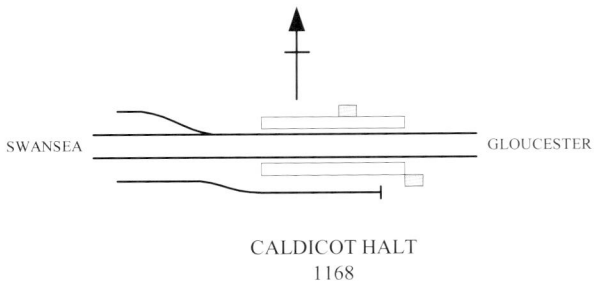

SWANSEA   GLOUCESTER

CALDICOT HALT
1168

1168   **CALDICOT HALT**   **[SWR]**
OP: 12/09/1932   Photo: E. 1962
CP: OPEN   Stations U.K.

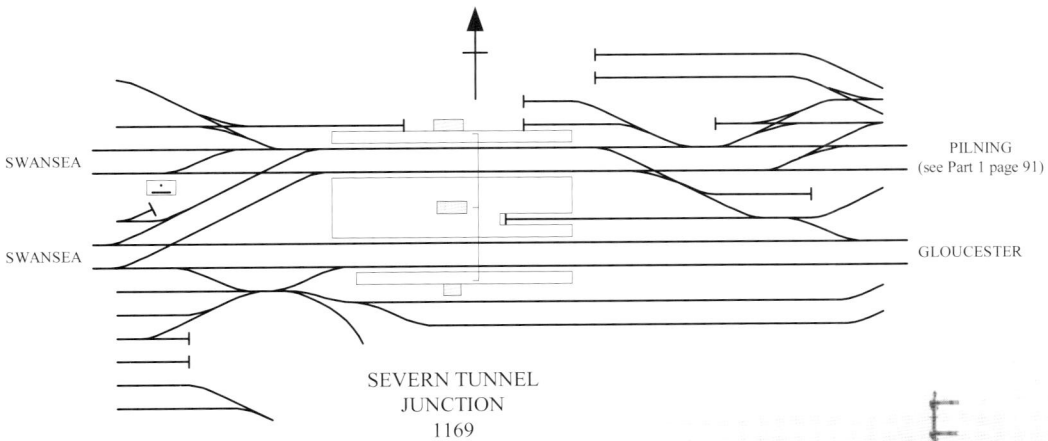

SWANSEA

PILNING
(see Part 1 page 91)

SWANSEA

GLOUCESTER

SEVERN TUNNEL
JUNCTION
1169

1169   **SEVERN TUNNEL JUNCTION**   **[SWR]**
OP: 01/12/1886   Photo: E. c.1955
CP: OPEN   LOSA

UNDY HALT
1170

1170   **UNDY HALT**   **[SWR]**
OP: 11/09/1933   Photo: E. 1958
CP: 31/10/1964   R.M.Casserley

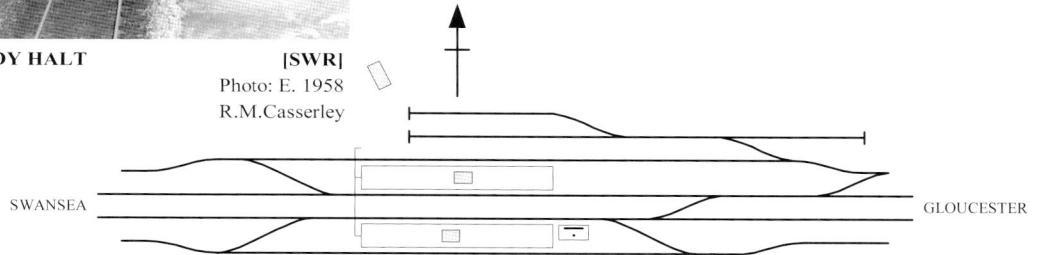

SWANSEA   GLOUCESTER

MAGOR
1171

1171   **MAGOR**   **[SWR]**
OP: 19/09/1851   Photo: E. c.1962
CP: 31/10/1964   LOSA

1172   **LLANWERN**   **[SWR]**
OP: 10/1855   Photo: W. c.1912
CP: 10/09/1960   LOSA

GS

SWANSEA   GLOUCESTER

LLANWERN
1172

1172   **LLANWERN**   **[SWR]**
Photo: E. 1961
M.Hale

1172   **LLANWERN**   **[SWR]**
Photo: E. c.1964
LOSA

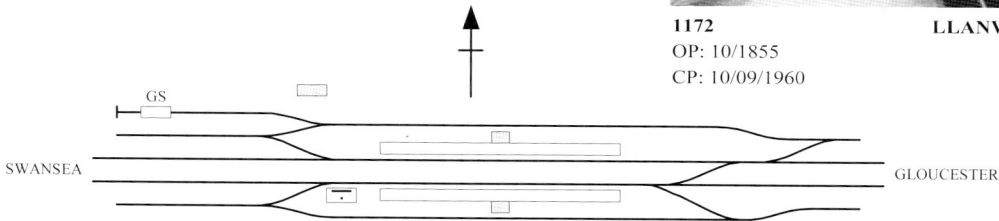

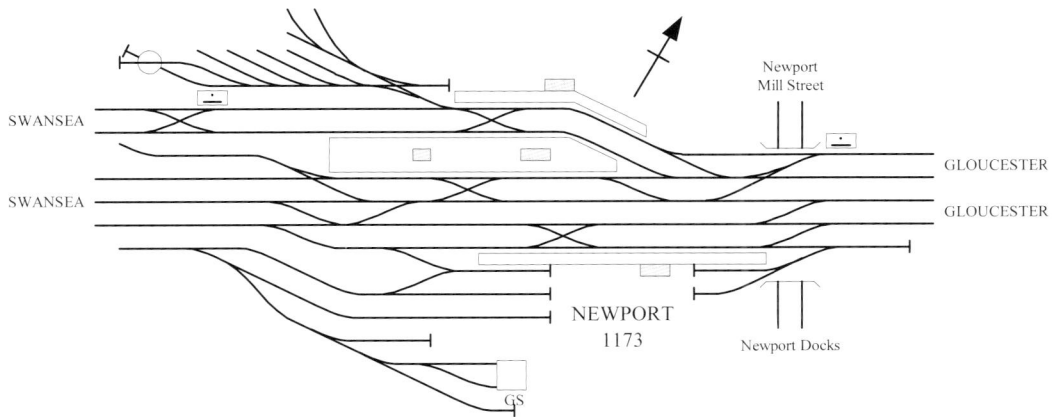

NEWPORT
1173

1173 **NEWPORT (HIGH STREET)** **[SWR]**
OP: 19/06/1850 Photo: NE. 1958
CP: OPEN Stations U.K.

1173 **NEWPORT (HIGH STREET)** **[SWR]**
Photo: SW. 1962
Stations U.K.

1173 **NEWPORT (HIGH STREET)** **[SWR]**
Photo: NE. 1962
Stations U.K.

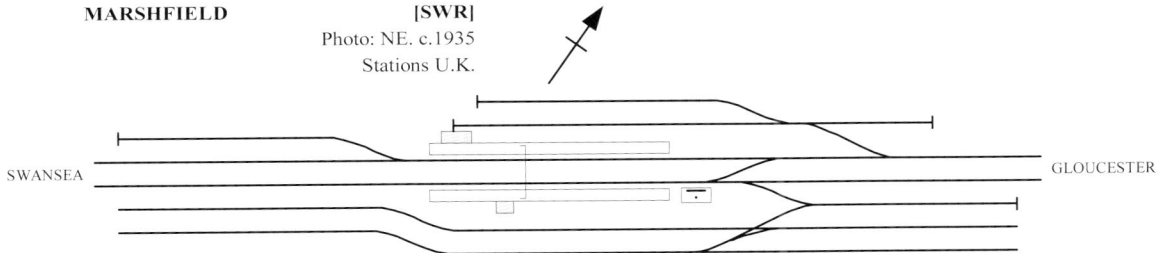

1174 **MARSHFIELD** **[SWR]**
OP: 02/09/1850 Photo: NE. c.1935
CP: 10/08/1959 Stations U.K.

MARSHFIELD
1174

SWANSEA

SWANSEA

PENARTH
(see page 503)

GLOUCESTER

GLOUCESTER

CARDIFF
(QUEEN STREET)
(see page 504)

CARDIFF
(CLARENCE ROAD)
(see page 503)

CARDIFF (GENERAL)
1175

1175   **CARDIFF (GENERAL)**   **[SWR]**
OP: 19/06/1850
CP: OPEN

Photo: W. 1953
R.C.Riley

1175   **CARDIFF (GENERAL)**   **[SWR]**
SE. c.1950
LOSA

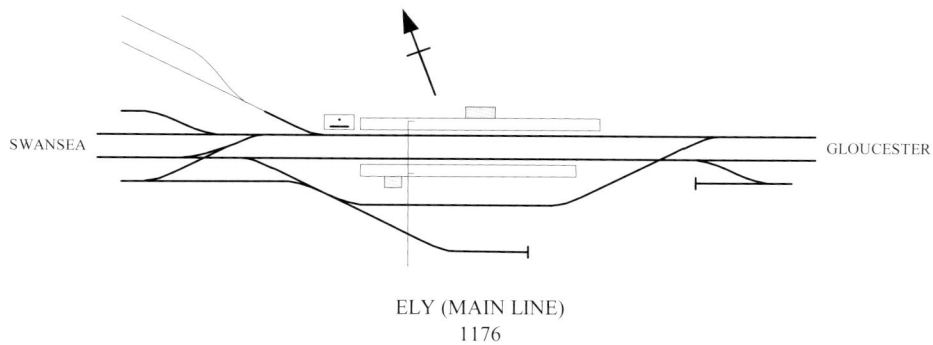

SWANSEA

GLOUCESTER

ELY (MAIN LINE)
1176

1176   **ELY (MAIN LINE)**   **[SWR]**
OP: 02/09/1850
CP: 08/09/1962

Photo: W. 1963
P.Garland

1176   **ELY (MAIN LINE)**   **[SWR]**
Photo: NW. 1963
P.Garland

1177   **ST. FAGANS**   **[SWR]**
OP: 01/04/1852   Photo: W. 1959
CP: 08/09/1962   R.M.Casserley

1177   **ST. FAGANS**   **[SWR]**
         Photo: E. 1959
         R.M.Casserley

SWANSEA   GLOUCESTER

ST. FAGANS
1177

1178   **PETERSTON**   **[SWR]**
OP: 19/06/1850   Photo: E. 1963
CP: 31/10/1964   P.Garland

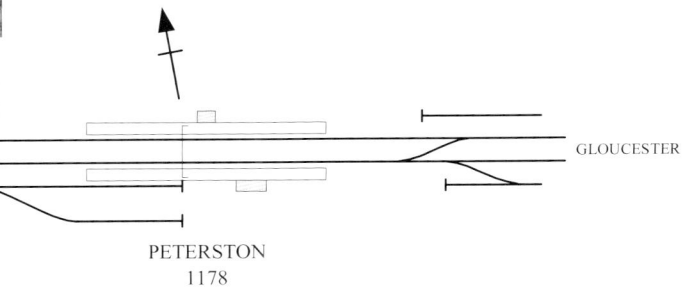

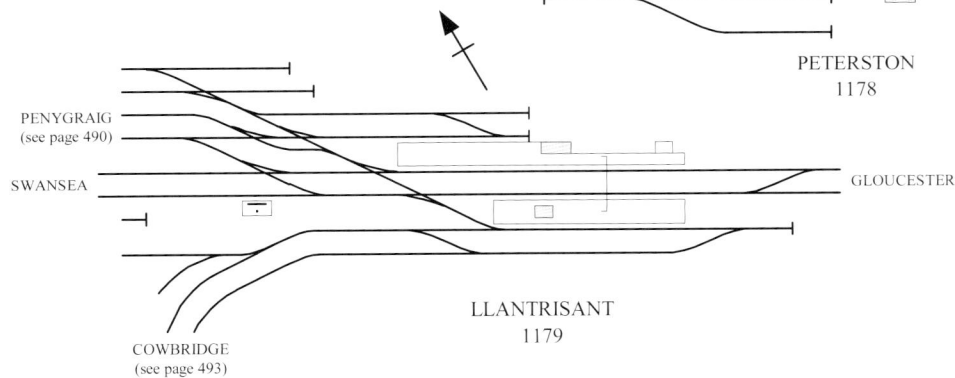

SWANSEA   GLOUCESTER

PETERSTON
1178

PENYGRAIG
(see page 490)

SWANSEA   GLOUCESTER

LLANTRISANT
1179

COWBRIDGE
(see page 493)

1179   **LLANTRISANT**   **[SWR]**
OP: 19/06/1850   Photo: NW. c.1951
CP: 31/10/1964   P.Garland

1179   **LLANTRISANT**   **[SWR]**
         Photo: SE. c.1960
         R.K.Blencowe

LLANHARAN
1180

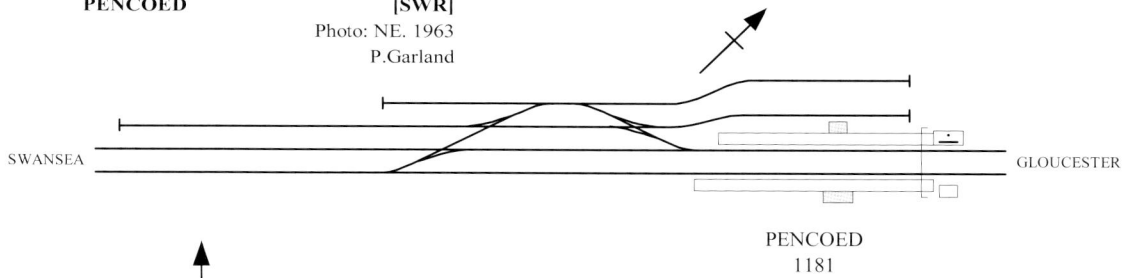

1181
PENCOED
OP: 02/09/1850
CP: 31/10/1964

[SWR]
Photo: NE. 1963
P.Garland

1180
LLANHARAN
OP: 01/09/1899
CP: 31/10/1964

[SWR]
Photo: E. 1958
Stations U.K.

PENCOED
1181

TREMAINS HALT
1182

1182
TREMAINS HALT
OP: 06/11/1939
CP: 11/09/1961 (Workmens trains)

[SWR]
Sketch: E. c.1941

1182
TREMAINS HALT

[SWR]
Photo: E. 1965
M.Hale

BRIDGEND
1183

1183   **BRIDGEND**   **[SWR]**
OP: 19/06/1850   Photo: NW. 1957
CP: OPEN   R.K.Blencowe

1183   **BRIDGEND**   **[SWR]**
          Photo: SE. 1960
          E.T.Gill

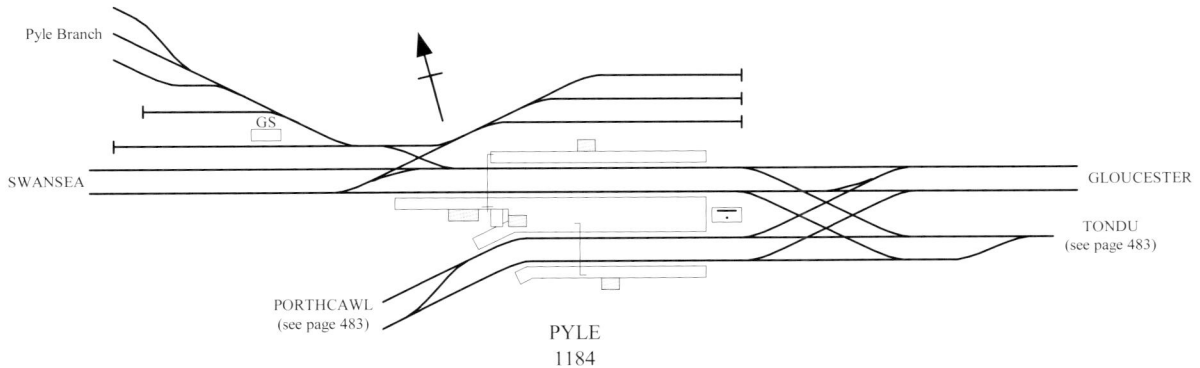

PYLE
1184

1184   **PYLE**   **[SWR]**
OP: 01/07/1886   Photo: E. 1959
CP: 31/10/1964   Stations U.K.

1184   **PYLE**   **[SWR]**
          Photo: E. 1959
          Stations U.K.

1184   **PYLE**   **[SWR]**

Photo: E. 1963
P.Garland

1185   **PORT TALBOT (GENERAL)**   **[SWR]**

OP: 19/06/1850   Photo: SE. 1955
CP: c.1961   Stations U.K.

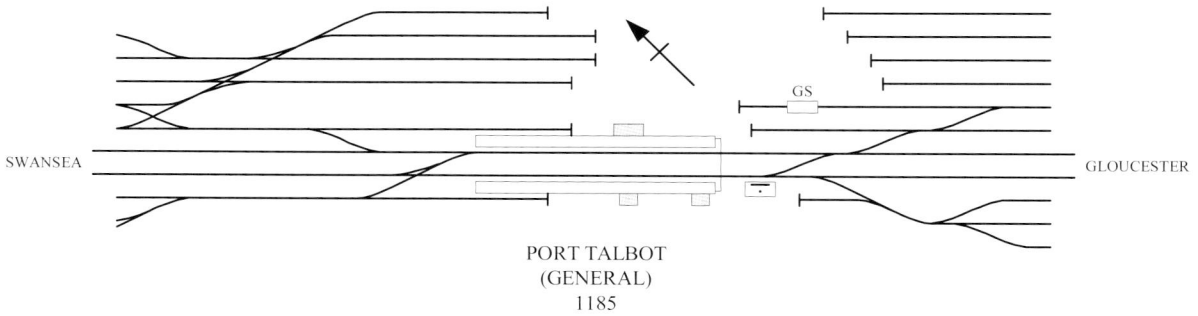

SWANSEA   GS   GLOUCESTER

PORT TALBOT
(GENERAL)
1185

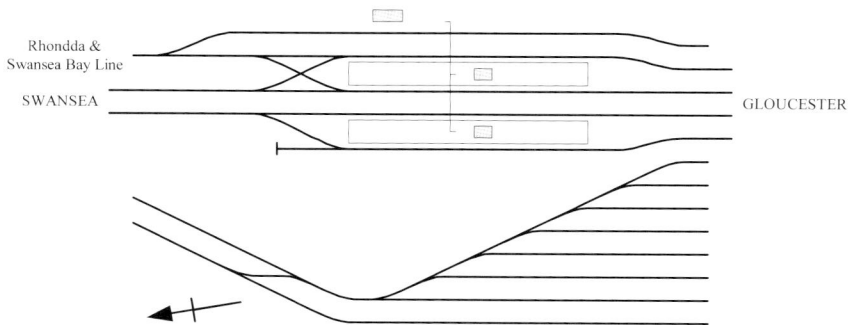

Rhondda &
Swansea Bay Line

SWANSEA   GLOUCESTER

BRITON FERRY
1186

1186   **BRITON FERRY**   **[SWR]**

OP: 08/07/1935   Photo: S. 1963
CP: 31/10/1964   P.Garland

1186   **BRITON FERRY**   **[SWR]**

Photo: S. c.1963
unknown

HIRWAUN
(see page 462)

SWANSEA

GLOUCESTER

GLOUCESTER

GS

NEATH (GENERAL)
1187

1187   **NEATH (GENERAL)**   **[SWR]**
OP: 04/06/1877   Photo: S. 1951
CP: OPEN   H.C.Casserley

1187   **NEATH (GENERAL)**   **[SWR]**
                                       Photo: N. 1963
                                       R.K.Blencowe

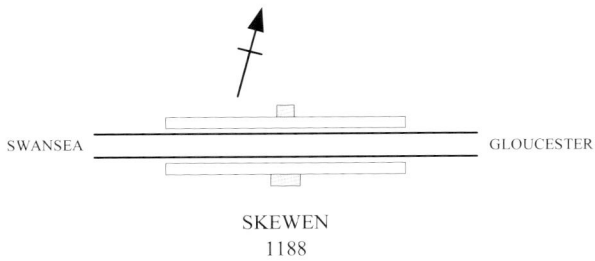

SWANSEA   GLOUCESTER

SKEWEN
1188

1188   **SKEWEN**   **[SWR]**
OP: 01/05/1910   Photo: E. 1963
CP: 31/10/1964   P.Garland

1189   **LLANSAMLET**   **[SWR]**
OP: 01/01/1885   Photo: NE. 1961
CP: 31/10/1964   Stations U.K.

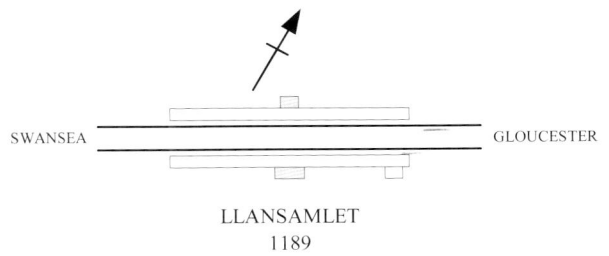

SWANSEA   GLOUCESTER

LLANSAMLET
1189

NEYLAND
(see page 421)

NEYLAND
(see page 421)

GLOUCESTER

GS

SWANSEA

LANDORE
1190

1190
OP: 09/05/1881
CP: 31/10/1964

LANDORE

[SWR]
Photo: SW. c.1935
Stations U.K.

1190

LANDORE

[SWR]
Photo: NE. 1960
P.Kingston

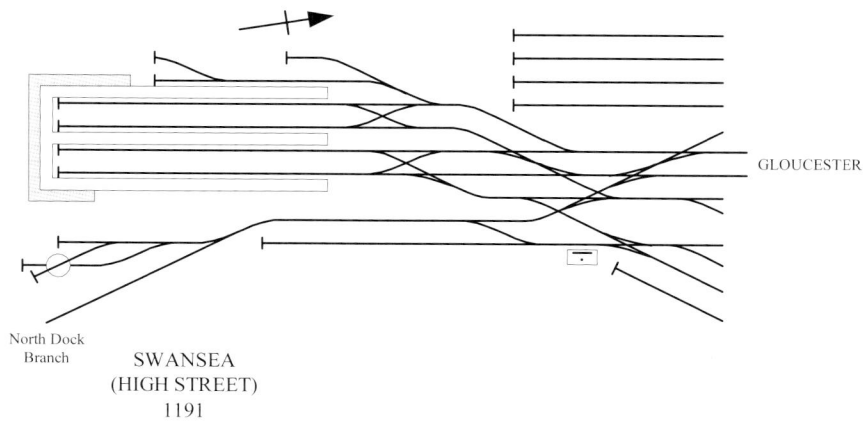

GLOUCESTER

North Dock
Branch

SWANSEA
(HIGH STREET)
1191

1191
OP: 19/06/1850
CP: OPEN

SWANSEA (HIGH STREET)

[SWR]
Photo: N. c.1930
Stations U.K.

1191

SWANSEA (HIGH STREET)

[SWR]
Photo: S. c.1970
D.Wittamore

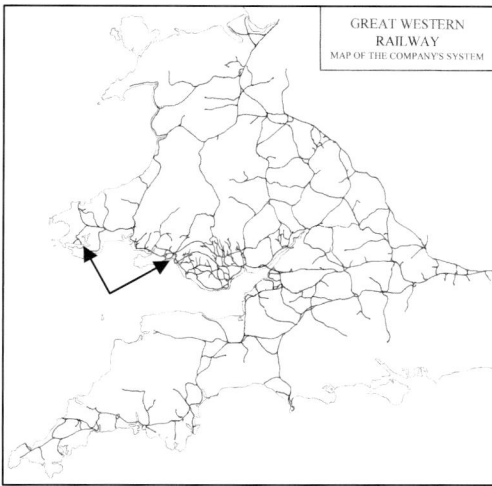

LANDORE (Exc) TO NEYLAND
SOUTH WALES MAIN LINE
South Wales Railway -
Great Western Railway (01/08/1863)
ACT: 04/08/1845 (Landore to Clarbeston Road)
ACT: 27/07/1846 (Clarbeston Road to Haverfordwest)
ACT: 17/06/1852 (Haverfordwest to Neyland)
OPG: 11/10/1852 (Landore to Carmarthen)
OPG: 02/01/1854 (Carmarthen to Haverfordwest)
OPG: 15/04/1856 (Haverfordwest to Neyland)
CP: 15/06/1964 (Johnston to Neyland)
CG: 15/06/1964 (Johnston to Neyland)

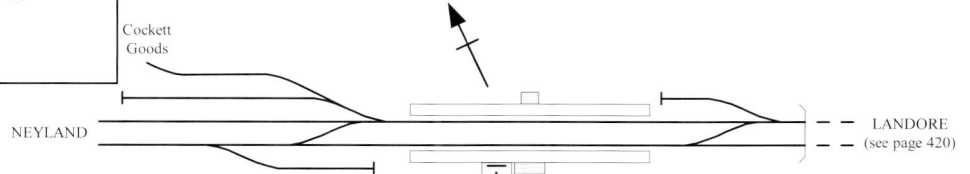

COCKETT
1192

1192	**COCKETT**	[SWR]
OP: 05/1871		Photo: E. 1956
CP: 13/06/1964		C.Mowat

1192　　　　**COCKETT**　　　　**[SWR]**
Photo: W. 1961
Stations U.K.

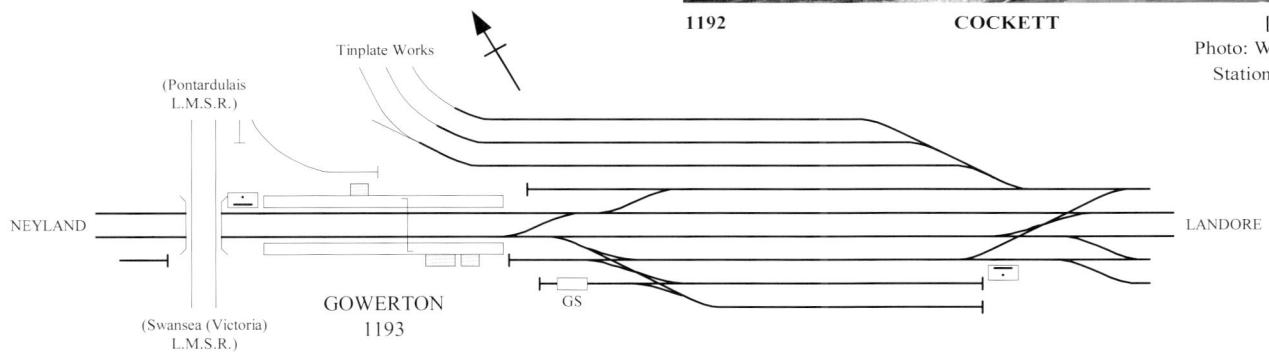

GOWERTON
1193

1193	**GOWERTON**	[SWR]
OP: 01/08/1854		Photo: W. c.1960
CP: OPEN		T.C.Cole

1193　　　　**GOWERTON**　　　　**[SWR]**
Photo: W. c.1930
unknown

LOUGHOR
1194

1194   **LOUGHOR**   **[SWR]**
OP: 11/10/1852   Photo: E. 1958
CP: 02/04/1960   H.C.Casserley

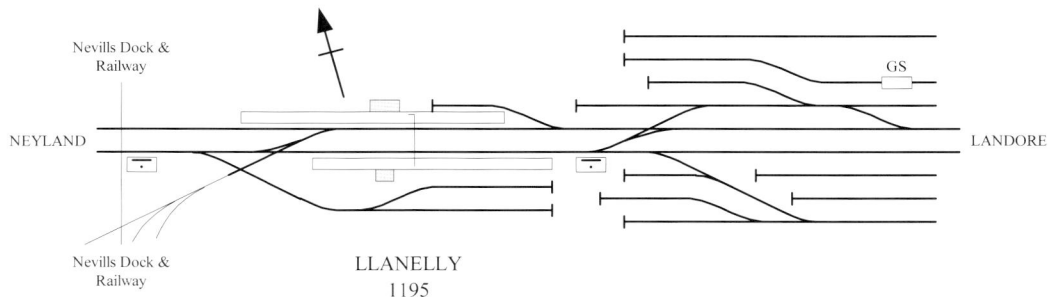

Nevills Dock &
Railway

NEYLAND

GS

LANDORE

Nevills Dock &
Railway

LLANELLY
1195

1195   **LLANELLY**   **[SWR]**
OP: 11/10/1852   Photo: W. 1956
CP: OPEN   C.Mowat

1195   **LLANELLY**   **[SWR]**
Photo: E. 1964
Stations U.K.

NEYLAND

LANDORE

PEMBREY &
BURRY PORT
1196

GS

Burry Port

1196   **PEMBREY & BURRY PORT**   **[SWR]**
OP: 11/10/1852   Photo: E. 1937
CP: OPEN   Stations U.K.

1196   **PEMBREY & BURRY PORT**   **[SWR]**
                               Photo: W. 1964
                               Stations U.K.

NEYLAND   LANDORE

LANDO
PLATFORM
1197

1197   **LANDO PLATFORM**   **[SWR]**
OP: 11/1915   Photo: NW. c.1960
CP: 13/06/1964 (Workmens trains)   LOSA

NEYLAND   LANDORE

KIDWELLY
FLATS HALT
1198

1198   **KIDWELLY FLATS HALT**   **[SWR]**
OP: 06/08/1941   Photo: N. 1960
CP: 11/11/1957 (Workmens trains)   M.Hale

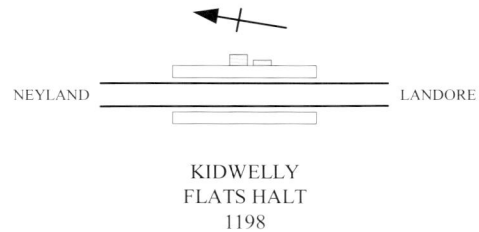

1199   **KIDWELLY**   **[SWR]**
OP: 11/10/1852   Photo: NW. 1947
CP: OPEN   H.C.Casserley

NEYLAND   GS   LANDORE

KIDWELLY
1199

NEYLAND

GS

LANDORE

FERRYSIDE
1200

1200   **FERRYSIDE**   **[SWR]**
OP: 11/10/1852   Photo: N. 1963
CP: OPEN   P.Garland

1201   **SARNAU**   **[SWR]**
OP: 06/06/1888   Photo: W. 1963
CP: 13/06/1964   P.Garland

GS

NEYLAND   LANDORE

SARNAU
1201

GS

NEYLAND   LANDORE

ST. CLEARS
1202

1202   **ST. CLEARS**   **[SWR]**
OP: 02/01/1854   Photo: W. 1961
CP: 14/06/1964   Stations U.K.

1202   **ST. CLEARS**   **[SWR]**
                                Photo: E. 1963
                                P.Garland

WHITLAND
1203

1203　　　　**WHITLAND**　　　　**[SWR]**
OP: 02/01/1854　　　　　　　　Photo: W. c.1911
CP: OPEN　　　　　　　　　　　　　LOSA

1203　　　　**WHITLAND**　　　　**[SWR]**
　　　　　　　　　　　　　　Photo: E. c.1950
　　　　　　　　　　　　　　　　LOSA

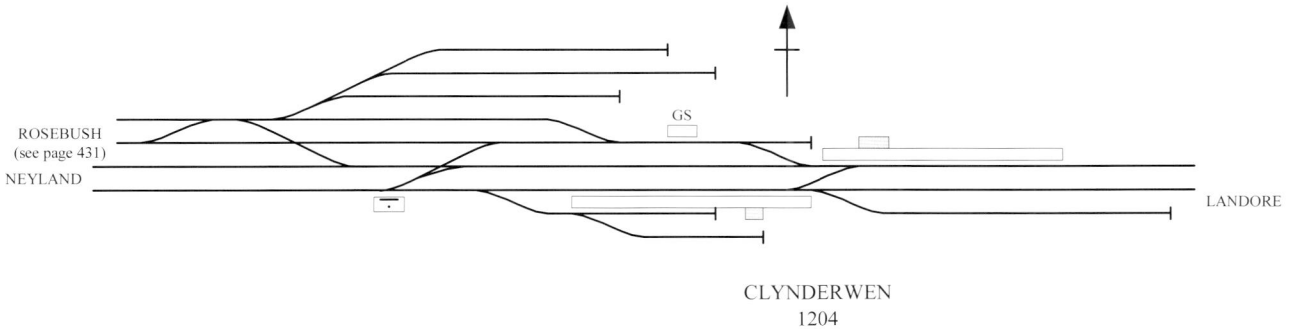

CLYNDERWEN
1204

1204　　　　**CLYNDERWEN**　　　　**[SWR]**
OP: 02/01/1854　　　　　　　Photo: W. c.1955
CP: OPEN　　　　　　　　　　　　LOSA

1204　　　　**CLYNDERWEN**　　　　**[SWR]**
　　　　　　　　　　　　Photo: W. c.1960
　　　　　　　　　　　　　　LOSA

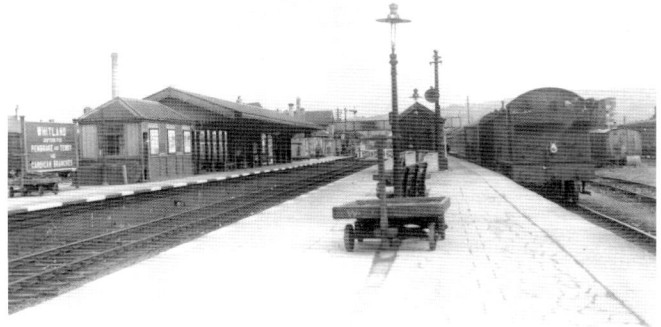

FISHGUARD
(see page 428)

NEYLAND

GS

CLARBESTON ROAD
1205

LANDORE

1205   **CLARBESTON ROAD**   **[SWR]**
OP: 27/07/1914   Photo: E. 1958
CP: OPEN   M.Hale

1205   **CLARBESTON ROAD**   **[SWR]**
                                  Photo: NW. 1959
                                  F.A.Blencowe

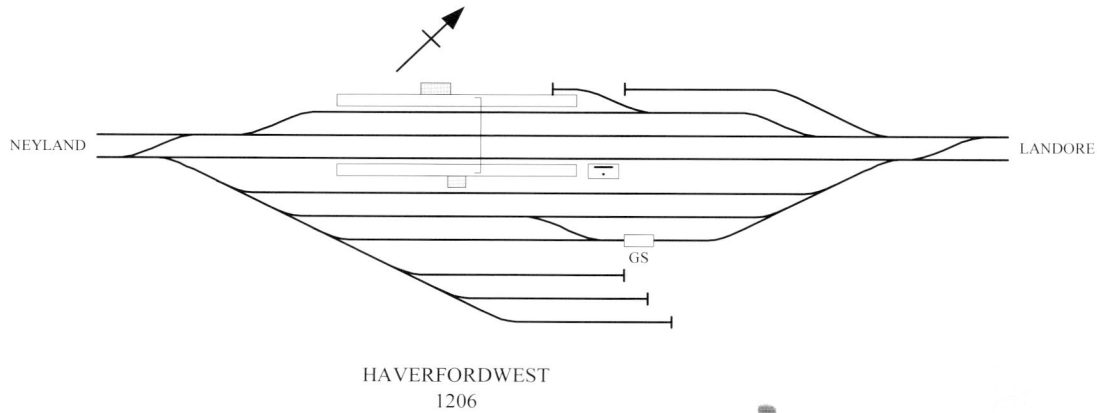

NEYLAND

GS

LANDORE

HAVERFORDWEST
1206

1207   **JOHNSTON (PEM.)**   **[SWR]**
OP: 15/04/1856   Photo: SE. c.1960
CP: OPEN   R.K.Blencowe

1206   **HAVERFORDWEST**   **[SWR]**
OP: 02/01/1854   Photo: NE. 1963
CP: OPEN   P.Garland

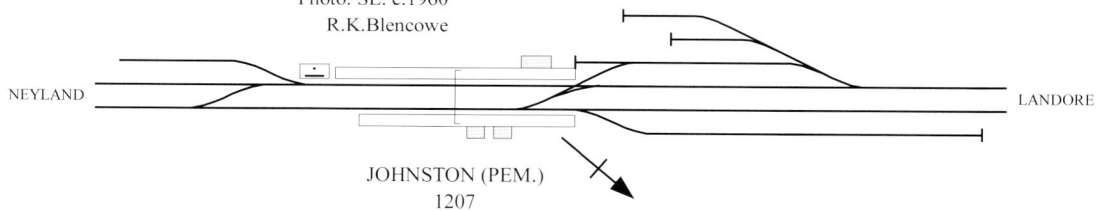

NEYLAND   LANDORE

JOHNSTON (PEM.)
1207

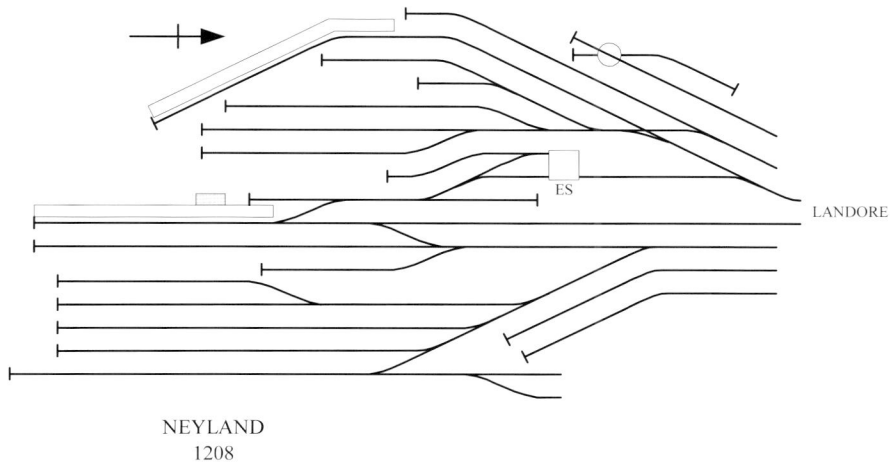

NEYLAND
1208

1208   **NEYLAND**   **[SWR]**
OP: 15/04/1856
CP: 14/06/1964   Photo: N. c.1955
       R.Carpenter

1208   **NEYLAND**   **[SWR]**
       Photo: S. 1958
       H.C.Casserley

GREAT WESTERN
RAILWAY
MAP OF THE COMPANY'S SYSTEM

JOHNSTON (Exc) TO MILFORD HAVEN
MILFORD HAVEN BRANCH
Milford Railway -
Great Western Railway (01/07/1896)
ACT: 05/06/1856
OP: 07/09/1863
OG: 07/09/1863
CP: OPEN
CG: OPEN

1209   **MILFORD HAVEN**   **[MilRly]**
OP: 07/09/1863
CP: OPEN   Photo: S. 1958
       H.C.Casserley

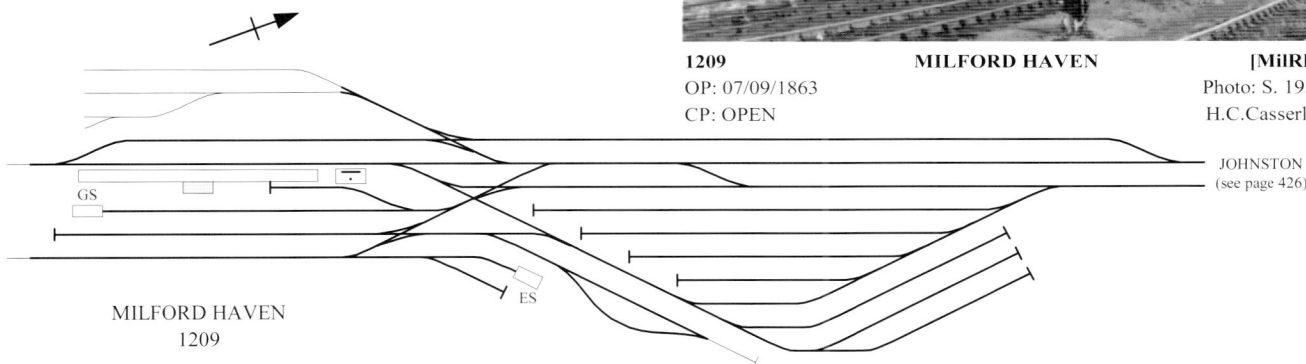

JOHNSTON
(see page 426)

MILFORD HAVEN
1209

GREAT WESTERN
RAILWAY
MAP OF THE COMPANY'S SYSTEM

**CLARBESTON ROAD (Exc) TO FISHGUARD HARBOUR
CLARBESTON ROAD & LETTERSTON LINE,
NORTH PEMBROKESHIRE & FISHGUARD LINE,
FISHGUARD HARBOUR LINES**
Great Western Railway
(Clarbeston Road to Letterston Junction) -
Rosebush & Fishguard Railway -
Great Western Railway (12/02/1898)
(Letterston Junction to 3 chains north of Fishguard & Goodwick)
Fishguard and Rosslare Railways and Harbours -
Great Western Railway (27/05/1898)
(Lines at Fishguard Harbour)
ACT: 12/08/1898 (Clarbeston Road to Letterston Junction)
ACT: 08/08/1878 (Letterston Junction to 3 chains north of
Fishguard & Goodwick)
ACT: 29/06/1893 (Fishguard Harbour Lines)
OPG: 30/08/1906 (Clarbeston Road to Letterston Junction)
OP: 01/08/1899 (Letterston to Fishguard & Goodwick)
OG: 01/07/1899 (Letterston to Fishguard & Goodwick)
OPG: 30/08/1906 (to Fishguard Harbour)
CP: 04/04/1964 (Local Services only)
CG: OPEN

1210	**WOLFS CASTLE HALT**	[GWR]
OP: 01/10/1913		Photo: NW. c.1963
CP: 04/04/1964		P.Garland

WOLFS CASTLE
HALT
1210

FISHGUARD — CLARBESTON ROAD
(see page 426)

WELSH HOOK
HALT
1211

FISHGUARD — CLARBESTON ROAD

1211	**WELSH HOOK HALT**	[GWR]
OP: 05/05/1924		Photo: SE. 1958
CP: 04/04/1964		R.M.Casserley

1212	**MATHRY ROAD**	[GWR]
OP: 01/08/1923		Photo: SW. 1962
CP: 04/04/1964		R.G.Nelson

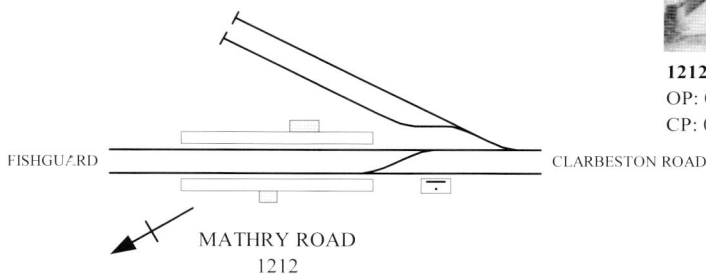

FISHGUARD — CLARBESTON ROAD

MATHRY ROAD
1212

JORDANSTON
HALT
1213

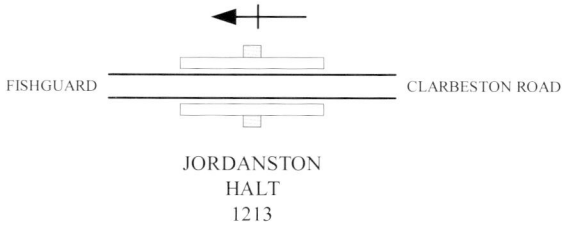

1213   **JORDANSTON HALT**   **[R&FR]**
OP: 01/10/1923   Photo: N. 1959
CP: 04/04/1964   M.Hale

1214   **FISHGUARD & GOODWICK**   **[R&FR]**
OP: 01/08/1899   Photo: S. 1959
CP: 03/08/1964 (Workmens trains)   Stations U.K.

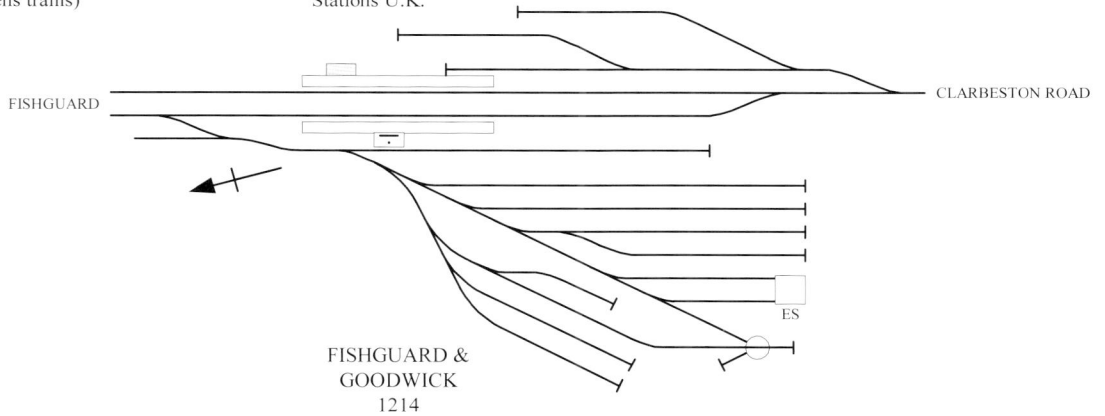

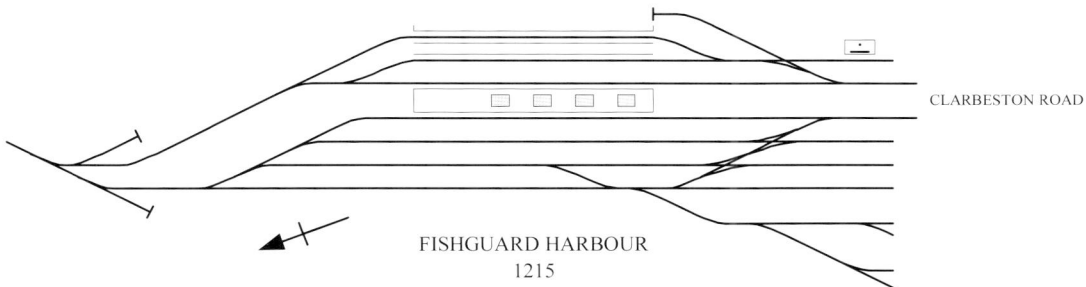

FISHGUARD

CLARBESTON ROAD

ES

FISHGUARD &
GOODWICK
1214

CLARBESTON ROAD

FISHGUARD HARBOUR
1215

1215   **FISHGUARD HARBOUR**   **[GWR]**
OP: 30/08/1906   Photo: S. c.1906
CP: OPEN   LOSA

1215   **FISHGUARD HARBOUR**   **[GWR]**
                                     Photo: N. 1964
                                     Stations U.K.

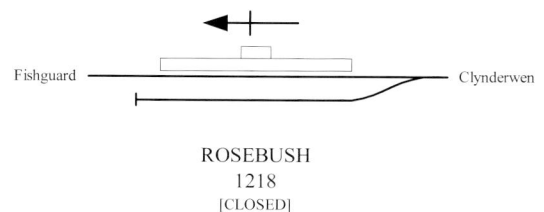

GREAT WESTERN
RAILWAY
MAP OF THE COMPANY'S SYSTEM

CLYNDERWEN (Exc) TO Letterston Junction
NORTH PEMBROKESHIRE AND FISHGUARD LINE
Narberth Road & Maenclochog Railway -
North Pembrokeshire & Fishguard Railway (1894) -
Great Western Railway (12/02/1898)
(Clynderwen to Rosebush)
Rosebush & Fishguard Railway -
(renamed North Pembrokeshire & Fishguard Railway 07/08/1884) -
Great Western Railway (12/02/1898)
(Rosebush to Letterston Junction)
ACT: 24/06/1872 (Clynderwen to Rosebush)
ACT: 08/08/1878 (Rosebush to Letterston Junction)
OPG: 19/09/1876 (Clynderwen to Rosebush)
CPG: 31/12/1882 (Clynderwen to Rosebush)
OP: 11/04/1895 (Clynderwen to Letterston)
OG: 14/03/1895 (Clynderwen to Letterston)
OP: 01/08/1899 (Letterston to Fishguard & Goodwick)
OG: 01/07/1899 (Letterston to Fishguard & Goodwick)
CP: 25/10/1937
CG: 16/05/1949 (Clynderwen to Puncheston)
CG: 03/11/1942 (Puncheston to Letterston)
CG: 01/03/1965 (Letterston to Letterston Junction)
OP: 05/1950 (Workmens trains, Letterston Junc. to Trecwn Junc.)
CP: 01/08/1964 (Workmens trains, Letterston Junc. to Trecwn Junc.)

Fishguard — LLANYCEFN — Clynderwen (see page 426)

LLANYCEFN
1216
[CLOSED]

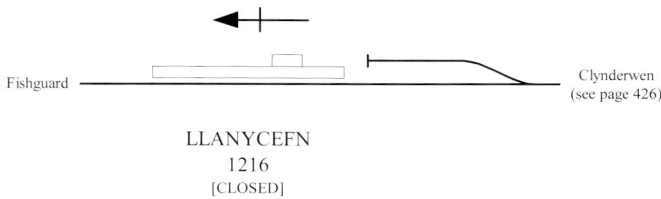

1216   **LLANYCEFN**   **[NR&MR]**
OP: 19/09/1876   Photo: SE. c.1905
CP: 25/10/1937   R.Carpenter

Fishguard — MAENCLOCHOG — Clynderwen

MAENCLOCHOG
1217
[CLOSED]

1217   **MAENCLOCHOG**   **[NR&MR]**
OP: 19/09/1876   Photo: N. c.1920
CP: 25/10/1937   John Gale

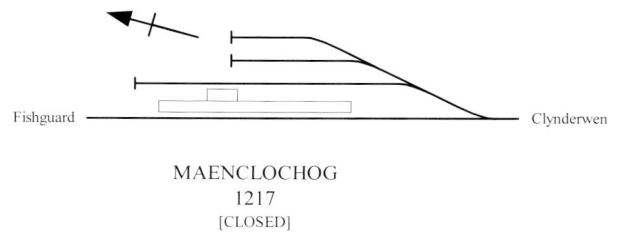

Fishguard — ROSEBUSH — Clynderwen

ROSEBUSH
1218
[CLOSED]

1218   **ROSEBUSH**   **[NR&MR]**
OP: 19/09/1876   Photo: NE. c.1920
CP: 25/10/1937   Stations U.K.

PUNCHESTON
1219
[CLOSED]

1219   **PUNCHESTON**   **[R&FR]**
OP: 11/04/1895   Photo: NE. c.1920
CP: 25/10/1937   John Gale

LETTERSTON
1220
[CLOSED]

1220   **LETTERSTON**   **[R&FR]**
OP: 11/04/1895   Photo: W. c.1920
CP: 25/10/1937   LOSA

1220   **LETTERSTON**   **[R&FR]**
                                     Photo: W. 1959
                                            M.Hale

WHITLAND (Exc) TO CARDIGAN
CARDIGAN BRANCH
Whitland & Taf Vale Railway -
(renamed Whitland & Cardigan Railway 1877) -
Great Western Railway (01/07/1890)
ACT: 12/07/1869 (Cardigan Junction to Crymmych Arms)
ACT: 1877 (Crymmych Arms to Cardigan)
OP: 12/07/1875 (Whitland to Crymmych Arms)
OP: 01/09/1886 (Crymmych Arms to Cardigan)
OG: 24/03/1873 (Whitland to Glogue)
OG: 07/1874 (Glogue to Crymmych Arms)
OG: 01/09/1886 (Crymmych Arms to Cardigan)
CP: 08/09/1962
CG: 27/05/1963

WHITLAND
(see page 425)

LLANFALTEG
1221

1221   **LLANFALTEG**   **[W&TVR]**
OP: 12/07/1875   Photo: S. 1961
CP: 08/09/1962   Stations U.K.

1222   **LOGIN**   **[W&TVR]**
OP: 12/07/1875   Photo: N. 1964
CP: 08/09/1962   P.Garland

CARDIGAN   WHITLAND

LOGIN
1222

CARDIGAN   WHITLAND

LLANGLYDWEN
1223

1223   **LLANGLYDWEN**   **[W&TVR]**
OP: 12/07/1875   Photo: SW. 1961
CP: 08/09/1962   Stations U.K.

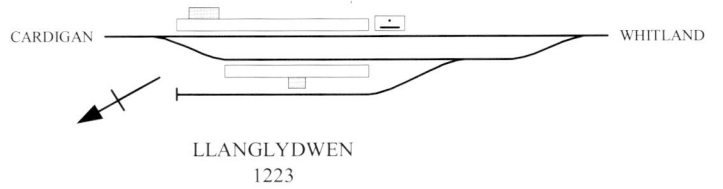

CARDIGAN   WHITLAND

RHYDOWEN
1224

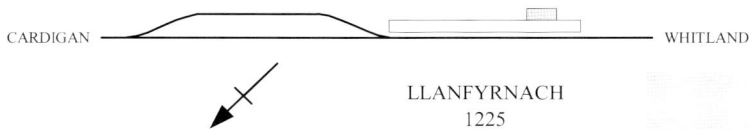

1224   **RHYDOWEN**   **[W&TVR]**
OP: 12/07/1875   Photo: NE. 1961
CP: 08/09/1962   Stations U.K.

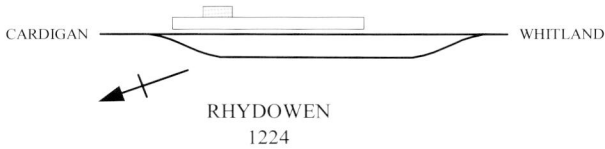

CARDIGAN   WHITLAND

LLANFYRNACH
1225

1225   **LLANFYRNACH**   **[W&TVR]**
OP: 12/07/1875   Photo: NE. 1961
CP: 08/09/1962   Stations U.K.

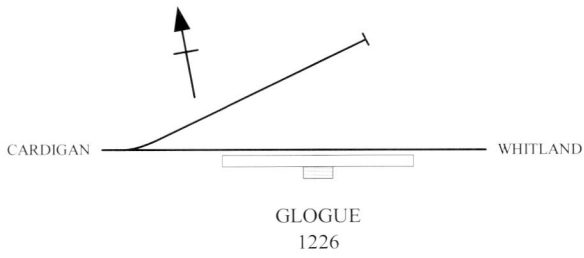

GLOGUE
1226

1226   **GLOGUE**   **[W&TVR]**
OP: 12/07/1875   Photo: W. 1958
CP: 08/09/1962   R.M.Casserley

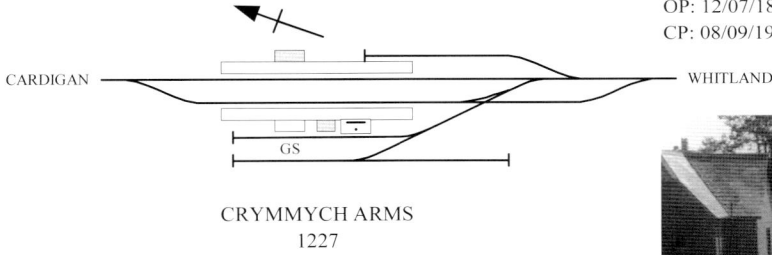

CRYMMYCH ARMS
1227

1227   **CRYMMYCH ARMS**   **[W&TVR]**
OP: 12/07/1875   Photo: S. 1959
CP: 08/09/1962   E.T.Gill

1228   **BONCATH**   **[W&CR]**
OP: 01/09/1886   Photo: SW. 1961
CP: 08/09/1962   Stations U.K.

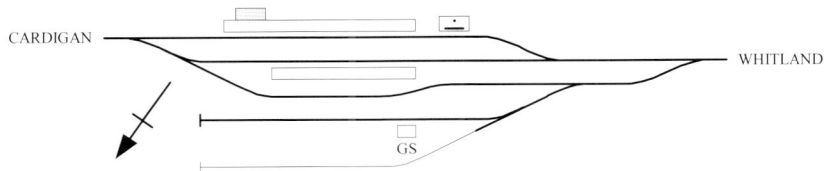

BONCATH
1228

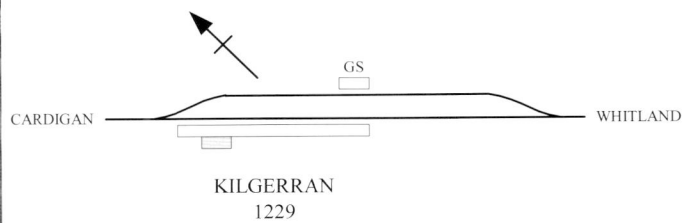

KILGERRAN
1229

1229   **KILGERRAN**   **[W&CR]**
OP: 01/09/1886   Photo: SE. 1961
CP: 08/09/1962   Stations U.K.

CARDIGAN
1230

1230	**CARDIGAN**	**[W&CR]**
OP: 01/09/1886		Photo: W. 1962
CP: 08/09/1962		R.G.Nelson

1230	**CARDIGAN**	**[W&CR]**
		Photo: E. c.1960
		LOSA

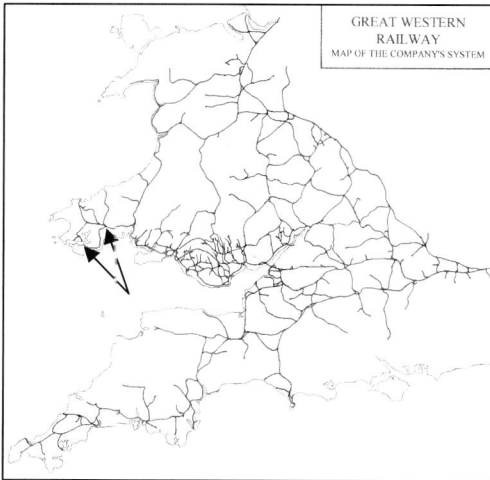

GREAT WESTERN
RAILWAY
MAP OF THE COMPANY'S SYSTEM

WHITLAND (Exc) TO PEMBROKE DOCK
PEMBROKE AND TENBY BRANCH
Pembroke & Tenby Railway -
Great Western Railway (01/07/1897)
ACT: 14/07/1864 (Whitland to Tenby)
ACT: 21/07/1859 (Tenby to Pembroke Dock)
OPG: 04/09/1866 (Whitland to Tenby)
OPG: 31/07/1863 (Tenby to Pembroke)
OPG: 09/08/1864 (Pembroke to Pembroke Dock)
CP: OPEN
CG: OPEN

1231	**NARBERTH**	**[P&TR]**
OP: 01/07/1878		Photo: SW. 1961
CP: OPEN		Stations U.K.

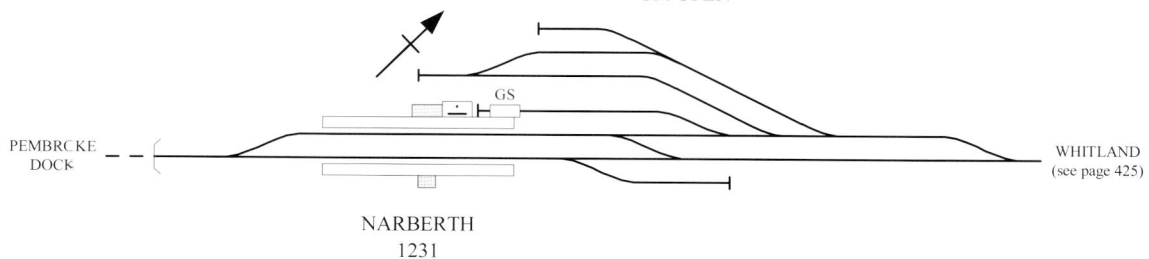

NARBERTH
1231

(see page 425)

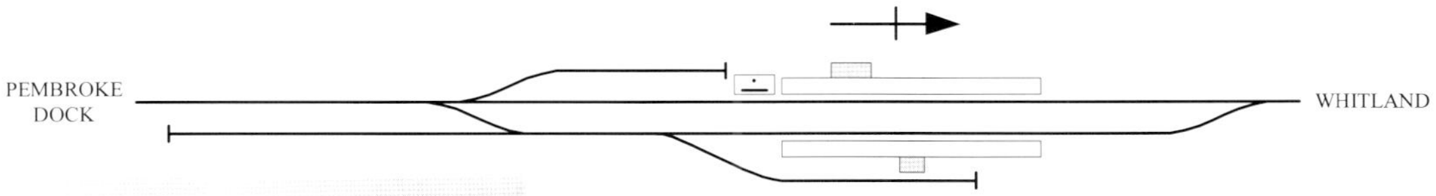

TEMPLETON
1232

1232   **TEMPLETON**   **[P&TR]**
OP: 1867   Photo: N. 1963
CP: 14/06/1964   P.Garland

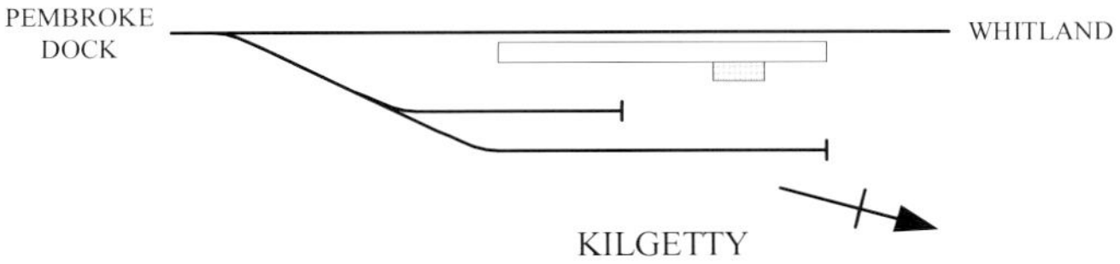

KILGETTY
1233

1233   **KILGETTY**   **[P&TR]**
OP: 04/09/1866   Photo: S. 1963
CP: OPEN   P.Garland

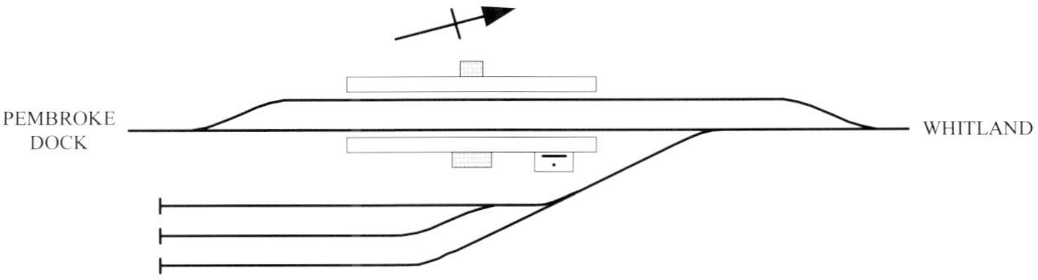

SAUNDERSFOOT
1234

1234   **SAUNDERSFOOT**   **[P&TR]**
OP: 04/09/1866   Photo: N. 1963
CP: OPEN   P.Garland

1235   **TENBY**   **[P&TR]**
OP: 04/09/1866   Photo: S. c.1920
CP: OPEN   HMRS (AAM104)

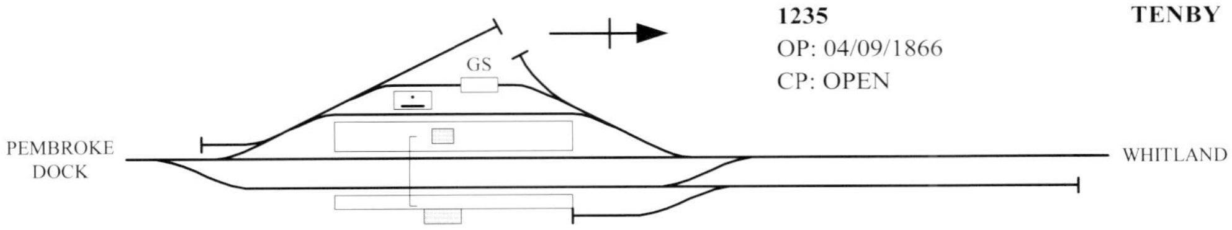

TENBY
1235

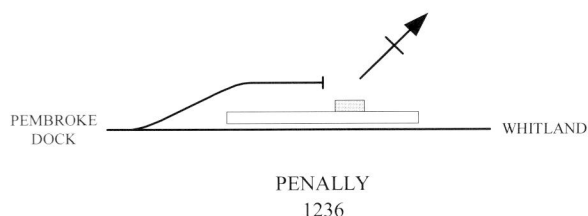

PENALLY
1236

1236   **PENALLY**   **[P&TR]**
OP: 31/07/1863   Photo: SW. 1961
CP: 14/06/1964   R.Carpenter

LYDSTEP HALT
1237

1237   **LYDSTEP HALT**   **[P&TR]**
OP: 1897   Photo: W. 1963
CP: 02/01/1956   P.Garland

MANORBIER
1238

1238   **MANORBIER**   **[P&TR]**
OP: 13/07/1863   Photo: W. c.1960
CP: OPEN   LOSA

1238   **MANORBIER**   **[P&TR]**
       Photo: E. 1962
       R.G.Nelson

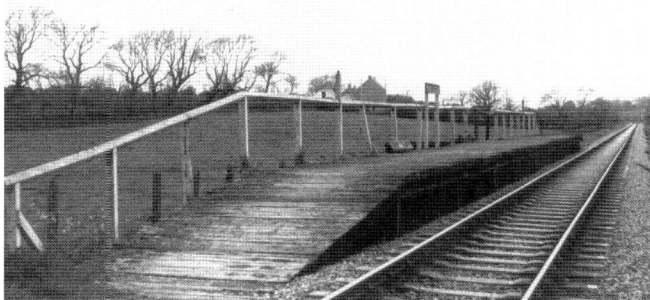

1239   **BEAVERS HILL HALT**   **[P&TR]**
OP: 01/05/1905   Photo: W. 1963
CP: 13/06/1964   P.Garland

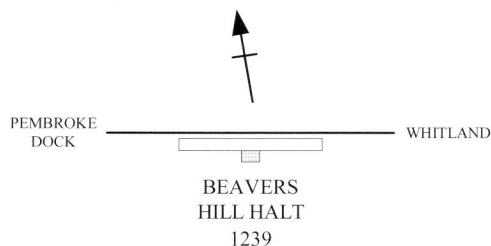

BEAVERS
HILL HALT
1239

LAMPHEY
1240

1240   **LAMPHEY**   **[P&TR]**
OP: 31/07/1863   Photo: W. 1963
CP: OPEN   P.Garland

1241   **PEMBROKE**   **[P&TR]**
OP: 31/07/1863   Photo: SE. 1963
CP: OPEN   P.Garland

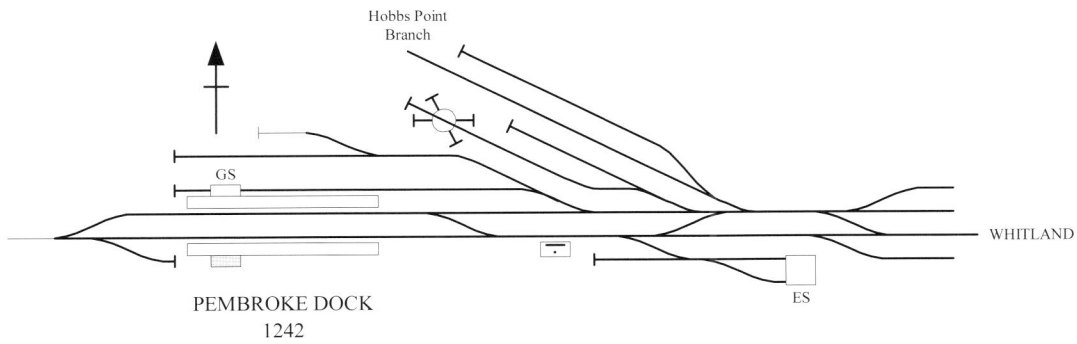

PEMBROKE
DOCK   WHITLAND

PEMBROKE
1241

Hobbs Point
Branch

GS

PEMBROKE DOCK   WHITLAND
1242

ES

1242   **PEMBROKE DOCK**   **[P&TR]**
OP: 09/08/1864   Photo: W. 1961
CP: OPEN   J.Harrold

1242   **PEMBROKE DOCK**   **[P&TR]**
     Photo: W. 1964
     C.Mowat

GREAT WESTERN
RAILWAY
MAP OF THE COMPANY'S SYSTEM

CARMARTHEN TO NEWCASTLE EMLYN
CARMARTHEN & NEWCASTLE EMLYN LINE
Carmarthen & Cardigan Railway -
Great Western Railway (01/07/1881)
(Carmarthen to Llandyssul)
Great Western Railway
(Llandyssul to Newcastle Emlyn)
ACT: 07/08/1854 (Carmarthen to Llandyssul)
ACT: 22/08/1881 (Llandyssul to Newcastle Emlyn)
OPG: 03/09/1860 (Carmarthen to Conwil)
OPG: 28/03/1864 (Conwil to Pencader)
OPG: 03/06/1864 (Pencader to Llandyssul)
OPG: 01/07/1895 (Llandyssul to Newcastle Emlyn)
CP: 20/02/1965 (Carmarthen to Pencader Junction)
CP: 13/09/1952 (Pencader Junction to Newcastle Emlyn)
CG: 22/09/1973 (Carmarthen to Newcastle Emlyn)

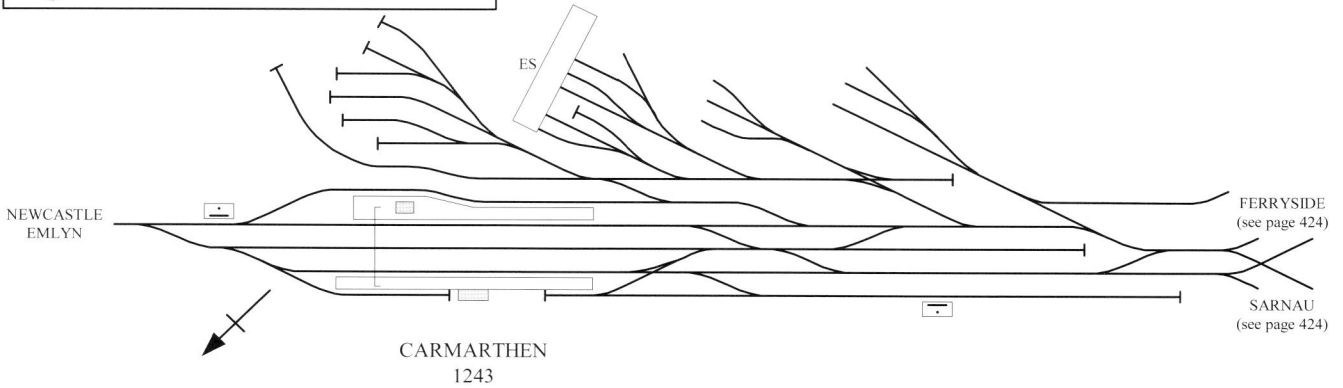

ES

NEWCASTLE
EMLYN

FERRYSIDE
(see page 424)

SARNAU
(see page 424)

CARMARTHEN
1243

1243	**CARMARTHEN**	[C&CR]
OP: 01/07/1902		Photo: NE. 1954
CP: OPEN		Stations U.K.

1243	**CARMARTHEN**	[C&CR]
		Photo: SW. 1961
		R.Dyer

NEWCASTLE
EMLYN

CARMARTHEN

BRONWYDD
ARMS
1244

1244	**BRONWYDD ARMS**	[C&CR]
OP: 01/07/1860		Photo: N. 1956
CP: 20/02/1965		H.C.Casserley

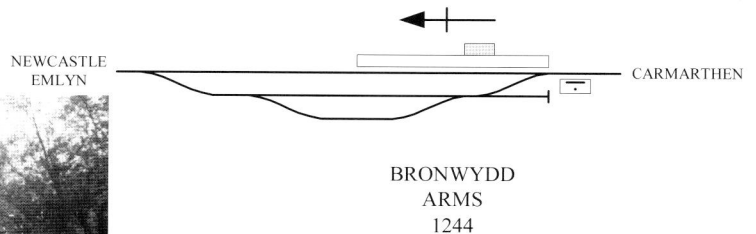

CONWIL
1245

1245   **CONWIL**   **[C&CR]**
OP: 01/07/1860   Photo: SE. 1937
CP: 20/02/1965   Stations U.K.

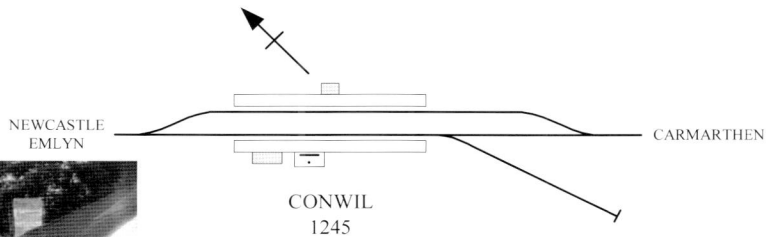

1246   **LLANPUMPSAINT**   **[C&CR]**
OP: 28/03/1864   Photo: SW. 1962
CP: 20/02/1965   M.Hale

LLANPUMPSAINT
1246

GS

PENCADER
1247

1247   **PENCADER**   **[C&CR]**
OP: 28/03/1864   Photo: N. 1948
CP: 20/02/1965   LOSA

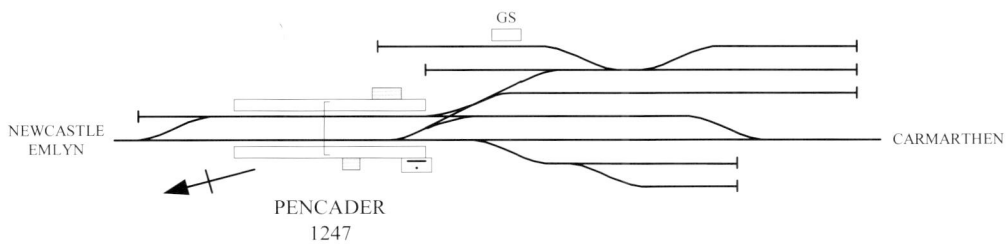

1247   **PENCADER**   **[C&CR]**
                          Photo: N. 1962
                          P.Garland

LLANDYSSUL
1248

1248   **LLANDYSSUL**   **[C&CR]**
OP: 03/06/1864   Photo: SE. 1937
CP: 13/09/1952   Stations U.K.

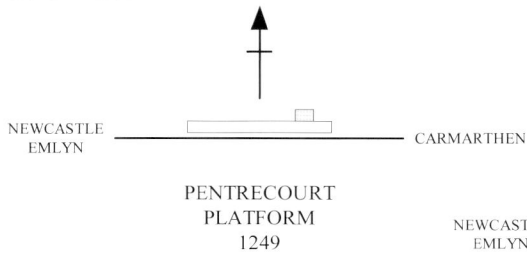

1249   **PENTRECOURT PLATFORM**   **[GWR]**
OP: 01/02/1912   Photo: W. c.1950
CP: 13/09/1952   unknown

NEWCASTLE
EMLYN   CARMARTHEN

PENTRECOURT
PLATFORM
1249

NEWCASTLE
EMLYN   CARMARTHEN

GS

HENLLAN
1250

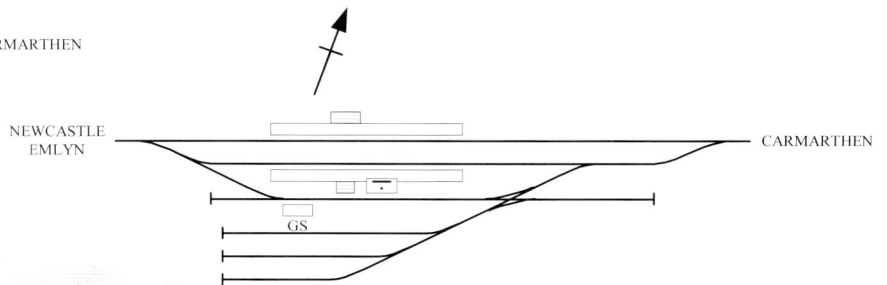

1250   **HENLLAN**   **[GWR]**
OP: 01/07/1895   Photo: E. c.1950
CP: 13/09/1952   LOSA

1251   **NEWCASTLE EMLYN**   **[GWR]**
OP: 01/07/1895   Photo: NE. 1963
CP: 13/09/1952   A.Attewell

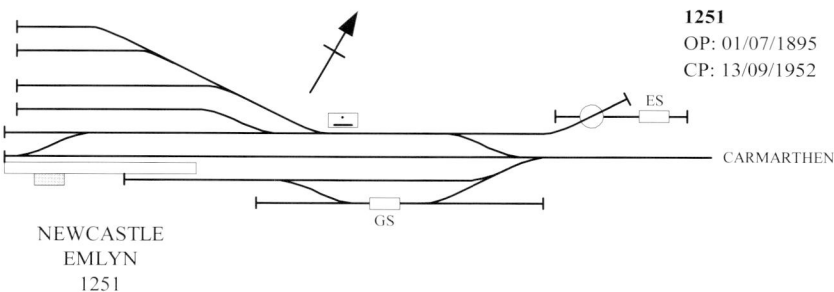

ES

GS

NEWCASTLE
EMLYN
1251

CARMARTHEN

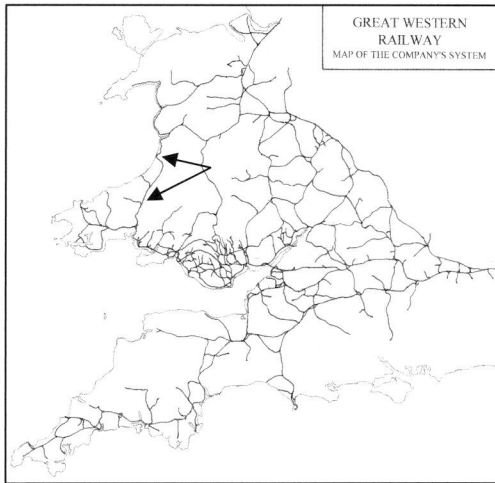

GREAT WESTERN
RAILWAY
MAP OF THE COMPANY'S SYSTEM

ACT: 23/07/1860 & 05/07/1865
OPG: 01/01/1866 (Pencader to Lampeter)
OPG: 01/09/1866 (Lampeter to Strata Florida)
OPG: 12/08/1867 (Strata Florida to Aberystwyth)
CP: 20/02/1965 (Pencader to Strata Florida)
CP: 12/12/1964 (Strata Florida to Aberystwyth)
CG: 22/09/1973 (Pencader to Lampeter)
CG: 16/03/1964 (Lampeter to Strata Florida) (Public Goods only)
CG: 02/12/1963 (Strata Florida to Aberystwyth)

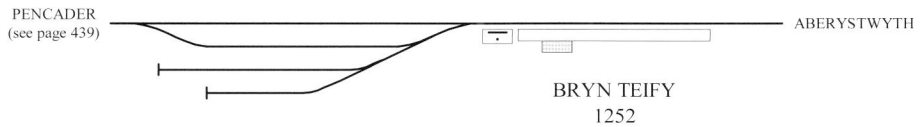

PENCADER
(see page 439)   ABERYSTWYTH

BRYN TEIFY
1252

1253   **MAESYCRUGIAU**   **[M&MR]**
OP: 01/01/1866   Photo: NE. 1937
CP: 20/02/1965   Stations U.K.

1252   **BRYN TEIFY**   **[M&MR]**
OP: 08/1869   Photo: NE. 1962
CP: 20/02/1965   D.K.Jones

PENCADER   ABERYSTWYTH

MAESYCRUGIAU
1253

1254   **LLANYBYTHER**   **[M&MR]**
OP: 01/01/1866   Photo: SW. 1937
CP: 20/02/1965   Stations U.K.

1254   **LLANYBYTHER**   **[M&MR]**
                          Photo: NE. 1958
                          C.Mowat

LLANYBYTHER
1254

PENCADER

GS

ABERYSTWYTH

PENCADER

ABERYSTWYTH

PENCARREG
HALT
1255

1255   **PENCARREG HALT**   **[M&MR]**
OP: 09/06/1930   Photo: NE. c.1960
CP: 20/02/1965   LOSA

1256   **LAMPETER**   **[M&MR]**
OP: 01/01/1866   Photo: S. 1958
CP: 20/02/1965   R.M.Casserley

PENCADER

GS

ABERYSTWYTH

LAMPETER
1256

PENCADER

ABERYSTWYTH

DERRY ORMOND
1257

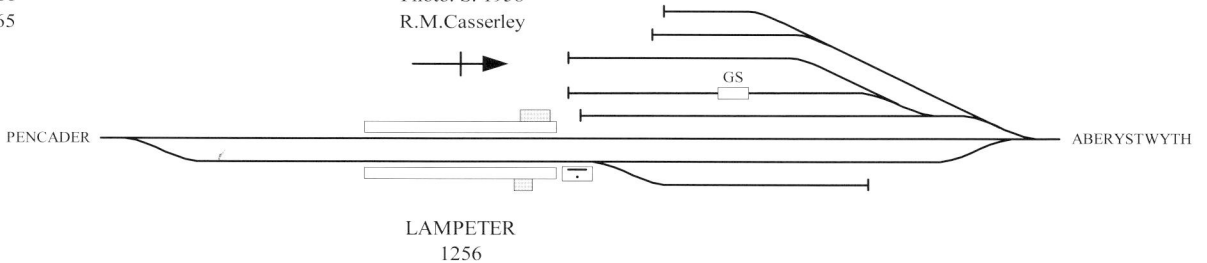

1257   **DERRY ORMOND**   **[M&MR]**
OP: 01/09/1866   Photo: W. 1965
CP: 20/02/1965   P.Garland

PENCADER ——————— ABERYSTWYTH

LLANGYBI
1258

1258   **LLANGYBI**   **[M&MR]**
OP: 08/1869   Photo: NE. 1937
CP: 20/02/1965   Stations U.K.

1259   **OLMARCH HALT**   **[M&MR]**
OP: 07/12/1929   Photo: SW. c.1960
CP: 20/02/1965   LOSA

PENCADER ——————— ABERYSTWYTH

OLMARCH
HALT
1259

PENCADER ——————— ABERYSTWYTH

GS

PONT LLANIO
1260

1260   **PONT LLANIO**   **[M&MR]**
OP: 01/09/1866   Photo: E. 1965
CP: 20/02/1965   P.Garland

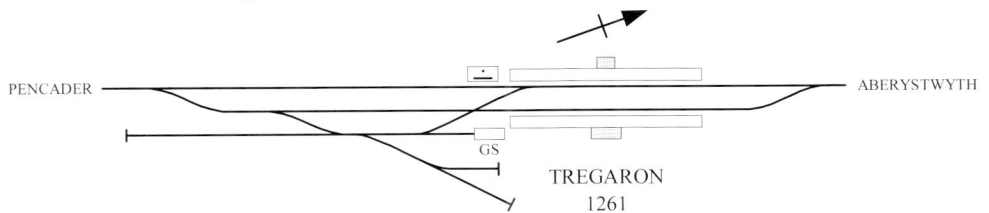

1261   **TREGARON**   **[M&MR]**
OP: 01/09/1866   Photo: S. 1937
CP: 20/02/1965   Stations U.K.

PENCADER ——————— ABERYSTWYTH

GS

TREGARON
1261

PENCADER — ABERYSTWYTH

ALLTDDU
HALT
1262

1262   **ALLTDDU HALT**   **[M&MR]**
OP: 23/09/1935   Photo: S. c.1960
CP: 20/02/1965   LOSA

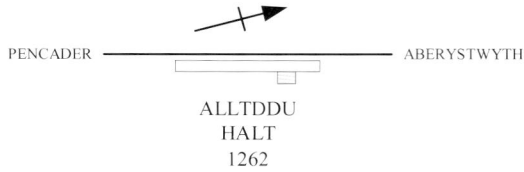

1263   **STRATA FLORIDA**   **[M&MR]**
OP: 01/09/1866   Photo: S. 1957
CP: 20/02/1965   D.K.Jones

PENCADER — ABERYSTWYTH
GS

STRATA FLORIDA
1263

PENCADER — ABERYSTWYTH

CARADOG
FALLS HALT
1264

1264   **CARADOG FALLS HALT**   **[M&MR]**
OP: 05/09/1932   Photo: NW. c.1960
CP: 12/12/1964   LOSA

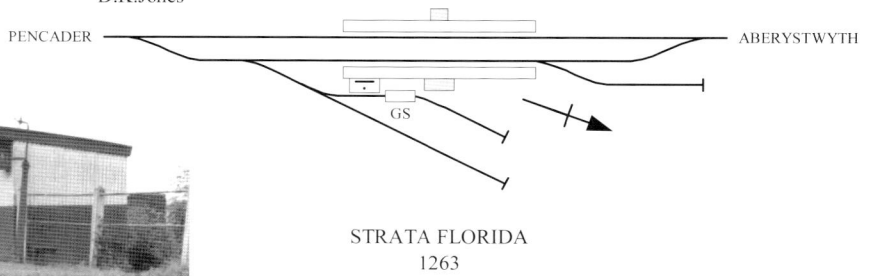

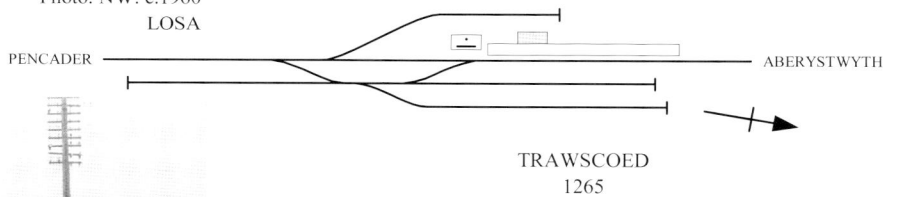

PENCADER — ABERYSTWYTH

TRAWSCOED
1265

1265   **TRAWSCOED**   **[M&MR]**
OP: 12/08/1867   Photo: S. 1955
CP: 12/12/1964   Stations U.K.

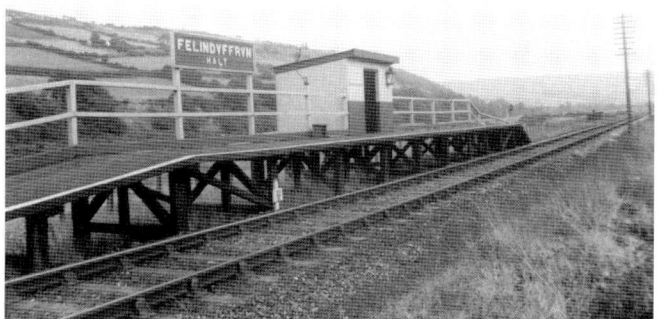

PENCADER — ABERYSTWYTH

FELINDYFFRYN
HALT
1266

1266   **FELINDYFFRYN HALT**   **[M&MR]**
OP: 10/06/1935   Photo: E. 1955
CP: 12/12/1964   Stations U.K.

PENCADER

LLANILAR
1267

1267   **LLANILAR**   **[M&MR]**
OP: 12/08/1867   Photo: SE. 1937
CP: 12/12/1964   Stations U.K.

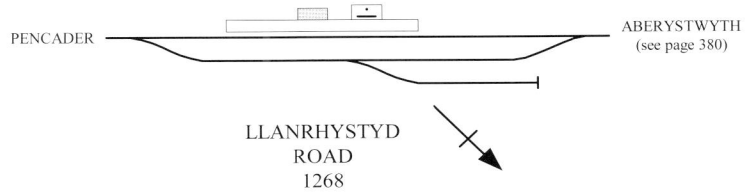

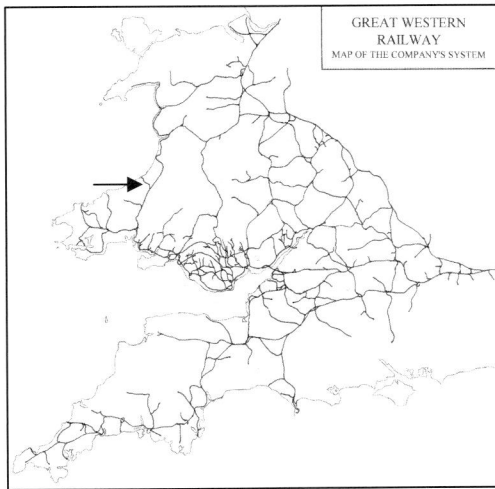

ABERYSTWYTH

1268   **LLANRHYSTYD ROAD**   **[M&MR]**
OP: 12/08/1867   Photo: NW. 1937
CP: 12/12/1964   Stations U.K.

PENCADER

ABERYSTWYTH
(see page 380)

LLANRHYSTYD
ROAD
1268

GREAT WESTERN
RAILWAY
MAP OF THE COMPANY'S SYSTEM

LAMPETER TO ABERAYRON
LAMPETER AND ABERAYRON BRANCH
Lampeter Aberayron & New Quay Light Railway -
Great Western Railway (01/07/1881)
ACT: 01/10/1906
OP: 12/05/1911
OG: 10/04/1911
CP: 10/02/1951
CG: 05/04/1965 (Public Goods only)

ABERAYRON

LAMPETER
(see page 442)

SILIAN HALT
1269

1269   **SILIAN HALT**   **[LA&NQ]**
OP: 12/05/1911   Photo: SE. 1954
CP: 10/02/1951   Stations U.K.

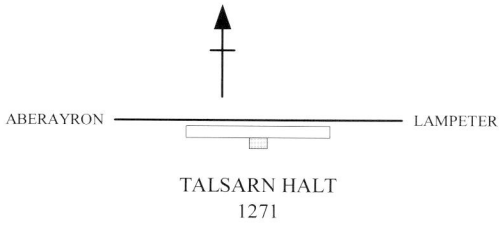

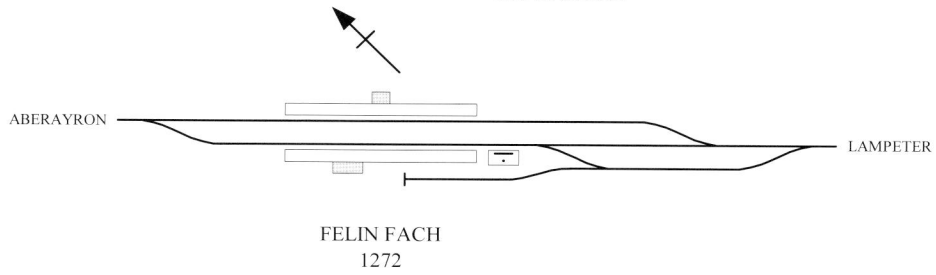

1270   **BLAENPLWYF HALT**   **[LA&NQ]**
OP: 12/05/1911   Photo: SE. c.1960
CP: 10/02/1951   LOSA

ABERAYRON ———————————— LAMPETER

BLAENPLWYF
HALT
1270

ABERAYRON ———————————— LAMPETER

TALSARN HALT
1271

1271   **TALSARN HALT**   **[LA&NQ]**
OP: 12/05/1911   Photo: E. c.1960
CP: 10/02/1951   LOSA

ABERAYRON ———————————— LAMPETER

FELIN FACH
1272

1272   **FELIN FACH**   **[LA&NQ]**
OP: 12/05/1911   Photo: SE. 1961
CP: 10/02/1951   Stations U.K.

1272   **FELIN FACH**   **[LA&NQ]**
                         Photo: NW. 1964
                         P.Garland

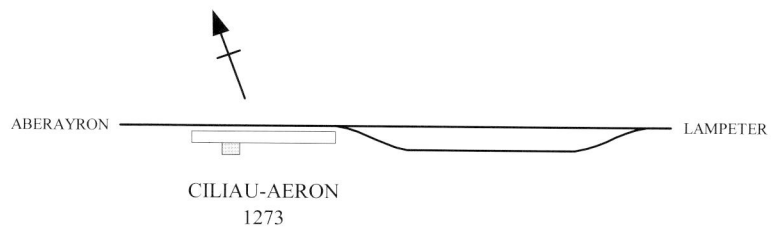

ABERAYRON ———————————— LAMPETER

CILIAU-AERON
1273

1273   **CILIAU-AERON**   **[LA&NQ]**
OP: 12/05/1911   Photo: E. 1964
CP: 10/02/1951   P.Garland

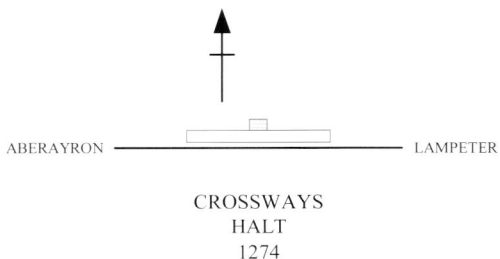

ABERAYRON ——————————————— LAMPETER

CROSSWAYS
HALT
1274

1274   **CROSSWAYS HALT**   **[LA&NQ]**
OP: 08/04/1929   Photo: W. 1961
CP: 10/02/1951   Stations U.K.

ABERAYRON ——————————————— LAMPETER

LLANERCH-AYRON
HALT
1275

1275   **LLANERCH-AYRON HALT**   **[LA&NQ]**
OP: 07/09/1911   Photo: NW. 1961
CP: 10/02/1951   Stations U.K.

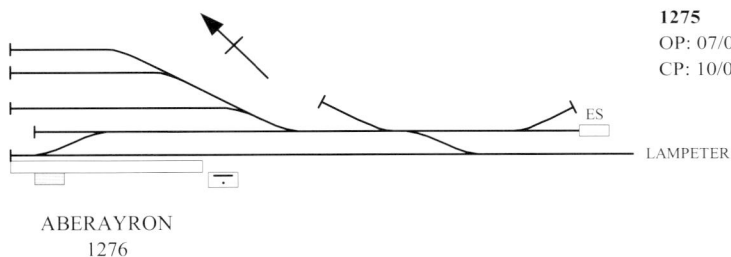

ES

LAMPETER

ABERAYRON
1276

1276   **ABERAYRON**   **[LA&NQ]**
OP: 02/05/1911   Photo: SE. 1954
CP: 10/02/1951   Stations U.K.

1276   **ABERAYRON**   **[LA&NQ]**
Photo: NW. 1960
A.Attewell

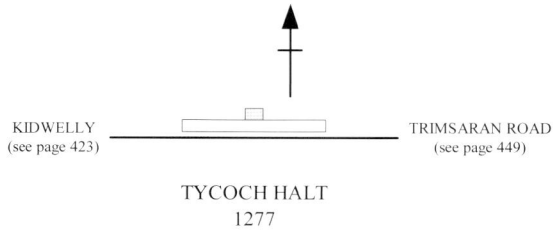

GREAT WESTERN
RAILWAY
MAP OF THE COMPANY'S SYSTEM

KIDWELLY (Exc) TO TRIMSARAN ROAD (Exc)
TYCOCH LOOP,
KIDWELLY BRANCH
Gwendraeth Valleys Railway -
Great Western Railway (01/01/1923)
(Tycoch Loop Junction to Tycoch Junction)
Burry Port & Gwendraeth Valley Railway -
Great Western Railway (01/01/1922)
(Tycoch Junction to Trimsaran Road)
ACT: 30/07/1866 (Tycoch Loop Junc. to Tycoch Junc.)
ACT: 30/04/1866 (Tycoch Junction to Trimsaran Road)
OP: c.1899 (Tycoch Halt, unadvertised trains only)
OG: c.1871 (Tycoch Loop Junction to Tycoch Junction)
OG: 06/1873 (Tycoch Junction to Trimsaran Road)
CP: 05/1949 (Tycoch Halt, unadvertised trains)
CG: 26/10/1964

KIDWELLY
(see page 423)

TRIMSARAN ROAD
(see page 449)

TYCOCH HALT
1277

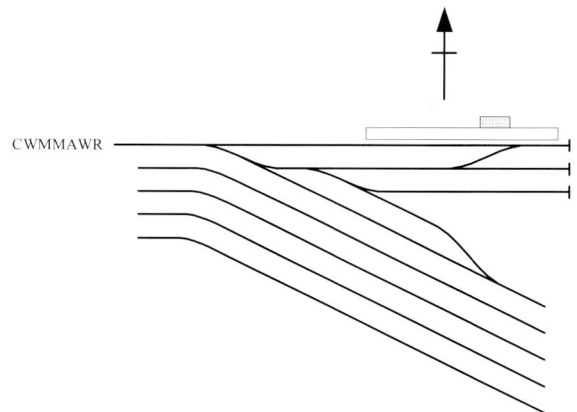

1277   **TYCOCH HALT**   **[BP&GVR]**
OP: c.1899   Photo: E. 1961
CP: 05/1949 (Workmens trains)   Stations U.K.

BURRY PORT TO CWMMAWR
BURRY PORT & GWENDRAETH VALLEY LINE
Burry Port & Gwendraeth Valley Railway -
Great Western Railway (01/01/1922)
ACT: 05/07/1865
OP: 1898 (Burry Port to Pontyberem), (Workmens trains)
OP: 02/08/1909 (Burry Port to Pontyberem), (Public Services)
OP: 01/01/1913 (Pontyberem to Cwmmawr)
OG: 07/1869 (Burry Port to Pontyberem)
OG: c.12/1869 (Pontyberem to Cwmmawr)
CP: 19/09/1953
CG: 07/06/1965 (Public Goods only)

CWMMAWR

BURRY PORT
1278

1278   **BURRY PORT**   **[BP&GVR]**
OP: 02/08/1909   Photo: W. 1958
CP: 19/09/1953   N.C.Simmons

PEMBREY HALT
1279

CRAIGLON
BRIDGE HALT
1280

1279   **PEMBREY HALT**   **[BP&GVR]**
OP: 02/08/1909   Photo: E. 1958
CP: 19/09/1953   M.Hale

1280   **CRAIGLON BRIDGE HALT**   **[BP&GVR]**
OP: 01/02/1932   Photo: N. c.1953
CP: 19/09/1953   LOSA

1281   **PINGED HALT**   **[BP&GVR]**
OP: 02/08/1909   Photo: S. 1955
CP: 19/09/1953   unknown

PINGED HALT
1281

TRIMSARAN ROAD
1282

KIDWELLY
(see page 448)

1282   **TRIMSARAN ROAD**   **[BP&GVR]**
OP: 02/08/1909   Photo: SW. c.1960
CP: 19/09/1953   LOSA

1283   **GLYN ABBEY HALT**   **[BP&GVR]**
OP: 02/08/1909   Photo: NE. 1953
CP: 19/09/1953   LOSA

GLYN ABBEY
HALT
1283

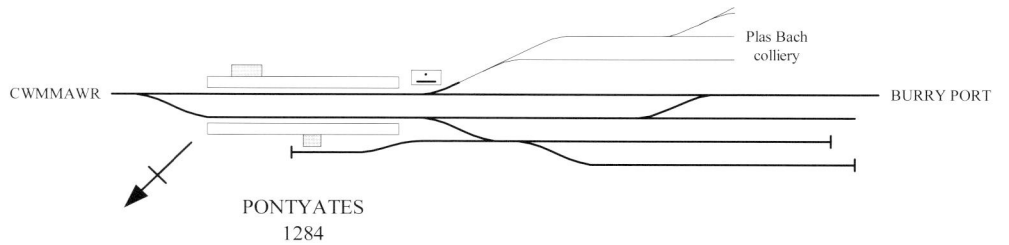

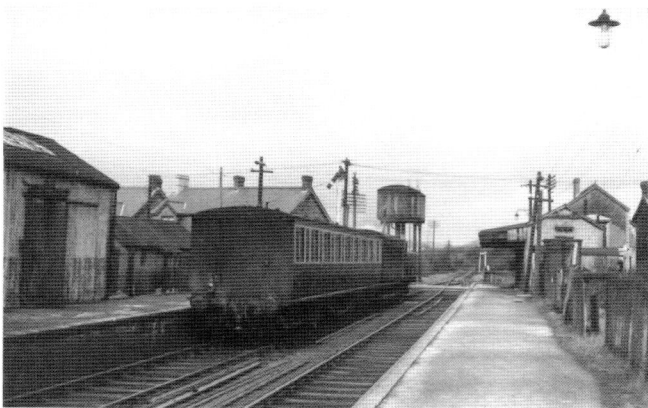

Plas Bach
colliery

CWMMAWR — — BURRY PORT

PONTYATES
1284

1284 **PONTYATES** **[BP&GVR]**
OP: 02/08/1909 Photo: NE. 1953
CP: 19/09/1953 C.H.Townley

1284 **PONTYATES** **[BP&GVR]**
Photo: NE. 1958
N.C.Simmons

1285 **PONTHENRY** **[BP&GVR]**
OP: 02/08/1909 Photo: NE. 1964
CP: 19/09/1953 Stations U.K.

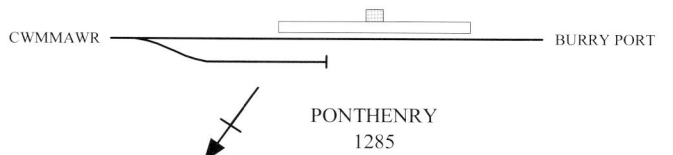

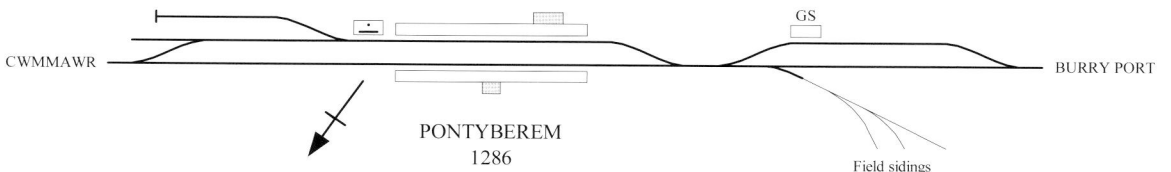

CWMMAWR — — BURRY PORT

PONTHENRY
1285

GS

CWMMAWR — — BURRY PORT

PONTYBEREM
1286

Field sidings

1286 **PONTYBEREM** **[BP&GVR]**
OP: 02/08/1909 Photo: SW. c.1909
CP: 19/09/1953 LOSA

1286 **PONTYBEREM** **[BP&GVR]**
Photo: SW. 1958
R.M.Casserley

CWMMAWR
1287

BURRY PORT

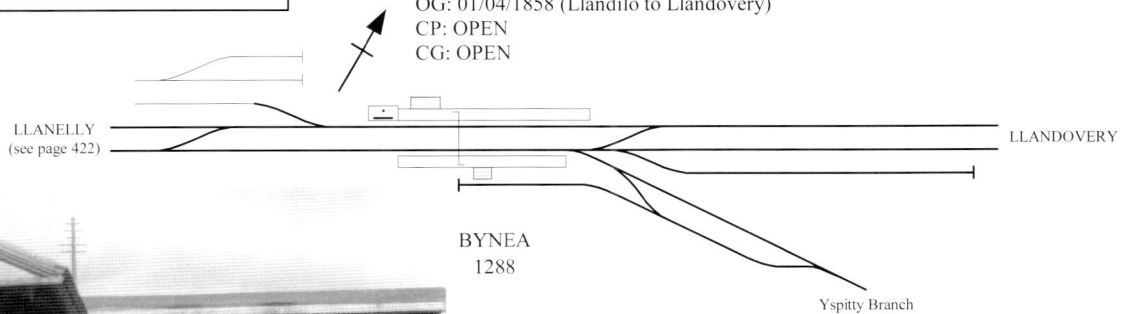

1287   **CWMMAWR**   **[BP&GVR]**
OP: 01/10/1913
CP: 19/09/1953
Photo: NE. 1947
H.C.Casserley

1287   **CWMMAWR**   **[BP&GVR]**
Photo: NE. 1950
C.H.Townley

GREAT WESTERN
RAILWAY
MAP OF THE COMPANY'S SYSTEM

LLANELLY (Exc) TO LLANDOVERY
LLANELLY TO LLANDILO LINE,
VALE OF TOWY LINE
Llanelly Railway -
Great Western Railway (01/07/1889)
(Genwen Junction to Llandilo)
Vale of Towy Railway -
LNWR (01/07/1884) -
Great Western & LNW Joint Railway (01/07/1889)
(Llandilo to Llandovery)
ACT: 21/08/1835 (Llanelly Dock to Llandilo)
ACT: 10/08/1854 (Llandilo to Llandovery)
OP: 01/05/1850 or earlier (Llanelly to Llandebie)
OP: 26/01/1857 (Llandebie to Llandilo)
OP: 01/04/1858 (Llandilo to Llandovery)
OG: 01/06/1839 (Llanelly to Pontardulais)
OG: 10/04/1840 (Pontardulais to Pantyffynnon)
OG: 06/05/1841 (Pantyffynnon to Mountain Branch Junc.)
OG: 24/01/1857 (Mountain Branch Junc. to Llandilo)
OG: 01/04/1858 (Llandilo to Llandovery)
CP: OPEN
CG: OPEN

LLANELLY
(see page 422)

LLANDOVERY

BYNEA
1288

Yspitty Branch

1288   **BYNEA**   **[LR]**
OP: 01/05/1850
CP: OPEN
Photo: NE. 1937
Stations U.K.

LLANELLY   LLANDOVERY

LLANGENNECH
1289

1289   **LLANGENNECH**   **[LR]**
OP: 07/1909   Photo: NE. 1961
CP: OPEN   Stations U.K.

1290   **PONTARDULAIS**   **[LR]**
OP: 01/05/1850   Photo: SW. 1963
CP: OPEN   F.G.Wood

LLANELLY   LLANDOVERY

GS

(Swansea L.M.S.R.)   PONTARDULAIS
                                     1290

1290   **PONTARDULAIS**   **[LR]**
                                         Photo: NE. 1955
                                          Stations U.K.

1290   **PONTARDULAIS**   **[LR]**
                                       Photo: NE. c.1960
                                             LOSA

PANTYFFYNNON
1291

1291   **PANTYFFYNNON**   **[LR]**
OP: 26/01/1857   Photo: N. 1951
CP: OPEN   H.C.Casserley

1291   **PANTYFFYNNON**   **[LR]**
       Photo: SW. 1955
       R.K.Blencowe

PARCYRHUN
HALT
1292

PHOTOGRAPH UNAVAILABLE

1293   **TIRYDAIL**   **[LR]**
OP: c.1897   Photo: N. 1956
CP: OPEN   C.Mowat

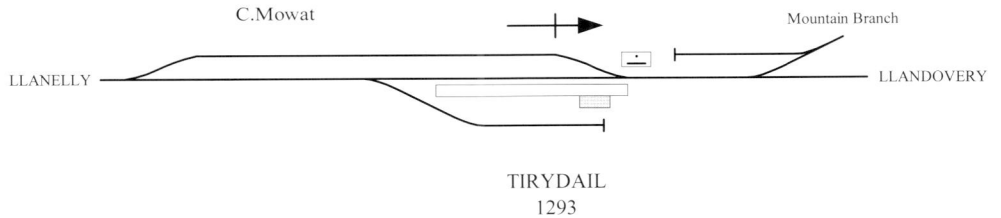

1292   **PARCYRHUN HALT**   **[LR]**
OP: 04/05/1936   Photo: None
CP: 13/06/1955   Available

TIRYDAIL
1293

LLANELLY   LLANDOVERY

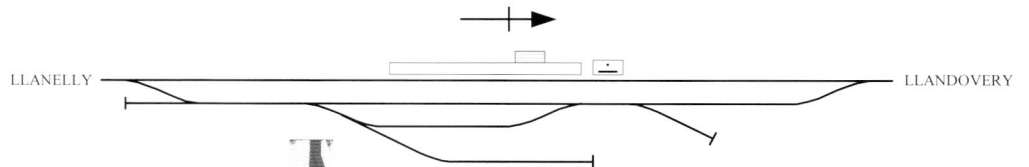

LLANDEBIE
1294

1294   **LLANDEBIE**   **[LR]**
OP: 26/01/1857   Photo: S. 1964
CP: OPEN   P.Garland

1295   **DERWYDD ROAD**   **[LR]**
OP: 26/01/1857   Photo: S. 1956
CP: 03/05/1954   C.Mowat

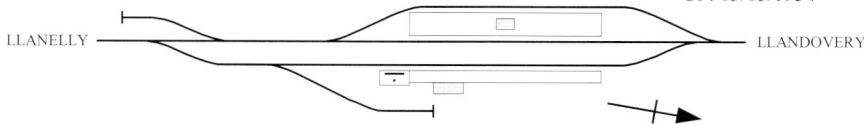

LLANELLY   LLANDOVERY

DERWYDD ROAD
1295

LLANELLY   LLANDOVERY

FFAIRFACH
1296

1296   **FFAIRFACH**   **[LR]**
OP: 26/01/1857   Photo: S. 1964
CP: OPEN   Stations U.K.

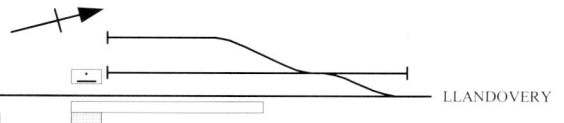

1297   **LLANDILO**   **[LR]**
OP: 26/01/1857   Photo: NE. 1964
CP: OPEN   P.Garland

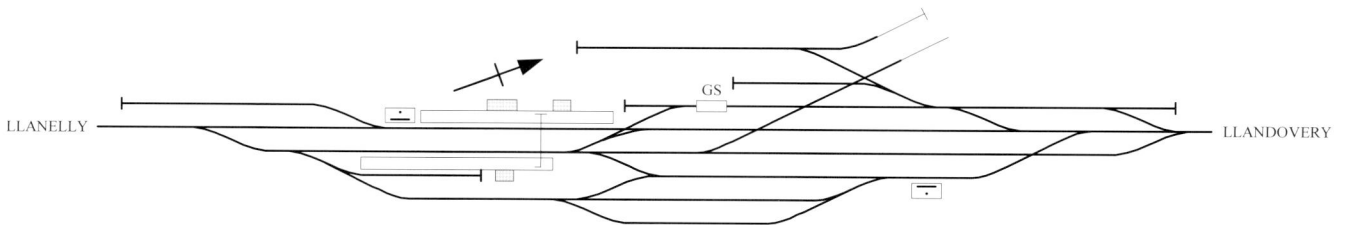

GS

LLANELLY   LLANDOVERY

LLANDILO
1297

TALLEY ROAD
HALT
1298

1298　　　　　**TALLEY ROAD HALT**　　　　　**[VTRJ]**
OP: c.08/1859　　　　　　　　　　　Photo: SW. c.1960
CP: OPEN　　　　　　　　　　　　　　　LOSA

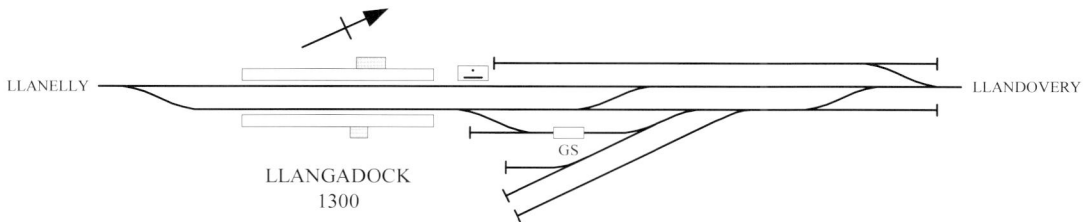

GLANRHYD
HALT
1299

1299　　　　　**GLANRHYD HALT**　　　　　**[VTRJ]**
OP: 01/05/1858　　　　　　　　　　Photo: SW. c.1960
CP: 07/03/1955　　　　　　　　　　　　　LOSA

LLANGADOCK
1300

1300　　　　　**LLANGADOCK**　　　　　**[VTRJ]**
OP: 01/04/1858　　　　　　　　　　Photo: SW. 1958
CP: OPEN　　　　　　　　　　　　R.M.Casserley

1300　　　　　**LLANGADOCK**　　　　　**[VTRJ]**
　　　　　　　　　　　　　　　　Photo: NE. c.1960
　　　　　　　　　　　　　　　　　　　　LOSA

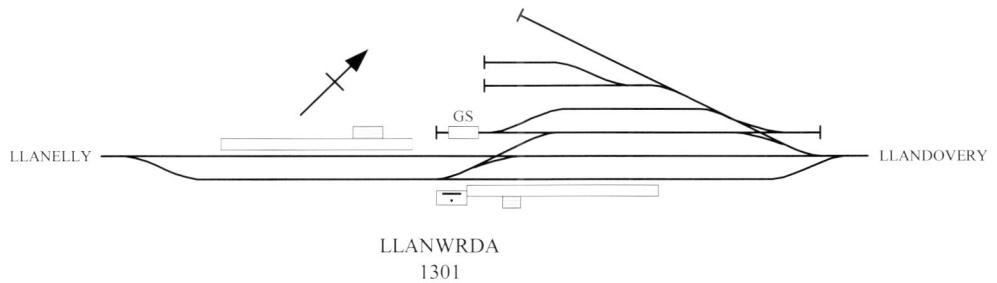

LLANWRDA
1301

1301　　　　　　**LLANWRDA**　　　　**[VTRJ]**
OP: 01/04/1858　　　　　　　　　　Photo: NE. 1958
CP: OPEN　　　　　　　　　　　　　　R.M.Casserley

1301　　　　　　**LLANWRDA**　　　　**[VTRJ]**
　　　　　　　　　　　　　　　　　Photo: SW. 1964
　　　　　　　　　　　　　　　　　Stations U.K.

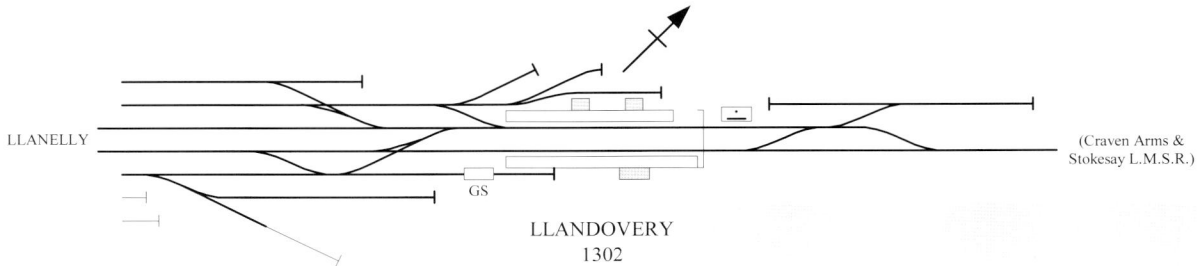

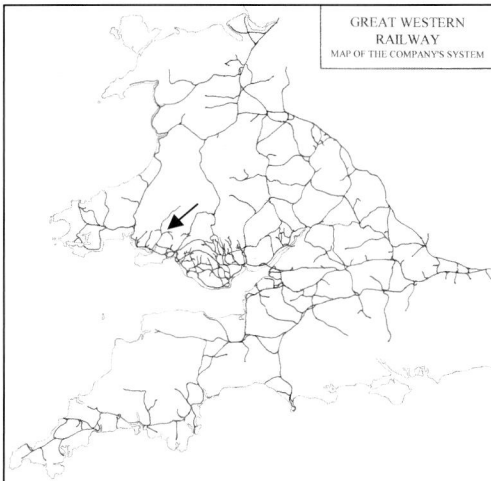

LLANELLY

(Craven Arms &
Stokesay L.M.S.R.)

GS

LLANDOVERY
1302

1302　　　　　　**LLANDOVERY**　　　　**[VTRJ]**
OP: 01/04/1858　　　　　　　　　　Photo: NE. 1964
CP: OPEN　　　　　　　　　　　　　　Stations U.K.

PANTYFFYNNON (Exc) TO BRYNAMMAN
GARNANT BRANCH
Llanelly Railway -
Great Western Railway (01/07/1889)

ACT: 21/08/1835
OP: 06/1842
OG: 10/04/1840 (Pantyffynnon to Garnant)
OG: 06/05/1841 (Garnant to Brynamman)
CP: 16/08/1958
CG: 30/01/1965 (Pantyffynnon to Garnant) (Public Goods only)
CG: 18/08/1958 (near Garnant to near Brynamman)
CG: 28/09/1964 (Brynamman, via LMSR)

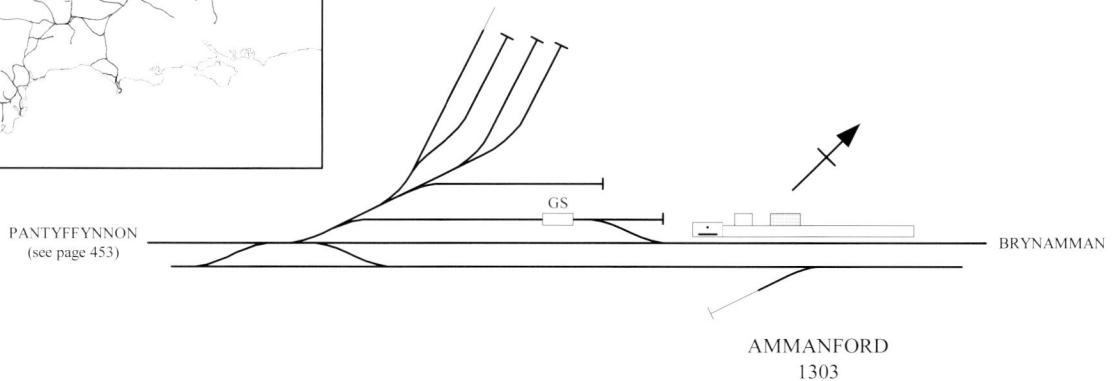

GREAT WESTERN
RAILWAY
MAP OF THE COMPANY'S SYSTEM

PANTYFFYNNON
(see page 453)

GS

BRYNAMMAN

AMMANFORD
1303

1303   **AMMANFORD**   **[LR]**
OP: 01/05/1850   Photo: SW. 1958
CP: 16/08/1958   N.C.Simmons

1304   **AMMANFORD COLLIERY HALT**   **[LR]**
OP: 01/05/1905   Photo: NE. 1958
CP: 16/08/1958   N.C.Simmons

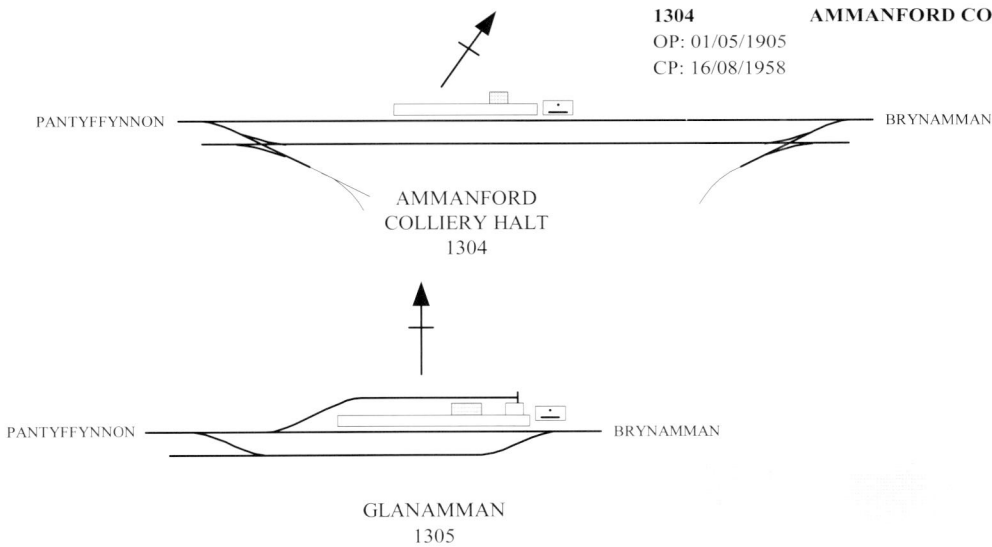

PANTYFFYNNON — BRYNAMMAN

AMMANFORD
COLLIERY HALT
1304

PANTYFFYNNON — BRYNAMMAN

GLANAMMAN
1305

1305   **GLANAMMAN**   **[LR]**
OP: 05/1851   Photo: W. 1958
CP: 16/08/1958   N.C.Simmons

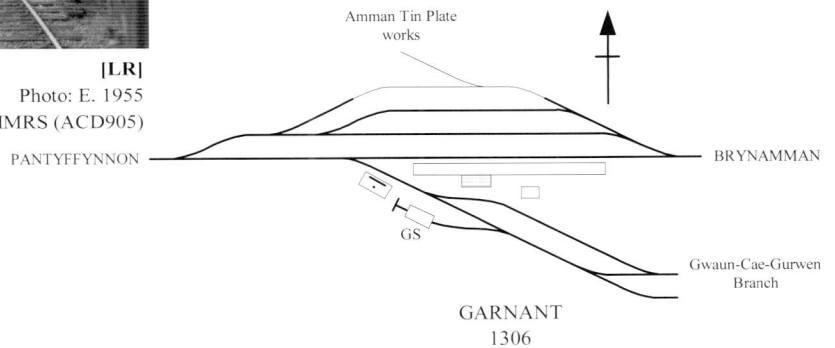

1306   **GARNANT**   **[LR]**
OP: 01/05/1850   Photo: E. 1955
CP: 16/08/1958   HMRS (ACD905)

Amman Tin Plate
works

PANTYFFYNNON — BRYNAMMAN

GS

Gwaun-Cae-Gurwen
Branch

GARNANT
1306

GS

PANTYFFYNNON

(Ystalyfera L.M.S.R.)

BRYNAMMAN
1307

1307   **BRYNAMMAN**   **[LR]**
OP: 20/03/1865   Photo: W. 1955
CP: 16/08/1958   R.Carpenter

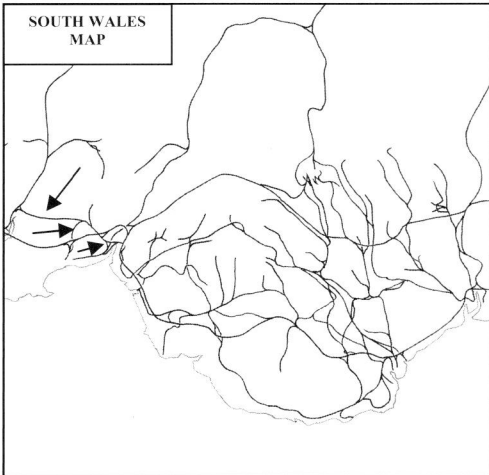

SOUTH WALES
MAP

Morlais Junction TO Skewen East Junction
SWANSEA DISTRICT LINE
Great Western Railway
ACT: 15/08/1904
OP: 14/07/1913
OG: 14/07/1913
CP: 09/06/1956 (Local Services only)
CPG: 04/10/1965 (Lonlas Junction to Skewen East Junction)

LLANGENNECH
(see page 452)

SKEWEN

PONT LLIW
1308
[CLOSED]

1308   **PONT LLIW**   **[GWR]**
OP: 14/07/1913   Photo: SE. 1958
CP: 22/09/1924   M.Hale

1309   **FELIN FRAN HALT**   **[GWR]**
OP: 02/01/1922   Photo: SE. 1959
CP: 09/06/1956   M.Hale

Pontardawe Branch

LLANGENNECH

SKEWEN
(see page 419)

FELIN FRAN HALT
1309

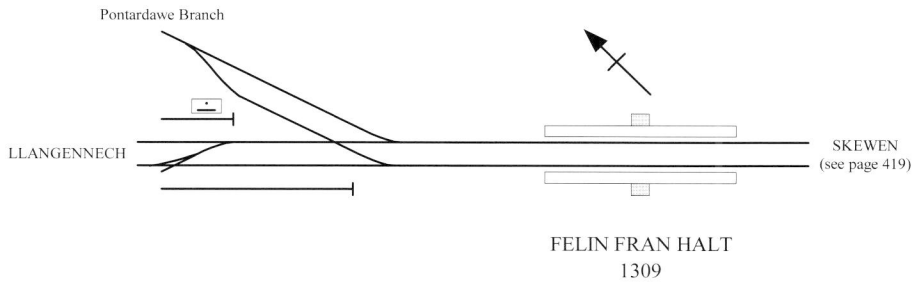

Lonlas Junction TO Jersey Marine Junction
JERSEY MARINE LOOP
Great Western Railway
ACT: 15/08/1904
OP: 22/09/1924
OG: 18/02/1912
CP: 04/10/1947 (Local Services only)
CG: 04/10/1965

1310   **LLANDARCY PLATFORM**   **[GWR]**
OP: 22/09/1924   Photo: E. c.1960
CP: 04/10/1947   LOSA

FELIN FRAN HALT
(see above)

BRITON FERRY
(see page 418)

Jersey Marine Loop

LLANDARCY
PLATFORM
1310

SWANSEA (HIGH STREET) (Exc) TO FELIN FRAN (Exc)
MORRISTON BRANCH
Great Western Railway
ACT: 25/07/1872 (Hafod Junction to Tyrcenol Junction)
ACT: 15/08/1904 (Tyrcenol Junction to Felin Fran West Junction)
OP: 09/05/1881 (Hafod Junction to Morriston)
OP: 02/01/1922 (to Felin Fran Halt)
OG: 09/05/1881 (Hafod Junction to Tyrcenol Junction)
OG: 09/05/1914 (Tyrcenol Junction to Felin Fran West Junction)
CP: 09/06/1956 (Local Services only)
CG: 04/10/1965

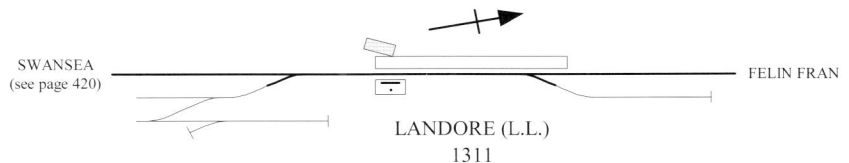

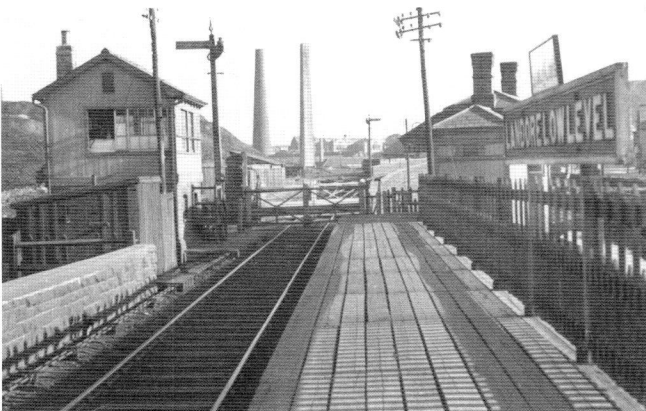

SWANSEA
(see page 420)

FELIN FRAN

LANDORE (L.L.)
1311

1311   **LANDORE (L.L.)**   **[GWR]**
OP: 09/05/1881   Photo: S. c.1935
CP: 09/06/1956   Stations U.K.

1311   **LANDORE (L.L.)**   **[GWR]**
                                     Photo: N. 1964
                                     Stations U.K.

PLAS MARL
1312

1312   **PLAS MARL**   **[GWR]**
OP: 09/05/1881   Photo: N. 1956
CP: 09/06/1956   C.Mowat

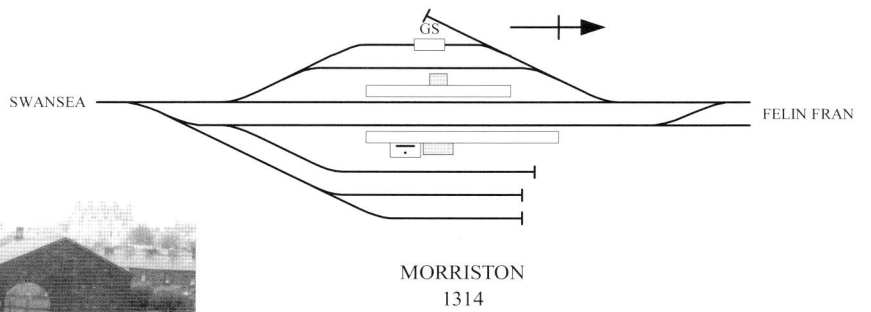

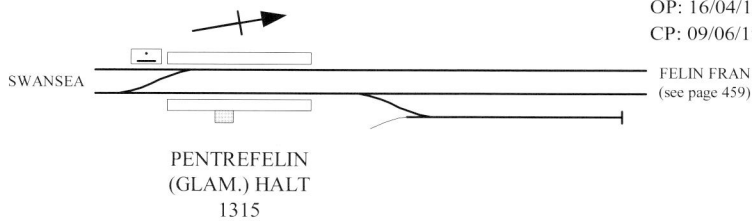

COPPER PIT
PLATFORM
1313

1313   **COPPER PIT PLATFORM**   **[GWR]**
OP: 02/1915   Photo: N. 1956
CP: 09/06/1956   C.Mowat

MORRISTON
1314

1314   **MORRISTON**   **[GWR]**
OP: 09/05/1881   Photo: S. 1961
CP: 09/06/1956   Stations U.K.

1315   **PENTREFELIN (GLAM.) HALT**   **[GWR]**
OP: 16/04/1928   Photo: N. 1956
CP: 09/06/1956   C.Mowat

FELIN FRAN
(see page 459)

PENTREFELIN
(GLAM.) HALT
1315

Wind Street Junction TO Neath Junction
VALE OF NEATH LINE
Swansea & Neath Railway -
Vale of Neath Railway (05/08/1863) -
Great Western Railway (01/02/1865)
ACT: 06/08/1861
OP: 01/08/1863
OG: 15/07/1863
CP: 28/09/1936 (Swansea (East Dock) to Neath (Riverside))
CP: 15/10/1962 (Neath (Riverside) to Brecon)
CG: OPEN

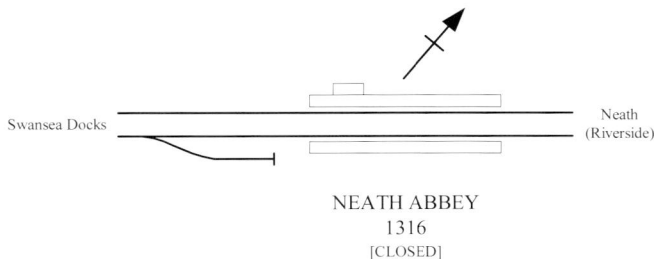

Swansea Docks

Neath (Riverside)

NEATH ABBEY
1316
[CLOSED]

1316   **NEATH ABBEY**   **[S&NR]**
OP: 01/08/1863   Photo: NE. c.1956
CP: 28/09/1936   D.K.Jones

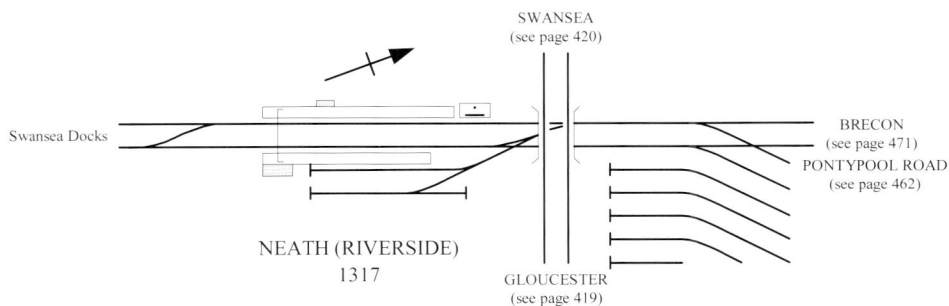

SWANSEA
(see page 420)

Swansea Docks

BRECON
(see page 471)
PONTYPOOL ROAD
(see page 462)

NEATH (RIVERSIDE)
1317

GLOUCESTER
(see page 419)

1317   **NEATH (RIVERSIDE)**   **[S&NR]**
OP: 01/08/1863   Photo: N. 1951
CP: 13/06/1964 (School trains)   LOSA

1317   **NEATH (RIVERSIDE)**   **[S&NR]**
        Photo: S. 1951
        LOSA

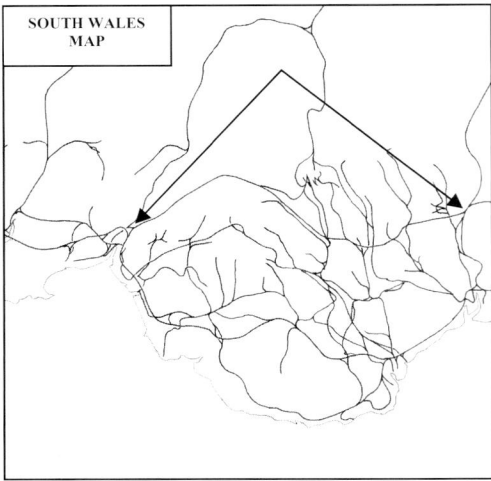

NEATH (GENERAL) (Exc) TO PONTYPOOL ROAD (Exc)
NEATH JUNCTION, VALE OF NEATH LINE

Vale of Neath Railway -
Great Western Railway (01/02/1865)
(Neath Loop Junction to Aberdare Canal Head)
Aberdare Valley Railway -
Vale of Neath Railway (01/01/1864) -
Great Western Railway (01/02/1865)
(Aberdare Canal Head to Middle Duffryn)
Newport Abergavenny & Hereford Railway -
West Midland Railway (01/07/1860) -
Great Western Railway (01/08/1863)
(Middle Duffryn to Pontypool Road)
ACT: 03/08/1946 (Neath to Aberdare Canal Head)
ACT: 02/07/1855 (Aberdare Canal Head to Middle Duffryn)
ACT: 08/1857 (Middle Duffryn to Quakers Yard)
ACT: 09/07/1847 (Pontypool Road to Quakers Yard)
OP: 24/09/1851 (Neath to Aberdare (H.L.))
OP: 05/10/1864 (Aberdare (H.L.) to Quakers Yard)
OP: 09/01/1858 (Quakers Yard to Pontllanfraith)
OP: 01/06/1857 (Pontllanfraith to Crumlin Junction)
OP: 20/08/1855 (Crumlin Junction to Pontypool Road)
OG: 24/09/1851 (Neath to Aberdare (H.L.)
OG: 06/1853 (Aberdare (H.L.) to Aberdare Canal Head)
OG: 11/1856 (Aberdare Canal Head to Middle Duffryn)
OG: 18/04/1864 (Middle Duffryn to Quakers Yard Junction)
OG: 09/01/1858 (Quakers Yard to Pontllanfraith)
OG: 01/06/1857 (Pontllanfraith to Crumlin Junction)
OG: 20/08/1855 (Crumlin Junction to Pontypool Road)
CP: 13/06/1964
CG: 15/08/1966 (Neath Loop Junction to Neath Junction)
CG: 1971 (Aberpergwm Colliery to Glyn Neath)
CG: 02/10/1967 (Glyn Neath to Hirwaun Pond Halt)
CG: 29/11/1971 (Aberdare to Mountain Ash)
CG: 01/03/1965 (Mountain Ash to Cresselly)
CG: 15/06/1964 (Cresselly to Ocean Colliery, Treharris)
CG: 15/06/1964 (Penalltau Junction to Fleur-de-lis Junction)
CG: 04/09/1967 (Feur-de-lis Junction to Sirhowy Junction)
CG: 15/06/1964 (Sirhowy Junction to Crumlin Junction)
CG: 09/02/1965 (Crumlin Junction to Hafodyrynys Colliery)
CG: 09/04/1979 (Hafodyrynys Colliery to Trosnant Junction)
CG: 15/06/1964 (Trosnant Junc. to Taff Vale Extension Junc.)

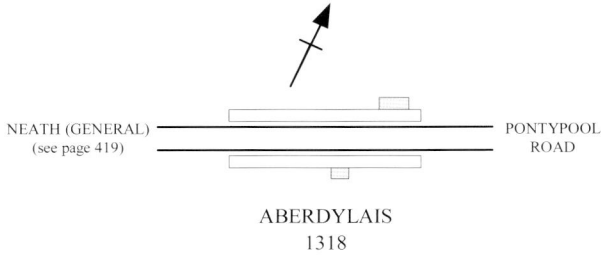

NEATH (GENERAL) ——————————— PONTYPOOL
(see page 419) ——————————— ROAD

ABERDYLAIS
1318

1318   **ABERDYLAIS**   **[VNR]**
OP: 24/09/1851   Photo: NE. 1959
CP: 13/06/1964   R.M.Casserley

NEATH ——————————— PONTYPOOL
(GENERAL) ——————————— ROAD

CLYNE HALT
1319

1319   **CLYNE HALT**   **[VNR]**
OP: 01/06/1905   Photo: NE. c.1920
CP: 13/06/1964   R.Grant

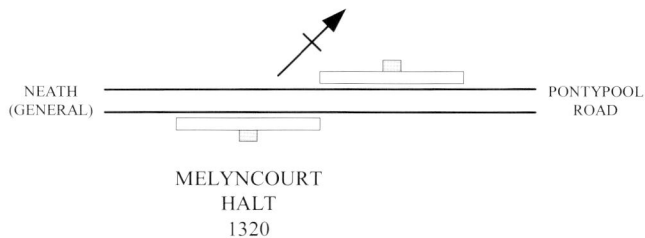

NEATH ——————————— PONTYPOOL
(GENERAL) ——————————— ROAD

MELYNCOURT
HALT
1320

1320   **MELYNCOURT HALT**   **[VNR]**
OP: 01/06/1905
CP: 13/06/1964   Photo: NE. c.1905
    LOSA

1320   **MELYNCOURT HALT**   **[VNR]**
    Photo: NE. 1961
    Stations U.K.

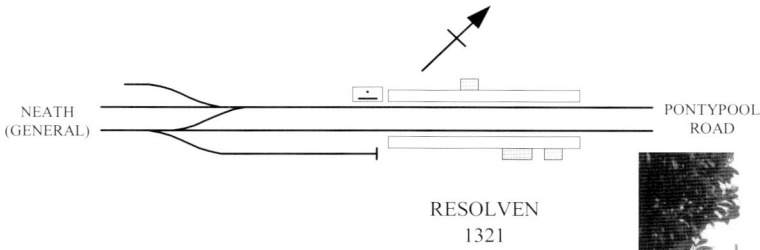

RESOLVEN
1321

1321   **RESOLVEN**   **[VNR]**
OP: 24/09/1851
CP: 13/06/1964   Photo: NE. 1961
    Stations U.K.

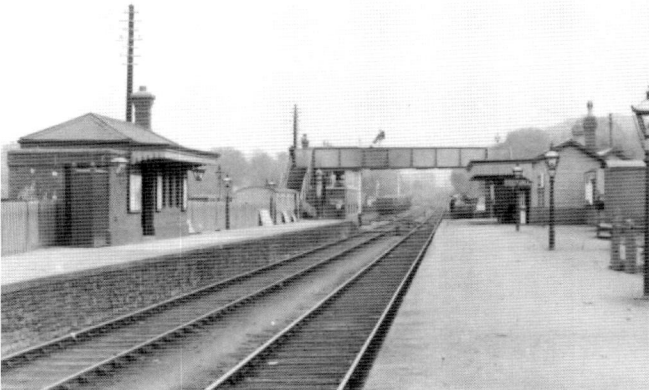

1322   **GLYN NEATH**   **[VNR]**
OP: 24/09/1851
CP: 13/06/1964   Photo: NE. c.1912
    LOSA

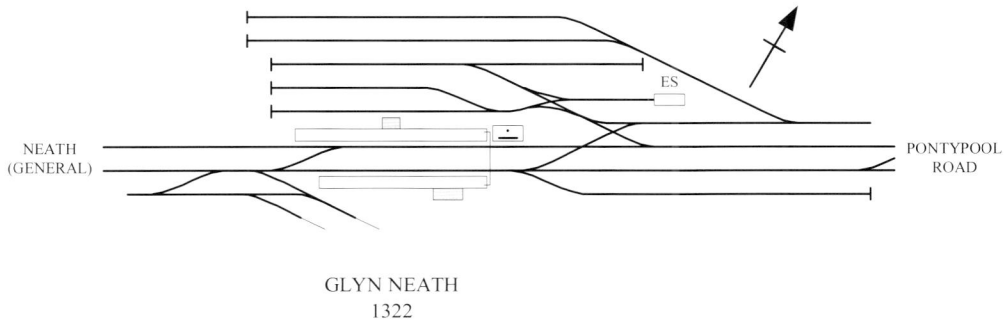

GLYN NEATH
1322

1323   **CWMRHYD-Y-GAU HALT**   **[VNR]**
NO INFORMATION AS CLOSED BY 1947
CP: by 10/1945

PONTWALBY
HALT
1324

1324   **PONTWALBY HALT**   **[VNR]**
OP: 01/05/1911   Photo: SW. c.1960
CP: 13/06/1964   M.Hale

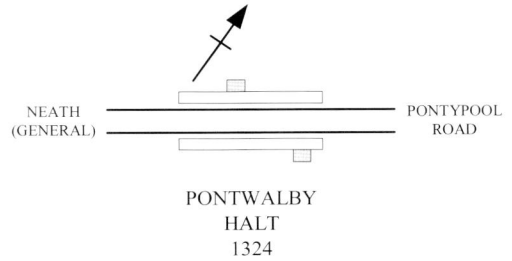

NEATH
(GENERAL)

PONTYPOOL
ROAD

RHIGOS HALT
1325

1325   **RHIGOS HALT**   **[VNR]**
OP: 01/05/1911   Photo: W. 1960
CP: 13/06/1964   M.Hale

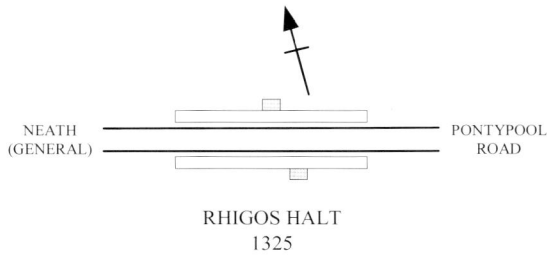

1326   **HIRWAUN POND HALT**   **[VNR]**
OP: 23/07/1941   Photo: W. 1961
CP: 13/06/1964 (Workmens trains)   M.Hale

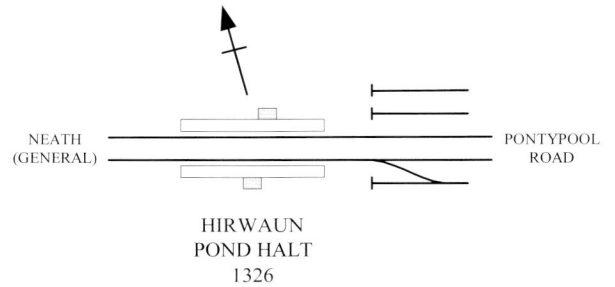

NEATH
(GENERAL)

PONTYPOOL
ROAD

HIRWAUN
POND HALT
1326

1327   **HIRWAUN**   **[VNR]**
OP: 24/09/1851   Photo: E. 1959
CP: 13/06/1964   Stations U.K.

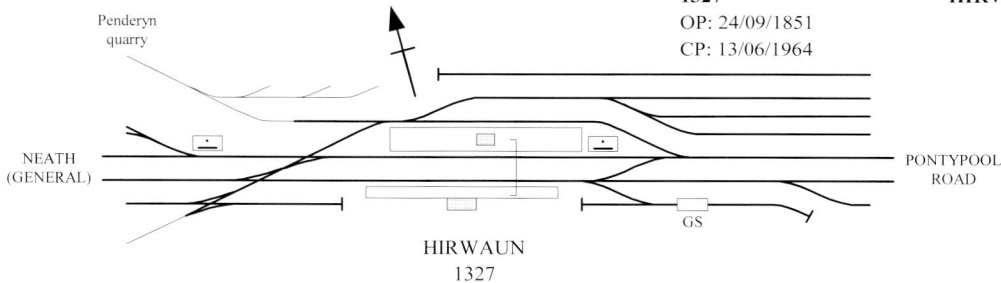

Penderyn
quarry

NEATH
(GENERAL)

PONTYPOOL
ROAD

GS

HIRWAUN
1327

NEATH
(GENERAL)

PONTYPOOL
ROAD

TRECYNON
HALT
1328

1328   **TRECYNON HALT**   **[VNR]**
OP: 01/05/1911   Photo: SE. 1961
CP: 13/06/1964   Stations U.K.

GS

NEATH
(GENERAL)

PONTYPOOL
ROAD

Aberdare (L.L.)   ABERDARE (H.L.)
(see page 518)   1329

1329   **ABERDARE (H.L.)**   **[VNR]**
OP: 24/09/1851   Photo: NW. 1964
CP: 13/06/1964   Stations U.K.

1329   **ABERDARE (H.L.)**   **[VNR]**
       Photo: SE. 1964
       Stations U.K.

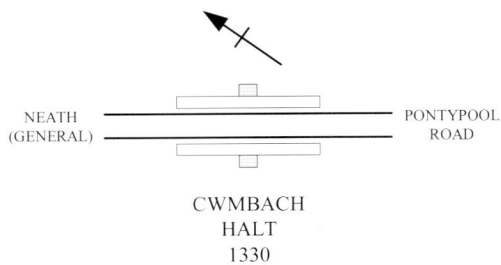

NEATH
(GENERAL)

PONTYPOOL
ROAD

CWMBACH
HALT
1330

1330   **CWMBACH HALT**   **[AVR]**
OP: 12/07/1914   Photo: SE. 1963
CP: 13/06/1964   P.Garland

MOUNTAIN ASH
(CARDIFF ROAD)
1331

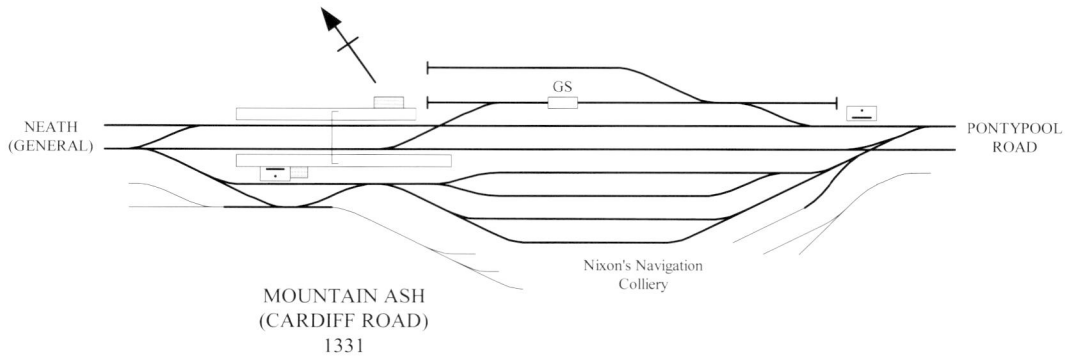

1331   **MOUNTAIN ASH (CARDIFF ROAD)**   **[NA&HR]**
OP: 05/10/1864   Photo: NW. 1960
CP: 13/06/1964   M.Hale

1331   **MOUNTAIN ASH (CARDIFF ROAD)**   **[NA&HR]**
                               Photo: SE. 1961
                              Stations U.K.

1332   **PENRHIWCEIBER (H.L.)**   **[NA&HR]**
OP: 15/06/1899   Photo: SE. 1964
CP: 13/06/1964   Stations U.K.

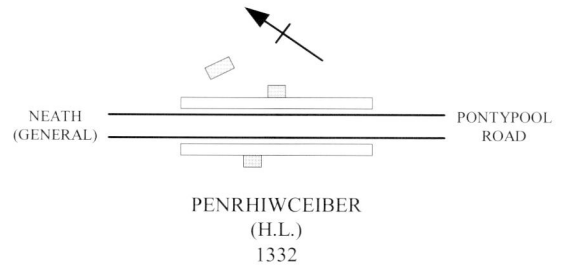

PENRHIWCEIBER
(H.L.)
1332

1333   **QUAKERS YARD (H.L.)**   **[NA&HR]**
OP: 05/10/1864   Photo: W. 1959
CP: 13/06/1964   H.C.Casserley

QUAKERS YARD
(H.L.)
1333

TREHARRIS
1334

1334   **TREHARRIS**   **[NA&HR]**
OP: 02/06/1890   Photo: E. 1958
CP: 13/06/1964   Stations U.K.

1334   **TREHARRIS**   **[NA&HR]**
Photo: W. 1963
P.Garland

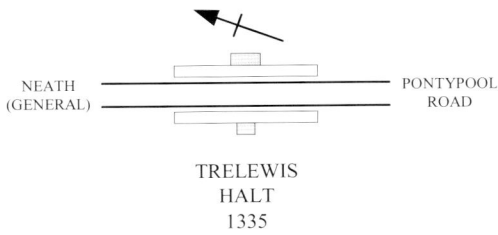

TRELEWIS
HALT
1335

1335   **TRELEWIS HALT**   **[NA&HR]**
OP: 09/07/1934   Photo: SE. 1958
CP: 13/06/1964   R.M.Casserley

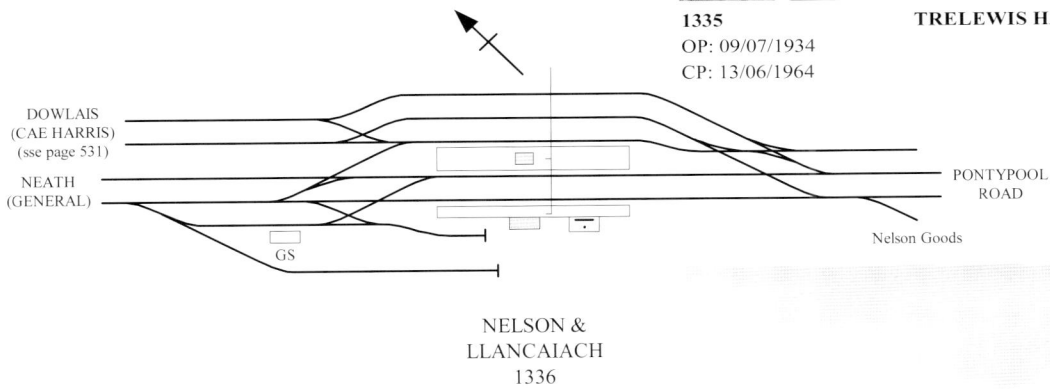

NELSON &
LLANCAIACH
1336

1336   **NELSON & LLANCAIACH**   **[NA&HR]**
OP: 01/07/1912   Photo: SE. 1959
CP: 13/06/1964   H.C.Casserley

RHYMNEY
(see page 523)

NEATH
(GENERAL)

YSTRAD
MYNACH
(see page 522)

CARDIFF
(QUEEN STREET)
(see page 522)

PONTYPOOL
ROAD

HENGOED (H.L.)
1337

1337   **HENGOED (H.L.)**   **[NA&HR]**
OP: 09/01/1858
CP: 13/06/1964   Photo: E. 1958
                                  Stations U.K.

1338   **PONTLLANFRAITH**   **[NA&HR]**
OP: 01/06/1857
CP: 13/06/1964   Photo: S. 1958
                                  R.M.Casserley

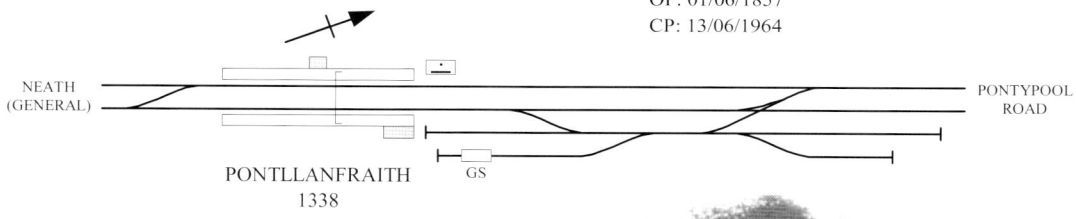

NEATH
(GENERAL)

PONTYPOOL
ROAD

GS

PONTLLANFRAITH
1338

1338   **PONTLLANFRAITH**   **[NA&HR]**
                                  Photo: N. 1958
                                  Stations U.K.

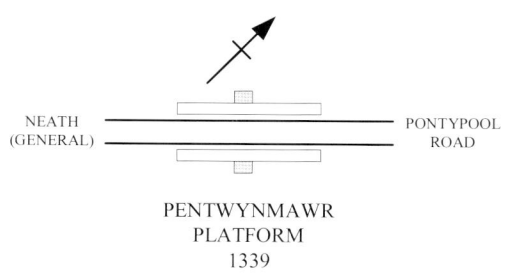

NEATH
(GENERAL)

PONTYPOOL
ROAD

PENTWYNMAWR
PLATFORM
1339

1339   **PENTWYNMAWR PLATFORM**   **[NA&HR]**
OP: 08/02/1926
CP: 13/06/1964   Photo: SW. 1959
                                  M.Hale

TREOWEN HALT
1340

NEATH (GENERAL) — — — — — — — — — — PONTYPOOL ROAD

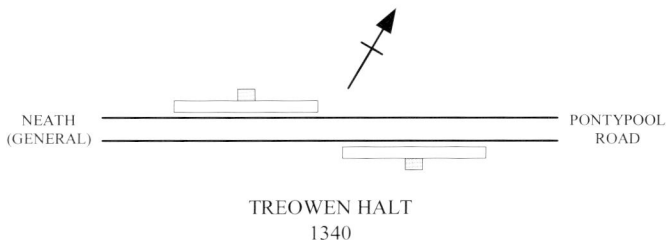

1340   **TREOWEN HALT**   **[NA&HR]**
OP: 14/03/1927   Photo: NE. 1959
CP: 09/07/1960   M.Hale

1341   **CRUMLIN (H.L.)**   **[NA&HR]**
OP: 15/10/1857   Photo: N. 1960
CP: 13/06/1964   H.C.Casserley

1341   **CRUMLIN (H.L.)**   **[NA&HR]**
Photo: S. 1964
F.A.Blencowe

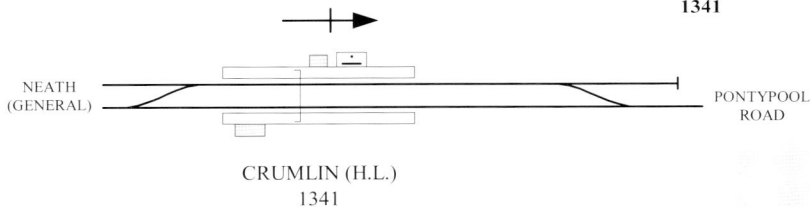

NEATH (GENERAL) — — — — — — — — PONTYPOOL ROAD

CRUMLIN (H.L.)
1341

NEATH (GENERAL) — — — — — — — — PONTYPOOL ROAD

HAFODYRYNYS
PLATFORM
1342

1342   **HAFODYRYNYS PLATFORM**   **[NA&HR]**
OP: 01/05/1913   Photo: E. 1960
CP: 13/06/1964   H.C.Casserley

1343   **CRUMLIN VALLEYS COLLIERY**   **[NA&HR]**
                         PLATFORM   Sketch: E. c.1955
OP: c.01/1921
CP: 1958 (Workmens trains)

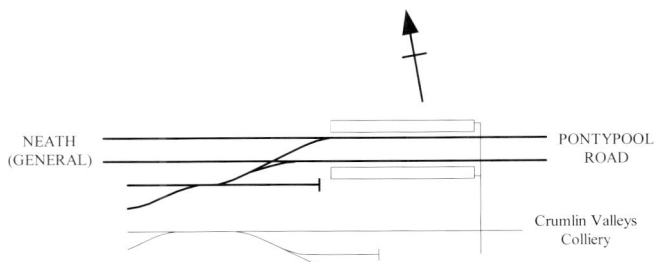

NEATH (GENERAL) — — — — — — — — PONTYPOOL ROAD

Crumlin Valleys Colliery

CRUMLIN VALLEYS
COLLIERY PLATFORM
1343

PONTYPOOL (CLARENCE STREET)
1344

BLAENAVON (see page 554)

NEATH (GENERAL)

LLANTARNAM (see page 554)

PONTYPOOL ROAD (see page 306)

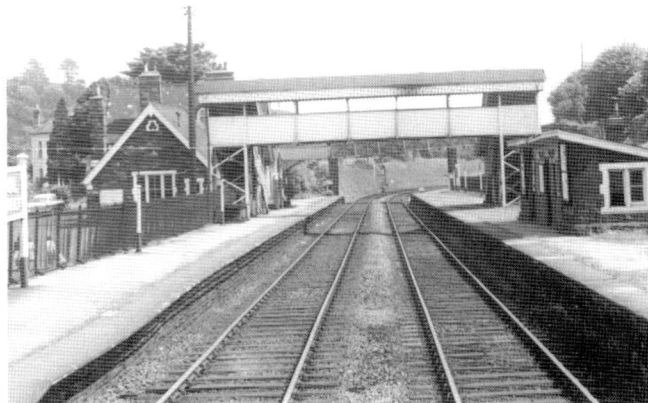

1344   PONTYPOOL (CLARENCE STREET)   [NA&HR]
OP: 20/08/1855
CP: 13/06/1964
Photo: W. 1957
Stations U.K.

1344   PONTYPOOL (CLARENCE STREET)   [NA&HR]
Photo: E. 1963
P.Garland

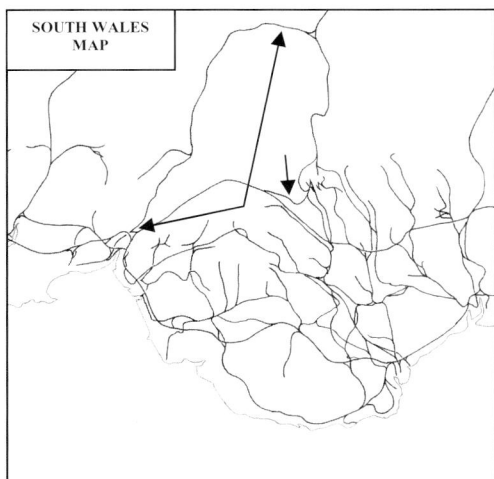

SOUTH WALES MAP

HIRWAUN (Exc) TO MERTHYR (Exc)
MERTHYR BRANCH
Vale of Neath Railway -
Great Western Railway (01/02/1865)
(Gelli Tarw Junction to Mardy Junction)
ACT: 03/08/1846
OP: 02/11/1853
OG: 02/11/1853
CP: 29/12/1962
CG: 29/12/1962

HIRWAUN (see page 464)

MERTHYR

LLWYDCOED
1345

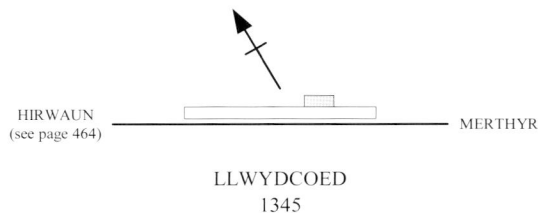

1345   LLWYDCOED   [VNR]
OP: 02/11/1853
CP: 29/12/1962
Photo: NW. 1961
Stations U.K.

HIRWAUN

MERTHYR (see page 509)

ABERNANT
1346

1346   ABERNANT   [VNR]
OP: 06/1854
CP: 29/12/1962
Photo: SE. 1961
Stations U.K.

NEATH (RIVERSIDE) (Exc) TO BRECON (Exc)
NEATH AND BRECON LINE
Neath & Brecon Railway -
Great Western Railway (01/01/1922)
ACT: 29/07/1862 (Neath to Onllwyn)
ACT: 13/07/1863 (Onllwyn to Brecon (Mount Street))
OP: 03/06/1867
OG: 02/09/1864 (Neath to Drym Colliery, Onllwyn)
OG: 03/06/1867 (Drym Colliery, Onllwyn to Brecon)
CP: 31/10/1962
CG: 07/10/1963 (Neath to Craigynos)
CG: 15/10/1962 (Craigynos to Brecon)

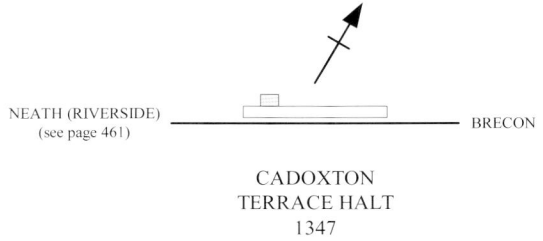

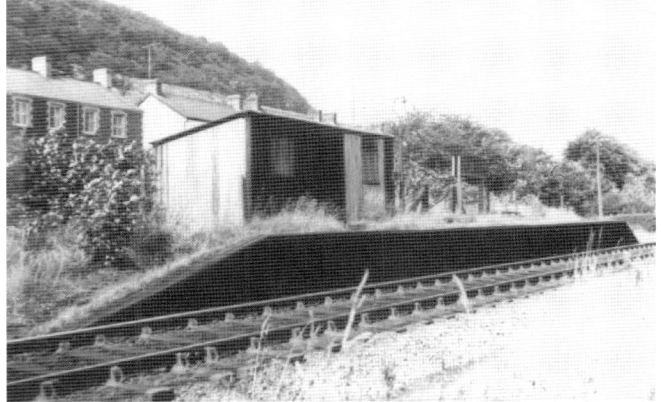

NEATH (RIVERSIDE)
(see page 461) ———————————————— BRECON

CADOXTON
TERRACE HALT
1347

NEATH
(RIVERSIDE) ———————————————— BRECON

PENSCYNOR
HALT
1348

1347   **CADOXTON TERRACE HALT**   **[N&BR]**
OP: 18/03/1929   Photo: N. 1959
CP: 13/10/1962   R.M.Casserley

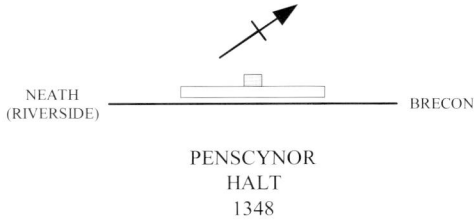

1348   **PENSCYNOR HALT**   **[N&BR]**
OP: 01/08/1929   Photo: NE. 1961
CP: 13/10/1962   Stations U.K.

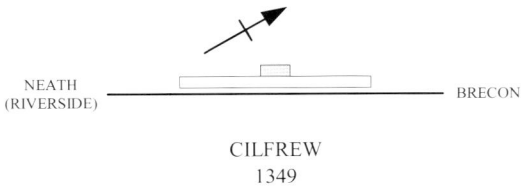

NEATH
(RIVERSIDE) ———————————————— BRECON

CILFREW
1349

1349   **CILFREW**   **[N&BR]**
OP: 12/1888   Photo: SW. 1961
CP: 13/10/1962   H.C.Casserley

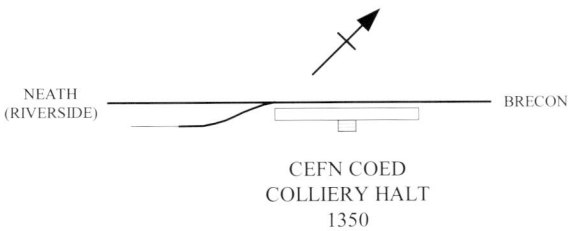

NEATH
(RIVERSIDE) ———————————————— BRECON

CEFN COED
COLLIERY HALT
1350

1350   **CEFN COED COLLIERY HALT**   **[N&BR]**
OP: 08/09/1930   Photo: SW. c.1960
CP: 13/10/1962   LOSA

CRYNANT
1351

1351   **CRYNANT**   **[N&BR]**
OP: 03/06/1867
CP: 13/10/1962

Photo: S. 1955
R.K.Blencowe

1351   **CRYNANT**   **[N&BR]**
Photo: N. 1956
Stations U.K.

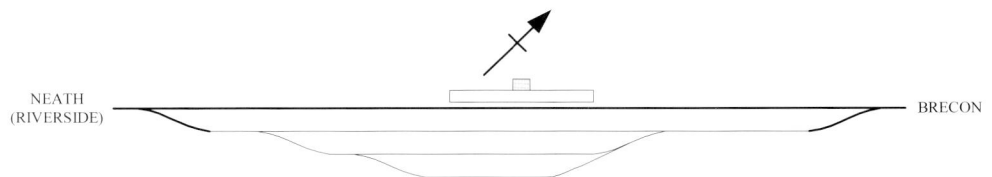

CRYNANT NEW
COLLIERY HALT
1352

1352   **CRYNANT NEW COLLIERY HALT**   **[N&BR]**
OP: 02/03/1931
CP: 1954 to 1956 (Workmens trains)

Photo: NE. 1965
M.Hale

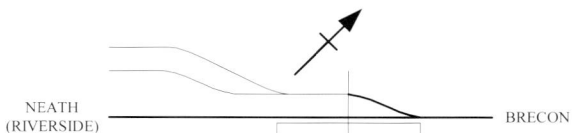

DILLWYN & BRYNTEG
PLATFORM
1353

1353   **DILLWYN & BRYNTEG PLATFORM**   **[N&BR]**
OP: by 09/1928
CP: 13/10/1962 (Workmens trains)

Photo: SW. 1962
M.Hale

Seven Sisters
Colliery

NEATH
(RIVERSIDE)

BRECON

SEVEN SISTERS
1354

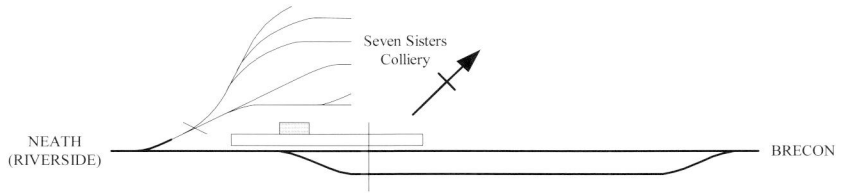

1354   **SEVEN SISTERS**   **[N&BR]**
OP: by 03/1875   Photo: NE. 1959
CP: 13/10/1962   M.Hale

NEATH
(RIVERSIDE)

BRECON

PANTYFFORDD
HALT
1355

1355   **PANTYFFORDD HALT**   **[N&BR]**
OP: 02/09/1929   Photo: NE. 1954
CP: 13/10/1962   unknown

NEATH
(GENERAL)

BRECON

ONLLWYN
1356

1356   **ONLLWYN**   **[N&BR]**
OP: 03/06/1867   Photo: SW. 1954
CP: 13/10/1962   unknown

1356   **ONLLWYN**   **[N&BR]**
    Photo: NE. c.1966
    LOSA

COLBREN JUNCTION
1357

1357   **COLBREN JUNCTION**   **[N&BR]**
OP: 10/11/1873
CP: 13/10/1962
Photo: SW. 1956
Stations U.K.

1357   **COLBREN JUNCTION**   **[N&BR]**
Photo: E. 1958
N.C.Simmons

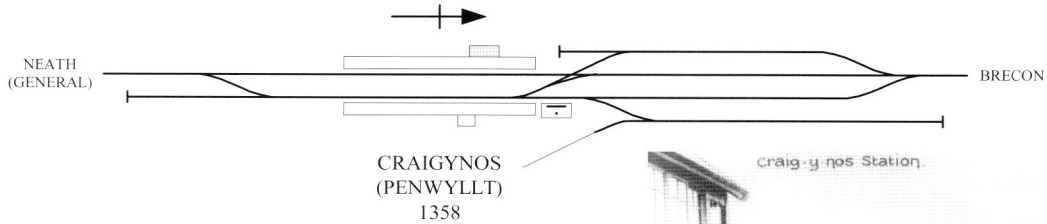

CRAIGYNOS
(PENWYLLT)
1358

1358   **CRAIGYNOS (PENWYLLT)**   **[N&BR]**
OP: 03/06/1867
CP: 13/10/1962
Photo: S. c.1910
LOSA

1359   **CRAY**   **[N&BR]**
OP: 02/1870
CP: 13/10/1962
Photo: NE. 1962
R.G.Nelson

CRAY
1359

DEVYNOCK &
SENNYBRIDGE
1360

1360   **DEVYNOCK & SENNYBRIDGE**   **[N&BR]**
OP: 03/06/1867   Photo: SW. 1961
CP: 13/10/1962   E.T.Gill

ABERCAMLAIS
HALT
1361

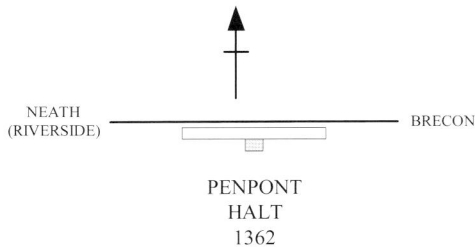

1361   **ABERCAMLAIS HALT**   **[N&BR]**
OP: 03/06/1867   Photo: E. 1949
CP: 13/10/1962 (Private)   WRRC Collection

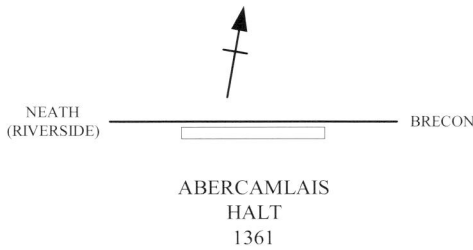

PENPONT
HALT
1362

1362   **PENPONT HALT**   **[N&BR]**
OP: 03/06/1867   Photo: E. 1949
CP: 13/10/1962 (Private)   WRRC Collection

1363   **ABERBRAN HALT**   **[N&BR]**
OP: 14/09/1868   Photo: SW. c.1960
CP: 13/10/1962   M.Hale

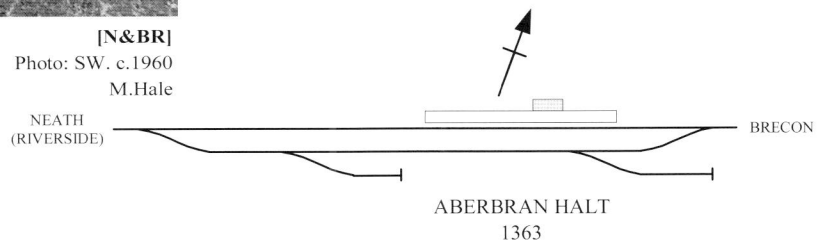

ABERBRAN HALT
1363

NEATH
(RIVERSIDE)

BRECON
(see page 542)

CRADOC
1364

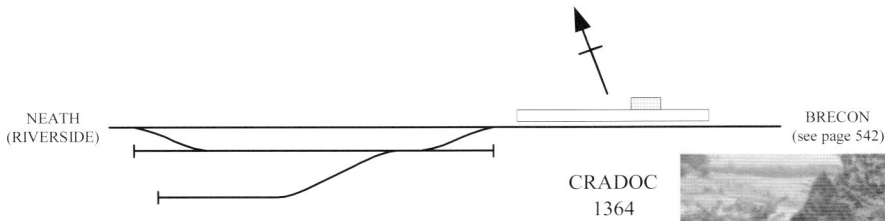

1364 **CRADOC** **[N&BR]**
OP: 01/03/1877 Photo: SE. 1956
CP: 13/10/1962 unknown

SOUTH WALES
MAP

COLBREN JUNCTION (Exc) TO Ynisygeinon Junction
YSTRADGYNLAIS BRANCH
Swansea Vale & Neath & Brecon Junction Railway -
Neath & Brecon Railway (26/07/1869) -
Great Western Railway (01/01/1922)
ACT: 29/07/1864
OP: 20/11/1873
OG: 20/11/1873
CP: 12/09/1932
CG: 30/11/1964 (Public Goods only)

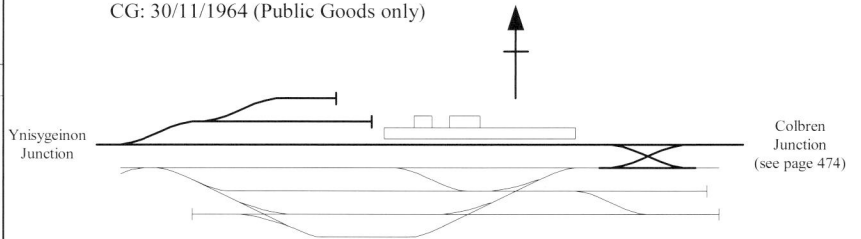

Ynisygeinon
Junction

Colbren
Junction
(see page 474)

ABERCRAVE
1365
[CLOSED]

1365 **ABERCRAVE** **[SV&N&BJR]**
OP: 02/03/1891 Photo: E. 1949
CP: 12/09/1932 L&GRP

1366 **YSTRADGYNLAIS** **[SV&N&BJR]**
OP: 20/11/1873 Photo: NE. 1956
CP: 12/09/1932 C.Mowat

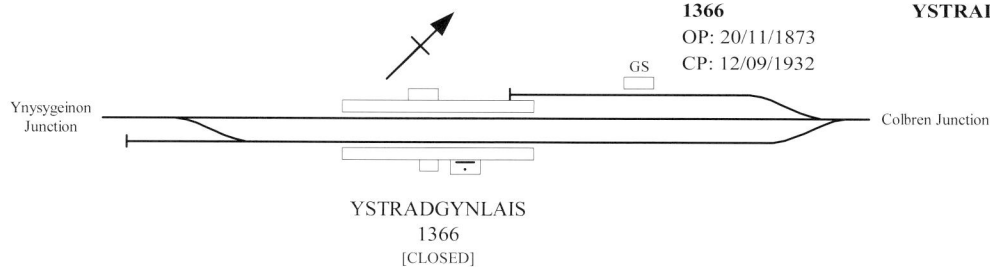

GS

Ynysygeinon
Junction

Colbren Junction

YSTRADGYNLAIS
1366
[CLOSED]

BRITON FERRY (Exc) TO BLAENRHONDDA
RHONDDA & SWANSEA BAY LINE
Rhondda & Swansea Bay Railway -
Great Western Railway (01/01/1922)

ACT: 28/07/1891 & 09/06/1893 (Briton Ferry to Burrows Junc.)
ACT: 10/08/1882 (Port Talbot Docks to Treherbert)
OP: 14/03/1895 (Briton Ferry to Burrows Junction)
OP: 02/11/1885 (Port Talbot Docks to Cymmer Afan)
OP: 02/06/1890 (Cymmer Afan to Blaengwynfi)
OP: 02/07/1890 (Blaengwynfi to Blaenrhondda)
OP: 14/07/1890 (Blaenrhondda to Treherbert)
OG: 30/12/1893 (Briton Ferry to Burrows Junction)
OG: 02/11/1885 (Port Talbot Docks to Cymmer Afan)
OG: 02/06/1890 (Cymmer Afan to Blaengwynfi)
OG: 02/07/1890 (Blaengwynfi to Treherbert)
CP: 01/12/1962 (Briton Ferry to Cymmer Afan)
CP: 24/02/1968 (Cymmer Afan to 5 miles 44 chains)
CP: 13/06/1960 (5 miles 44 chains to 4 miles 8 chains)
CP: 24/02/1968 (4 miles 8 chains to Treherbert)
CG: 03/12/1962 (Briton Ferry to Aberavon (Seaside))
CG: 03/08/1964 (Aberavon (Seaside) to 13 miles 68 chains)
CG: 29/07/1963 (13 miles 68 chains to Cwmavon)
CMin: 07/1964 (Cwmavon to Duffryn Rhondda Colliery)
CMin: 22/01/1970 (Duffryn Rhondda Colliery to Cymmer Afan)
CG: 13/06/1960 (5 miles 44 chains to 4 miles 8 chains)
CG: 24/02/1968 (4 miles 8 chains to R&SB Junction, Treherbert)

1367   **ABERAVON (SEASIDE)**   **[R&SB]**
OP: 03/1899   Photo: NW. 1955
CP: 01/12/1962   Stations U.K.

ABERAVON
(SEASIDE)
1367

1367   **ABERAVON (SEASIDE)**   **[R&SB]**
Photo: SE. 1959
M.Hale

1368   **ABERAVON (TOWN)**   **[R&SB]**
OP: 25/06/1885   Photo: NE. c.1955
CP: 01/12/1962   LOSA

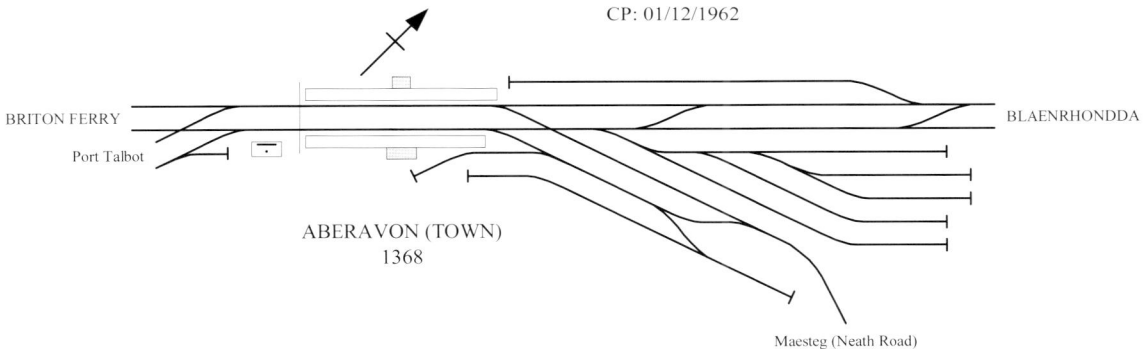

ABERAVON (TOWN)
1368

CWMAVON (GLAM.)
1369

1369　　　　CWMAVON (GLAM.)　　　　[R&SB]
OP: 25/06/1885　　　　　　　　　　Photo: NE. 1960
CP: 01/12/1962　　　　　　　　　　R.M.Casserley

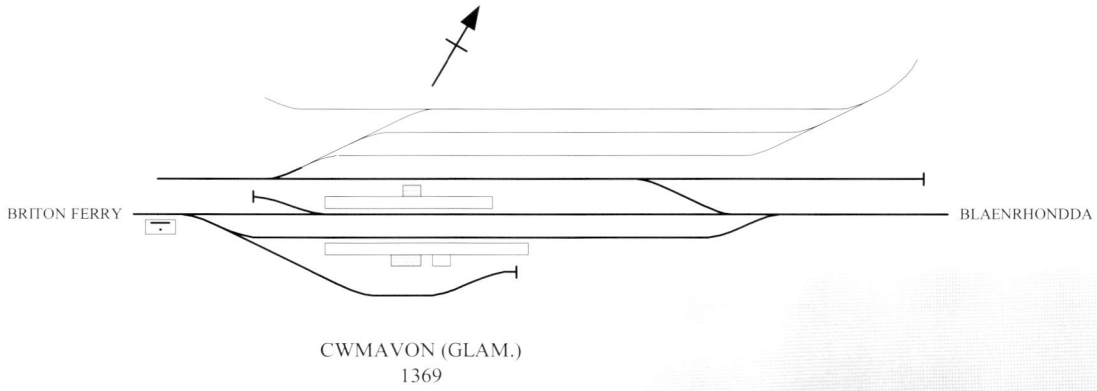

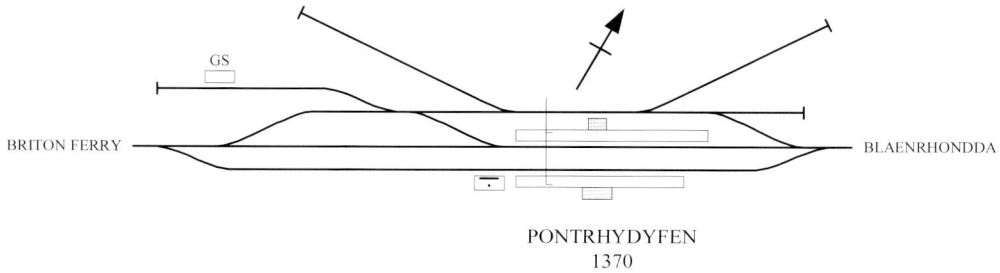

1370　　　　PONTRHYDYFEN　　　　[R&SB]
OP: 25/06/1885　　　　　　　　　Photo: NE. 1960
CP: 01/12/1962　　　　　　　　　H.C.Casserley

GS

BRITON FERRY　　　　　　　　　　　　　BLAENRHONDDA

PONTRHYDYFEN
1370

BRITON FERRY　　　　　　　　　　　　BLAENRHONDDA

CYNONVILLE
HALT
1371

1371　　　　CYNONVILLE HALT　　　　[R&SB]
OP: by 1898　　　　　　　　　　Photo: NE. 1964
CP: 02/01/1956　　　　　　　　　Stations U.K.

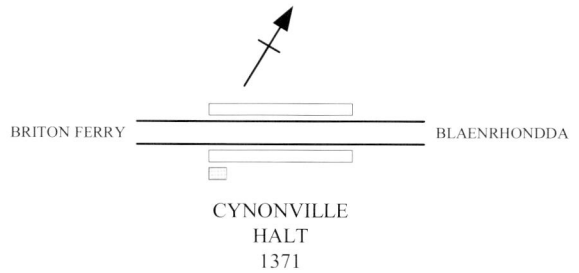

BRITON FERRY　　　　　　　　　　　　BLAENRHONDDA

DUFFRYN RHONDDA
HALT
1372

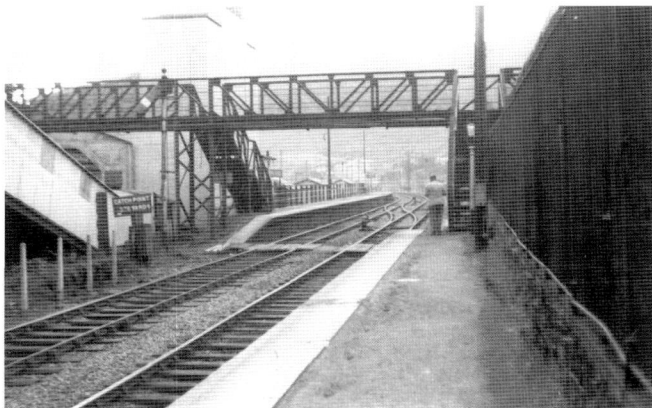

1372   **DUFFRYN RHONDDA HALT**   **[R&SB]**
OP: by 1898   Photo: E. 1964
CP: 07/11/1966 (Workmens trains)   Stations U.K.

1372   **DUFFRYN RHONDDA HALT**   **[R&SB]**
Photo: W. c.1965
LOSA

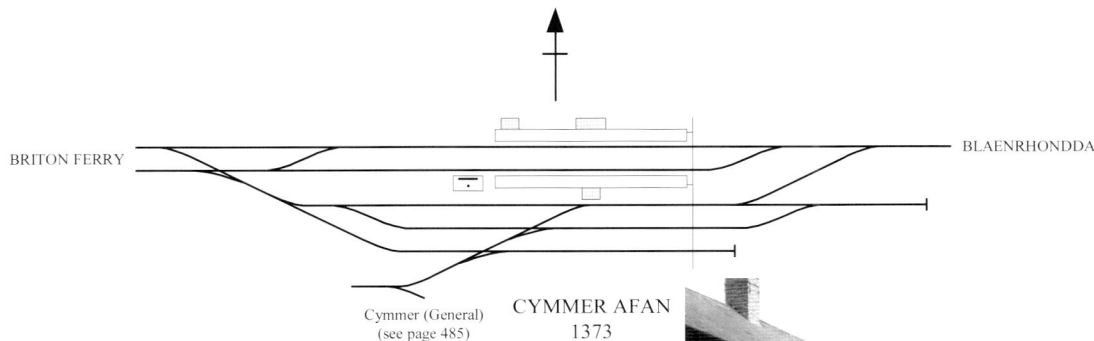

BRITON FERRY   BLAENRHONDDA

Cymmer (General)
(see page 485)   **CYMMER AFAN**
1373

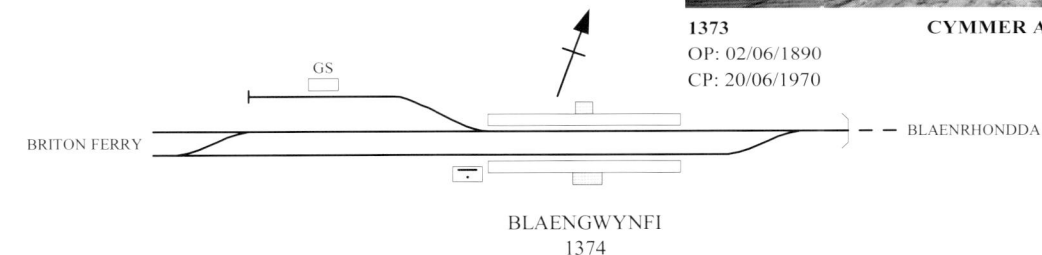

1373   **CYMMER AFAN**   **[R&SB]**
OP: 02/06/1890   Photo: E. 1959
CP: 20/06/1970   H.C.Casserley

GS

BRITON FERRY   BLAENRHONDDA

BLAENGWYNFI
1374

1374   **BLAENGWYNFI**   **[R&SB]**
OP: 02/06/1890   Photo: W. c.1960
CP: 24/02/1968   LOSA

1374   **BLAENGWYNFI**   **[R&SB]**
Photo: N. 1964
Stations U.K.

BRITON FERRY

TREHERBERT
(see page 512)

BLAENRHONDDA
1375

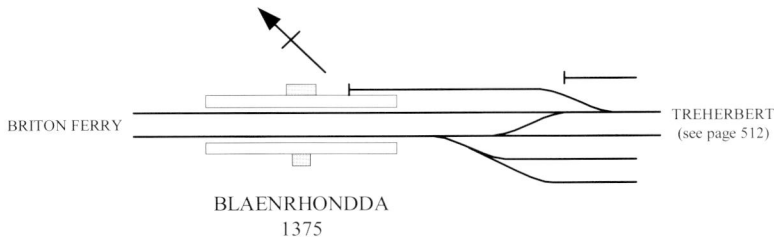

1375   **BLAENRHONDDA**   **[R&SB]**
OP: 02/07/1890   Photo: NW. 1954
CP: 24/02/1968   unknown

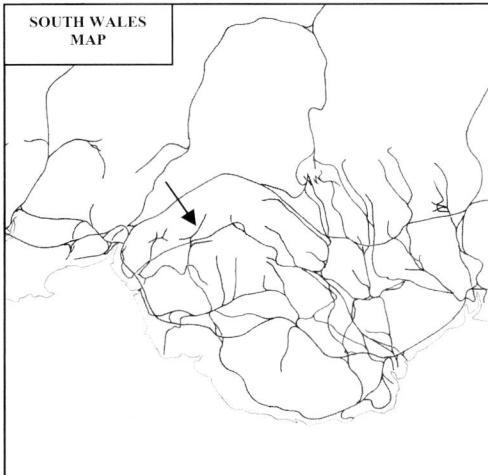

SOUTH WALES MAP

CYMMER CORRWG TO NORTH RHONDDA HALT
SOUTH WALES MINERAL RAILWAY

South Wales Mineral Railway -
Great Western Railway (01/01/1923)

ACT: 10/08/1853
OP: 28/03/1918 (Public Services) (Cymmer Corrwg to Glyncorrwg)
OP: 27/08/1923 (Workmens trains) (Glyncorrwg to North Rhondda Halt)
OG: 10/03/1863
CP: 1955 (Workmens trains) (Cymmer Corrwg to Glyncorrwg)
CP: 30/10/1964 (Workmens trains) (Glyncorrwg to South Pit Halt)
CP: 03/1963 (Workmens trains) (South Pit Halt to North Rhondda Halt)
CG: 30/08/1965 (Public Goods only)

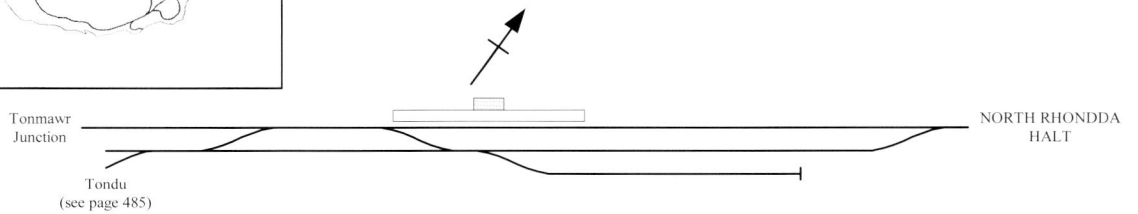

Tonmawr
Junction

NORTH RHONDDA
HALT

Tondu
(see page 485)

CYMMER CORRWG
1376

1376   **CYMMER CORRWG**   **[SWMR]**
OP: 28/03/1918   Photo: SW. 1959
CP: 1955 (Workmens trains)   H.C.Casserley

1377   **NANTEWLAETH COLLIERY HALT**   **[SWMR]**
OP: by 28/10/1940   Photo: N. 1959
CP: 18/09/1955 (Workmens trains)   R.M.Casserley

CYMMER CORRWG

NORTH RHONDDA
HALT

NANTEWLAETH
COLLIERY HALT
1377

CYMMER CORRWG

ES

NORTH RHONDDA
HALT

GLYNCORRWG
1378

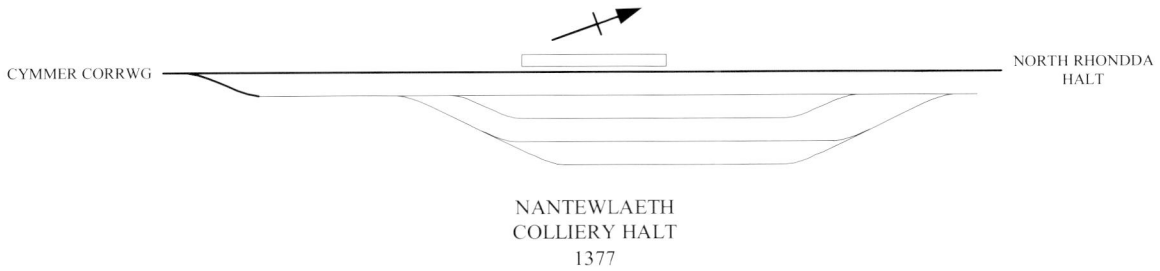

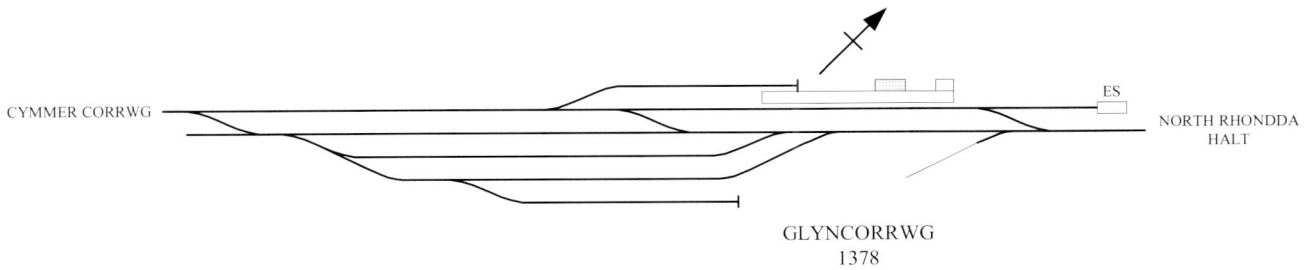

1378   **GLYNCORRWG**   **[SWMR]**
OP: 28/03/1918
CP: 30/10/1964 (Workmens trains)
Photo: NE. 1960
Stations U.K.

1378   **GLYNCORRWG**   **[SWMR]**
Photo: SW. 1959
H.C.Casserley

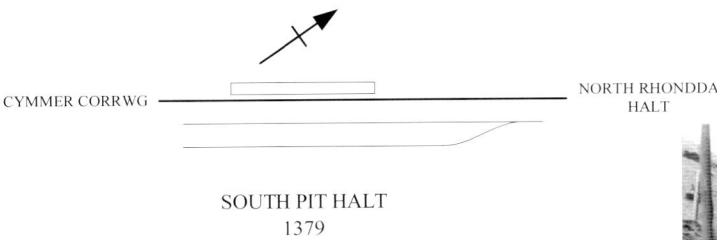

CYMMER CORRWG

NORTH RHONDDA
HALT

SOUTH PIT HALT
1379

1379   **SOUTH PIT HALT**   **[SWMR]**
OP: by 27/08/1923
CP: 1956 (Workmens trains)
Photo: NE. c.1960
M.Hale

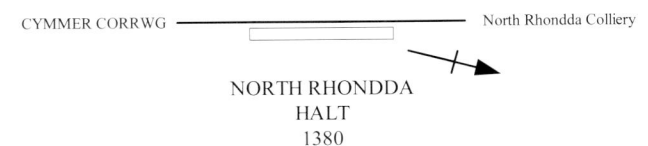

CYMMER CORRWG

North Rhondda Colliery

NORTH RHONDDA
HALT
1380

1380   **NORTH RHONDDA HALT**   **[SWMR]**
OP: 27/08/1923
CP: 03/1963 (Workmens trains)
Photo: S. 1960
Stations U.K.

SOUTH WALES MAP

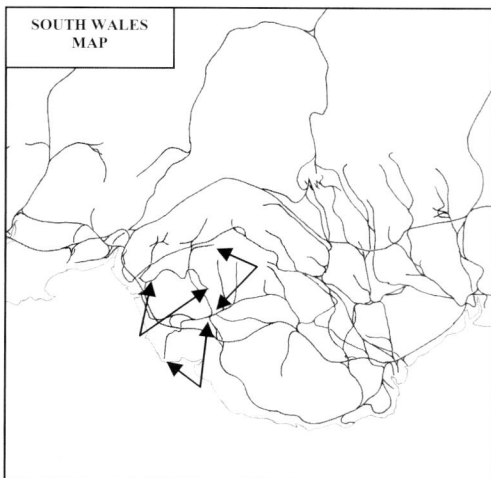

PORT TALBOT (CENTRAL) TO LLETTY BRONGU (Exc)
PORT TALBOT TO PONTYRHYLL
Port Talbot Railway & Docks -
Great Western Railway (01/01/1922)

ACT: 31/07/1894
OP: 14/02/1898
OG: 31/08/1897
CP: 11/09/1933 (Port Talbot to Maesteg)
CP: 12/09/1932 (Maesteg to Pontyrhyll)
CG: 01/02/1960 (Port Talbot (Central) to Tonygroes East Junction)
CG: 27/03/1963 (Tonygroes East Junction to Dufffryn Junction)
CG: 28/08/1964 (Dufffryn Junction to Cwmdu)
CG: 09/05/1960 (Cwmdu to Lletty Brongu)

1381   **PORT TALBOT (CENTRAL)**   **[PTR&D]**
NO INFORMATION AS CLOSED BY 1947

CP: 11/09/1933

Port Talbot   Lletty Brongu

GS

MAESTEG
(NEATH ROAD)
1382
[CLOSED]

1382   **MAESTEG (NEATH ROAD)**   **[PTR&D]**
OP: 14/02/1898   Photo: SE. 1956
CP: 11/09/1933   C.Mowat

1383   **CWMDU**   **[PTR&D]**
OP: 09/06/1913   Photo: NW. 1962
CP: 12/09/1932   C.H.Townley

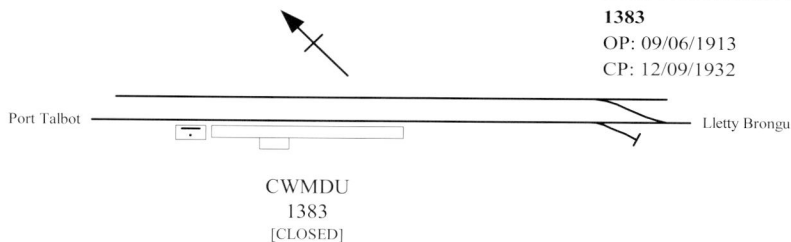

Port Talbot   Lletty Brongu

CWMDU
1383
[CLOSED]

PORTHCAWL TO TONDU (Exc)
PORTHCAWL BRANCH,
OGMORE VALE EXTENSION LINE
Llynvi Valley Railway -
Llynvi & Ogmore Railway (28/06/1866) -
Great Western Railway (01/07/1883)

ACT: 15/06/1855
OP: 01/08/1865
OG: 10/08/1861
CP: 07/09/1963
CG: 01/02/1965 (Porthcawl to Pyle East Junction)
CG: 19/11/1973 (Pyle East Junction to Cefn Junction)

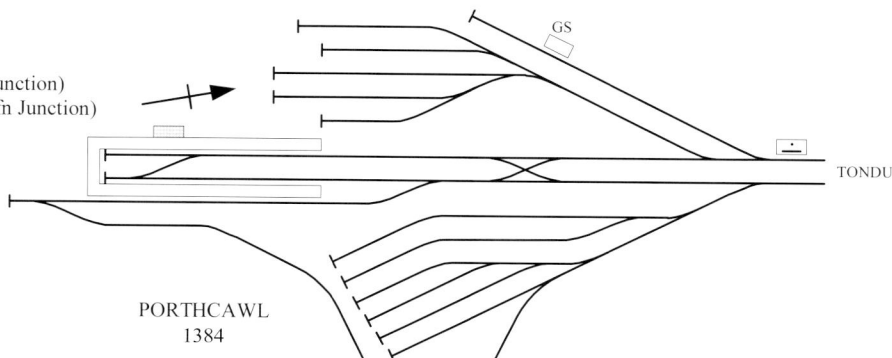

GS

TONDU

PORTHCAWL
1384

1384 **PORTHCAWL** **[LVR]**
OP: 06/03/1916 Photo: N. 1963
CP: 07/09/1963 P.Garland

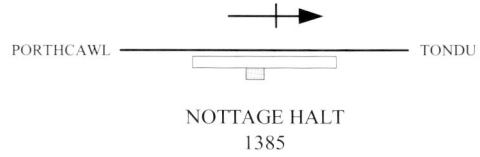

PORTHCAWL ←————————→ TONDU

NOTTAGE HALT
1385

1385 **NOTTAGE HALT** **[LVR]**
OP: c.1897 Photo: N. 1963
CP: 07/09/1963 P.Garland

1386 **KENFIG HILL** **[LVR]**
OP: 01/08/1865 Photo: E. 1960
CP: 03/05/1958 M.Hale

PORTHCAWL TONDU
(see page 484)

KENFIG HILL
1386

BRIDGEND (Exc) TO ABERGWYNFI
BRIDGEND TO ABERGWYNFI LINE
Llynvi Valley Railway -
Llynvi & Ogmore Railway (28/06/1866) -
Great Western Railway (01/07/1883)
(Bridgend to Nantyffyllon)
Llynvi & Ogmore Railway (28/06/1866) -
Great Western Railway (01/07/1883)
(Nantyffyllon to Abergwynfi)
ACT: 15/06/1855 (Bridgend to Nantyffyllon)
ACT: 21/07/1873 (Nantyffyllon to Abergwynfi)
OP: 25/02/1864 (Bridgend to Nantyffyllon)
OP: 16/07/1880 (Nantyffyllon to Cymmer (General))
OP: 22/03/1886 (Cymmer (General) to Abergwynfi)
OG: 10/08/1861 (Bridgend to Nantyffyllon)
OG: 01/07/1878 (Nantyffyllon to Cymmer (General))
OG: 22/03/1886 (Cymmer (General) to Abergwynfi)
CP: 20/06/1970 (Public Services) (Bridgend to Cymmer)
CP: 11/06/1960 (Cymmer to Abergwynfi)
CMin: 19/07/1976 (Maesteg to Caerau)
CMin: 25/06/1970 (Caerau to Cymmer)
CMin: 29/09/1969 (Cymmer to Abergwynfi)

1387 **TONDU** **[LVR]**
OP: 25/02/1864 Photo: S. 1958
CP: 20/06/1970 Stations U.K.

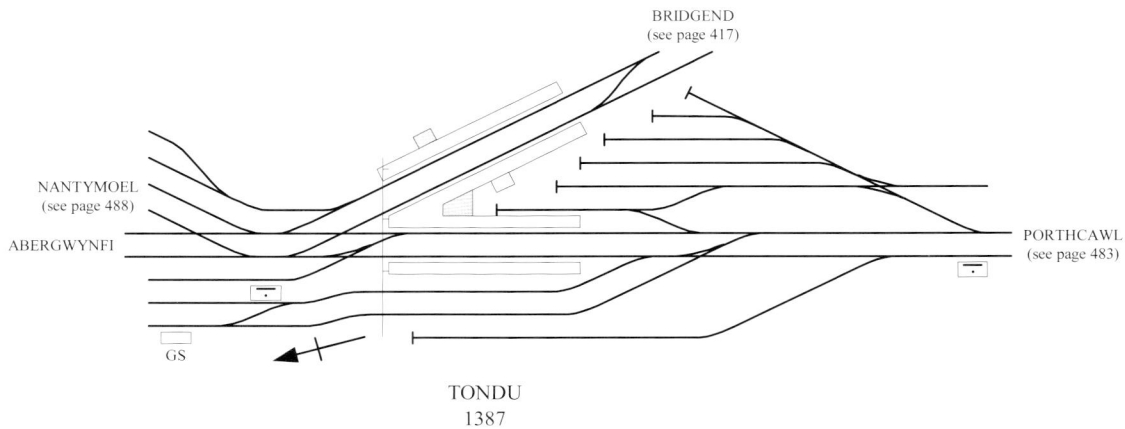

BRIDGEND
(see page 417)

NANTYMOEL
(see page 488)

ABERGWYNFI

PORTHCAWL
(see page 483)

GS

TONDU
1387

1387   **TONDU**   **[LVR]**
Photo: SE. 1962
H.B.Priestley

1387   **TONDU**   **[LVR]**
Photo: S. 1960
Stations U.K.

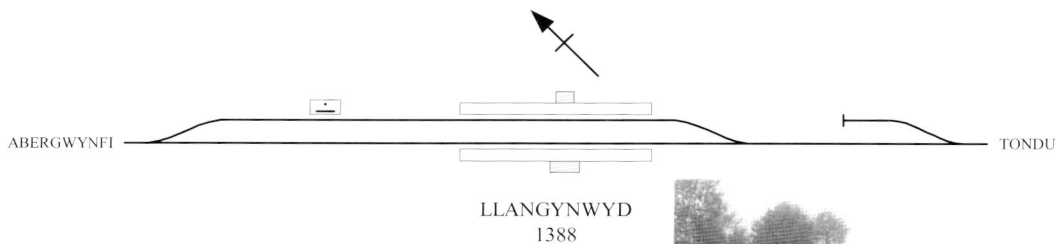

ABERGWYNFI   TONDU

LLANGYNWYD
1388

1388   **LLANGYNWYD**   **[LVR]**
OP: 1897   Photo: NW. 1963
CP: 20/06/1970   P.Garland

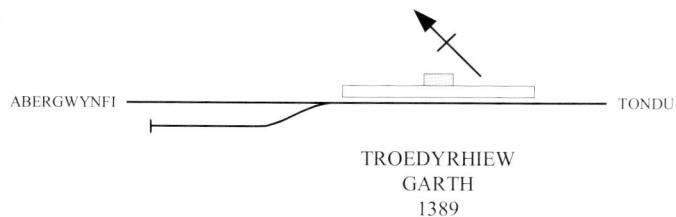

1389   **TROEDYRHIEW GARTH**   **[LVR]**
OP: 10/1873
CP: 20/06/1970   Photo: SE. 1959
                                 R.M.Casserley

ABERGWYNFI   TONDU

TROEDYRHIEW
GARTH
1389

MAESTEG
(CASTLE STREET)
1390

ABERGWYNFI

TONDU

GS

1390   **MAESTEG (CASTLE STREET)**   **[LVR]**
OP: 25/02/1864   Photo: SE. 1960
CP: 20/06/1970   H.C.Casserley

1391   **NANTYFFYLLON**   **[LVR]**
OP: 19/07/1880   Photo: N. 1960
CP: 20/06/1970   H.C.Casserley

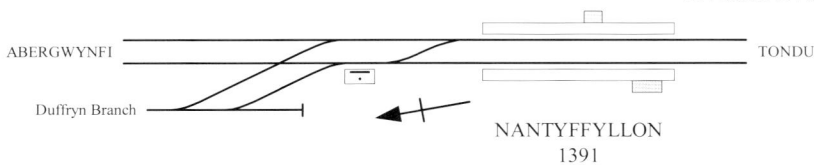

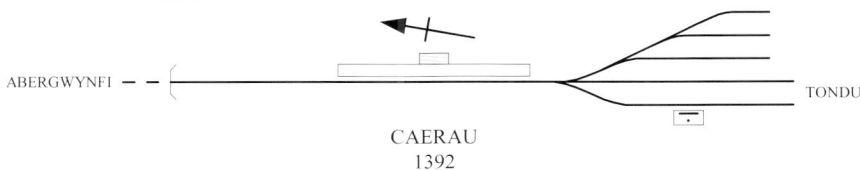

ABERGWYNFI

TONDU

Duffryn Branch

NANTYFFYLLON
1391

ABERGWYNFI

TONDU

CAERAU
1392

1392   **CAERAU**   **[L&OR]**
OP: 01/04/1901   Photo: N. 1963
CP: 20/06/1970   P.Garland

1393   **CYMMER (GENERAL)**   **[L&OR]**
OP: 19/07/1880   Photo: NW. 1951
CP: 11/06/1960   R.Carpenter

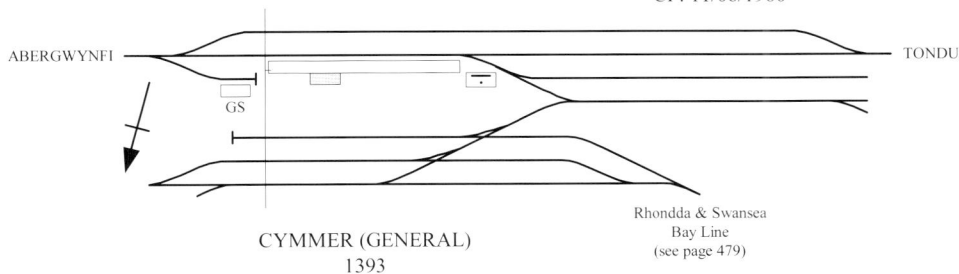

ABERGWYNFI

TONDU

GS

Rhondda & Swansea
Bay Line
(see page 479)

CYMMER (GENERAL)
1393

GS

Avon Colliery

TONDU

ABERGWYNFI
1394

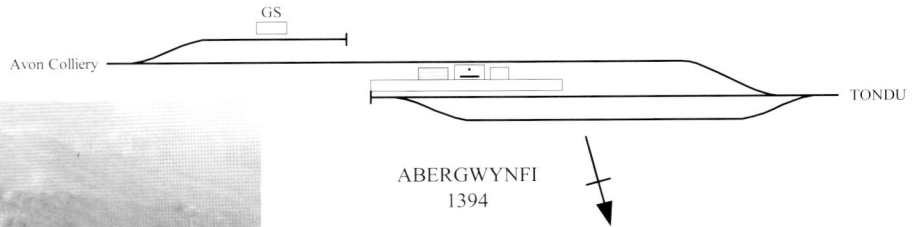

1394   **ABERGWYNFI**   **[L&OR]**
OP: 22/03/1886   Photo: W. c.1958
CP: 11/06/1960   A.Attewell

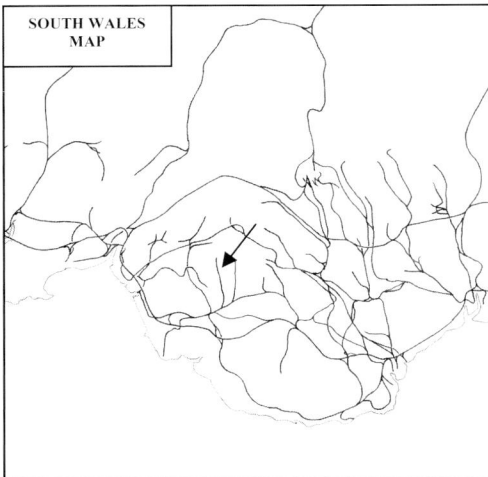

SOUTH WALES
MAP

BRYNMENYN (Exc) TO BLAENGARW
GARW BRANCH
Ogmore Valley Railway -
Llynvi & Ogmore Railway (28/06/1866) -
Great Western Railway (01/07/1883)
ACT: 23/07/1866
OP: 25/10/1886 (Brynmenyn to Pontyrhyll)
OP: 01/06/1889 (Pontyrhyll to Pontycymmer)
OP: 01/05/1902 (Pontycymmer to Blaengarw)
OG: 25/10/1876
CP: 07/02/1953
CG: 19/07/1965 (Public Goods only) (Brynmenyn to Pontycymmer)
CG: 02/07/1962 (Public Goods only) (Pontycymmer to Blaengarw)

BLAENGARW

BRYNMENYN
(see page 488)

LLANGEINOR
1395

1395   **LLANGEINOR**   **[OVR]**
OP: 25/10/1886   Photo: NE. 1962
CP: 07/02/1953   M.Hale

1396   **PONTYRHYLL**   **[OVR]**
OP: 25/10/1886   Photo: SE. c.1900
CP: 07/02/1953   R.G.Simmonds

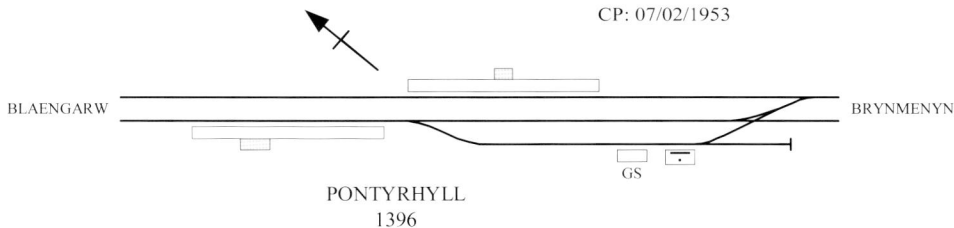

BLAENGARW

BRYNMENYN

GS

PONTYRHYLL
1396

1396   **PONTYRHYLL**   **[OVR]**
Photo: NW. 1962
M.Hale

1397   **PONTYCYMMER**   **[OVR]**
OP: 01/06/1889   Photo: S. 1959
CP: 07/02/1953   H.C.Casserley

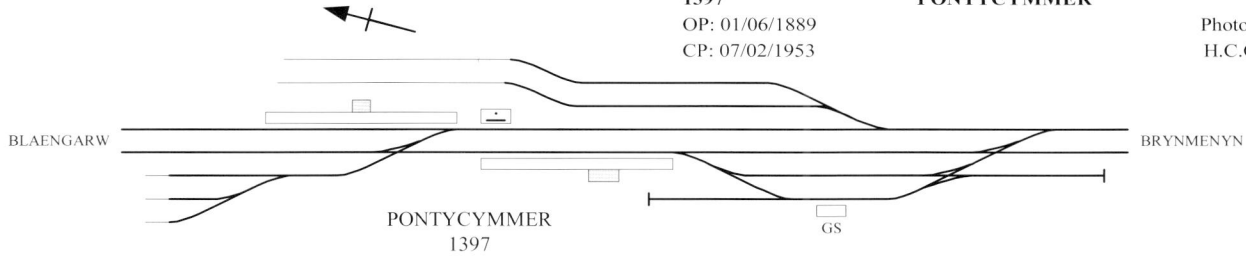

BLAENGARW   BRYNMENYN

GS

PONTYCYMMER
1397

1398   **BLAENGARW**   **[OVR]**
OP: 26/05/1902   Photo: S. 1959
CP: 07/02/1953   H.C.Casserley

1397   **PONTYCYMMER**   **[OVR]**
Photo: S. 1960
Stations U.K.

GS

BRYNMENYN

BLAENGARW
1398

1398   **BLAENGARW**   **[OVR]**
Photo: N. 1965
M.Hale

**TONDU (Exc) TO NANTYMOEL
BLACKMILL BRANCH,
OGMORE BRANCH**
Ogmore Valley Railway -
Llynvi & Ogmore Railway (28/06/1866) -
Great Western Railway (01/07/1883)
ACT: 13/07/1863
OP: 01/08/1865
OG: 01/08/1865
CP: 03/05/1958
CG: 19/07/1965 (Public Goods only) (Tondu to Brynmenyn)
CG: 23/11/1964 (Public Goods only) (Brynmenyn to Ogmore Vale)
CG: 19/11/1962 (Public Goods only) (Ogmore Vale to Nantymoel)

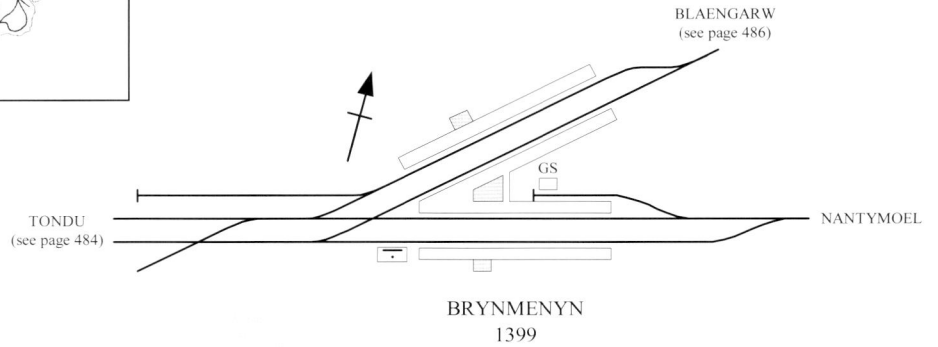

BLAENGARW
(see page 486)

GS

TONDU
(see page 484)

NANTYMOEL

BRYNMENYN
1399

1399   **BRYNMENYN**   **[OVR]**
OP: 12/05/1873   Photo: NE. 1958
CP: 03/05/1958   Stations U.K.

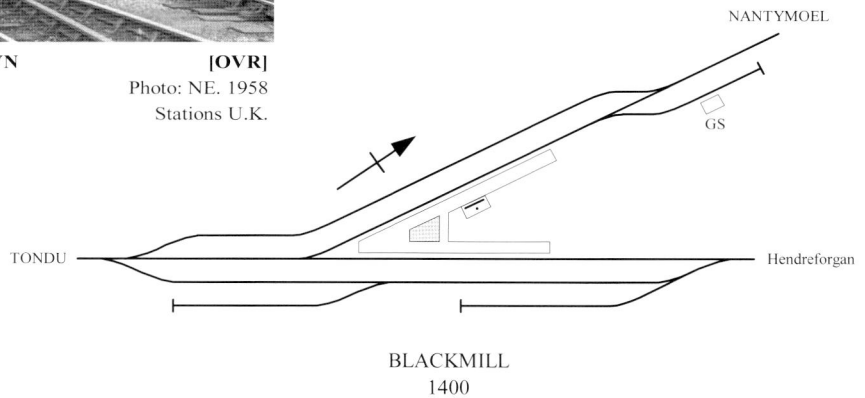

NANTYMOEL

GS

TONDU

Hendreforgan

BLACKMILL
1400

1400   **BLACKMILL**   **[OVR]**
OP: 12/05/1873   Photo: NE. 1957
CP: 03/05/1958   W.A.Camwell

1400   **BLACKMILL**   **[OVR]**
Photo: SW. 1958
D.Lawrence

LEWISTOWN
HALT
1401

TONDU ——————————— NANTYMOEL

1401 **LEWISTOWN HALT** **[OVR]**
OP: 10/08/1942 Photo: SW. 1962
CP: 04/06/1951 M.Hale

GS

TONDU   NANTYMOEL

OGMORE VALE
1402

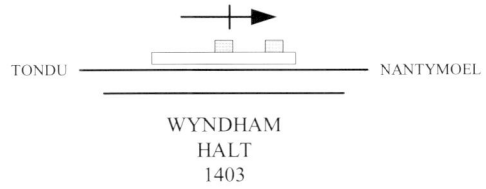

1402 **OGMORE VALE** **[OVR]**
OP: 12/05/1873 Photo: S. 1958
CP: 03/05/1958 M.Hale

TONDU ——————————— NANTYMOEL

WYNDHAM
HALT
1403

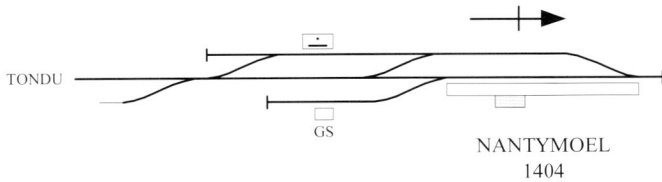

1403 **WYNDHAM HALT** **[OVR]**
OP: 10/08/1942 Photo: S. 1958
CP: 03/05/1958 M.Hale

TONDU

GS

NANTYMOEL
1404

1404 **NANTYMOEL** **[OVR]**
OP: 12/05/1873 Photo: S. 1956
CP: 03/05/1958 R.M.Casserley

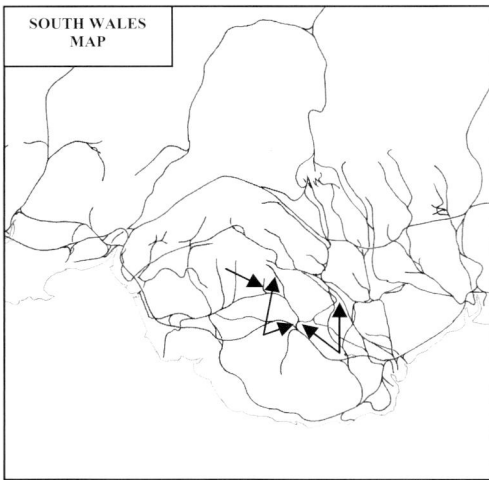

SOUTH WALES
MAP

HENDREFORGAN (Exc) TO GILFACH GOCH COLLIERS PLATFORM
GILFACH BRANCH
Ely Valley Extension Railway -
Ogmore Valley Railway (05/07/1865) -
Llynvi & Ogmore Railway (28/06/1866) -
Great Western Railway (01/07/1883)
ACT: 28/07/1863
OP: 01/09/1875 (Hendreforgan to Gilfach Goch)
OP: 1912 (Gilfach Goch Colliers Platform) (Workmens trains only)
OG: 16/10/1865
CP: 22/09/1930 (Public Services and Workmens trains)
CG: 05/06/1961

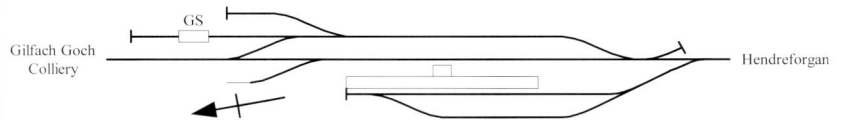

GS

Gilfach Goch
Colliery

Hendreforgan

GILFACH GOCH
1405
[CLOSED]

1405	**GILFACH GOCH**	[EVER]
OP: 01/09/1875		Photo: N. 1951
CP: by 06/1954 (Excursion trains)		W.A.Camwell

1406	**GILFACH GOCH COLLIERS PLATFORM**	[EVER]
	NO INFORMATION AS CLOSED BY 1947	
CP: c.1930		

LLANTRISANT (Exc) TO PENYGRAIG
ELY VALLEY LINE
Ely Valley Railway -
Great Western Railway (01/07/1903)
ACT: 13/07/1857 (Llantrisant to Penygraig)
OP: 01/05/1901
OG: 02/08/1860 (to Penrhiwfer Colliery)
OG: 12/12/1862 (Penrhiwfer Colliery to Penygraig)
CP: 07/16/1958
CG: 12/10/1964 (Public Goods only)

PENYGRAIG

LLANTRISANT
(see page 415)

COED ELY
1407

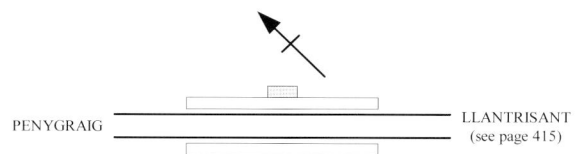

1407	**COED ELY**	[EVR]
OP: 13/07/1925		Photo: NW. 1958
CP: 07/06/1958		Stations U.K.

1408	**TONYREFAIL**	[EVR]
OP: 01/05/1901		Photo: S. 1958
CP: 07/06/1958		Stations U.K.

TONYREFAIL
1408

PENYGRAIG
1409

1409	PENYGRAIG	[EVR]
OP: 01/05/1901		Photo: S. 1951
CP: 07/06/1958		R.C.Riley

1409	PENYGRAIG	[EVR]
		Photo: N. 1958
		Stations U.K.

LLANTRISANT (Exc) TO TONTEG HALT (Exc)
LLANTRISANT BRANCH
Ely Valley Railway -
Great Western Railway (01/07/1903)
(Mwyndy Junction to Maesaraul Junction)
Llantrisant & Taff Vale Junction Railway -
Taff Vale Railway (26/08/1889) -
Great Western Railway (01/01/1922)
(Maesaraul Junction to near Tonteg)
Great Western Railway
(connection to Treforest Branch Junction)
ACT: 14/06/1858 (Mwyndy Junction to Maesaraul Junction)
ACT: 07/06/1861 (Maesaraul Junction to near Tonteg)
ACT: 26/07/1929 (connection to Treforest Branch Junction)
OP: 18/09/1865
OP: 05/05/1930 (connection to Treforest Branch Junction)
OG: 02/08/1860 (Llantrisant to Maesaraul Junction)
OMin: 01/12/1863 (Maesaraul Junction to west of Llantwit Fardre)
OMin: 17/09/1863 (Llantwit Fardre to near Tonteg)
OG: 05/05/1930 (connection to Treforest Branch Junction)
CP: 29/03/1952
CG: 07/10/1963 (Public Goods only)

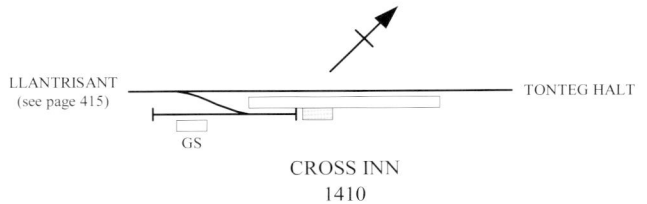

CROSS INN
1410

1410	CROSS INN	[L&TVJR]
OP: 06/09/1869		Photo: SW. 1958
CP: 29/03/1952		Stations U.K.

BEDDAU HALT
1411

PHOTOGRAPH UNAVAILABLE

1411   **BEDDAU HALT**   **[L&TVJR]**
OP: 07/1910   Photo: None
CP: 29/03/1952   Available

1412   **LLANTWIT FARDRE**   **[L&TVJR]**
OP: 01/1867   Photo: SW. 1958
CP: 29/03/1952   Stations U.K.

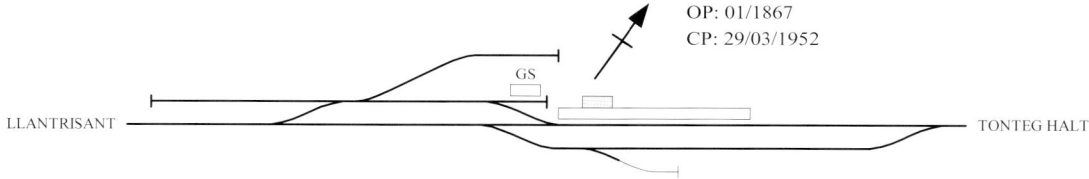

LLANTWIT FARDRE
1412

CHURCH VILLAGE
HALT
1413

1413   **CHURCH VILLAGE HALT**   **[L&TVJR]**
OP: 01/10/1887   Photo: E. c.1956
CP: 29/03/1952   LOSA

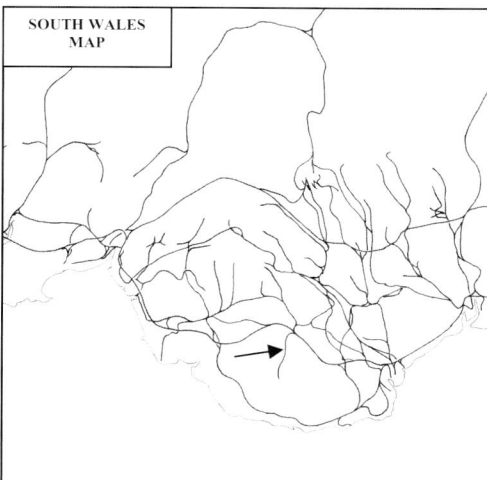

LLANTRISANT (Exc) TO COWBRIDGE
ABERTHAW BRANCH
Cowbridge Railway -
Taff Vale Railway (01/07/1889) -
Great Western Railway (01/01/1922)
(Llantrisant to Cowbridge old station)
Cowbridge & Aberthaw Railway -
Taff Vale Railway (01/01/1895) -
Great Western Railway (01/01/1922)
(Cowbridge station)
ACT: 29/07/1862 (Llantrisant to Cowbridge old station)
ACT: 12/08/1889 (Cowbridge)
OP: 18/09/1865 (Llantrisant to Cowbridge old station)
OPG: 01/10/1892 (Cowbridge)
OG: 08/02/1865 (Llantrisant to Cowbridge old station)
CP: 24/11/1951
CG: 01/02/1965 (Public Goods only) (Llantrisant to Cowbridge)
CG: 1946 (line through Cowbridge)

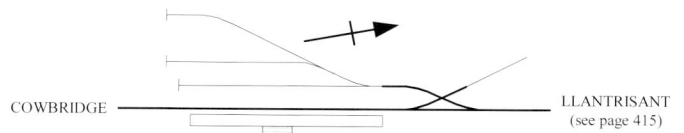

SOUTH WALES MAP

LLANHARRY
1414

1414   **LLANHARRY**   **[CR]**
OP: 02/03/1891   Photo: N. 1961
CP: 24/11/1951   R.J.Leonard

1415   **YSTRADOWEN**   **[CR]**
OP: 18/09/1865   Photo: W. c.1910
CP: 24/11/1951   LOSA

YSTRADOWEN
1415

1416   **TRERHYNGYLL & MAENDY**   **[CR]**
OP: 01/05/1905   Photo: N. 1960
CP: 24/11/1951   R.J.Leonard

TRERHYNGYLL
& MAENDY
1416

1417   **COWBRIDGE**   **[C&AR]**
OP: 01/10/1892   Photo: N. c.1950
CP: 24/11/1951   W.A.Camwell

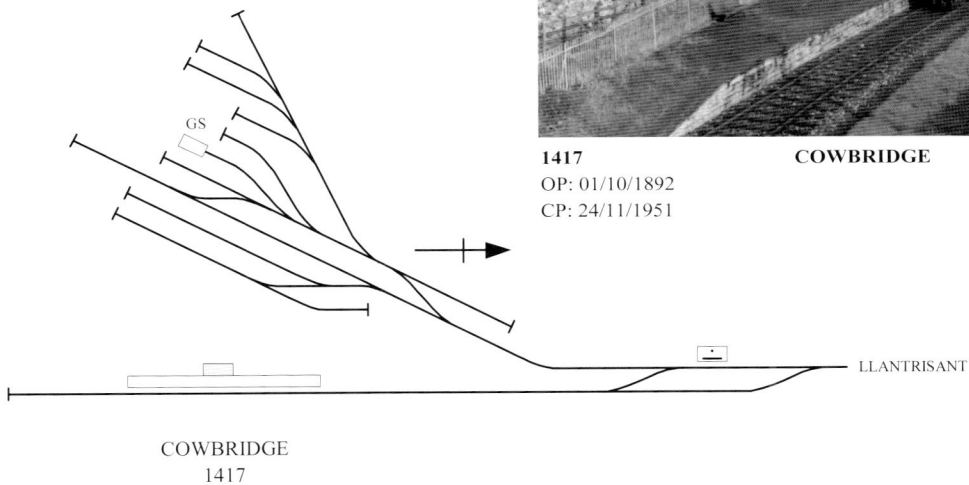

COWBRIDGE
1417

BRIDGEND (Exc) TO BARRY (Exc)
COWBRIDGE ROAD JUNCTION TO BRIDGEND,
VALE OF GLAMORGAN LINE
Vale of Glamorgan Railway -
Great Western Railway (01/01/1922)
ACT: 26/08/1889
ACT: 20/06/1895 (Bridgend to Cowbridge Road Junction)
OP: 01/12/1897
OG: 01/12/1897
CP: 13/06/1964 (Local Services only)
CG: OPEN

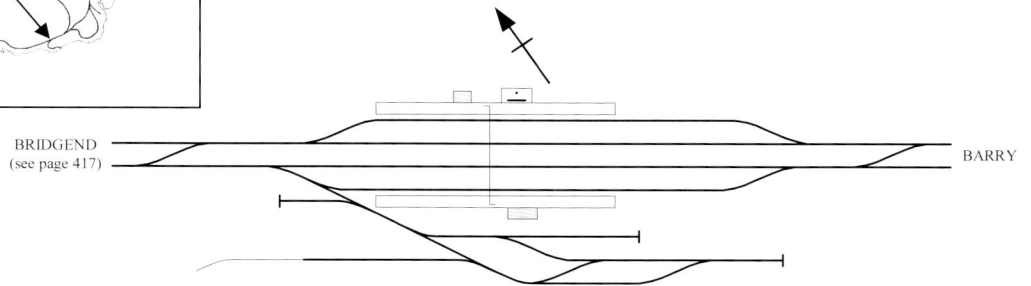

BRIDGEND
(see page 417)

BARRY

SOUTHERNDOWN
ROAD
1418

1418   **SOUTHERNDOWN ROAD**   **[VofGR]**
OP: 01/12/1897   Photo: SE. 1958
CP: 21/10/1961   Stations U.K.

BRIDGEND   BARRY

LLANDOW HALT
1419

1419   **LLANDOW HALT**   **[VofGR]**
OP: 01/05/1915   Photo: N. 1962
CP: 13/06/1964   M.Hale

BRIDGEND   BARRY

LLANDOW (WICK
ROAD) HALT
1420

1420   **LLANDOW (WICK ROAD) HALT**   **[VofGR]**
OP: 19/04/1943   Photo: N. 1958
CP: 13/06/1964   Stations U.K.

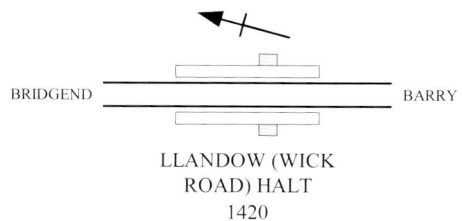

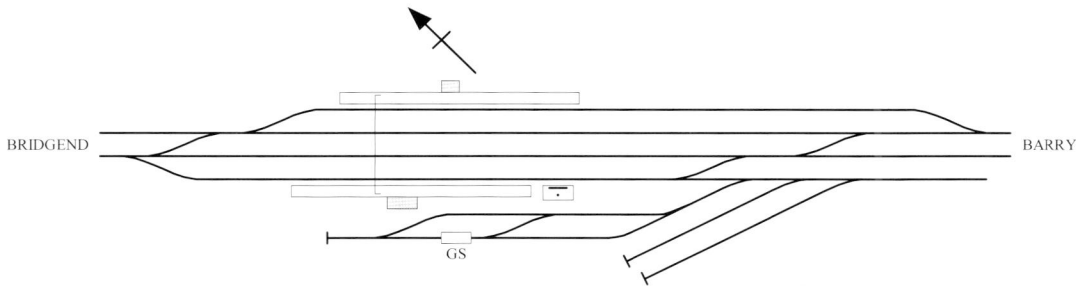

LLANTWIT MAJOR
1421

1421　　　**LLANTWIT MAJOR**　　　**[VofGR]**
OP: 01/12/1897　　　Photo: SE. 1961
CP: 13/06/1964　　　　　　　M.Hale

1422　　　**ST. ATHAN**　　　**[VofGR]**
OP: 01/09/1939　　　Photo: SE. 1958
CP: 13/06/1964　　　Stations U.K.

ST. ATHAN
1422

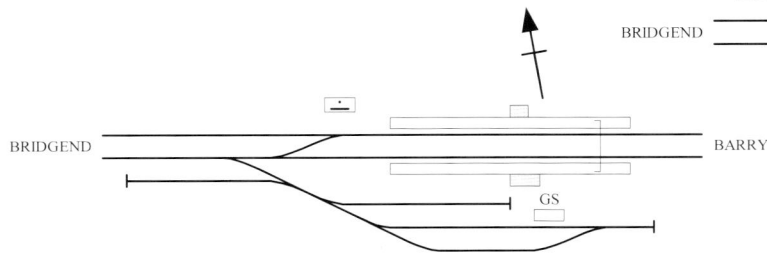

GILESTON
1423

1423　　　**GILESTON**　　　**[VofGR]**
OP: 01/12/1897　　　Photo: E. 1958
CP: 13/06/1964　　　Stations U.K.

1424　　　**ABERTHAW**　　　**[VofGR]**
OP: 01/12/1897　　　Photo: SE. 1958
CP: 13/06/1964　　　Stations U.K.

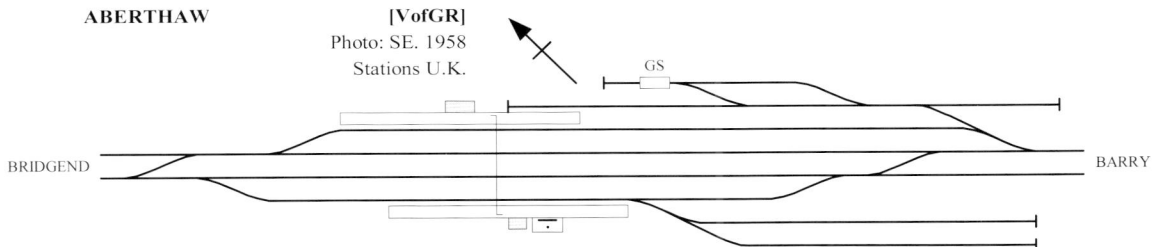

ABERTHAW
1424

RHOOSE
1425

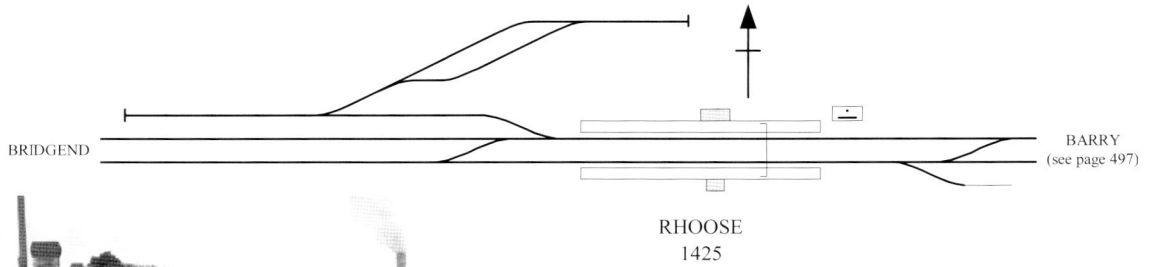

1425 **RHOOSE** **[VofGR]**
OP: 01/12/1897
CP: 13/06/1964
Photo: E. 1958
Stations U.K.

SOUTH WALES
MAP

BARRY PIER TO TREHAFOD (Exc)
BARRY LINE, CADOXTON & TREHAFOD LINE
Barry Railway -
Great Western Railway (01/01/1922)
ACT: 17/08/1896 (Barry Pier to Barry Island)
ACT: 14/08/1884 (Barry Island to Trehafod Junction)
OP: 27/06/1889 (Barry Pier to Barry Island)
OP: 03/08/1896 (Barry Island to Barry)
OP: 08/02/1889 (Barry to Barry Docks)
OP: 20/12/1888 (Barry Docks to Cadoxton)
OP: 16/03/1896 (Cadoxton to Trehafod)
OG: 27/01/1897 (Barry Island to Barry)
OG: 13/05/1889 (Barry to Trehafod)
CP: 18/10/1971 (Barry Pier to Barry Island)
CP: 10/09/1962 (Cadoxton to Tonteg Halt)
CP: 10/07/1930 (Tonteg Halt to Trehafod)
CG: 17/06/1963 (Cadoxton to Tonteg Halt)
CG: 06/1951 (Tonteg Halt to Maesycoed Street Goods)
CG: 04/06/1956 (Maesycoed Street Goods to Trehafod)

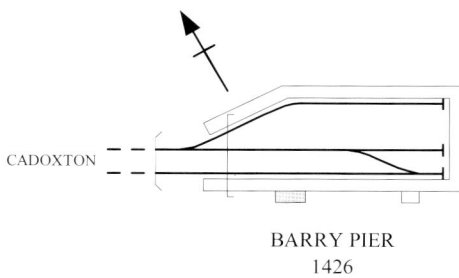

BARRY PIER
1426

1426 **BARRY PIER** **[BR]**
OP: 27/06/1899
CP: 11/10/1971 (Excursion train)
Photo: E. 1957
Stations U.K.

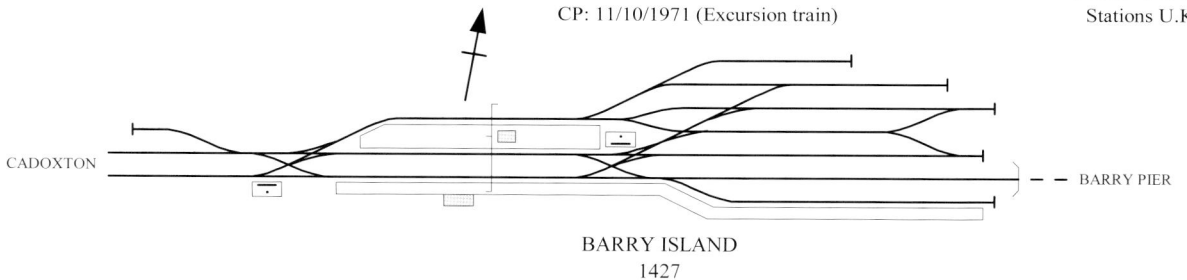

BARRY ISLAND
1427

1427
OP: 03/08/1896
CP: OPEN

BARRY ISLAND [BR]

Photo: E. 1957
R.K.Blencowe

1427

BARRY ISLAND [BR]

Photo: E. 1950
P.Garland

BARRY
1428

CADOXTON

CADOXTON

BARRY PIER

BRIDGEND
(see page 496)

BRIDGEND
(see page 496)

1428
OP: 08/02/1889
CP: OPEN

BARRY [BR]

Photo: NE. 1953
R.C.Riley

1429
OP: 20/12/1888
CP: OPEN

BARRY DOCKS [BR]

Photo: W. c.1962
LOSA

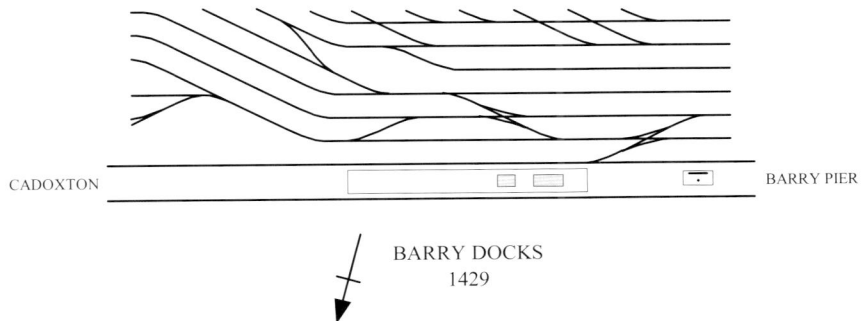

CADOXTON

BARRY PIER

BARRY DOCKS
1429

CARDIFF
(see page 501)

TREHAFOD

BARRY PIER

CADOXTON
1430

1430   **CADOXTON**   **[BR]**
OP: 20/12/1888
CP: OPEN
Photo: NE. 1958
Stations U.K.

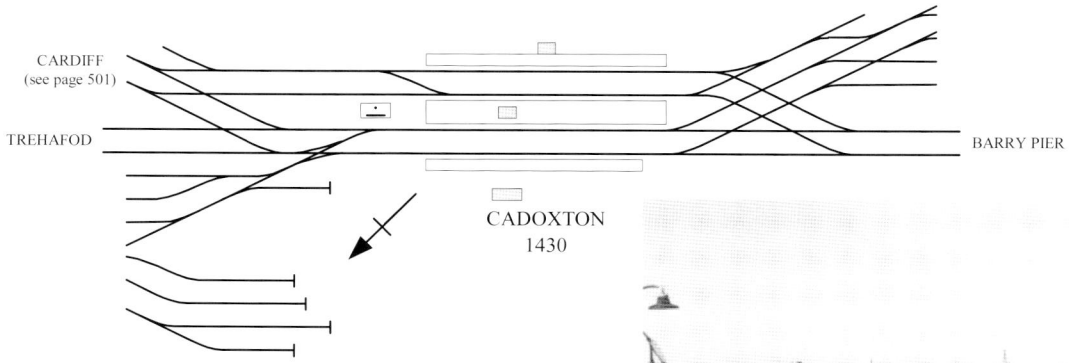

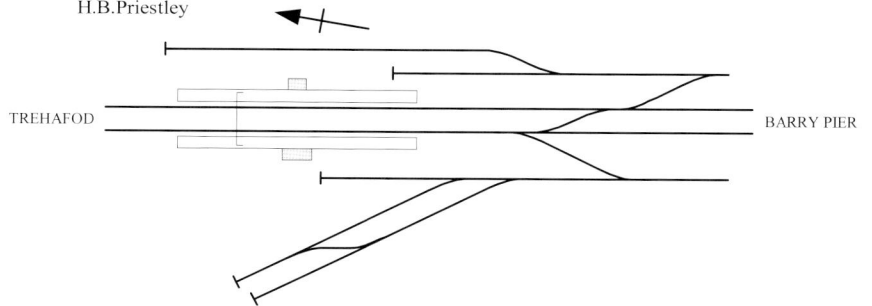

1431   **WENVOE**   **[BR]**
OP: 16/03/1896
CP: 09/09/1962
Photo: S. 1927
H.B.Priestley

TREHAFOD

BARRY PIER

WENVOE
1431

TREHAFOD

BARRY PIER

CREIGIAU
1432

1432   **CREIGIAU**   **[BR]**
OP: 16/03/1896
CP: 09/09/1962
Photo: N. 1959
R.M.Casserley

TREHAFOD

GS

BARRY PIER

EFAIL ISAF
1433

1433
OP: 16/03/1896
CP: 09/09/1962

EFAIL ISAF   **[BR]**

Photo: NE. 1958
Stations U.K.

1433   **EFAIL ISAF**   **[BR]**

Photo: S. 1959
R.M.Casserley

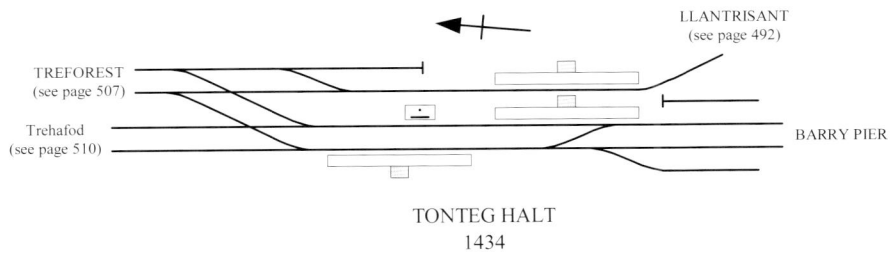

LLANTRISANT
(see page 492)

TREFOREST
(see page 507)

Trehafod
(see page 510)

BARRY PIER

TONTEG HALT
1434

1434
OP: 05/05/1930
CP: 09/09/1962

TONTEG HALT   **[BR, GWR]**

Photo: S. 1954
unknown

1434   **TONTEG HALT**   **[BR, GWR]**

Photo: S. 1958
Stations U.K.

Cadoxton Junction TO Cogan Junction
BARRY LINE
Barry Railway -
Great Western Railway (01/01/1922)
ACT: 31/07/1885
OP: 20/12/1888
OG: 13/05/1889
CP: OPEN
CG: OPEN

CADOXTON
(see page 498)

GRANGETOWN

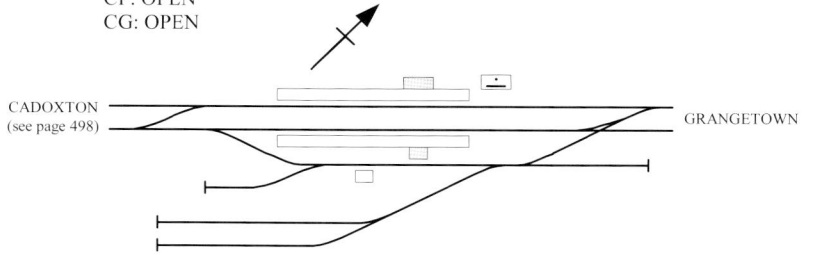

DINAS POWIS
1435

1435	**DINAS POWIS**	**[BR]**
OP: 20/12/1888		Photo: NE. 1956
CP: OPEN		HMRS (AEP834)

1436	**COGAN**	**[BR]**
OP: 20/12/1888		Photo: N. c.1960
CP: OPEN		LOSA

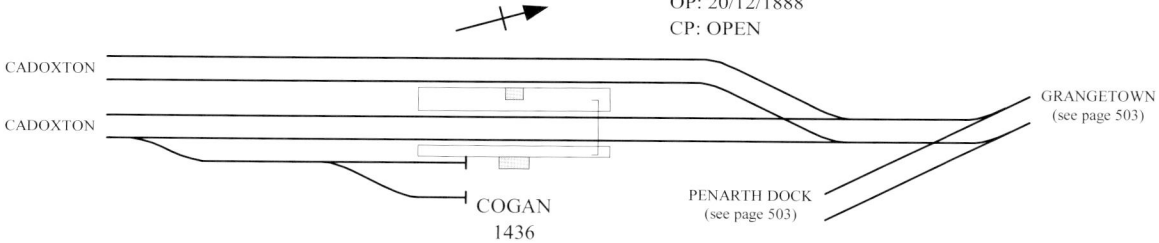

CADOXTON

CADOXTON

COGAN
1436

GRANGETOWN
(see page 503)

PENARTH DOCK
(see page 503)

CADOXTON (Exc) TO NINIAN PARK HALT
PENARTH BRANCH, BARRY LINE, PENARTH CURVE
Cardiff Penarth & Barry Junction Railway -
Taff Vale Railway (01/07/1889) -
Great Western Railway (01/01/1922)
(Biglis Junction to Penarth)
Penarth Extension Railway -
Great Western Railway (01/01/1923)
(Penarth to Penarth Dock)
Penarth Harbour Dock & Railway -
Leased to Taff Vale Railway (22/06/1863) -
Great Western Railway (01/01/1922)
(Penarth Dock to Radyr)
ACT: 06/08/1885 (Biglis Junction to Penarth)
ACT: 11/08/1876 (Penarth to Llandough Junction)
ACT: 21/07/1856 (Llandough Junction to Radyr Junction)
OP: 08/07/1889 (Biglis Junction to Sully)
OP: 24/12/1888 (Sully to Lavernock)
OP: 01/12/1887 (Lavernock to Penarth)
OP: 20/02/1878 (Penarth to Cardiff (General))
OP: 02/11/1912 (Ninian Park Halt)
OG: 08/07/1889 (Biglis Junction to Sully)
OG: 05/11/1888 (Sully to Lavernock)
OG: 01/12/1887 (Lavernock to Penarth)
OG: 01/01/1878 (Penarth to Llandough Junction)
OG: 18/07/1859 (Penarth Dock to Radyr Junction)
CP: 04/05/1968 (Biglis Junctiom to Penarth)
CG: 07/10/1963 (Biglis Junction to Penarth)

1437	**SULLY**	**[CP&BJR]**
OP: 24/12/1888		Photo: NW. 1962
CP: 04/05/1968		M.Hale

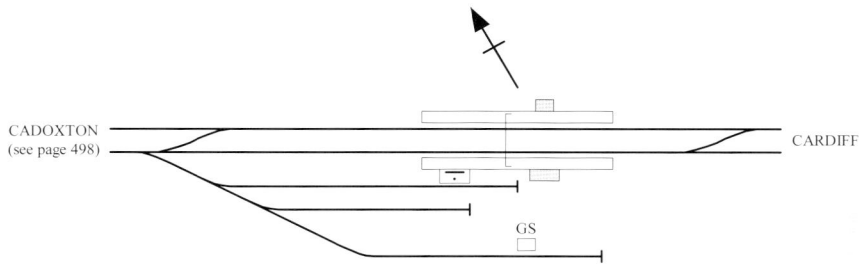

SULLY
1437

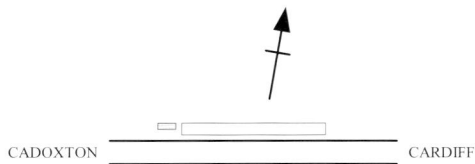

SWANBRIDGE
HALT
1438

1438　　　　**SWANBRIDGE HALT**　　　　**[CP&BJR]**
OP: 06/1906　　　　　　　　　　　　Photo: E. c.1960
CP: 04/05/1968　　　　　　　　　　　　　　　LOSA

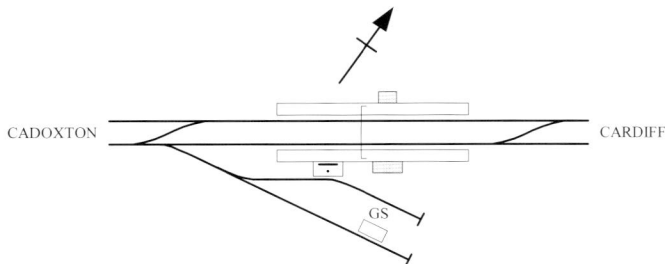

LAVERNOCK
1439

1439　　　　　**LAVERNOCK**　　　　　**[CP&BJR]**
OP: 01/12/1887　　　　　　　　　　Photo: NE. 1958
CP: 04/05/1968　　　　　　　　　　　Stations U.K.

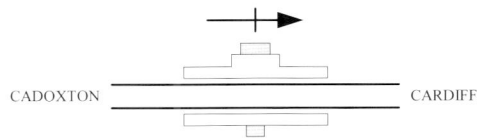

LOWER PENARTH
HALT
1440

1440　　　**LOWER PENARTH HALT**　　　**[CP&BJR]**
OP: 02/01/1897　　　　　　　　　　Photo: N. c.1920
CP: 14/06/1954　　　　　　　　　　　　　　　LOSA

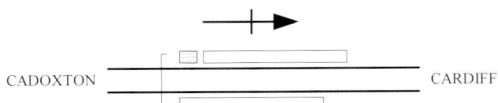

ALBERTA PLACE
HALT
1441

1441　　　　**ALBERTA PLACE HALT**　　　　**[CP&BJR]**
OP: 19/09/1904　　　　　　　　　　Photo: S. 1962
CP: 04/05/1968　　　　　　　　　　　　　　M.Hale

CADOXTON

CARDIFF

PENARTH
1442

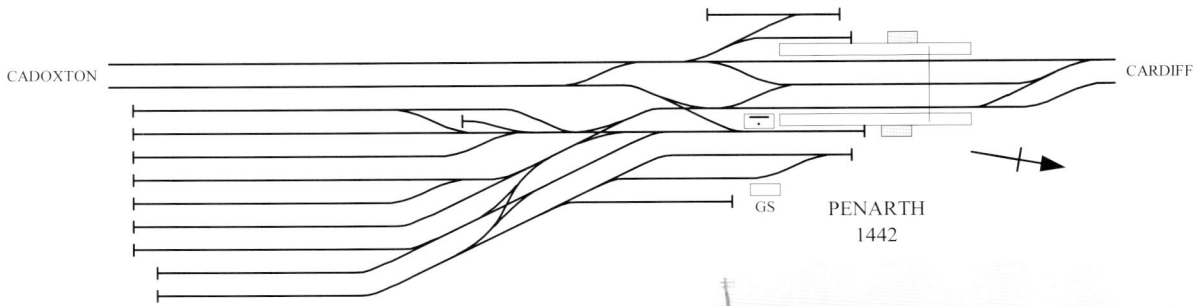

1442   **PENARTH**   **[PER]**
OP: 20/02/1878   Photo: N. c.1960
CP: OPEN   LOSA

1443   **DINGLE ROAD HALT**   **[PER]**
OP: 01/03/1904   Photo: SE. 1958
CP: OPEN   Stations U.K.

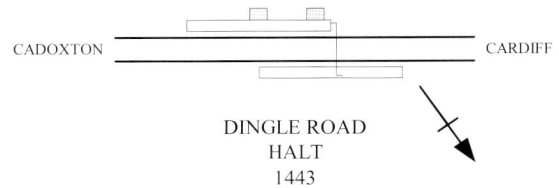

CADOXTON

CARDIFF

DINGLE ROAD
HALT
1443

CADOXTON

CARDIFF

Penarth Dock

PENARTH DOCK
1444

1444   **PENARTH DOCK**   **[PER]**
OP: 20/02/1878   Photo: NW. 1957
CP: 30/12/1961   M.Hale

1444   **PENARTH DOCK**   **[PER]**
Photo: SE. 1958
Stations U.K.

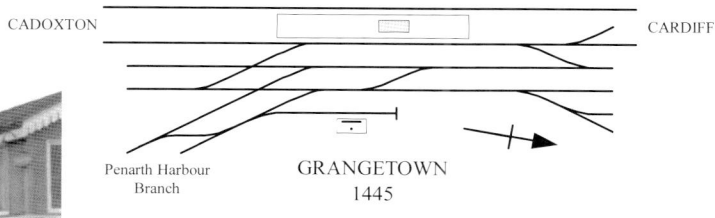

1445   **GRANGETOWN**   **[PHD&R]**
OP: 1904   Photo: S. 1964
CP: OPEN   Stations U.K.

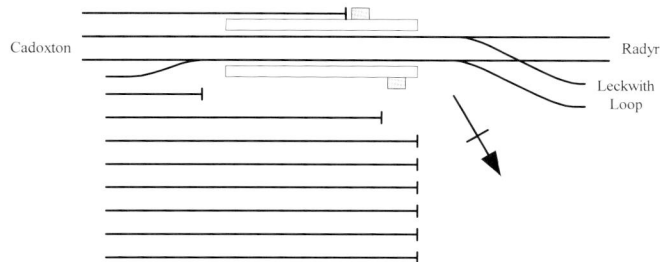

CADOXTON

CARDIFF

Penarth Harbour
Branch

GRANGETOWN
1445

Cadoxton

Radyr

Leckwith
Loop

NINIAN PARK
HALT
1446

1446   **NINIAN PARK HALT**   **[PHD&R]**
OP: 02/11/1912   Photo: NW. 1962
CP: OPEN   M.Hale

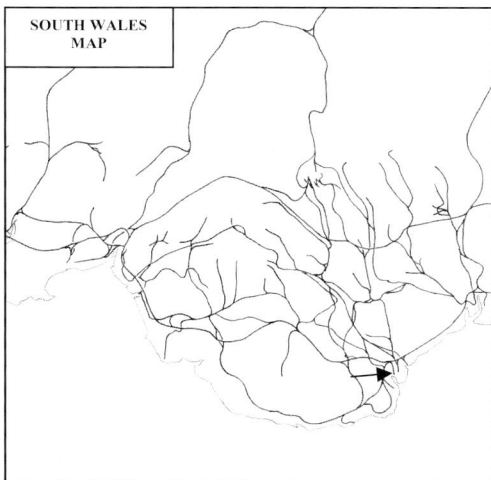

SOUTH WALES
MAP

CARDIFF (GENERAL) TO CARDIFF (CLARENCE ROAD)
RIVERSIDE BRANCH
Great Western Railway

ACT: 06/08/1880
OP: 02/04/1894
OG: 02/04/1894
CP: 14/03/1964
CG: 08/07/1968

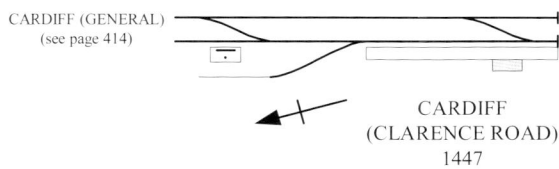

CARDIFF (GENERAL)
(see page 414)

CARDIFF
(CLARENCE ROAD)
1447

1447   **CARDIFF (CLARENCE ROAD)**   **[GWR]**
OP: 02/04/1894   Photo: N. 1949
CP: 14/03/1964   R.Carpenter

1447   **CARDIFF (CLARENCE ROAD)**   **[GWR]**
Photo: N. 1963
P.Garland

CARDIFF (BUTE ROAD) TO MERTHYR
CARDIFF AND MERTHYR LINE, MERTHYR BRANCH
Taff Vale Railway -
Great Western Railway (01/01/1922)
(Cardiff (Bute Road) to Brandy Bridge Junction (Merthyr))
Great Western & Taff Vale Joint Railway -
Great Western Railway (01/01/1922)
(Brandy Bridge Junction to Mardy Junction)
Vale of Neath Railway -
Great Western Railway (01/02/1865)
(Mardy Junction to Merthyr)
ACT: 21/06/1836 (Cardiff (Bute Road) to Brandy Bridge Junc.)
ACT: 15/07/1867 (Brandy Bridge Junction to Mardy Junction)
ACT: 03/08/1846 (Mardy Junction to Merthyr)
OPG: 09/10/1840 (Cardiff (Bute Road) to Abercynon)
OPG: 12/04/1841 (Abercynon to Merthyr (Plymouth Street))
OPG: 01/08/1877 (Brandy Bridge Junction to Mardy Junction)
OPG: 02/11/1853 (Mardy Junction to Merthyr (High Street))
CP: OPEN
CG: OPEN

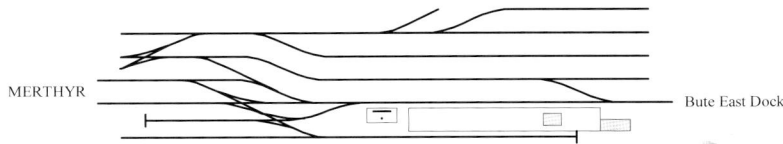

MERTHYR

Bute East Dock

CARDIFF
(BUTE ROAD)
1448

1448   **CARDIFF (BUTE ROAD)**   **[TVR]**
OP: 1929   Photo: N. 1963
CP: OPEN   M.Hale

CAERPHILLY
(see page 520)

MERTHYR

MERTHYR

CARDIFF
(BUTE ROAD)

CARDIFF
(QUEEN STREET)
1449

1449   **CARDIFF (QUEEN STREET)**   **[TVR]**
OP: 09/04/1840   Photo: N. 1963
CP: OPEN   P.Garland

1449   **CARDIFF (QUEEN STREET)**   **[TVR]**
Photo: S. c.1960
LOSA

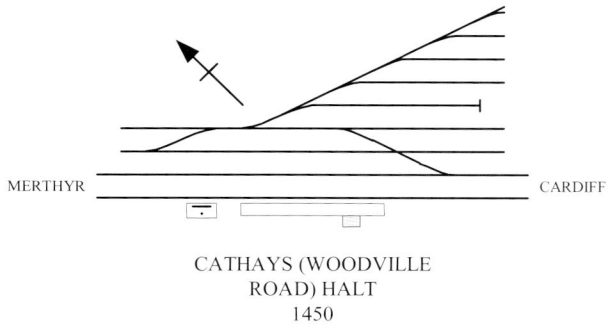

CATHAYS (WOODVILLE
ROAD) HALT
1450

1450   CATHAYS (WOODVILLE ROAD) HALT   [TVR]
OP: 12/07/1906   Photo: NW. 1957
CP: 13/09/1958   Stations U.K.

1451   MAINDY (NORTH ROAD) HALT   [TVR]
OP: 01/12/1906   Photo: S. 1955
CP: 13/09/1958   R.K.Blencowe

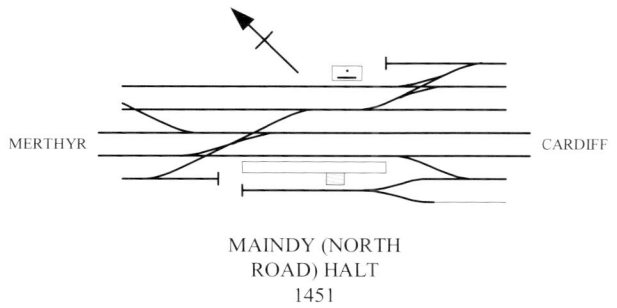

MAINDY (NORTH
ROAD) HALT
1451

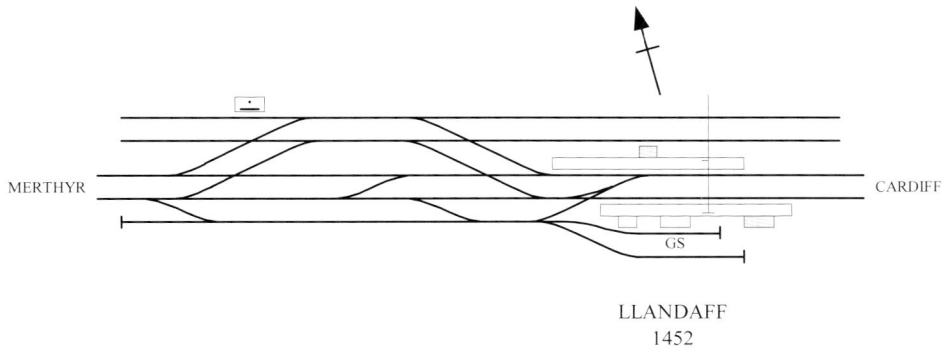

LLANDAFF
1452

1452   LLANDAFF   [TVR]
OP: 09/10/1840   Photo: W. 1959
CP: OPEN   Stations U.K.

1452   LLANDAFF   [TVR]
                                                  Photo: E. c.1960
                                                  LOSA

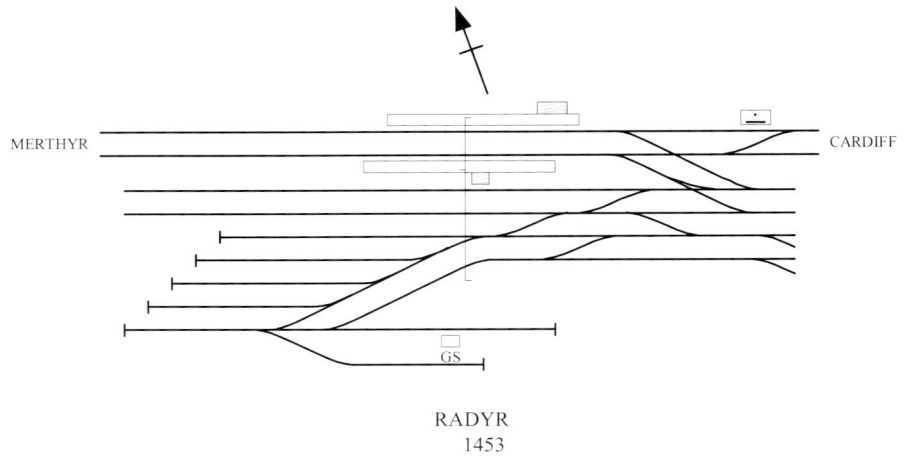

RADYR
1453

1453   **RADYR**   **[TVR]**
OP: 01/06/1883   Photo: E. 1951
CP: OPEN   P.Garland

1453   **RADYR**   **[TVR]**
       Photo: W. c.1958
       LOSA

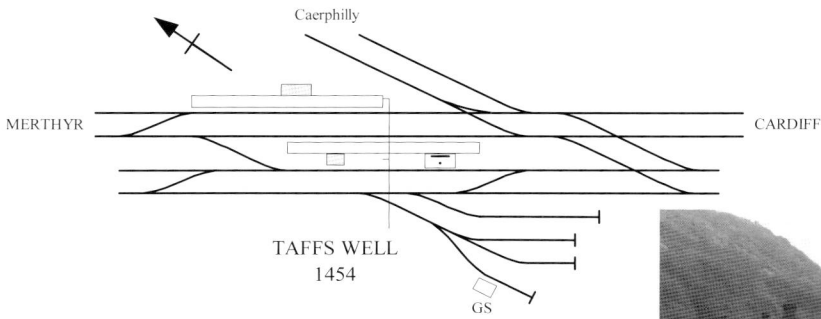

TAFFS WELL
1454

1454   **TAFFS WELL**   **[TVR]**
OP: 22/06/1863   Photo: SE. c.1960
CP: OPEN   LOSA

1455   **TREFOREST ESTATE**   **[TVR]**
OP: 05/01/1942   Photo: NW. 1958
CP: OPEN   Stations U.K.

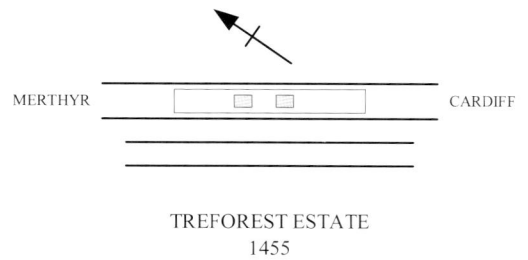

TREFOREST ESTATE
1455

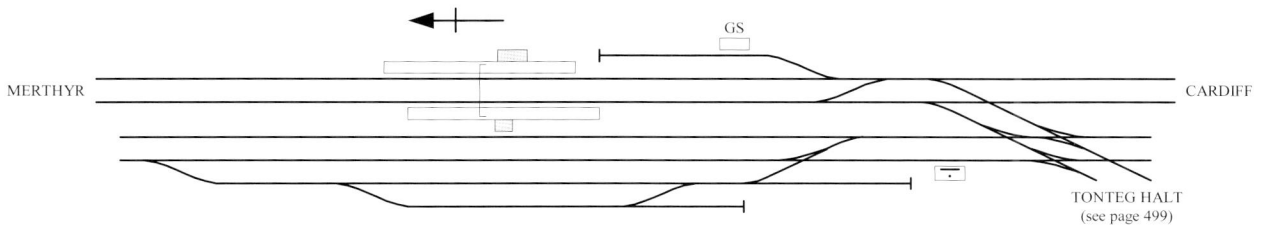

TREFOREST
1456

1456   **TREFOREST**   **[TVR]**
OP: c.1885   Photo: N. 1959
CP: OPEN   Stations U.K.

1457   **PONTYPRIDD**   **[TVR]**
OP: 09/10/1840   Photo: NW. 1959
CP: OPEN   Stations U.K.

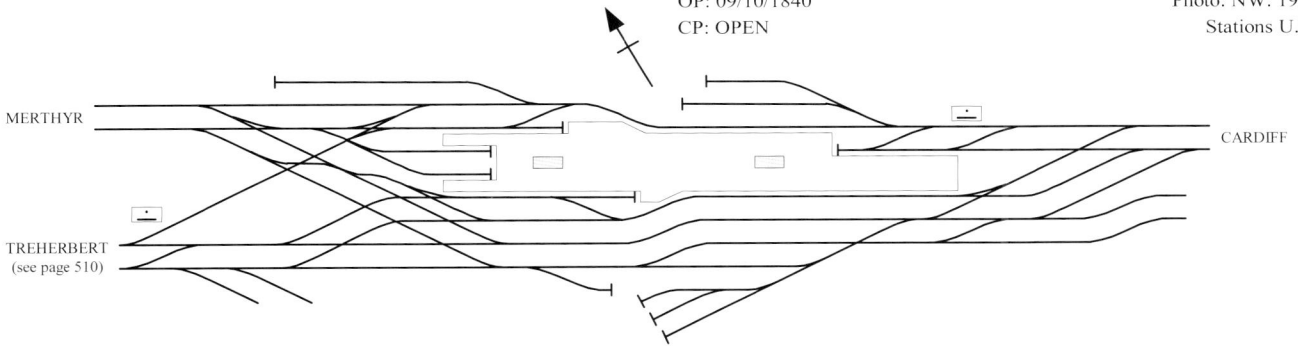

PONTYPRIDD
1457

1457   **PONTYPRIDD**   **[TVR]**
Photo: SE. 1958
Stations U.K.

1457   **PONTYPRIDD**   **[TVR]**
Photo: SE. c.1960
LOSA

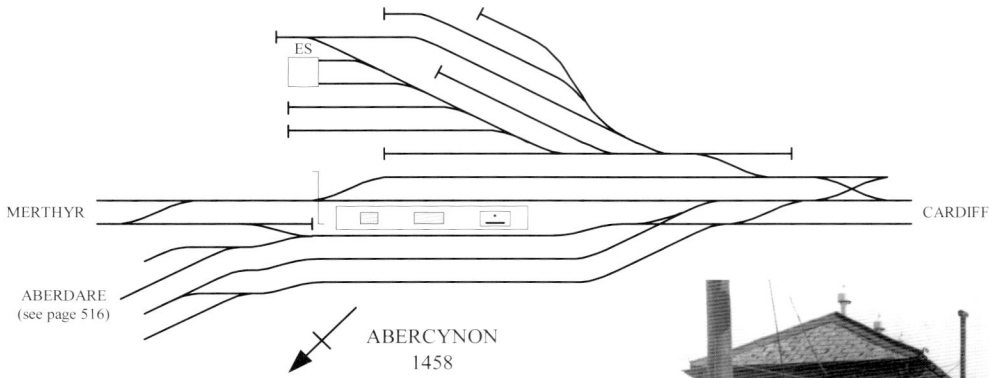

ABERCYNON
1458

1458   **ABERCYNON**   **[TVR]**
OP: 1875   Photo: NE. c.1958
CP: OPEN   LOSA

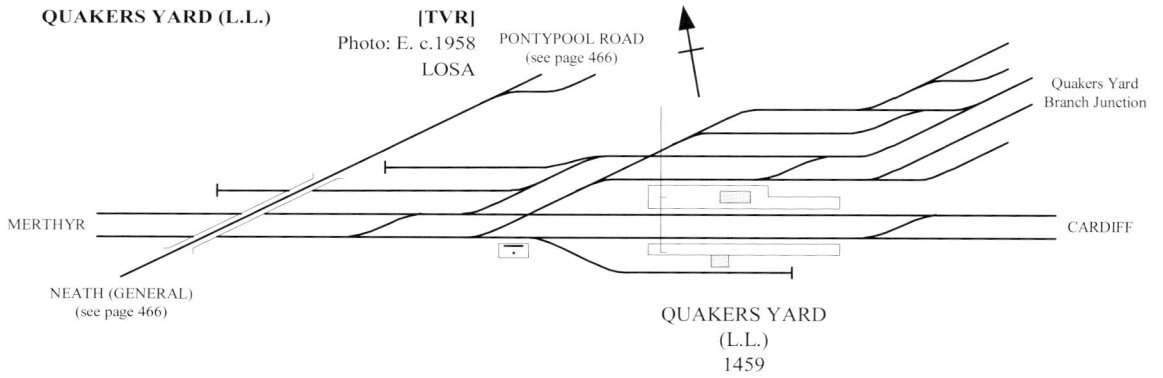

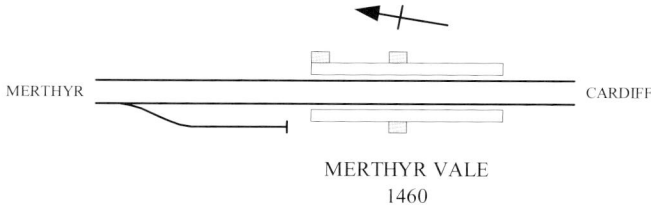

1459   **QUAKERS YARD (L.L.)**   **[TVR]**
OP: 09/01/1858   Photo: E. c.1958
CP: OPEN   LOSA

QUAKERS YARD
(L.L.)
1459

MERTHYR VALE
1460

1460   **MERTHYR VALE**   **[TVR]**
OP: 01/06/1883   Photo: S. 1964
CP: OPEN   Stations U.K.

1460   **MERTHYR VALE**   **[TVR]**
       Photo: N. c.1960
       LOSA

TROEDYRHIW
1461

1461   **TROEDYRHIW**   **[TVR]**
OP: 12/04/1841   Photo: S. c.1960
CP: OPEN   LOSA

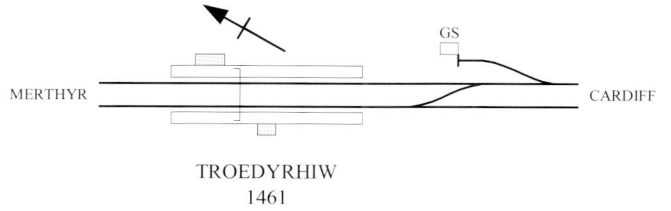

1461   **TROEDYRHIW**   **[TVR]**
Photo: N. c.1960
LOSA

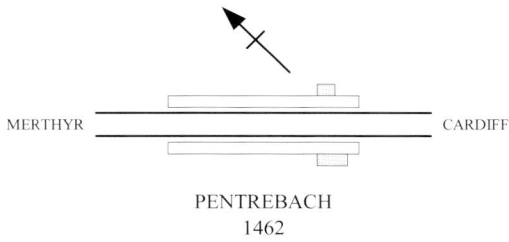

PENTREBACH
1462

1462   **PENTREBACH**   **[TVR]**
OP: 01/08/1886   Photo: NW. 1958
CP: OPEN   Stations U.K.

1462   **PENTREBACH**   **[TVR]**
Photo: NW. 1958
M.Hale

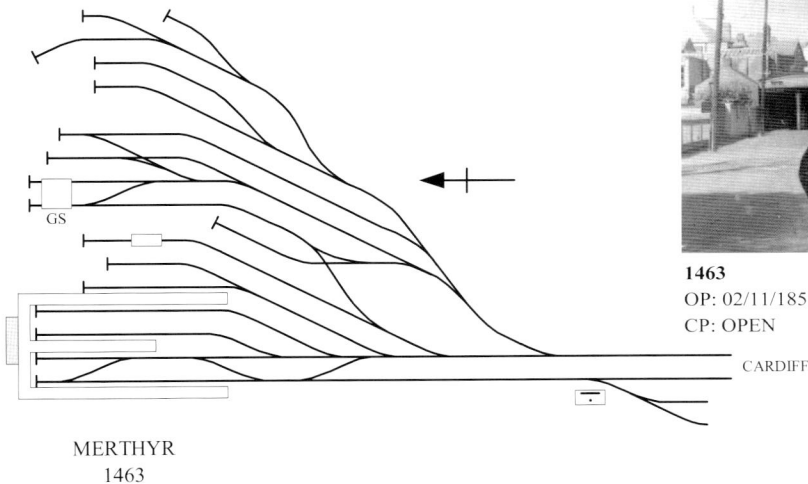

1463   **MERTHYR**   **[VNR]**
OP: 02/11/1853   Photo: N. 1950
CP: OPEN   LOSA

MERTHYR
1463

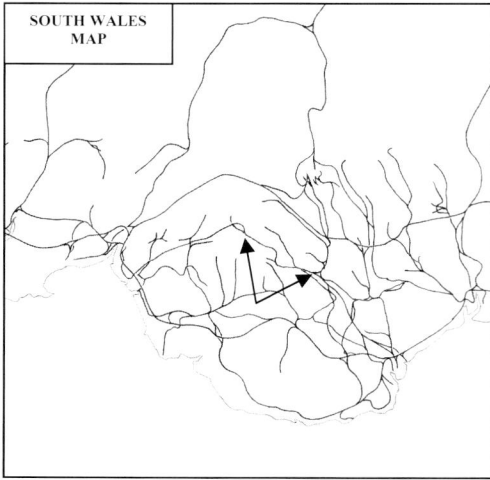

PONTYPRIDD (Exc) TO TREHERBERT
TREHERBERT BRANCH
Taff Vale Railway -
Great Western Railway (01/01/1922)
ACT: 21/06/1836 (Pontypridd to Dinas (Rhondda))
ACT: 26/08/1846 (Dinas (Rhondda) to Treherbert)
OP: 07/01/1863
OG: 06/1841 (Pontypridd to Dinas (Rhondda))
OG: 07/08/1856 (Dinas (Rhondda) to Treherbert)
CP: OPEN
CG: OPEN

SOUTH WALES
MAP

TREHERBERT

PONTYPRIDD
(see page 507)

TREHAFOD
1464

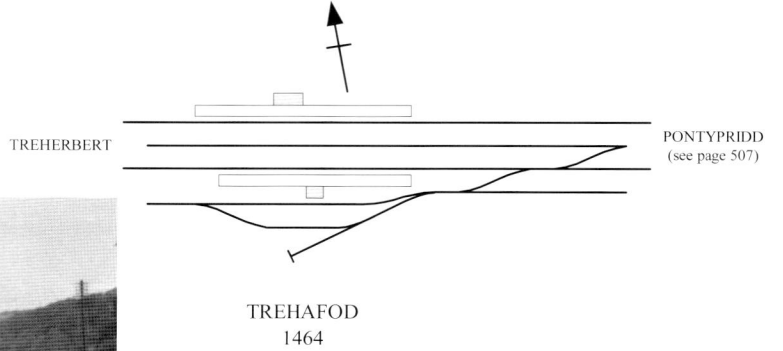

1464   **TREHAFOD**   **[TVR]**
OP: 17/10/1892
CP: OPEN
Photo: W. 1958
Stations U.K.

1465   **PORTH**   **[TVR]**
OP: 01/07/1876
CP: OPEN
Photo: SE. 1963
P.Garland

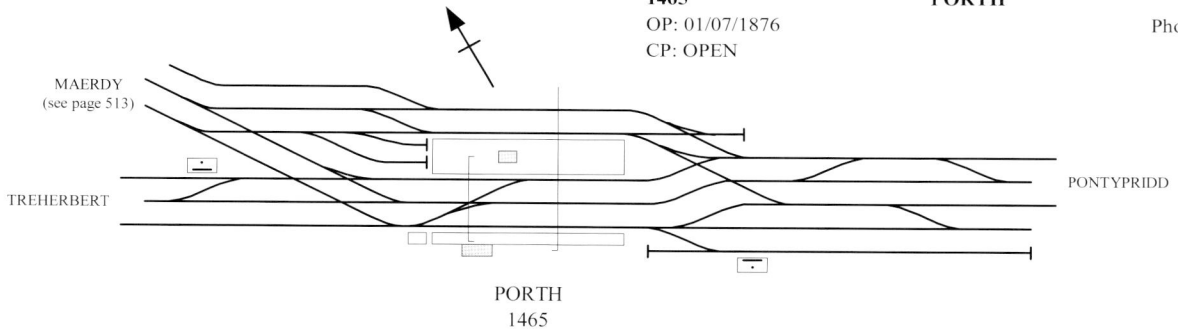

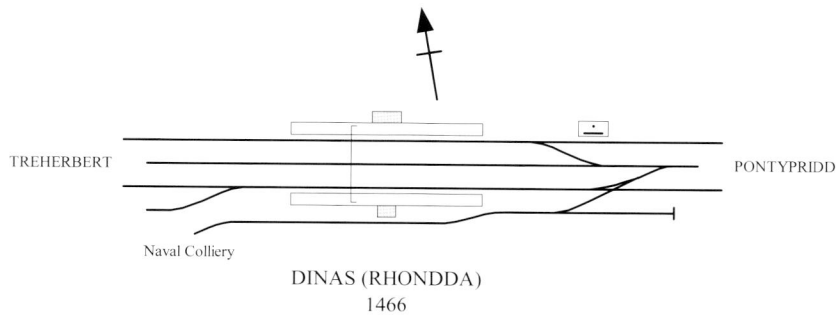

MAERDY
(see page 513)

TREHERBERT

PONTYPRIDD

PORTH
1465

TREHERBERT

PONTYPRIDD

Naval Colliery

DINAS (RHONDDA)
1466

1466   **DINAS (RHONDDA)**   **[TVR]**
OP: 02/08/1886   Photo: W. 1959
CP: OPEN   M.Hale

1467   **TONYPANDY & TREALAW**   **[TVR]**
OP: 09/03/1908   Photo: W. 1958
CP: OPEN   Stations U.K.

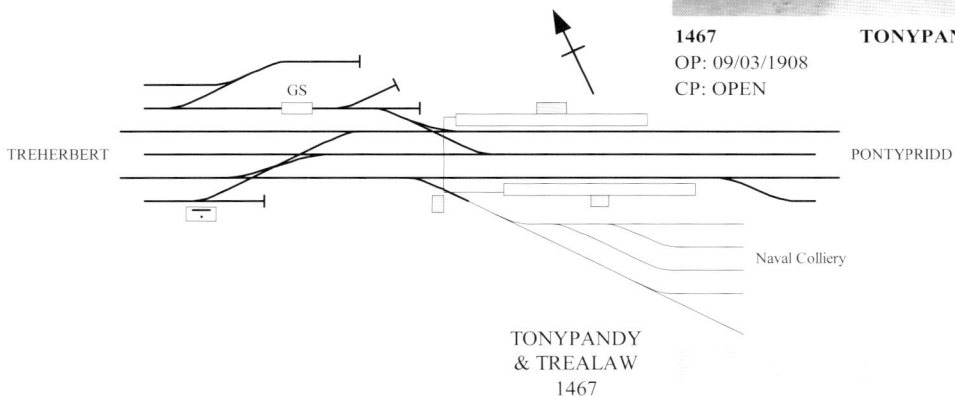

TREHERBERT   GS   PONTYPRIDD

Naval Colliery

TONYPANDY
& TREALAW
1467

1467   **TONYPANDY & TREALAW**   **[TVR]**
Photo: W. 1958
Stations U.K.

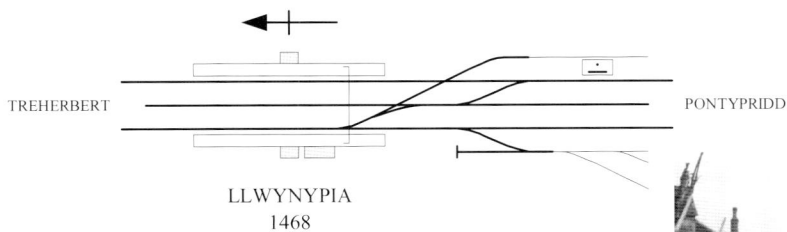

TREHERBERT   PONTYPRIDD

LLWYNYPIA
1468

1468   **LLWYNYPIA**   **[TVR]**
OP: 05/1871   Photo: S. 1959
CP: OPEN   M.Hale

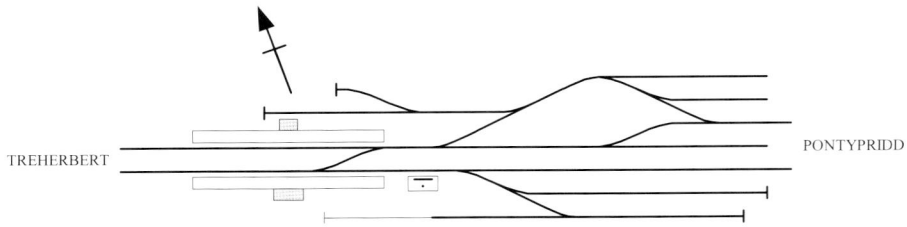

YSTRAD (RHONDDA)
1469

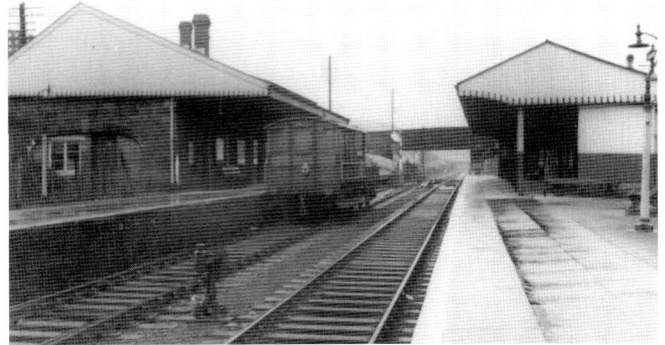

1470 **TREORCHY** **[TVR]**
OP: 03/03/1884 Photo: SE. 1954
CP: OPEN LOSA

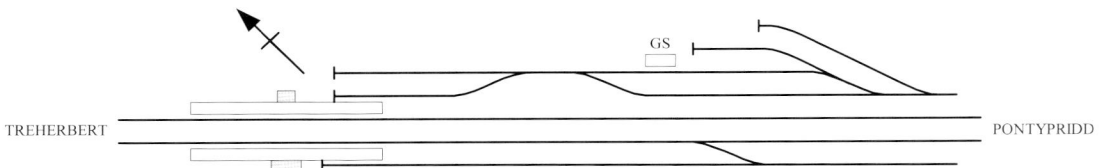

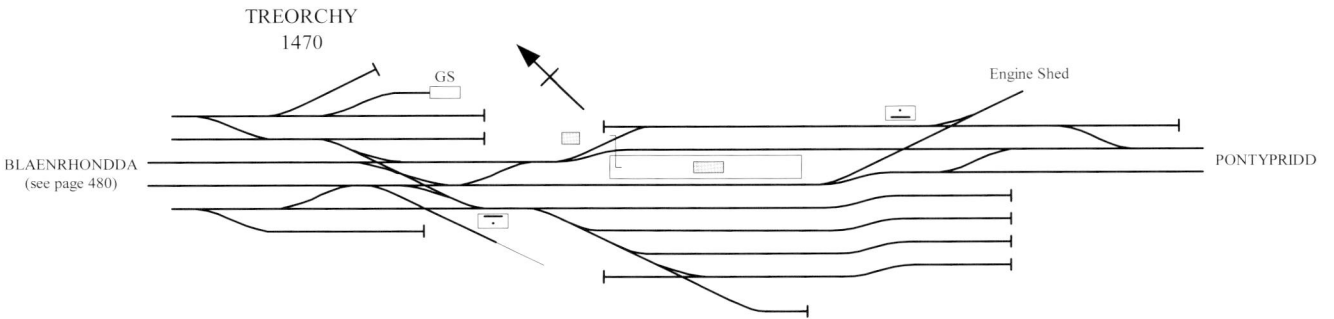

1469 **YSTRAD (RHONDDA)** **[TVR]**
OP: 12/01/1863 Photo: NW. c.1960
CP: OPEN LOSA

TREORCHY
1470

TREHERBERT
1471

1471 **TREHERBERT** **[TVR]**
OP: 17/10/1901 Photo: SE. 1954
CP: OPEN LOSA

1471 **TREHERBERT** **[TVR]**
Photo: SE. 1962
W.A.Brown

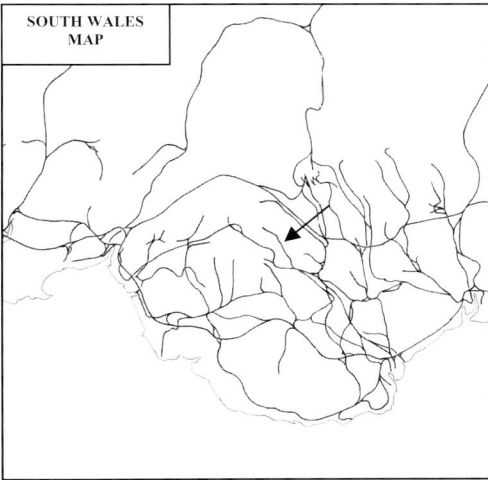
SOUTH WALES MAP

PORTH (Exc) TO MAERDY
MAERDY BRANCH
Taff Vale Railway -
Great Western Railway (01/01/1922)
ACT: 26/08/1846 (Porth to Ferndale)
ACT: 25/06/1886 (Purchase of Private line to Maerdy)
OP: 05/06/1876 (Porth to Ferndale)
OP: 18/06/1889 (Ferndale to Maerdy)
OG: 1849 (Porth to Ynyshir)
OG: 1856 (Ynyshir to Ferndale)
OG: 05/1877 (Ferndale to Maerdy as a Private line)
CP: 13/06/1964
CG: OPEN

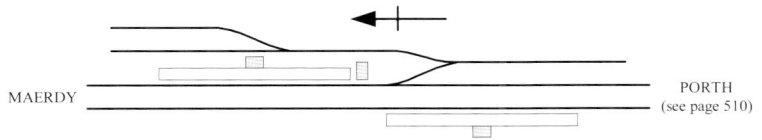

MAERDY

PORTH
(see page 510)

YNYSHIR
1472

1472	YNYSHIR	[TVR]
OP: 07/1885		Photo: S. 1963
CP: 13/06/1964		P.Garland

1472	YNYSHIR	[TVR]
		Photo: S. 1963
		P.Garland

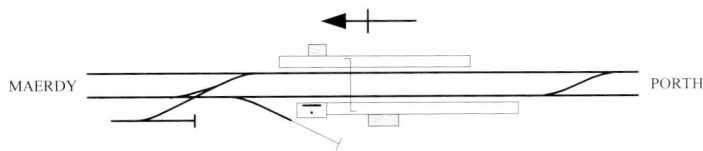

MAERDY

PORTH

TYLORSTOWN
1473

1473	TYLORSTOWN	[TVR]
OP: 24/05/1882		Photo: N. 1955
CP: 13/06/1964		R.K.Blencowe

1473	TYLORSTOWN	[TVR]
		Photo: S. 1963
		P.Garland

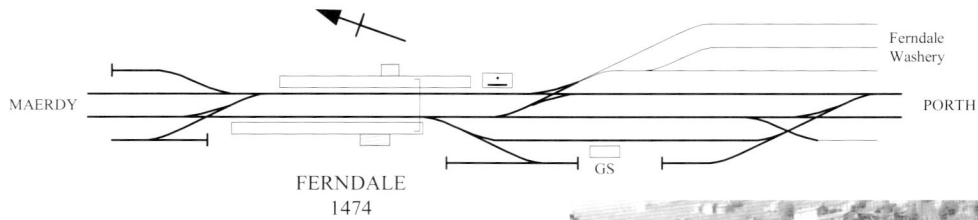

FERNDALE
1474

1475   **MAERDY**   **[TVR]**
OP: 18/06/1889
CP: 13/06/1964
Photo: N. 1956
C.Mowat

1474   **FERNDALE**   **[TVR]**
OP: 05/06/1876
CP: 13/06/1964
Photo: NW. c.1960
LOSA

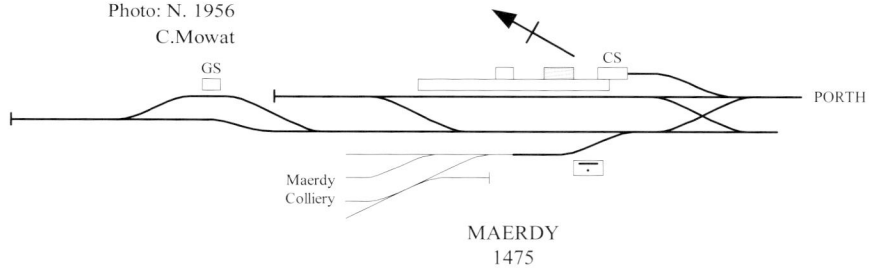

MAERDY
1475

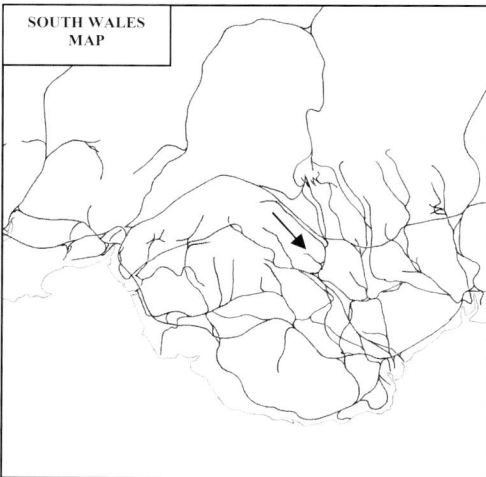

SOUTH WALES
MAP

PONTYPRIDD (Exc) TO OLD YNYSYBWL HALT
YNYSYBWL BRANCH
Taff Vale Railway -
Great Western Railway (01/01/1922)
ACT: 17/08/1894 (Clydach Court Jc. to Clydach Court Loop Jc.)
ACT: 21/07/1873 (from Stormstown Junction to end of Branch)
OP: 17/10/1904 (Clydach Court Jc. to Clydach Court Loop Jc.)
OP: 01/01/1890 (from Abercynon to Ynysybwl)
OP: 17/10/1904 (Ynysybwl to Old Ynysybwl Halt)
OG: 05/1900 (Clydach Court Jc. to Clydach Court Loop Jc.)
OG: 1886 (from Stormstown Junction to Mynachty Colliery)
CP: 26/07/1952 (including Ynysybwl Loop)
CG: 26/07/1952 (Clydach Court Jc. to Clydach Court Loop Jc.)
CG: 02/01/1959 (from Stormstown Jc. to Ynysybwl) (Public
            Goods only)
CG: 22/09/1949 (Ynysybwl to Mynachty Colliery)

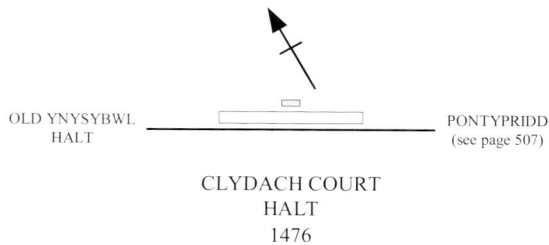

CLYDACH COURT
HALT
1476

1476   **CLYDACH COURT HALT**   **[TVR]**
OP: 10/1915
CP: 26/07/1952
Photo: SE. 1952
R.C.Riley

YNYSYBWL (NEW
ROAD) HALT
1477

1477   **YNYSYBWL (NEW ROAD) HALT**   **[TVR]**
OP: 06/07/1910   Photo: N. 1959
CP: 26/07/1952   M.Hale

ROBERTSTOWN
HALT
1478

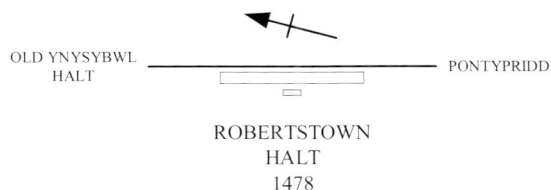

1478   **ROBERTSTOWN HALT**   **[TVR]**
OP: 17/10/1904   Sketch: W. c.1910
CP: 26/07/1952

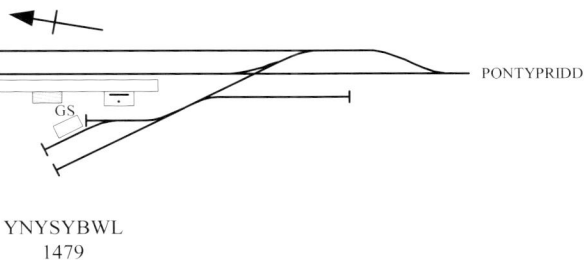

YNYSYBWL
1479

1479   **YNYSYBWL**   **[TVR]**
OP: 01/01/1890   Photo: S. 1952
CP: 26/07/1952   R.C.Riley

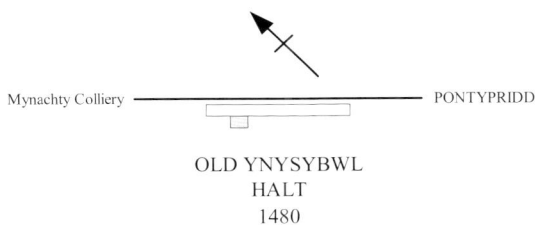

OLD YNYSYBWL
HALT
1480

1480   **OLD YNYSYBWL HALT**   **[TVR]**
OP: 17/10/1904   Sketch: NW. c.1947
CP: 26/07/1952

1480   **OLD YNYSYBWL HALT**   **[TVR]**
                                      Photo: SE. 1951
                                       H.C.Casserley

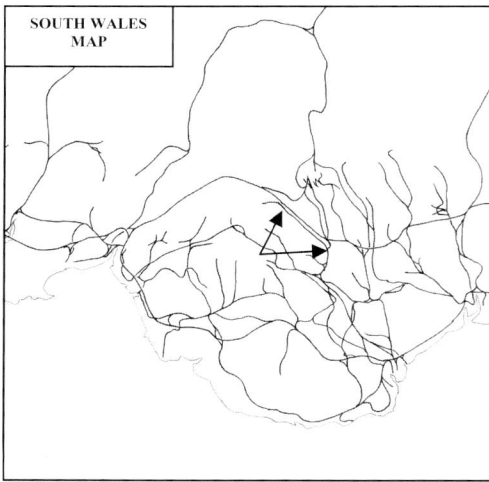

ABERCYNON (Exc) TO ABERDARE
ABERDARE BRANCH
Aberdare Railway -
Taff Vale Railway (30/06/1902) -
Great Western Railway (01/01/1922)
ACT: 31/07/1845
OP: 06/08/1846
OG: 06/08/1846
CP: 14/03/1964
CG: 03/08/1964 (Public Goods only)

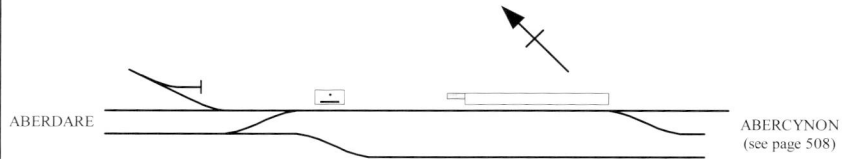

ABERDARE
ABERCYNON
(see page 508)

PONTCYNON
BRIDGE HALT
1481

1481	PONTCYNON BRIDGE HALT	[AberRly]
OP: 26/12/1904		Photo: SE. 1961
CP: 14/03/1964		Stations U.K.

1482	MATTHEWSTOWN HALT	[AberRly]
OP: 01/10/1914		Photo: W. 1958
CP: 14/03/1964		Stations U.K.

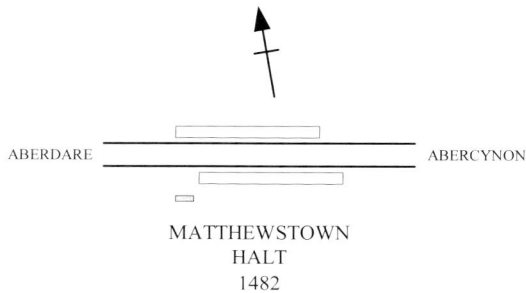

ABERDARE
ABERCYNON

MATTHEWSTOWN
HALT
1482

1483	PENRHIWCEIBER (L.L.)	[AberRly]
OP: 01/06/1883		Photo: NW. 1959
CP: 14/03/1964		H.C.Casserley

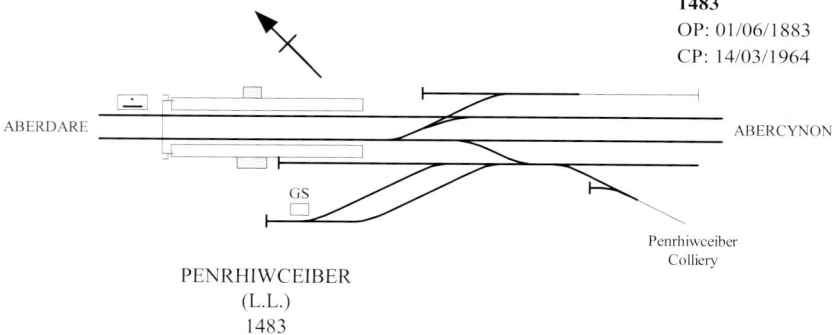

ABERDARE
ABERCYNON

GS

Penrhiwceiber
Colliery

PENRHIWCEIBER
(L.L.)
1483

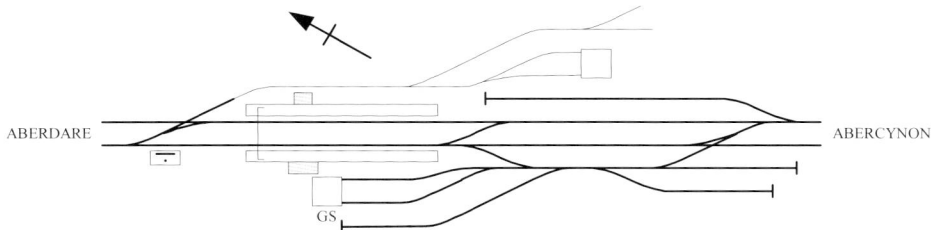

MOUNTAIN ASH
(OXFORD STREET)
1484

1484   **MOUNTAIN ASH (OXFORD STREET)**   **[AberRly]**
OP: 06/08/1846   Photo: SE. 1958
CP: 14/03/1964   D.Lawrence

1484   **MOUNTAIN ASH (OXFORD STREET)**   **[AberRly]**
Photo: N. 1961
Stations U.K.

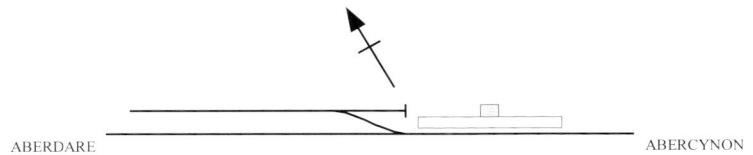

ABERCWMBOI
HALT
1485

1485   **ABERCWMBOI HALT**   **[AberRly]**
OP: 26/12/1904   Photo: NW. 1922
CP: 31/03/1956   D.K.Jones

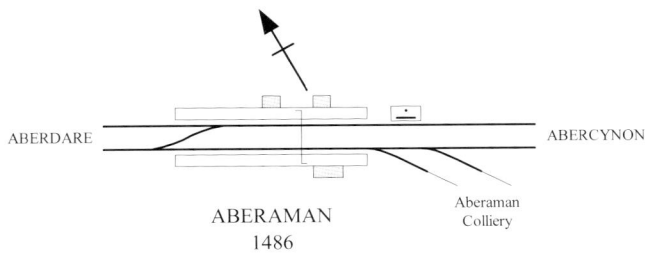

ABERAMAN
1486

Aberaman
Colliery

1486   **ABERAMAN**   **[AberRly]**
OP: 26/08/1889   Photo: NW. 1959
CP: 14/03/1964   M.Hale

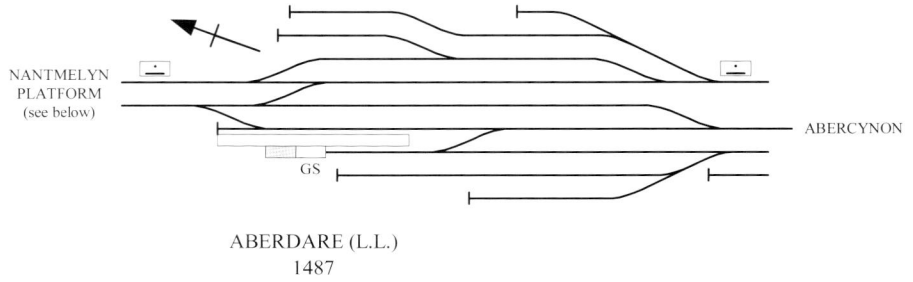

ABERDARE (L.L.)
1487

1487	ABERDARE (L.L.)	[AberRly]
OP: 1914		Photo: N. 1959
CP: 14/03/1964		Stations U.K.

1487	ABERDARE (L.L.)	[AberRly]
		Photo: S. 1959
		Stations U.K.

SOUTH WALES MAP

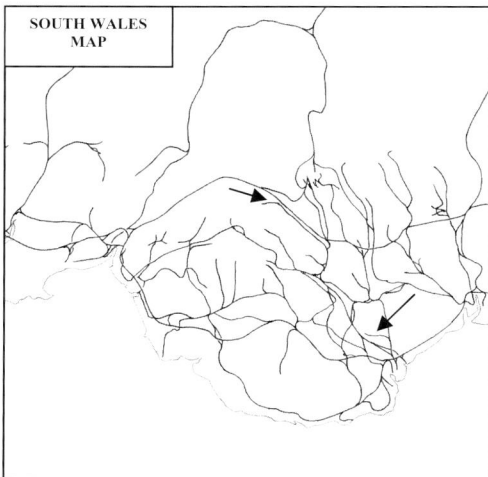

ABERDARE (Exc) TO NANTMELYN PLATFORM
DARE VALLEY BRANCH
Dare Valley Railway -
Taff Vale Railway (01/07/1889) -
Great Western Railway (01/01/1922)

ACT: 21/07/1863
OP: 01/06/1904
OMin: 01/07/1866
CP: 01/04/1949
CMin: 02/1957

GADLYS ROAD
PLATFORM
1488

1488	GADLYS ROAD PLATFORM	[DVR]
OP: 12/07/1914		Sketch: NE. c.1950
CP: 01/04/1949 (Workmens trains)		

PHOTOGRAPH UNAVAILABLE

1489	NANTMELYN PLATFORM	[DVR]
OP: 01/06/1904		Photo: None
CP: 01/04/1949 (Workmens trains)		Available

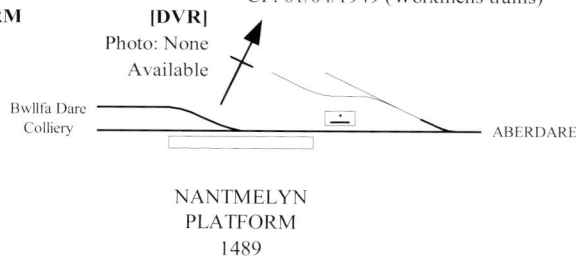

NANTMELYN
PLATFORM
1489

Heath Junction TO CORYTON HALT
CARDIFF RAILWAY
Cardiff Railway -
Great Western Railway (01/01/1922)
ACT: 06/08/1897
OP: 01/03/1911
OG: 15/05/1909
CP: OPEN
CG: 20/07/1931 (beyond Whitchurch)
CG: 02/12/1963 (Whitchurch)

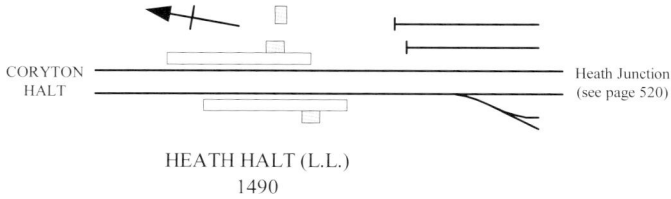

CORYTON
HALT

Heath Junction
(see page 520)

HEATH HALT (L.L.)
1490

1490   **HEATH HALT (L.L.)**   **[CardRly]**
OP: 01/03/1911   Photo: N. 1958
CP: OPEN   Stations U.K.

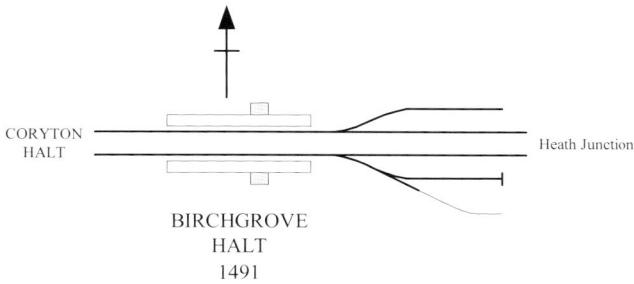

CORYTON
HALT

Heath Junction

BIRCHGROVE
HALT
1491

1491   **BIRCHGROVE HALT**   **[CardRly]**
OP: 10/06/1929   Photo: W. 1964
CP: OPEN   Stations U.K.

1492   **RHIWBINA HALT**   **[CardRly]**
OP: 01/03/1911   Photo: E. 1960
CP: OPEN   M.Hale

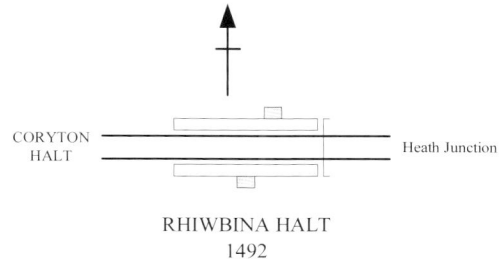

CORYTON
HALT

Heath Junction

RHIWBINA HALT
1492

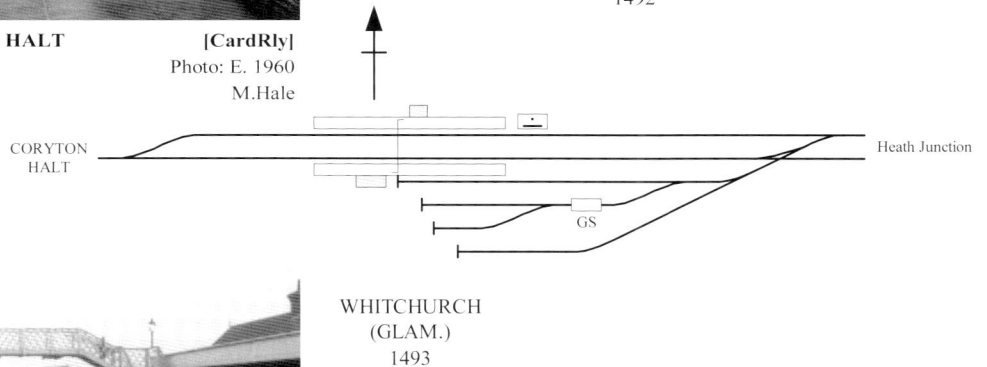

CORYTON
HALT

Heath Junction

GS

WHITCHURCH
(GLAM.)
1493

1493   **WHITCHURCH (GLAM.)**   **[CardRly]**
OP: 01/03/1911   Photo: E. 1958
CP: OPEN   Stations U.K.

CORYTON
HALT (GLAM.)
1494

Nantgarw Colliery — Heath Junction

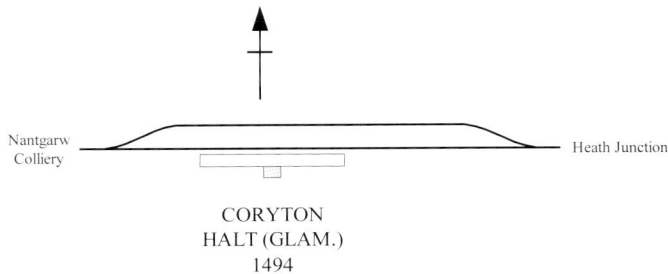

1494   **CORYTON HALT (GLAM.)**   **[CardRly]**
OP: 01/03/1911
CP: OPEN   Photo: E. 1954
     R.Carpenter

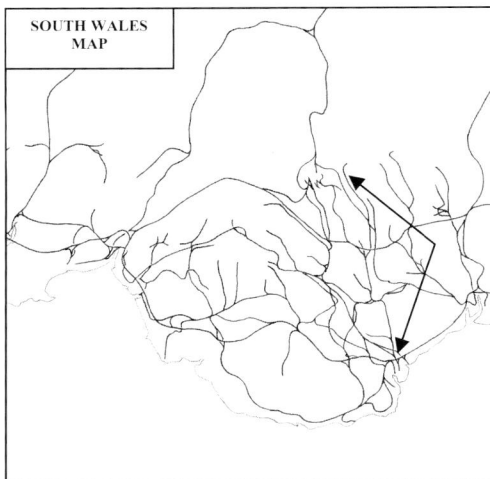

SOUTH WALES
MAP

CARDIFF (QUEEN STREET) (Exc) TO RHYMNEY
CARDIFF AND RHYMNEY LINE
Rhymney Railway -
Great Western Railway (01/01/1922)
ACT: 25/07/1864 (Gaol Lane Junc. (Cardiff) to Aber Junction)
ACT: 02/07/1855 (Aber Junction to Hengoed Junction)
ACT: 24/07/1854 (Hengoed Junction to Rhymney)
OP: 01/04/1871 (Cardiff to Aber Junction)
OP: 31/03/1858 (from Aber Junction to Rhymney)
OG: 01/04/1871 (Cardiff to Aber Junction)
OG: 25/02/1858 (from Aber Junction to Hengoed Junction)
OG: 28/12/1857 (Hengoed Junction to Rhymney)
CP: OPEN
CG: OPEN

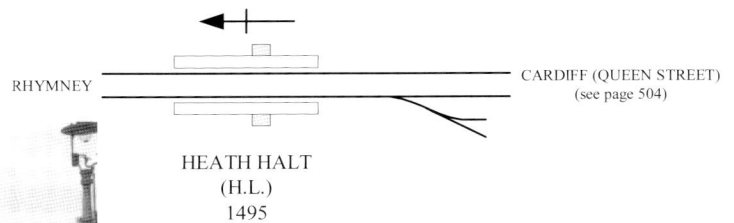

RHYMNEY — CARDIFF (QUEEN STREET)
(see page 504)

HEATH HALT
(H.L.)
1495

1495   **HEATH HALT (H.L.)**   **[RR]**
OP: 10/1915
CP: OPEN   Photo: N. 1958
     Stations U.K.

1496   **LLANISHEN**   **[RR]**
OP: 01/04/1871
CP: OPEN   Photo: N. 1963
     P.Garland

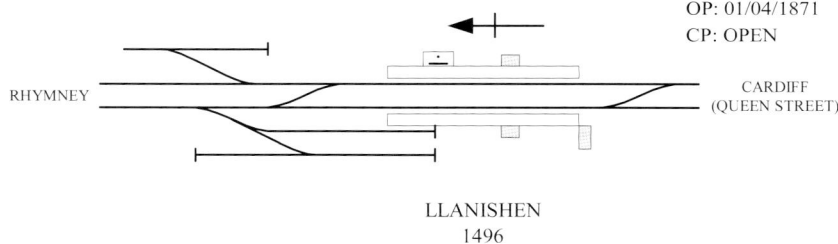

RHYMNEY — CARDIFF (QUEEN STREET)

LLANISHEN
1496

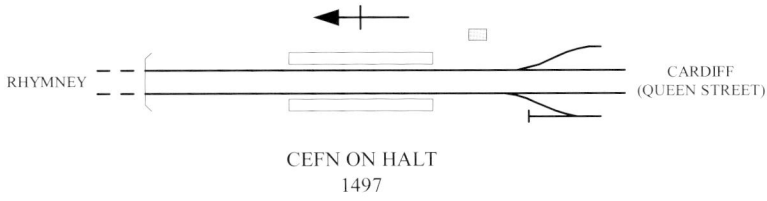

CEFN ON HALT
1497

1497   **CEFN ON HALT**   **[RR]**
OP: 10/1915   Photo: N. c.1960
CP: 27/09/1986   LOSA

1497   **CEFN ON HALT**   **[RR]**
Photo: S. c.1960
LOSA

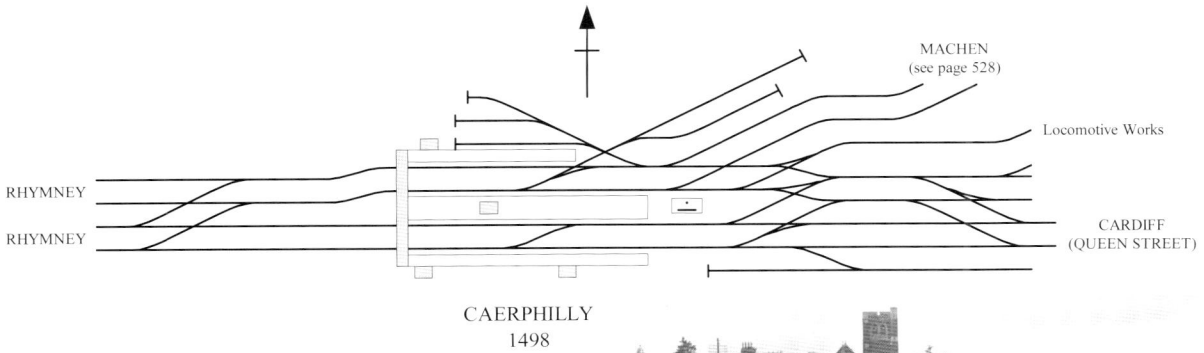

MACHEN
(see page 528)

Locomotive Works

CARDIFF
(QUEEN STREET)

CAERPHILLY
1498

1498   **CAERPHILLY**   **[RR]**
OP: 01/04/1871   Photo: W. 1952
CP: OPEN   R.C.Riley

1499   **ABER JUNCTION HALT**   **[RR]**
OP: 01/04/1908   Photo: N. c.1950
CP: OPEN   L&GRP

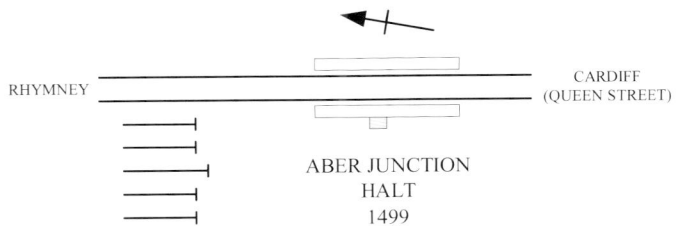

RHYMNEY

CARDIFF
(QUEEN STREET)

ABER JUNCTION
HALT
1499

LLANBRADACH
1500

RHYMNEY

CARDIFF
(QUEEN STREET)

GS

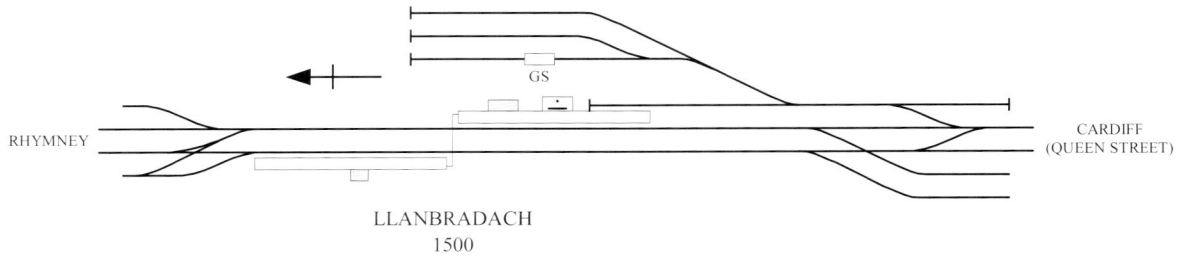

1500	LLANBRADACH	[RR]
OP: 01/03/1893		Photo: N. 1952
CP: OPEN		R.C.Riley

1500	LLANBRADACH	[RR]
		Photo: N. c.1960
		LOSA

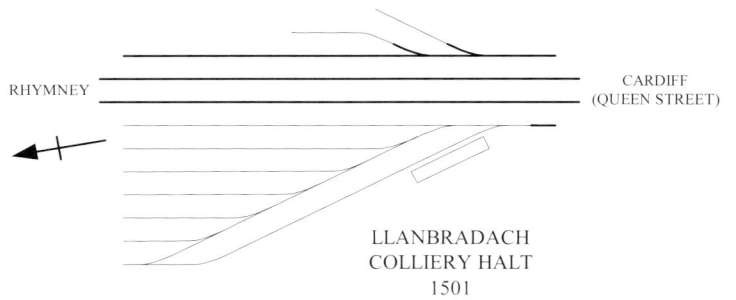

RHYMNEY

CARDIFF
(QUEEN STREET)

LLANBRADACH
COLLIERY HALT
1501

PHOTOGRAPH UNAVAILABLE

1501	LLANBRADACH COLLIERY HALT	[RR]
OP: by 09/1928		Photo: None
CP: by 06/1954 (Workmens trains)		Available

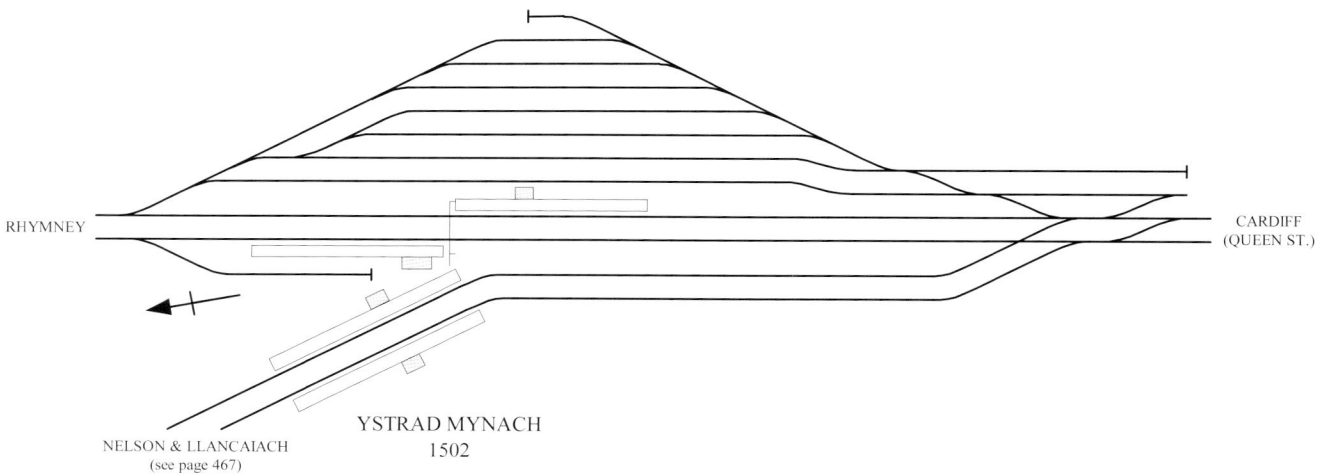

RHYMNEY

CARDIFF
(QUEEN ST.)

YSTRAD MYNACH
1502

NELSON & LLANCAIACH
(see page 467)

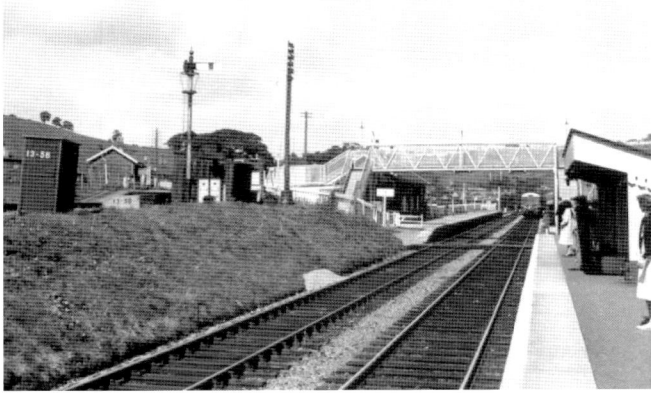

1502   **YSTRAD MYNACH**   **[RR]**
OP: 31/03/1858   Photo: N. 1963
CP: OPEN   P.Garland

1502   **YSTRAD MYNACH**   **[RR]**
Photo: N. c.1936
Stations U.K.

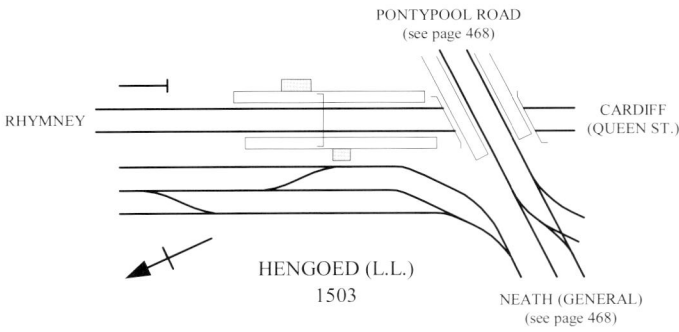

PONTYPOOL ROAD
(see page 468)

RHYMNEY

CARDIFF
(QUEEN ST.)

HENGOED (L.L.)
1503

NEATH (GENERAL)
(see page 468)

1503   **HENGOED (L.L.)**   **[RR]**
OP: 31/03/1858   Photo: N. 1952
CP: OPEN   R.C.Riley

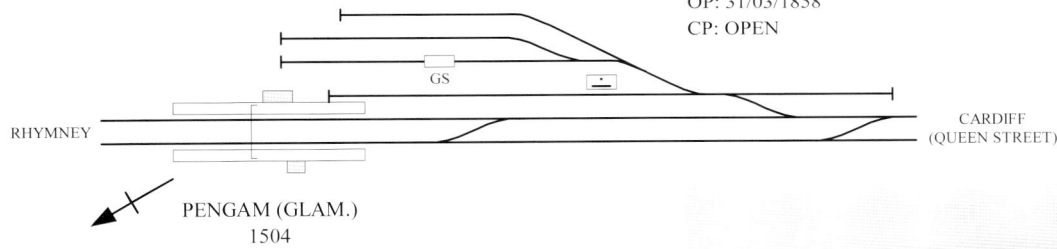

GS

RHYMNEY

CARDIFF
(QUEEN STREET)

PENGAM (GLAM.)
1504

1504   **PENGAM (GLAM.)**   **[RR]**
OP: 31/03/1858   Photo: N. 1960
CP: OPEN   M.Hale

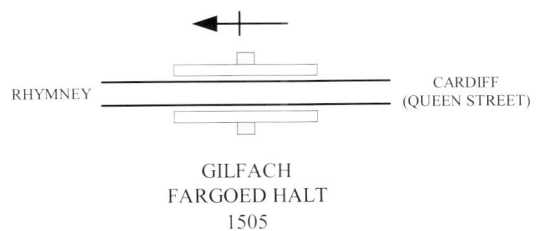

RHYMNEY

CARDIFF
(QUEEN STREET)

GILFACH
FARGOED HALT
1505

1505   **GILFACH FARGOED HALT**   **[RR]**
OP: 01/04/1908   Photo: N. 1958
CP: OPEN   Stations U.K.

BARGOED
1506

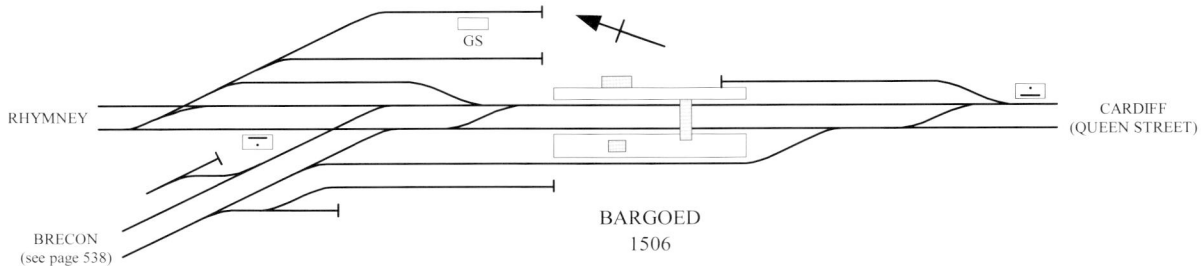

1506   **BARGOED**   **[RR]**
OP: 31/03/1858   Photo: S. 1964
CP: OPEN   Stations U.K.

1506   **BARGOED**   **[RR]**
Photo: N. c.1960
LOSA

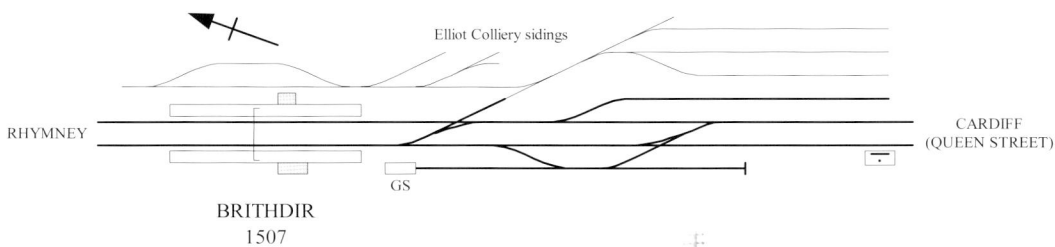

Elliot Colliery sidings

RHYMNEY   CARDIFF
(QUEEN STREET)
GS

BRITHDIR
1507

1507   **BRITHDIR**   **[RR]**
OP: by 03/1871   Photo: N. 1962
CP: OPEN   M.Hale

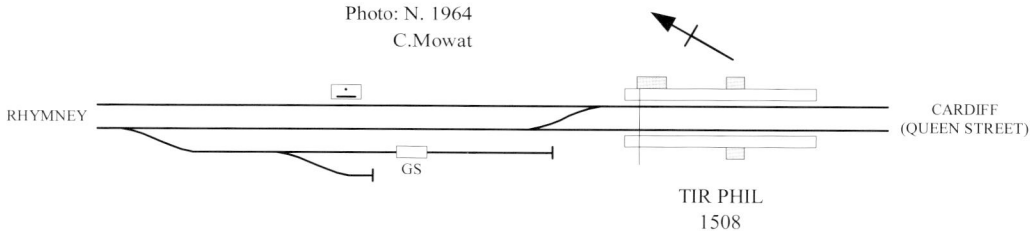

1508   **TIR PHIL**   **[RR]**
OP: 31/03/1858   Photo: N. 1964
CP: OPEN   C.Mowat

RHYMNEY   CARDIFF
(QUEEN STREET)
GS

TIR PHIL
1508

RHYMNEY

BRECON
(see page 538)

RHYMNEY   CARDIFF
                                            (QUEEN STREET)

GS

PONTLOTTYN
1509

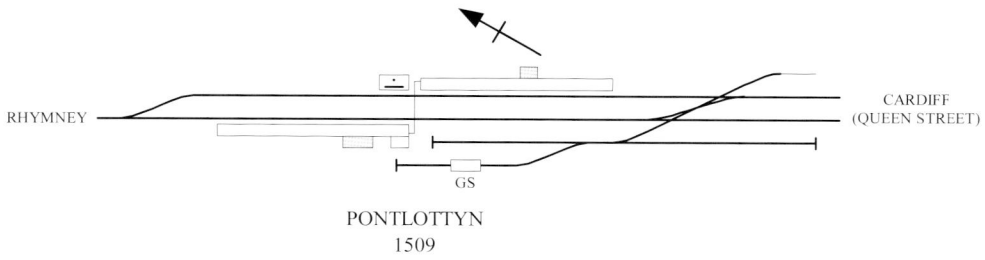

1509   **PONTLOTTYN**   **[RR]**
OP: 09/1859   Photo: NW. 1958
CP: OPEN   Stations U.K.

1509   **PONTLOTTYN**   **[RR]**
                                  Photo: SE. 1962
                                       M.Hale

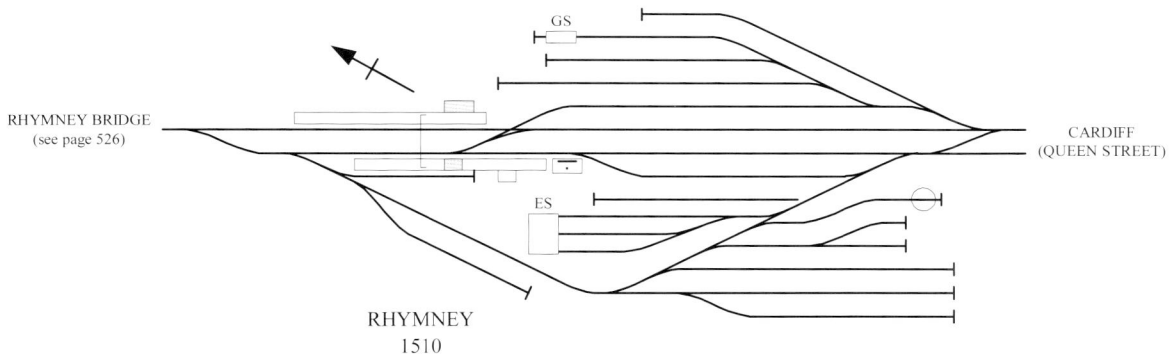

GS

RHYMNEY BRIDGE   CARDIFF
(see page 526)   (QUEEN STREET)

ES

RHYMNEY
1510

1510   **RHYMNEY**   **[RR]**
OP: 31/03/1858   Photo: N. 1963
CP: OPEN   P.Garland

1510   **RHYMNEY**   **[RR]**
                                   Photo: S. 1963
                                     P.Garland

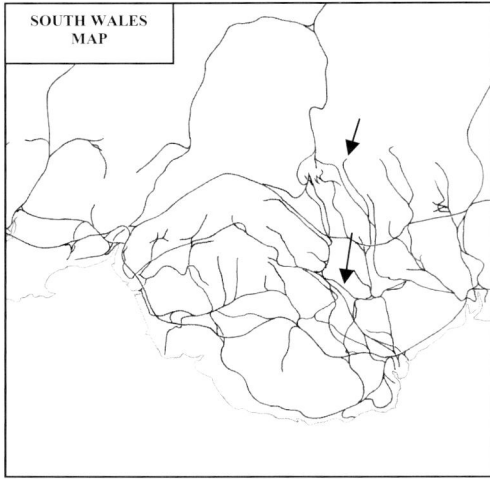

SOUTH WALES MAP

RHYMNEY (Exc) TO RHYMNEY BRIDGE
RHYMNEY AND NANTYBWCH LINE
Rhymney Railway -
LNW & Rhymney Joint Railway (15/07/1867) -
Great Western & LMS Joint Railway (01/01/1922)
ACT: 25/07/1864 (Rhymney to 8 chains west of Nantybwch)
OP: 05/09/1871
OG: 05/09/1871
CP: 19/09/1953 (to Rhymney Bridge)
CG: 19/09/1953 (to Rhymney Bridge)

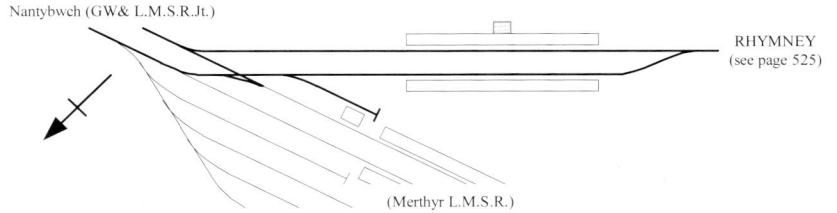

Nantybwch (GW& L.M.S.R.Jt.)

RHYMNEY
(see page 525)

(Merthyr L.M.S.R.)

RHYMNEY BRIDGE
1511

1511	RHYMNEY BRIDGE	[LNW&RJR]
OP: 02/10/1871		Photo: SE. c.1935
CP: 19/09/1953		Stations U.K.

CAERPHILLY (Exc) TO PONTYPRIDD (Exc)
CAERPHILLY AND PONTYPRIDD LINE
Pontypridd Caerphilly & Newport Railway -
Alexandra (Newport & South Wales) Dock & Railway (31/12/1897) -
Great Western Railway (25/03/1922)
ACT: 08/08/1878 (Walnut Tree Branch Junction to PC&N Junction)
OP: 28/12/1887
OG: 07/07/1884
CP: 15/09/1956
CG: 02/01/1967 (Walnut Tree Junction to Glyntaff Goods)
CG: 31/07/1967 (Glyntaff Goods to PC&N Junction, Pontypridd)

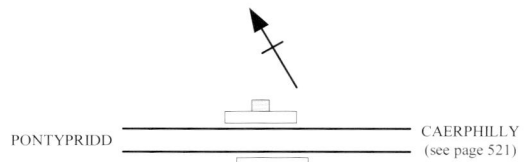

PONTYPRIDD

CAERPHILLY
(see page 521)

NANTGARW
HALT
1512

1512	NANTGARW HALT	[PC&NR]
OP: 01/09/1904		Photo: NW. 1952
CP: 15/09/1956		L&GRP

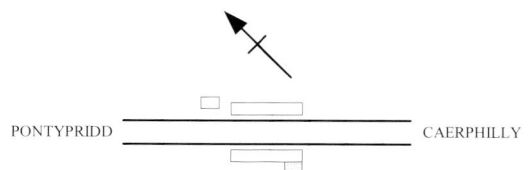

PONTYPRIDD

CAERPHILLY

GROESWEN
HALT
1513

1513   **GROESWEN HALT**   **[PC&NR]**
OP: 01/09/1904   Photo: SE. 1958
CP: 15/09/1956   R.M.Casserley

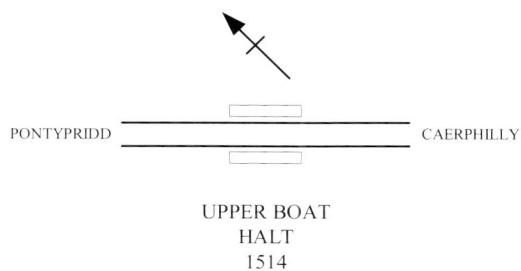

PONTYPRIDD   CAERPHILLY

UPPER BOAT
HALT
1514

1514   **UPPER BOAT HALT**   **[PC&NR]**
OP: 01/09/1904   Photo: SE. 1957
CP: 15/09/1956   R.K.Blencowe

1515   **DYNEA HALT**   **[PC&NR]**
OP: 01/09/1904   Photo: SE. 1956
CP: 15/09/1956   R.K.Blencowe

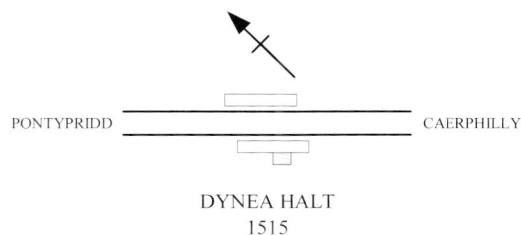

PONTYPRIDD   CAERPHILLY

DYNEA HALT
1515

PONTYPRIDD   CAERPHILLY

RHYDYFELIN
HALT
1516

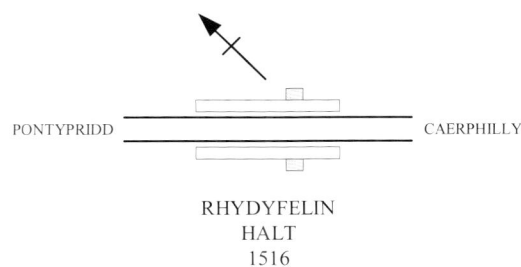

1516   **RHYDYFELIN HALT**   **[PC&NR]**
OP: 14/05/1928   Sketch: NW. c.1948
CP: 02/02/1953

PONTYPRIDD
(see page 507)   CAERPHILLY

TREFOREST
HALT
1517

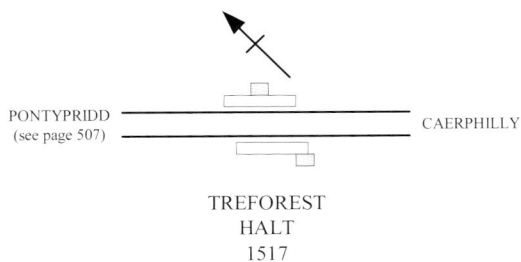

1517   **TREFOREST HALT**   **[PC&NR]**
OP: 01/09/1904   Photo: NW. 1952
CP: 15/09/1956   L&GRP

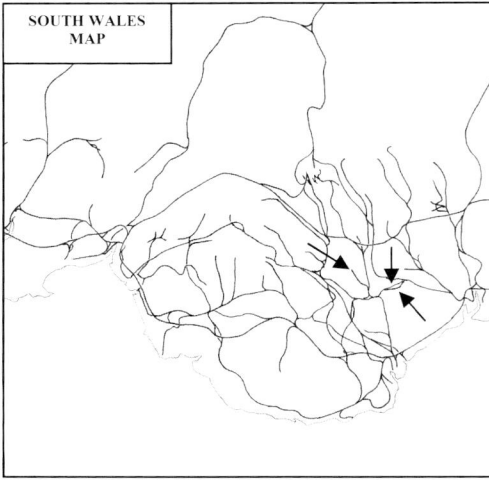

CAERPHILLY (Exc) TO MACHEN (Exc)
CAERPHILLY BRANCH
Rumney Railway -
Brecon & Merthyr Railway (28/07/1863) -
Great Western Railway (01/01/1922)
ACT: 01/08/1861
OP: 28/12/1887
OG: 1864
CP: 15/09/1956 (Public Services)
CP: 01/07/1963 (Workmens trains)
CG: 20/11/1967 (Caerphilly to Gwaunybara Junction)
CG: 20/07/1964 (Gwaunybara Junction to Machen)

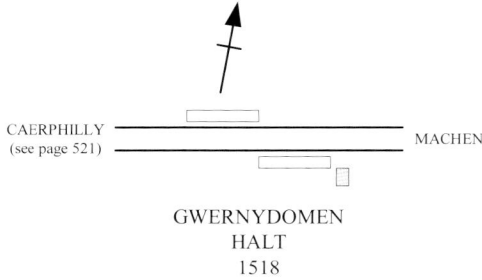

CAERPHILLY (see page 521) — MACHEN

GWERNYDOMEN
HALT
1518

1518	GWERNYDOMEN HALT	[B&MR]
OP: 10/1908		Photo: E. 1957
CP: 15/09/1956		M.Hale

CAERPHILLY — MACHEN

WATERLOO
HALT
1519

1519	WATERLOO HALT	[B&MR]
OP: 10/1908		Photo: SW. 1959
CP: 15/09/1956		Stations U.K.

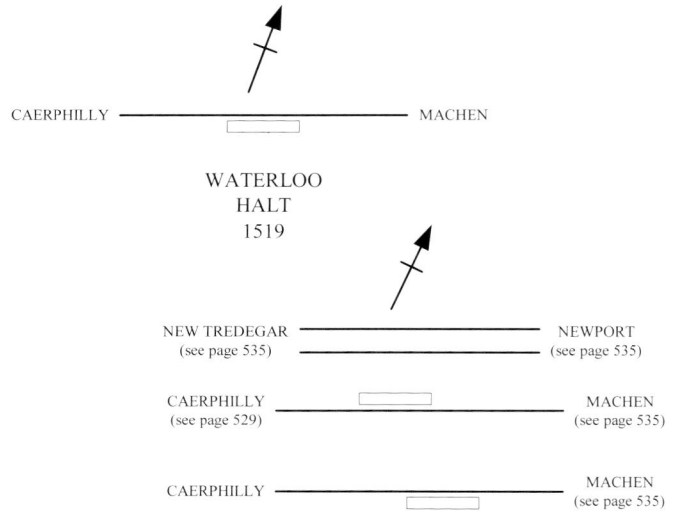

NEW TREDEGAR (see page 535) — NEWPORT (see page 535)

CAERPHILLY (see page 529) — MACHEN (see page 535)

CAERPHILLY — MACHEN (see page 535)

WHITE HART
HALT
1520

1520	WHITE HART HALT	[PC&NR]
OP: 12/05/1947		Photo: E. c.1947
CP: 28/06/1952		L&GRP

1520	WHITE HART HALT	[B&MR]
		Photo: E. 1952
		R.Carpenter

CAERPHILLY (Exc) TO MACHEN (Exc)
CAERPHILLY BRANCH DOWN LOOP LINE
Pontypridd Caerphilly & Newport Railway -
Brecon & Merthyr Railway (14/09/1891) -
Great Western Railway (01/01/1922)
ACT: 1887 (Gwaunybara Junction to Machen)
OP: 14/09/1891
OG: 01/11/1890
CP: 15/09/1956 (Public Services)
CG: 20/11/1967

CAERPHILLY
(see page 528) ——————— MACHEN

FOUNTAIN
BRIDGE HALT
1521

1521   **FOUNTAIN BRIDGE HALT**   **[PC&NR]**
OP: 10/1908   Photo: SW. 1956
CP: 15/09/1956   S.C.Philips

CAERPHILLY (Exc) TO SENGHENYDD
SENGHENYDD BRANCH
Rhymney Railway -
Great Western Railway (01/01/1922)
ACT: 25/07/1890 (Senghenydd Branch Junction to end of line)
OP: 01/02/1894
OG: 01/02/1894
CP: 13/06/1964
CG: 01/03/1965 (Public Goods only) (to Abertridwr)
CG: 02/07/1962 (Public Goods only) (Abertidwr to Senghenydd)

1522   **PENYRHEOL**   **[RR]**
OP: 01/02/1894   Photo: E. 1952
CP: 13/06/1964   R.C.Riley

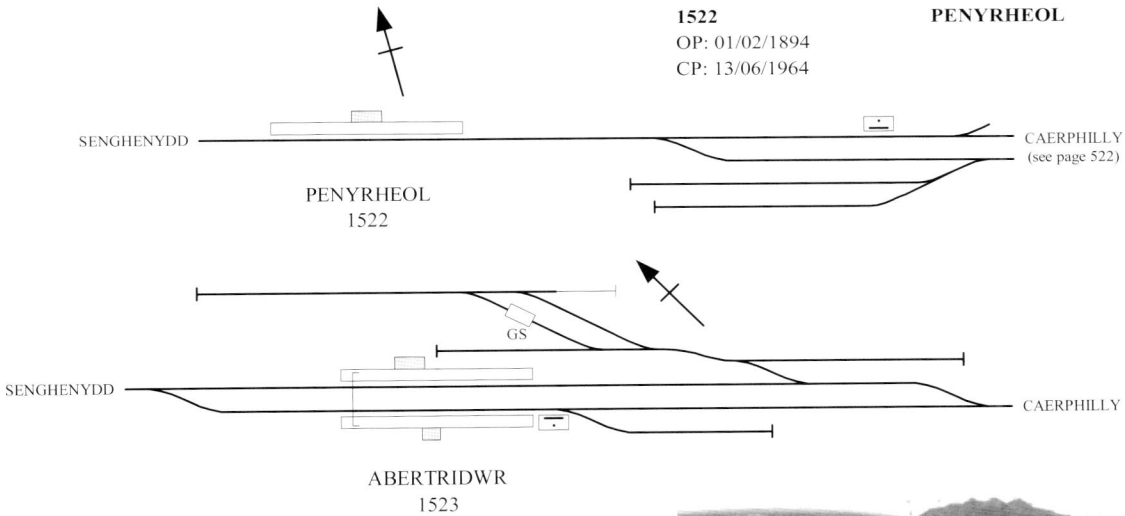

SENGHENYDD ——————— CAERPHILLY
(see page 522)

PENYRHEOL
1522

GS

SENGHENYDD ——————— CAERPHILLY

ABERTRIDWR
1523

1523   **ABERTRIDWR**   **[RR]**
OP: 01/02/1894   Photo: NW. 1963
CP: 13/06/1964   P.Garland

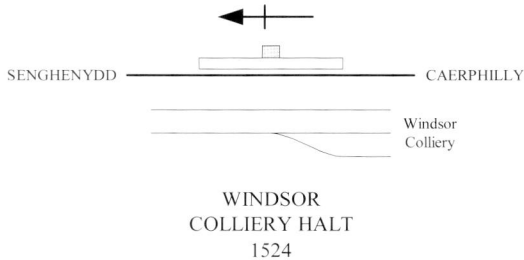

WINDSOR
COLLIERY HALT
1524

1524	**WINDSOR COLLIERY HALT**	[RR]
OP: 04/10/1943		Photo: S. 1962
CP: 13/06/1964 (Workmens trains)		M.Hale

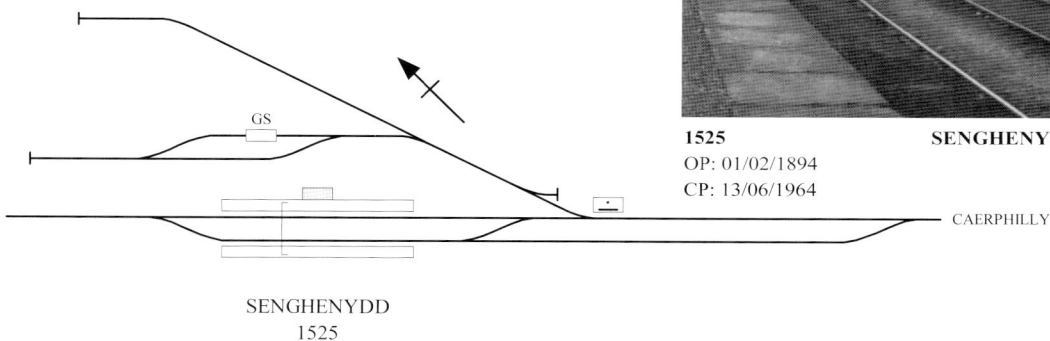

1525	**SENGHENYDD**	[RR]
OP: 01/02/1894		Photo: NW. c.1910
CP: 13/06/1964		unknown

SENGHENYDD
1525

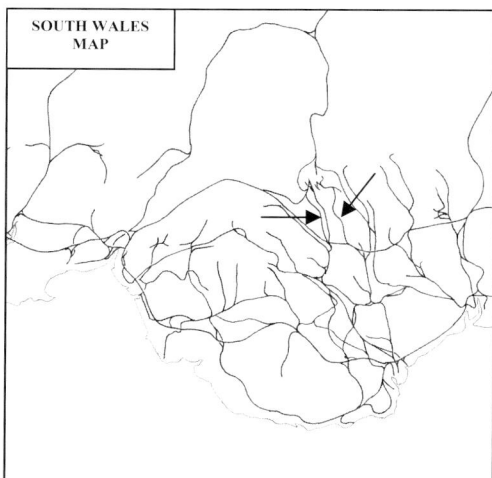

SOUTH WALES
MAP

QUAKERS YARD (H.L.) (Exc) TO MERTHYR (Exc)
QUAKERS YARD AND MERTHYR LINE
Great Western & Rhymney Joint Railway -
Great Western Railway (01/01/1922)
ACT: 18/08/1882 (Quakers Yard Junc. to Merthyr Joint Line Junc.
OP: 01/04/1886
OG: 01/04/1886
CP: 03/02/1951 (Public Services)
CP: 01/11/1954 (Workmens trains from Merthyr to Troedyrhiw Halt)
CG: 03/02/1951 (Quakers Yard to Aberfan)
CG: 01/11/1954 (Aberfan to Abercanaid)
CMin: 09/05/1960 (Abercanaid to Merthyr Joint Line Junc.)

PHOTOGRAPH UNAVAILABLE

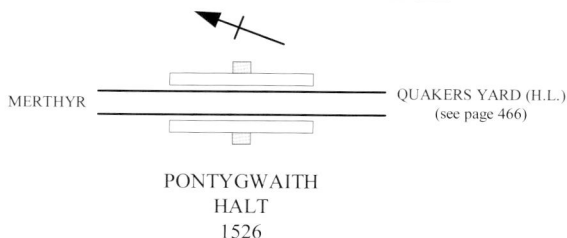

PONTYGWAITH
HALT
1526

1526	**PONTYGWAITH HALT**	[GW&RJR]
OP: 11/09/1933		Photo: None
CP: 03/02/1951		Available

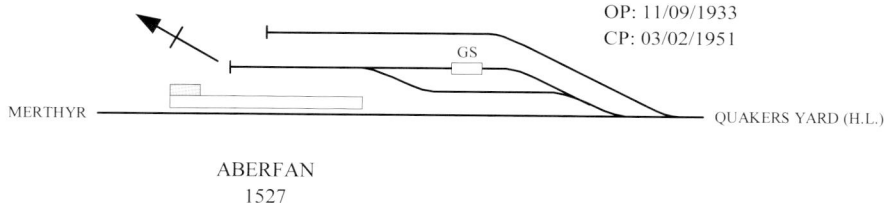

ABERFAN
1527

1527   **ABERFAN**   **[GW&RJR]**
OP: 01/04/1886   Photo: N. c.1900
CP: 03/02/1951   WRRC Collection

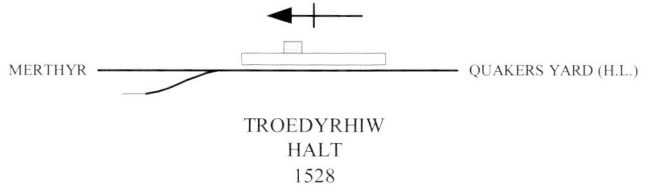

TROEDYRHIW
HALT
1528

PHOTOGRAPH UNAVAILABLE

1528   **TROEDYRHIW HALT**   **[GW&RJR]**
OP: 18/02/1907   Photo: None
CP: 03/02/1951   Available

G. W. R. Station.   Abercanaid

1529   **ABERCANAID**   **[GW&RJR]**
OP: 01/04/1886   Photo: SE. c.1910
CP: 03/02/1951   WRRC Collection

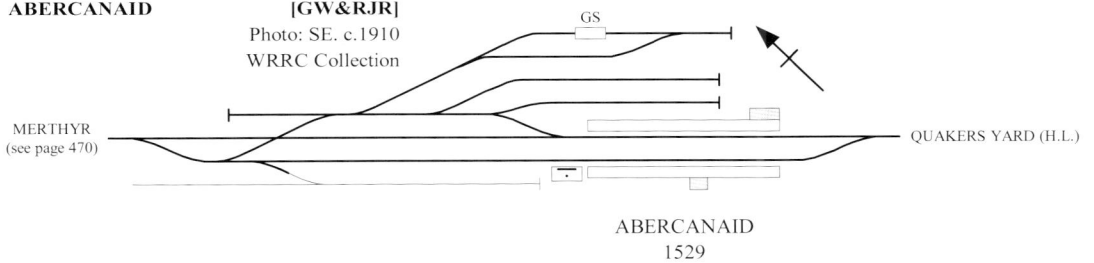

ABERCANAID
1529

NELSON & LLANCAIACH (Exc) TO DOWLAIS (CAE HARRIS)
TAFF BARGOED BRANCH
Great Western & Rhymney Joint Railway -
Great Western Railway (01/01/1922)
ACT: 15/07/1867
OP: 02/02/1876 (Public Services)
OG: 20/12/1875
CP: 13/06/1964
CG: 07/10/1963

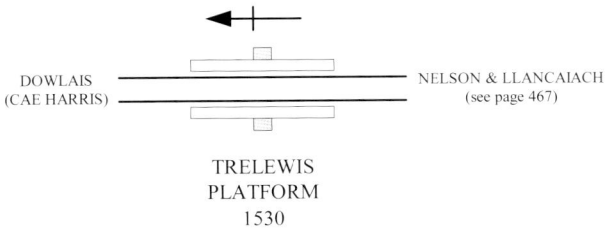

TRELEWIS
PLATFORM
1530

1530   **TRELEWIS PLATFORM**   **[GW&RJR]**
OP: 10/07/1911   Photo: N. 1958
CP: 13/06/1964   Stations U.K.

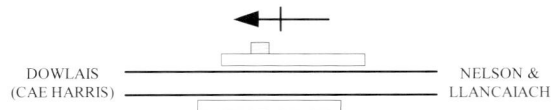

TAFF MERTHYR
COLLIERY HALT
1531

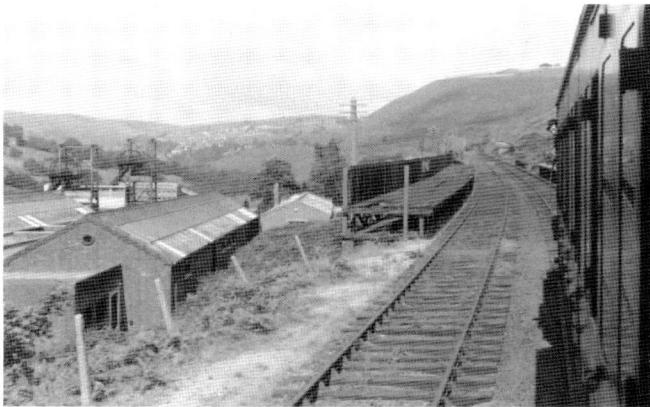

1531   **TAFF MERTHYR COLLIERY HALT**   **[GW&RJR]**
OP: by 09/1928   Photo: N. 1963
CP: 13/06/1964 (Workmens trains)   P.Garland

1531   **TAFF MERTHYR COLLIERY HALT**   **[GW&RJR]**
Photo: S. 1965
M.Hale

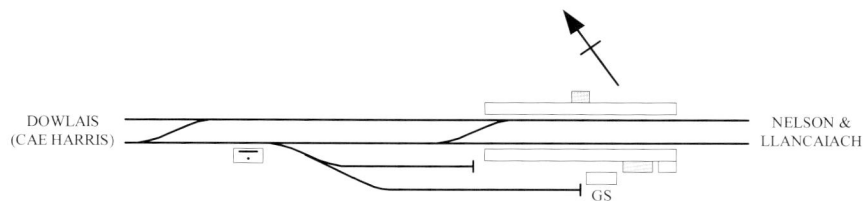

BEDLINOG
1532

1532   **BEDLINOG**   **[GW&RJR]**
OP: 02/02/1876   Photo: S. c.1910
CP: 13/06/1964   LOSA

1532   **BEDLINOG**   **[GW&RJR]**
Photo: SE. 1960
H.C.Casserley

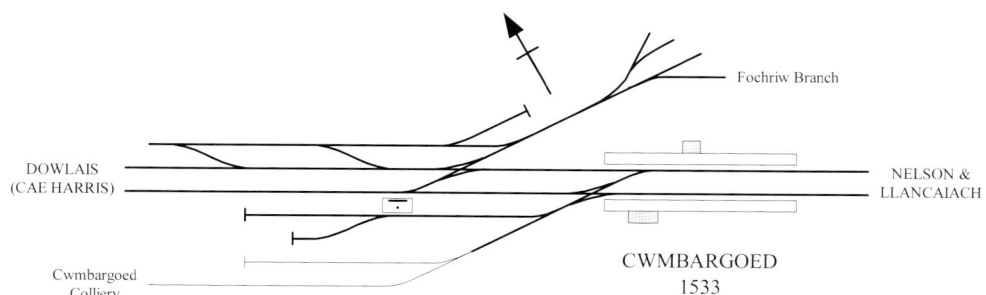

CWMBARGOED
1533

1533　　　　　　**CWM BARGOED**　　　　**[GW&RJR]**
OP: 02/02/1876　　　　　　　　　　　Photo: SE. 1958
CP: 13/06/1964　　　　　　　　　　　　　　　　M.Hale

1533　　　　　　**CWM BARGOED**　　　　**[GW&RJR]**
　　　　　　　　　　　　　　　　　Photo: NW. 1963
　　　　　　　　　　　　　　　　　　　　P.Garland

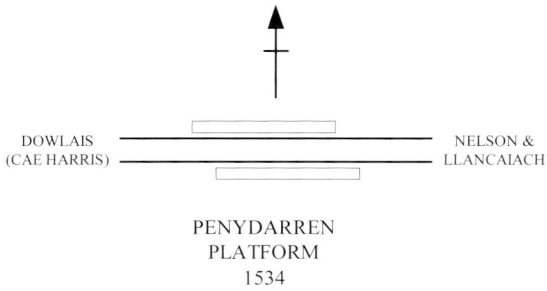

DOWLAIS
(CAE HARRIS)

NELSON &
LLANCAIACH

**PENYDARREN
PLATFORM
1534**

1534　　　**PENYDARREN PLATFORM**　　**[GW&RJR]**
OP: by 09/1928　　　　　　　　　　　Photo: W. 1958
CP: after 1954 (Workmens trains)　　　　　　　M.Hale

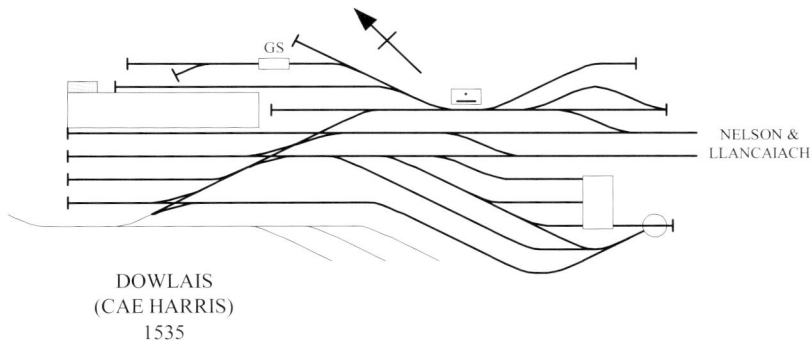

GS

NELSON &
LLANCAIACH

**DOWLAIS
(CAE HARRIS)
1535**

1535　　　**DOWLAIS (CAE HARRIS)**　　**[GW&RJR]**
OP: 02/02/1876　　　　　　　　　　　Photo: NW. 1957
CP: 13/06/1964　　　　　　　　　　　R.M.Casserley

1535　　　**DOWLAIS (CAE HARRIS)**　　**[GW&RJR]**
　　　　　　　　　　　　　　　　　Photo: W. 1959
　　　　　　　　　　　　　　　　　R.Stewartson

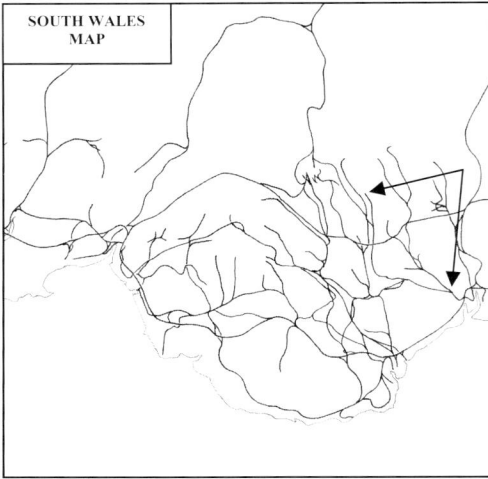

Bassaleg Junction TO NEW TREDEGAR
BASSALEG JUNCTION AND RHYMNEY LINE
Rumney Railway -
Brecon & Merthyr Railway (28/07/1863) -
Great Western Railway (01/01/1922)
ACT: 01/08/1861
OPG: 13/06/1865 (Bassaleg Junction to Pengam)
OPG: 16/04/1866 (Pengam to New Tredegar)
CP: 29/12/1962
CG: 16/07/1964 (Public Goods only) (Bassaleg Jc. to Bedwas)
CG: 31/12/1962 (Bedwas to Maesycwmmer Junction)
CG: 31/12/1962 (Public Goods only)
     (Maesycwmmer Junc. to Aberbargoed Junc.)
CG: 31/12/1962 (Aberbargoed Junction to New Tredegar)

1536
OP: 13/06/1865
CP: 29/12/1962

BASSALEG

[B&MR]
Photo: W. 1958
D.K.Jones

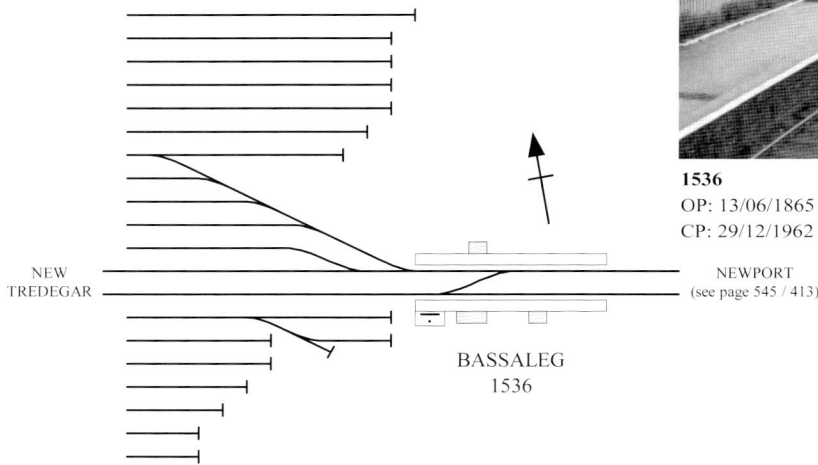

NEW TREDEGAR

NEWPORT
(see page 545 / 413)

BASSALEG
1536

NEW TREDEGAR

NEWPORT

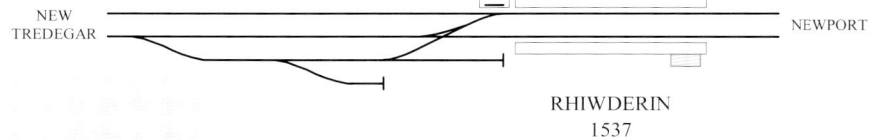

RHIWDERIN
1537

1537
OP: 13/06/1865
CP: 27/02/1954

RHIWDERIN

[B&MR]
Photo: W. 1949
L&GRP

1538
OP: 13/06/1865
CP: 14/09/1957

CHURCH ROAD

[B&MR]
Photo: E. c.1920
LOSA

NEW TREDEGAR

NEWPORT

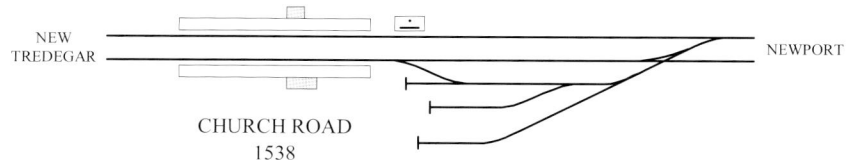

CHURCH ROAD
1538

NEW
TREDEGAR

NEWPORT

CAERPHILLY (see page 529)
CAERPHILLY (see page 528)

GS

MACHEN
1539

1539
OP: 13/06/1865
CP: 29/12/1962

MACHEN

[B&MR]
Photo: W. 1958
H.C.Casserley

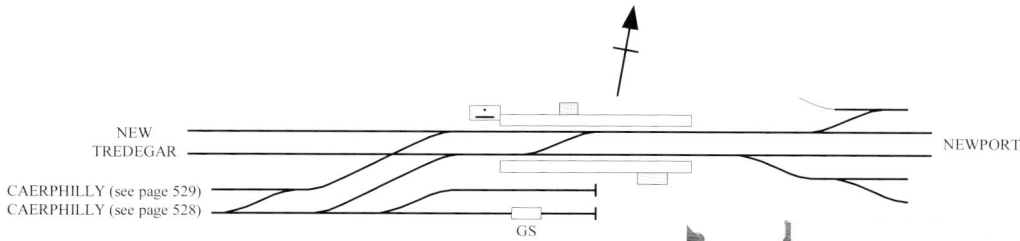

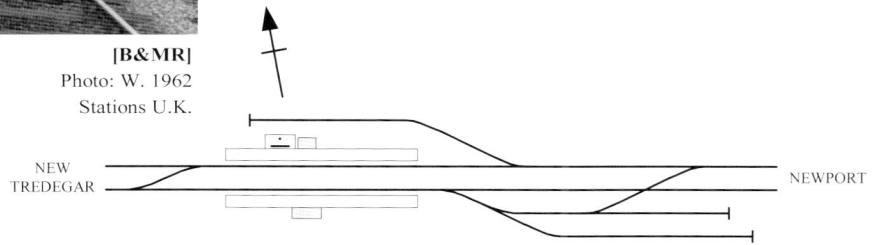

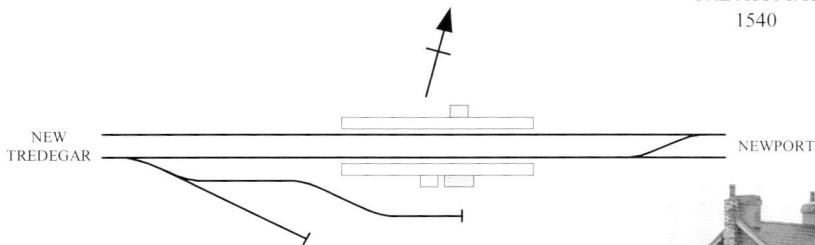

1540
OP: 04/01/1915
CP: 29/12/1962

TRETHOMAS

[B&MR]
Photo: W. 1962
Stations U.K.

NEW
TREDEGAR

NEWPORT

TRETHOMAS
1540

NEW
TREDEGAR

NEWPORT

BEDWAS
1541

1541
OP: 13/06/1865
CP: 29/12/1962

BEDWAS

[B&MR]
Photo: W. 1958
M.Hale

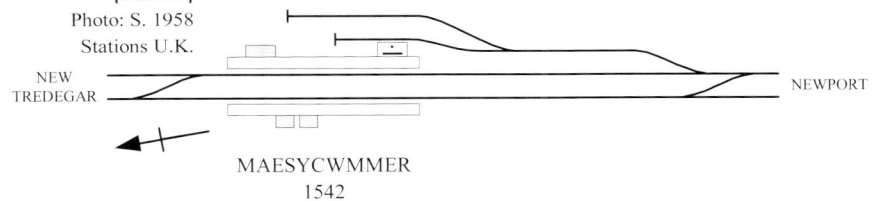

1542
OP: 13/06/1865
CP: 29/12/1962

MAESYCWMMER

[B&MR]
Photo: S. 1958
Stations U.K.

NEW
TREDEGAR

NEWPORT

MAESYCWMMER
1542

1543   **FLEUR-DE-LIS PLATFORM**   **[B&MR]**
OP: 29/03/1926   Photo: N c.1950
CP: 29/12/1962   unknown

1543   **FLEUR-DE-LIS PLATFORM**   **[B&MR]**
Photo: S. 1959
R.M.Casserley

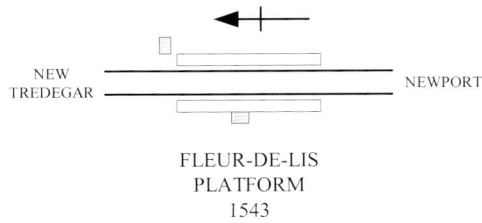

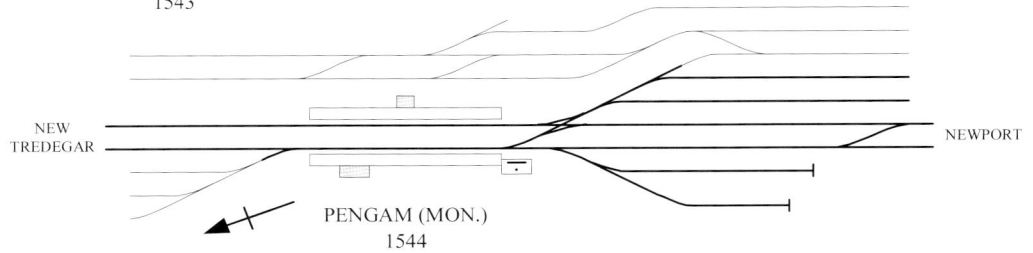

NEW TREDEGAR   NEWPORT

FLEUR-DE-LIS
PLATFORM
1543

NEW TREDEGAR   NEWPORT

PENGAM (MON.)
1544

NEW TREDEGAR   NEWPORT

BARGOED
COLLIERY HALT
1545

1544   **PENGAM (MON.)**   **[B&MR]**
OP: 13/06/1865   Photo: S. 1958
CP: 29/12/1962   Stations U.K.

1545   **BARGOED COLLIERY HALT**   **[B&MR]**
OP: by 09/1926   Photo: S. 1962
CP: 29/12/1962 (Workmens trains)   Stations U.K.

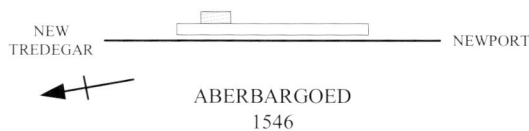

NEW TREDEGAR   NEWPORT

ABERBARGOED
1546

1546   **ABERBARGOED**   **[B&MR]**
OP: 16/04/1866   Photo: S. 1962
CP: 29/12/1962   Stations U.K.

CWMSYFIOG
COLLIERY HALT
1547

1548   **CWMSYFIOG**   **[B&MR]**
OP: 05/07/1937   Photo: S. 1958
CP: 29/12/1962   M.Hale

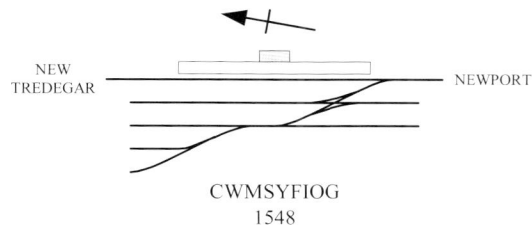

ELLIOT PIT
HALT
1549

NEW TREDEGAR
1550

1547   **CWMSYFIOG COLLIERY HALT**   **[B&MR]**
OP: 01/02/1908   Photo: S. 1958
CP: 29/12/1962 (Workmens trains)   Stations U.K.

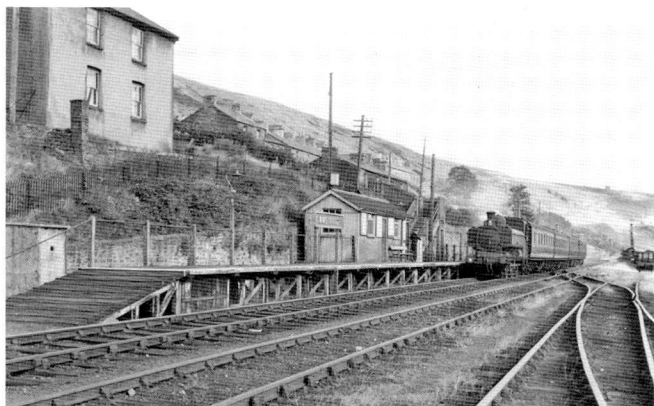

CWMSYFIOG
1548

1549   **ELLIOT PIT HALT**   **[B&MR]**
OP: c.1909   Photo: SE. 1962
CP: 29/12/1962 (Workmens trains)   Stations U.K.

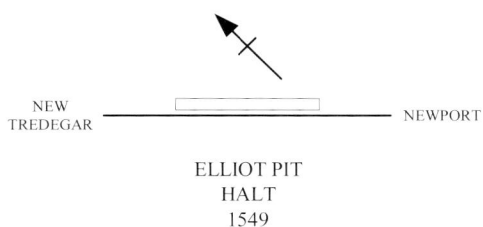

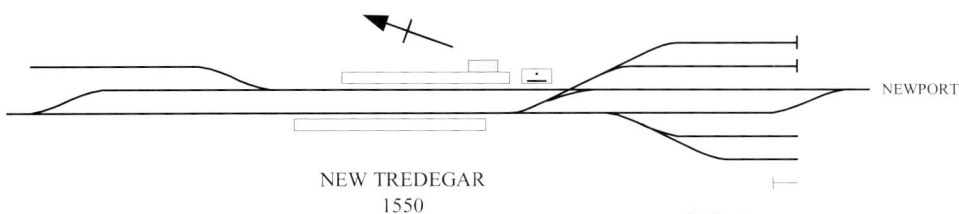

1550   **NEW TREDEGAR**   **[B&MR]**
OP: 16/04/1866   Photo: S. c.1930
CP: 29/12/1962   P.Rutherford

SOUTH WALES MAP

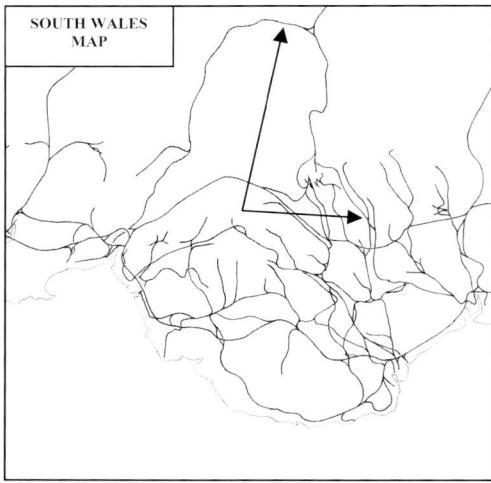

BARGOED (Exc) TO BRECON
BARGOED AND PANT LINE,
BRECON AND DOWLAIS LINE
RhymneyRailway -
Great Western Railway (01/01/1922)
(Bargoed North Junction to 20 miles 30 chains near Ogilvie)
Brecon & Merthyr Railway -
Great Western Railway (01/01/1922)
(20miles 30 chains near Ogilvie to Brecon)
ACT: 11/07/1861 (Bargoed North Junc. to 20 miles 30 chains)
ACT: 06/08/1861 (20 miles 30 chains to Pontsticill Junction)
ACT: 01/08/1859 (Pontsticill Junction to near Talybont)
ACT: 15/05/1860 (Near Talybont to Brecon)
OPG: 01/09/1868 (Bargoed to Dowlais Top)
OPG: 01/08/1867 (Dowlais Top to Pant)
OP: 19/03/1863 (unofficial opening) (Pant to Talybont)
OP: 23/04/1863 (Pant to Brecon (Watton))
OG: 20/01/1863 (Pant to Brecon (Watton))
OP: 01/03/1871 (to Brecon (Free Street))
CP: 29/12/1962
CG: 23/08/1965 (Public Goods only) (Bargoed to Darran & Deri)
CG: 01/04/1963 (Darran & Deri to Pant)
CG: 04/05/1964 (Pant to Brecon (Watton))
CG: 31/12/1962 (Brecon (Watton) to Brecon (Mount Street))

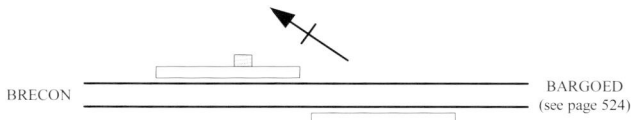

BRECON

BARGOED
(see page 524)

GROESFAEN
COLLIERY HALT
1551

1551   GROESFAEN COLLIERY HALT   [RR]
OP: by 09/1926   Photo: S. 1962
CP: 29/12/1962 (Workmens trains)   M.Hale

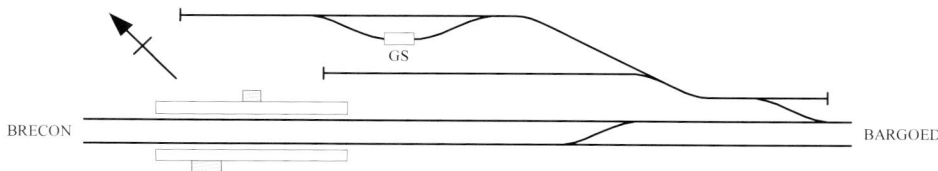

1552   DARRAN & DERI   [RR]
OP: 01/09/1868   Photo: NW. 1960
CP: 29/12/1962   M.Hale

GS

BRECON

BARGOED

DARRAN & DERI
1552

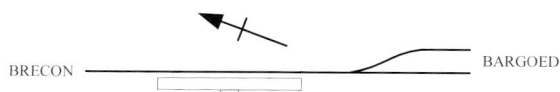

BRECON

BARGOED

OGILVIE
VILLAGE HALT
1553

1553   OGILVIE VILLAGE HALT   [B&MR]
OP: 16/05/1935   Photo: N. 1962
CP: 29/12/1962   M.Hale

OGILVIE
COLLIERY HALT
1554

1554   **OGILVIE COLLIERY HALT**   **[B&MR]**
OP: 08/06/1925   Photo: E. 1964
CP: 29/12/1962 (Workmens trains)   Stations U.K.

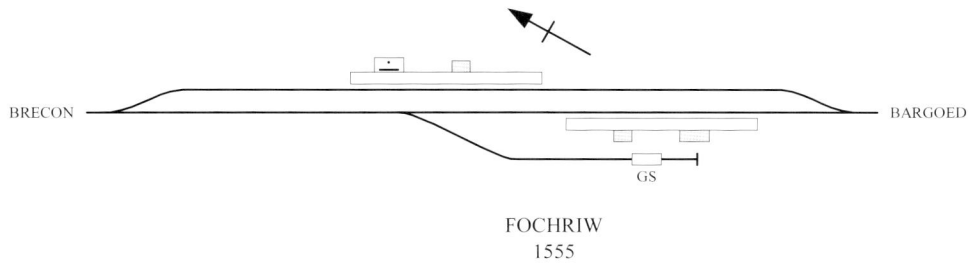

FOCHRIW
1555

1555   **FOCHRIW**   **[B&MR]**
OP: 01/09/1868   Photo: S. 1960
CP: 29/12/1962   E.T.Gill

1555   **FOCHRIW**   **[B&MR]**
                                 Photo: SE. 1960
                                 E.T.Gill

1556   **PANTYWAUN HALT**   **[B&MR]**
OP: 22/12/1941   Photo: SE. 1956
CP: 29/12/1962   H.C.Casserley

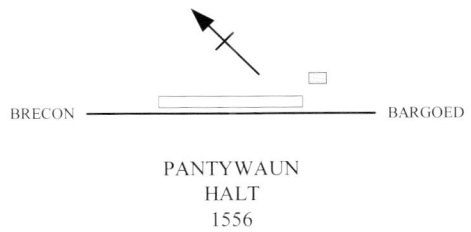

PANTYWAUN
HALT
1556

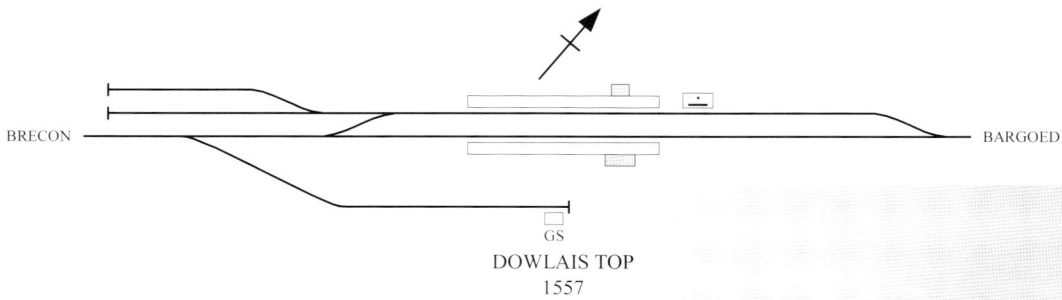

DOWLAIS TOP
1557

BRECON

BARGOED

GS

1557
OP: 01/08/1867
CP: 29/12/1962

DOWLAIS TOP

[B&MR]
Photo: NE. 1958
H.C.Casserley

1558
OP: 05/1889
CP: 29/12/1962

PANT

[B&MR]
Photo: NW. 1958
R.M.Casserley

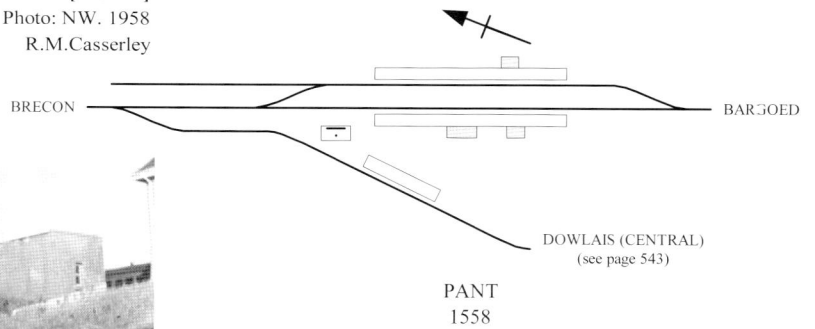

BRECON

BARGOED

DOWLAIS (CENTRAL)
(see page 543)

PANT
1558

1558
OP: 05/1889
CP: 29/12/1962

PANT

[B&MR]
Photo: N. 1957
R.M.Casserley

1559
OP: 01/08/1867
CP: 29/12/1962

PONTSTICILL JUNCTION

[B&MR]
Photo: N c.1960
J.Tarrant

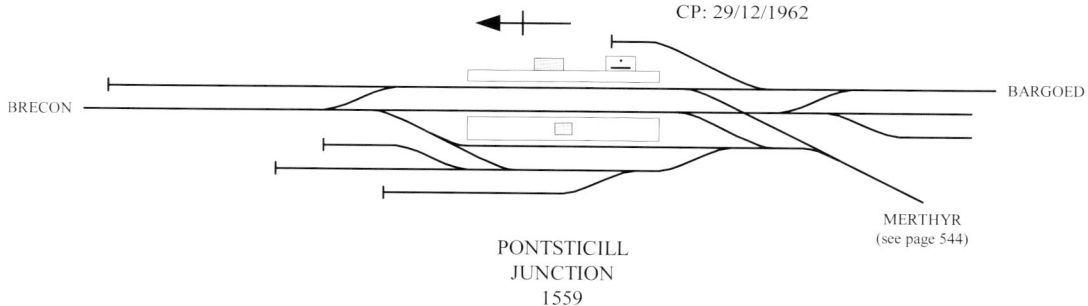

BRECON

BARGOED

MERTHYR
(see page 544)

PONTSTICILL
JUNCTION
1559

BRECON —————— BARGOED

DOLYGAER
1560

1560   **DOLYGAER**   **[B&MR]**
OP: 23/04/1863   Photo: N c.1963
CP: 29/12/1962   LOSA

1561   **TORPANTAU**   **[B&MR]**
OP: 06/1869   Photo: S. 1961
CP: 29/12/1962   LOSA

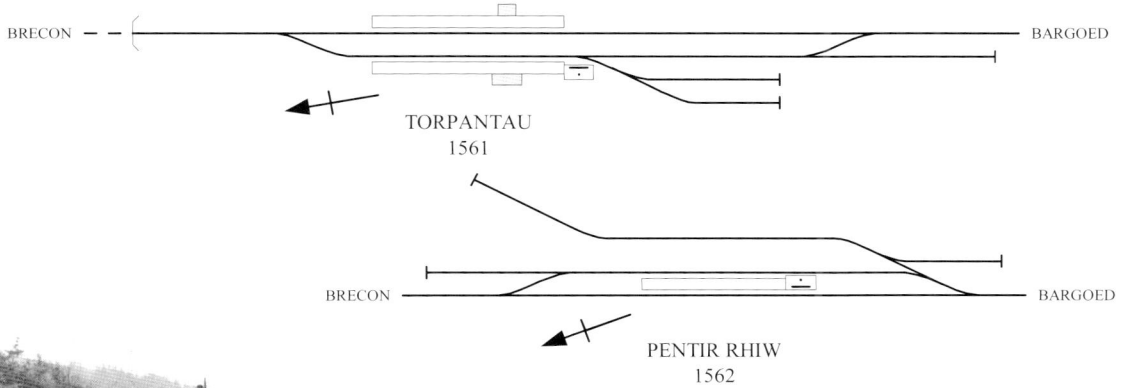

BRECON ———— BARGOED

TORPANTAU
1561

BRECON ———— BARGOED

PENTIR RHIW
1562

1562   **PENTIR RHIW**   **[B&MR]**
OP: 06/1909   Photo: S. c.1961
CP: 29/12/1962   LOSA

1563   **TALYBONT-ON-USK**   **[B&MR]**
OP: 23/04/1863   Photo: NE. 1957
CP: 29/12/1962   M.Hale

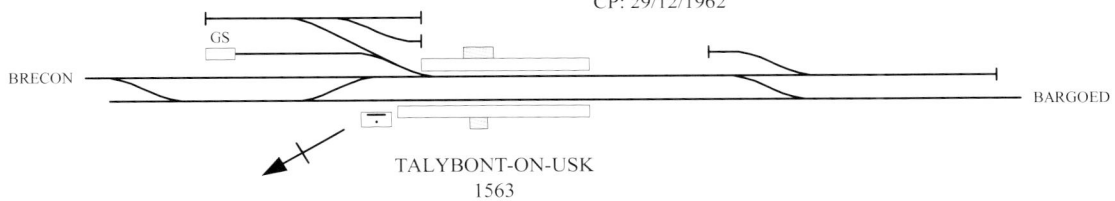

GS

BRECON ———— BARGOED

TALYBONT-ON-USK
1563

MOAT LANE JUNCTION
(see page 407)

BRECON – –   BARGOED

TALYLLYN
JUNCTION
1564

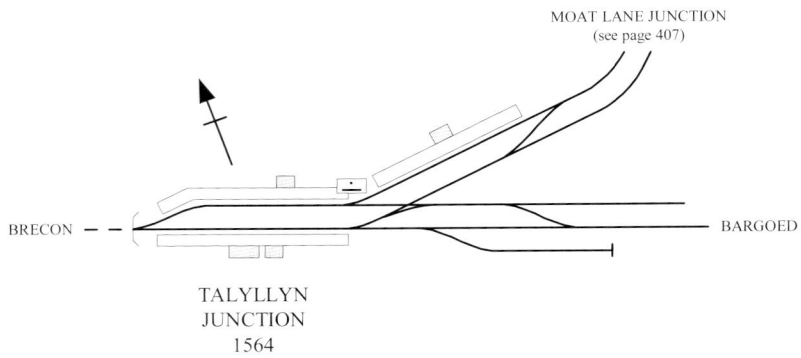

1564   **TALYLLYN JUNCTION**   **[B&MR]**
OP: 01/10/1869   Photo: E. c.1960
CP: 29/12/1962   E.T.Gill

1564   **TALYLLYN JUNCTION**   **[B&MR]**
                                        Photo: W. c.1961
                                                LOSA

1565   **GROESFFORDD HALT**   **[B&MR]**
OP: 08/09/1934   Photo: SE. c.1961
CP: 29/12/1962   LOSA

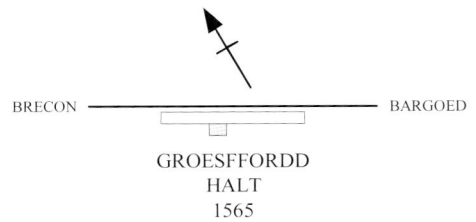

BRECON   BARGOED

GROESFFORDD
HALT
1565

1566   **BRECON**   **[B&MR]**
OP: 01/03/1871   Photo: E. 1961
CP: 29/12/1962   R.G.Nelson

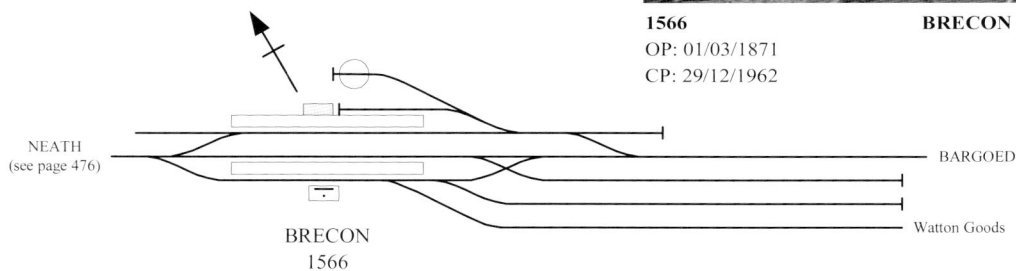

NEATH
(see page 476)

BARGOED

Watton Goods

BRECON
1566

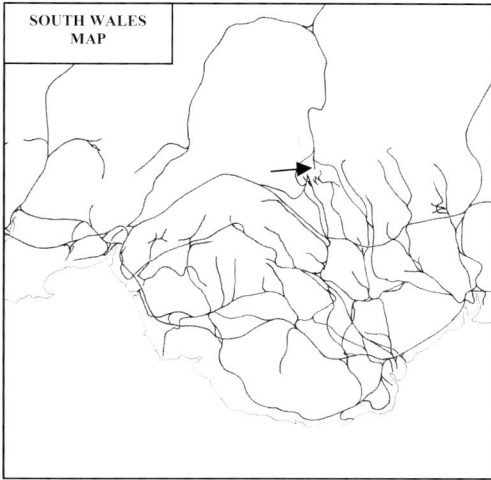

SOUTH WALES
MAP

PANT (Exc) TO DOWLAIS (CENTRAL)
BRECON AND DOWLAIS LINE
Brecon & Merthyr Railway -
Great Western Railway (01/01/1922)
ACT: 05/07/1865
OP: 23/06/1869
OG: 23/06/1869
CP: 28/06/1952 (Public Services only)
CP: 30/04/1960 (Workmens trains)
CG: 04/05/1964

PANT
(see page 540)

DOWLAIS
(CENTRAL)

PANTYSCALLOG
HALT
1567

1567   **PANTYSCALLOG HALT**   **[B&MR]**
OP: 01/10/1910   Photo: SE. 1958
CP: 30/04/1960 (Workmens trains)   Stations U.K.

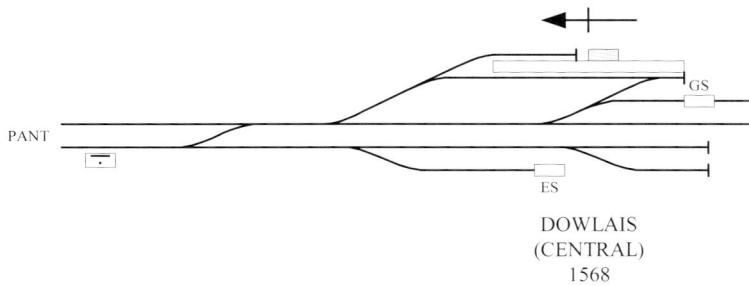

PANT

GS

ES

DOWLAIS
(CENTRAL)
1568

1568   **DOWLAIS (CENTRAL)**   **[B&MR]**
OP: 23/06/1869   Photo: S. 1962
CP: 30/04/1960 (Workmens trains)   R.Carpenter

1568   **DOWLAIS (CENTRAL)**   **[B&MR]**
     Photo: N. 1960
     E.T.Gill

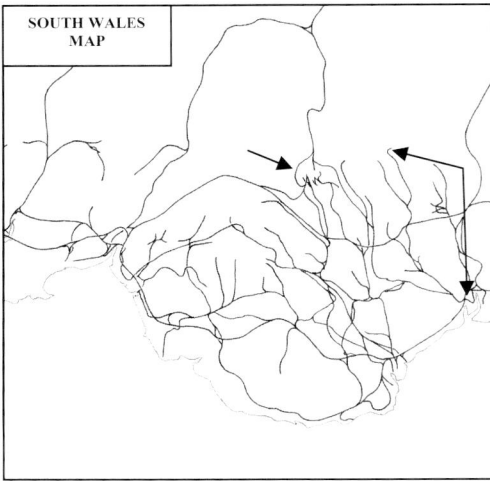

PONTSTICILL JUNCTION (Exc) TO MERTHYR (Exc)
PONTSTICILL LOOP,
MORLAIS JUNCTION TO RHYDYCAR JUNCTION
Brecon & Merthyr Railway -
Great Western Railway (01/01/1922)
(Pontsticill Junction to Morlais Junction)
Brecon & Merthyr Railway -
Brecon & Merthyr & LNW Joint Railway (19/07/1875) -
Great Western & LMS Joint Railway (01/01/1922)
(Morlais Junction to Rhydycar Junction)
ACT: 28/07/1862
OPG: 01/08/1867 (Pontsticill Junction to Cefn Coed)
OPG: 01/08/1868 (Cefn Coed to Rhydycar Junction)
CP: 11/11/1961
CG: 04/05/1964 (Pontsticill Junction to Vaynor Quarry)
CG: 03/01/1966 (Vaynor Quarry to Rhydycar Junction)

MERTHYR ——————————————— PONTSTICILL JUNCTION
(see page 540)

PONTSARN
1569

1569   **PONTSARN**   **[BM&LNWJ]**
OP: 06/1869   Photo: E. 1957
CP: 11/11/1961   Stations U.K.

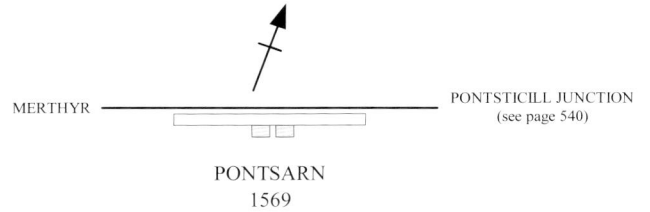

1570   **CEFN COED**   **[BM&LNWJ]**
OP: 01/08/1867   Photo: SW. 1951
CP: 11/11/1961   H.C.Casserley

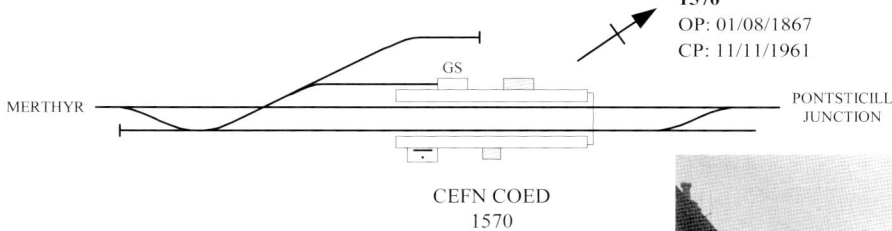

GS

MERTHYR ——————————————— PONTSTICILL
JUNCTION

CEFN COED
1570

1571   **HEOLGERRIG HALT**   **[BM&LNWJ]**
OP: 31/05/1937   Photo: S. 1958
CP: 11/11/1961   Stations U.K.

1570   **CEFN COED**   **[BM&LNWJ]**
                                   Photo: NE. 1958
                                   Stations U.K.

MERTHYR ——————————————— PONTSTICILL
(see page 509)   JUNCTION

HEOLGERRIG
HALT
1571

NEWPORT (HIGH STREET) (Exc) TO BRYNMAWR (Exc)
GAER BRANCH,
WESTERN VALLEYS LINE,
BRYNMAWR & WESTERN VALLEYS LINE

Monmouthshire Railway & Canal Company -
Great Western Railway (01/08/1880)
(Gaer Junction to Park Junction)
Monmouthshire Railway & Canal Company -
Great Western Railway (01/08/1880)
(Park Junction to Nantyglo)
Brynmawr & Western Valleys Railway -
Great Western & LNW Joint Railway (31/07/1902)
(Nantyglo to Brynmawr & Western Valleys Junction)

ACT: 11/08/1876 (Gaer Junction to Park Junction)
ACT: 31/07/1845 (Park Junction to Nantyglo)
ACT: 13/07/1899 (Nantyglo to Brynmawr & Western Valleys Jc.)
OP: 11/03/1880 (Gaer Junction to Park Junction)
OP: 23/12/1850 (Newport to Blaina as a Tramway)
OP: 16/05/1859 (Blaina to Nantyglo)
OP: 28/05/1906 (Nantyglo to Brynmawr)
OG: 11/03/1880 (Gaer Junction to Park Junction)
OG: 1855 (Newport to Nantyglo)
OG: 12/07/1905 (Nantyglo to Brynmawr)
CP: 29/12/1962 (Gaer Junction to Bassaleg Junction)
CP: 28/04/1962 (Bassaleg Junction to Brynmawr)
CG: 07/04/1969 (Public Goods only) (Newport to Newbridge)
CG: 03/10/1966 (Public Goods only) (Newbridge to Abertillery)
CG: 23/03/1964 (Abertillery to Blaina)
CG: 04/12/1963 (Blaina to Brynmawr)

1572   **BASSALEG JUNCTION**   **[MR&CC]**
OP: 23/12/1850   Photo: SE. 1960
CP: 28/04/1962   M.Hale

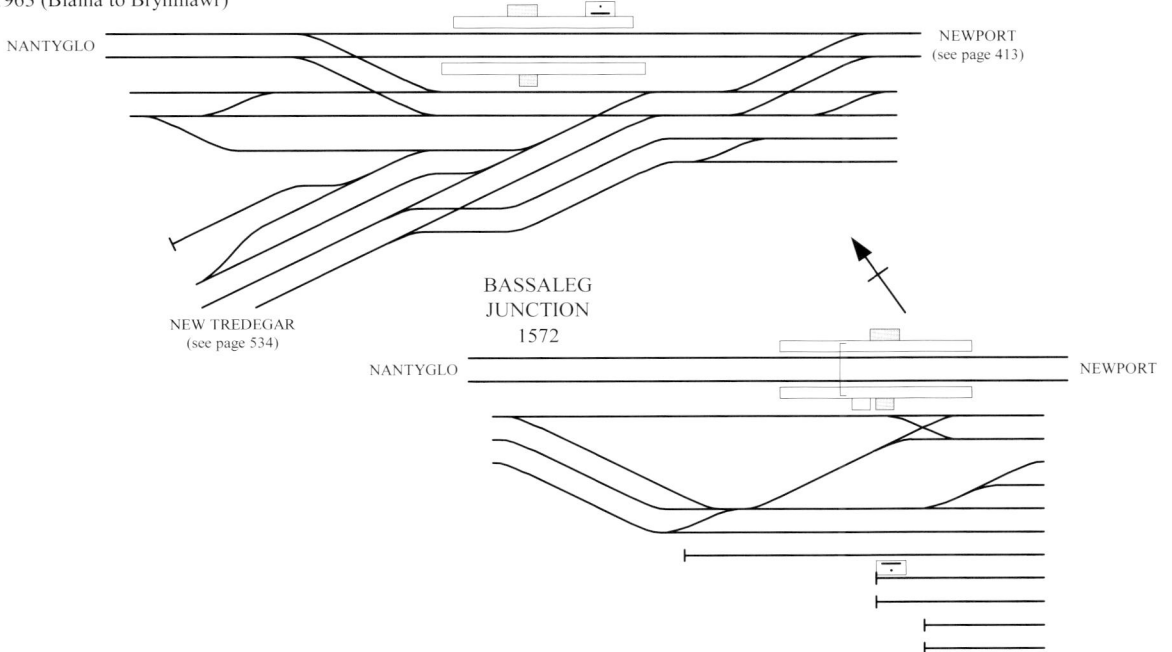

NANTYGLO

NEWPORT
(see page 413)

NEW TREDEGAR
(see page 534)

BASSALEG
JUNCTION
1572

NANTYGLO

NEWPORT

ROGERSTONE
1573

1573   **ROGERSTONE**   **[MR&CC]**
OP: 1900   Photo: NW. c.1912
CP: 28/04/1962   LOSA

1573   **ROGERSTONE**   **[MR&CC]**
                             Photo: NW. c.1964
                             LOSA

TYNYCWM
HALT
1574

1574   **TYNYCWM HALT**   **[MR&CC]**
OP: 17/04/1935   Photo: E. 1962
CP: 28/04/1962   M.Hale

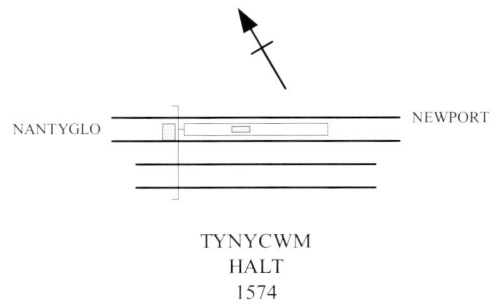

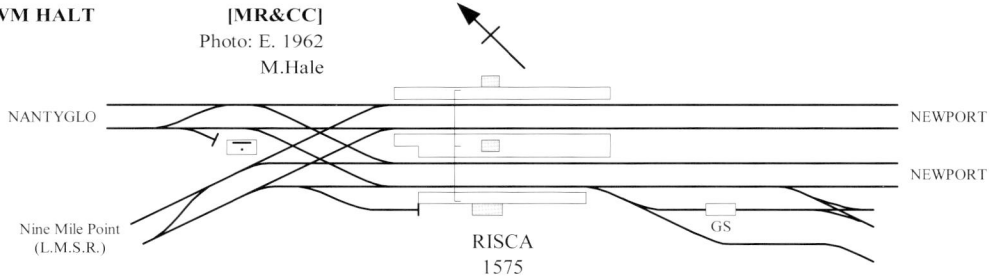

NANTYGLO   NEWPORT
     NEWPORT
Nine Mile Point
(L.M.S.R.)   GS

RISCA
1575

1575   **RISCA**   **[MR&CC]**
OP: 23/12/1850   Photo: SE. c.1964
CP: 28/04/1962   LOSA

1575   **RISCA**   **[MR&CC]**
Photo: SE. c.1964
LOSA

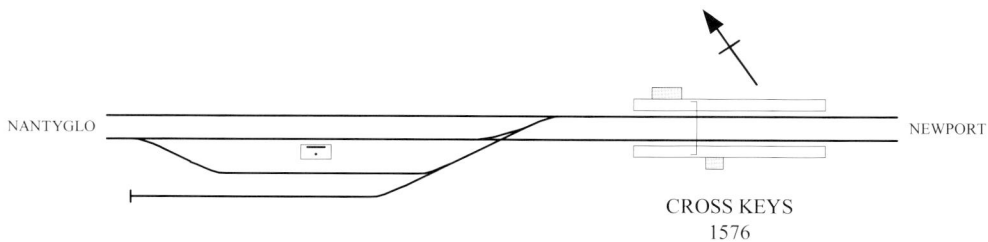

NANTYGLO   NEWPORT

CROSS KEYS
1576

1576   **CROSS KEYS**   **[MR&CC]**
OP: 09/1851   Photo: NW. 1958
CP: 28/04/1962   Stations U.K.

1576   **CROSS KEYS**   **[MR&CC]**
Photo: SE. c.1964
LOSA

1577   **CWMCARN**   **[MR&CC]**
OP: 02/03/1925   Photo: N. 1962
CP: 28/04/1962   M.Hale

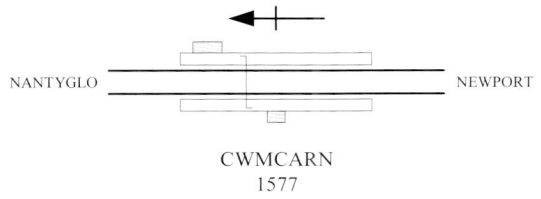

CWMCARN
1577

1578   **ABERCARN**   **[MR&CC]**
OP: 08/1867   Photo: SW. 1958
CP: 28/04/1962   Stations U.K.

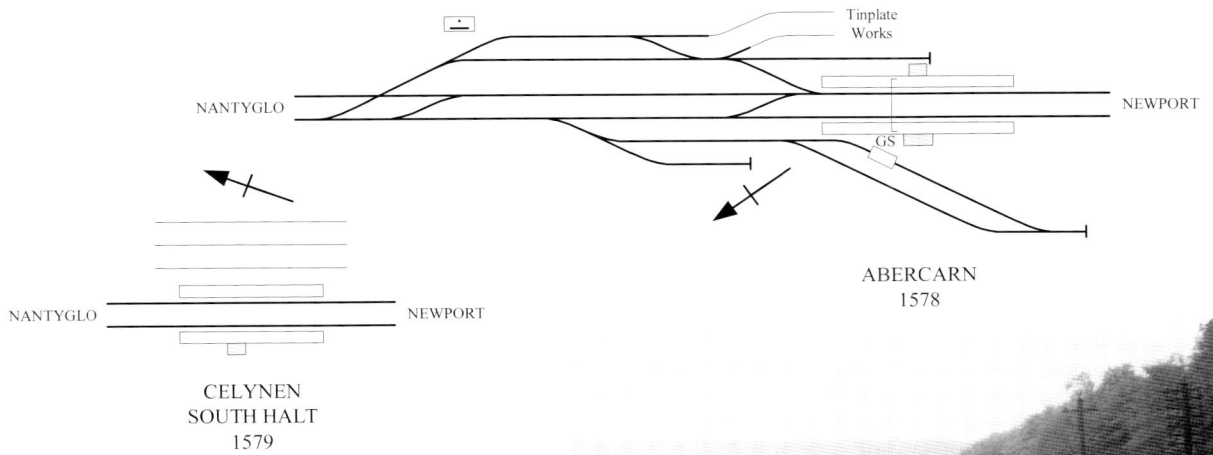

ABERCARN
1578

CELYNEN
SOUTH HALT
1579

1579   **CELYNEN SOUTH HALT**   **[MR&CC]**
OP: 14/08/1933   Photo: S. 1958
CP: 28/04/1962   Stations U.K.

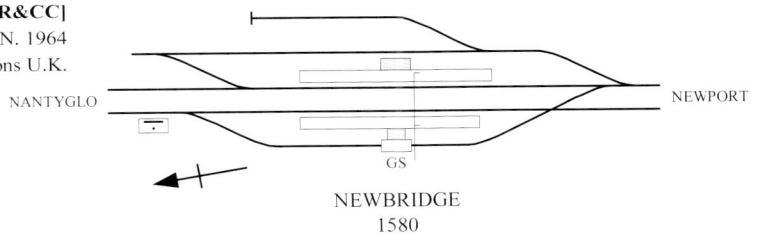

1580   **NEWBRIDGE**   **[MR&CC]**
OP: 23/12/1850   Photo: N. 1964
CP: 28/04/1962   Stations U.K.

NEWBRIDGE
1580

NANTYGLO   NEWPORT

CELYNEN
NORTH HALT
1581

1581   **CELYNEN NORTH HALT**   **[MR&CC]**
OP: 10/08/1936   Photo: N. 1958
CP: 28/04/1962 (Workmens trains)   Stations U.K.

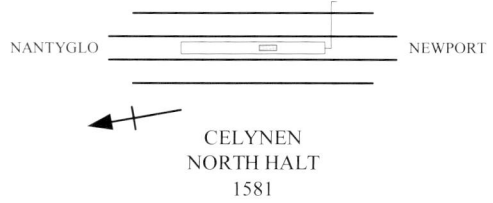

1582   **CRUMLIN (L.L.)**   **[MR&CC]**
OP: 23/12/1850   Photo: S. 1955
CP: 28/04/1962   R.M.Casserley

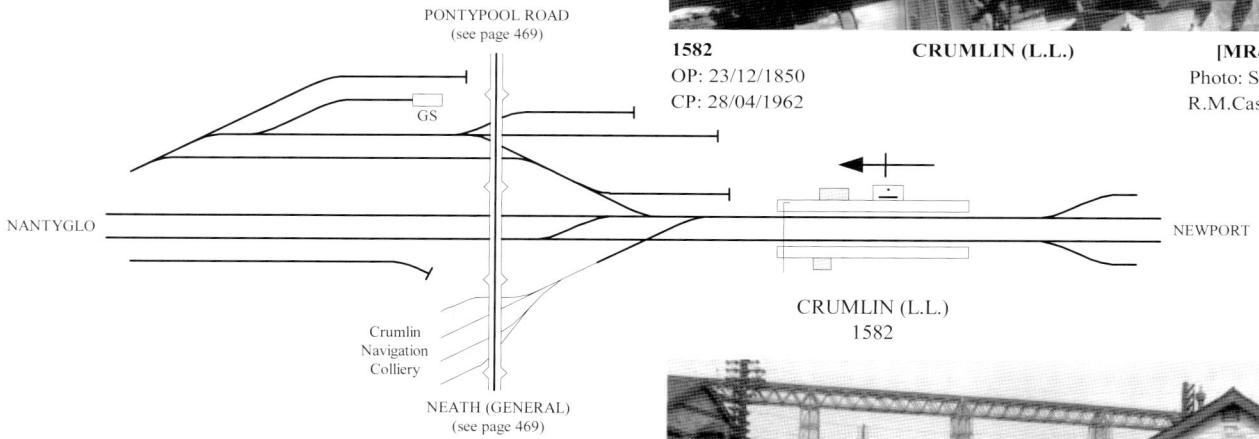

PONTYPOOL ROAD
(see page 469)

GS

NANTYGLO   NEWPORT

Crumlin
Navigation
Colliery

NEATH (GENERAL)
(see page 469)

CRUMLIN (L.L.)
1582

1582   **CRUMLIN (L.L.)**   **[MR&CC]**
                         Photo: N. 1965
                         M.M.Lloyd

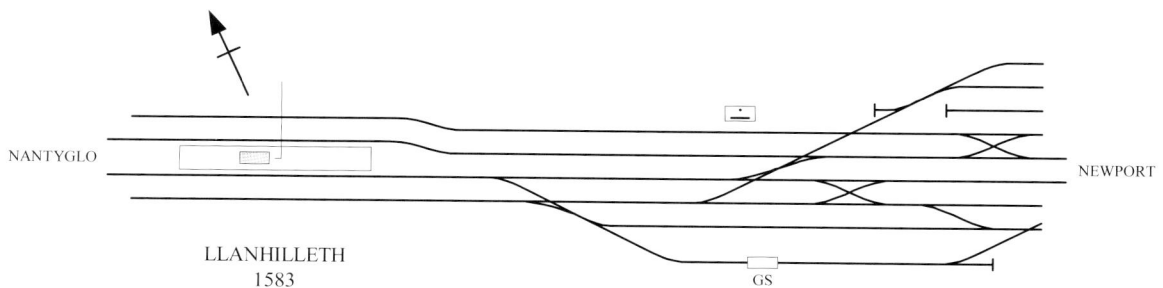

1583   **LLANHILLETH**   **[MR&CC]**
OP: 01/10/1901   Photo: SE. 1962
CP: 28/04/1962   Stations U.K.

NANTYGLO   NEWPORT

LLANHILLETH
1583

GS

NANTYGLO

NEWPORT

GS

EBBW VALE
(see page 551)

ABERBEEG
1584

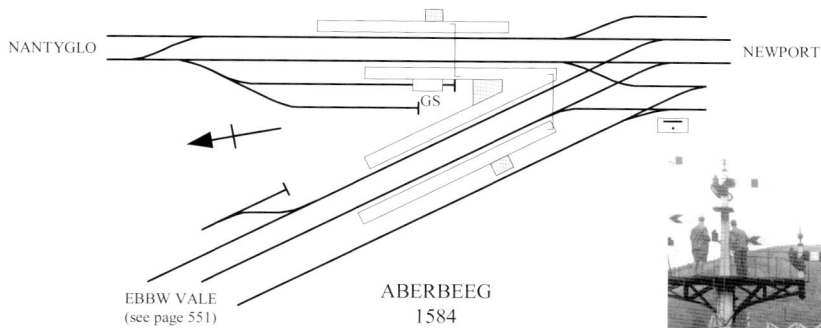

1584   ABERBEEG   [MR&CC]
OP: 23/12/1850   Photo: N. 1962
CP: 28/04/1962   Stations U.K.

1584   ABERBEEG   [MR&CC]
                                     Photo: NW. 1962
                                     P.Garland

1584   ABERBEEG   [MR&CC]
                                     Photo: S. 1962
                                     Stations U.K.

NANTYGLO   NEWPORT

SIX BELLS HALT
1585

1585   SIX BELLS HALT   [MR&CC]
OP: 27/09/1937   Photo: N. 1962
CP: 28/04/1962   M.Hale

1586   ABERTILLERY   [MR&CC]
OP: c.1892   Photo: SE. c.1935
CP: 28/04/1962   Stations U.K.

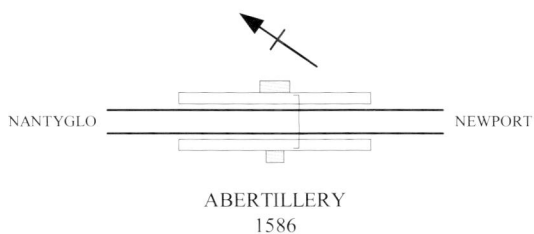

NANTYGLO   NEWPORT

ABERTILLERY
1586

1587   **BOURNVILLE (MON.) HALT**   **[MR&CC]**
OP: 07/1897   Photo: S. c.1964
CP: 28/04/1962   LOSA

1587   **BOURNVILLE (MON.) HALT**   **[MR&CC]**
                                 Photo: N. c.1964
                                 LOSA

NANTYGLO   NEWPORT

BOURNVILLE
(MON.) HALT
1587

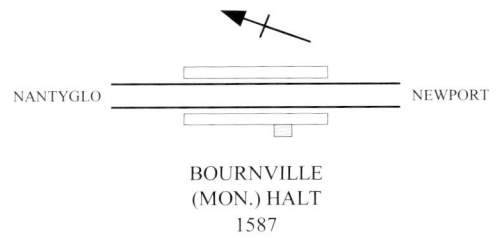

1588   **BLAINA**   **[MR&CC]**
OP: 23/12/1850   Photo: S. 1962
CP: 28/04/1962   R.K.Blencowe

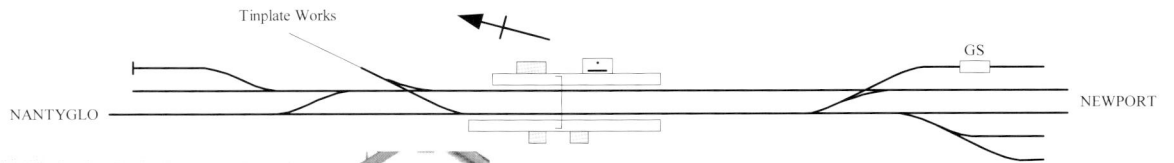

Tinplate Works   GS

NANTYGLO   NEWPORT

BLAINA
1588

1588   **BLAINA**   **[MR&CC]**
                             Photo: N. c.1964
                             LOSA

1589   **NANTYGLO**   **[MR&CC]**
OP: 16/05/1859   Photo: S. 1957
CP: 28/04/1962   R.M.Casserley

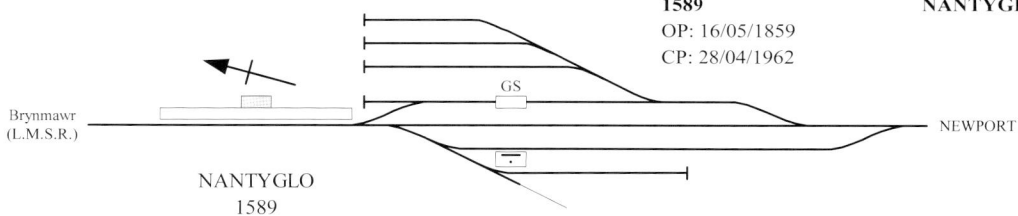

Brynmawr
(L.M.S.R.)   GS   NEWPORT

NANTYGLO
1589

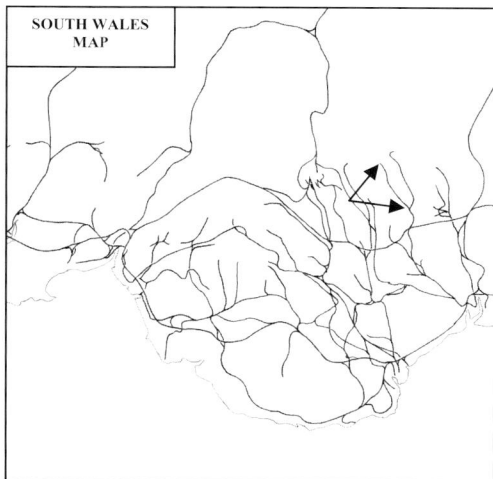

ABERBEEG (Exc) TO EBBW VALE
EBBW VALE BRANCH
Monmouthshire Railway & Canal Company -
Great Western Railway (01/08/1880)
ACT: 31/07/1845
OP: 19/04/1852 (as a Tramway)
OG: 1855
CP: 28/04/1962
CG: 04/11/1963 (Aberbeeg to Cwm (Public Goods only)
CG: 07/10/1963 (Cwm to Ebbw Vale (Public Goods only)

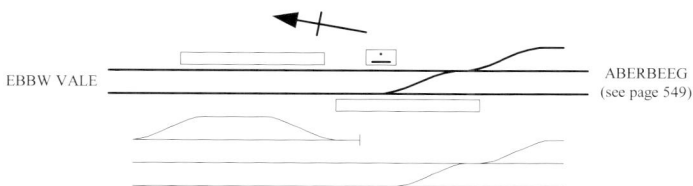

EBBW VALE   ABERBEEG
                                                                (see page 549)

MARINE COLLIERY
PLATFORM
1590

1590	MARINE COLLIERY PLATFORM	[MR&CC]
OP: c.1890		Photo: S. 1962
CP: 02/10/1961 (Workmens trains)		Stations U.K.

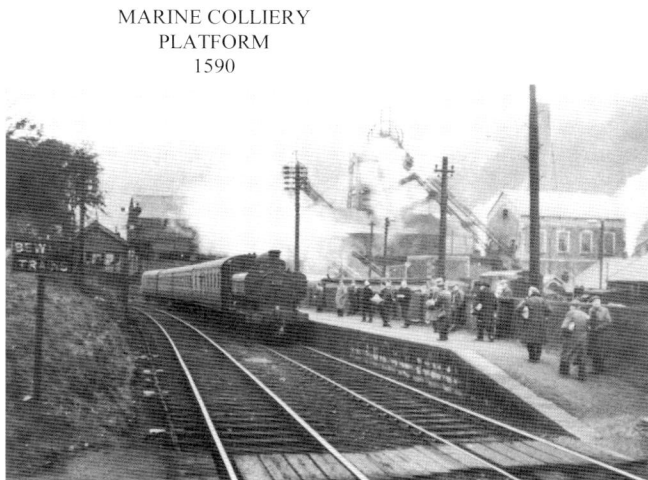

1590	MARINE COLLIERY PLATFORM	[MR&CC]
		Photo: S. 1961
		M.Hale

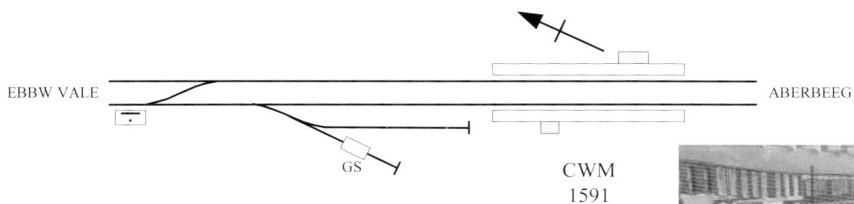

EBBW VALE   ABERBEEG

GS

CWM
1591

1591	CWM	[MR&CC]
OP: 19/04/1852		Photo: S. 1962
CP: 28/04/1962		Stations U.K.

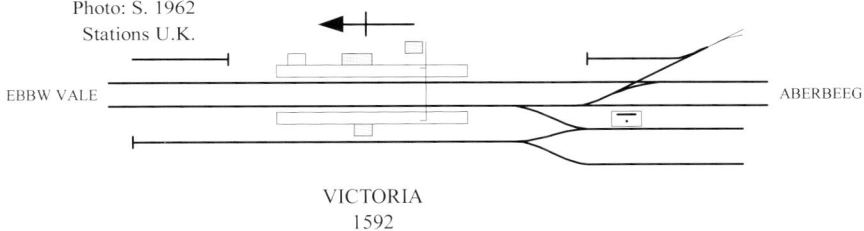

1592	VICTORIA	[MR&CC]
OP: 08/1852		Photo: S. 1962
CP: 28/04/1962		Stations U.K.

EBBW VALE   ABERBEEG

VICTORIA
1592

TYLLWYN HALT
1593

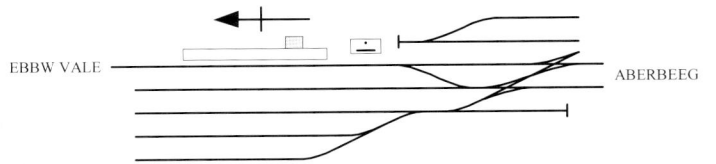

1593	TYLLWYN HALT	[MR&CC]
OP: 29/11/1943		Photo: S. 1962
CP: 28/04/1962		Stations U.K.

1594	EBBW VALE	[MR&CC]
OP: 19/04/1852		Photo: N. 1959
CP: 28/04/1962		Stations U.K.

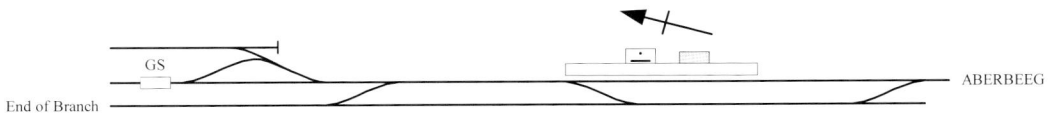

EBBW VALE
1594

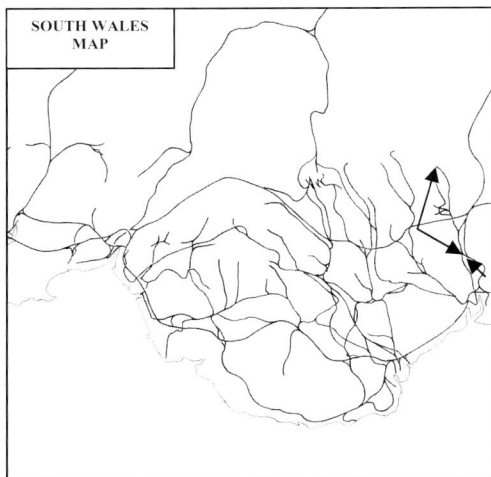

SOUTH WALES
MAP

Llantarnam Junction TO Cwmbran Junction
CWMBRAN BRANCH
Pontypool Caerleon & Newport Railway -
Great Western Railway (13/07/1876)
ACT: 05/07/1865
OP: 04/1878
OG: 04/1878
CP: 28/04/1962
CG: OPEN

1595	CWMBRAN	[PC&NR]
OP: 01/08/1880		Photo: SE. 1910
CP: 28/04/1962		Stations U.K.

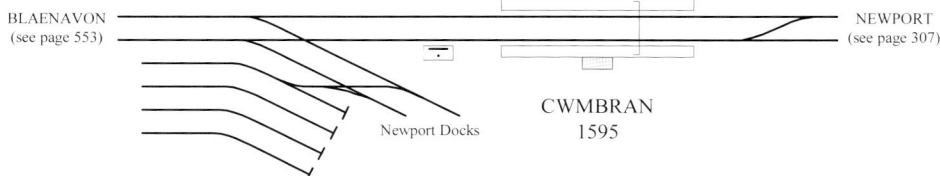

CWMBRAN
1595

Cwmbran Junction TO BLAENAVON
EASTERN VALLEYS LINE
Monmouthshire Railway & Canal Company -
Great Western Railway (01/08/1880)
ACT: 31/07/1845
OP: 01/07/1852 (Newport to Pontypool (Crane Street))
OP: 02/10/1854 (Pontypool (Crane Street) to Blaenavon)
OG: 01/07/1852 (Newport to Pontypool (Crane Street))
OG: 01/06/1854 (Pontypool (Crane Street) to Blaenavon)
CP: 28/04/1962
CG: 07/04/1969 (Trevethin Junction to Pontnewynydd Junction)
CG: 05/1962 (Pontnewynydd Junction to Snatchwood Sidings)
CG: 07/03/1960 (Snatchwood Sidings to Blaenavon)

1596   **UPPER PONTNEWYDD**   **[MR&CC]**
OP: 01/07/1852   Photo: N. 1960
CP: 28/04/1962   R.K.Blencowe

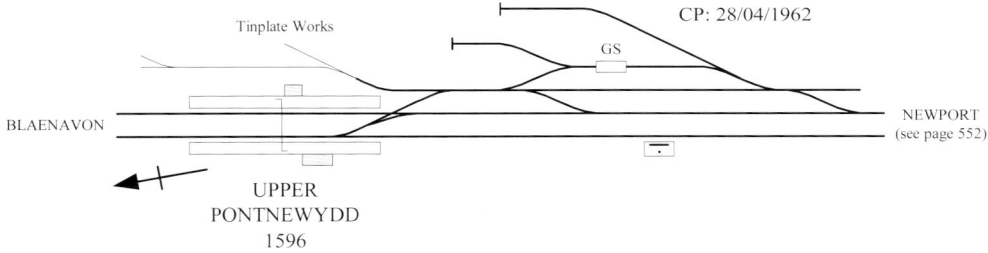

UPPER
PONTNEWYDD
1596

PONTRHYDYRUN
HALT
1597

1597   **PONTRHYDYRUN HALT**   **[MR&CC]**
OP: 17/07/1933   Photo: S. 1961
CP: 28/04/1962   M.Hale

SEBASTOPOL
1598

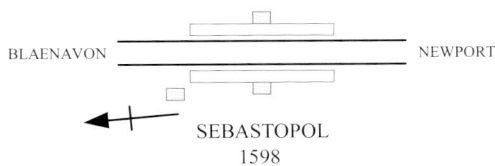

1598   **SEBASTOPOL**   **[MR&CC]**
OP: 28/05/1928   Photo: N. 1961
CP: 28/04/1962   M.Hale

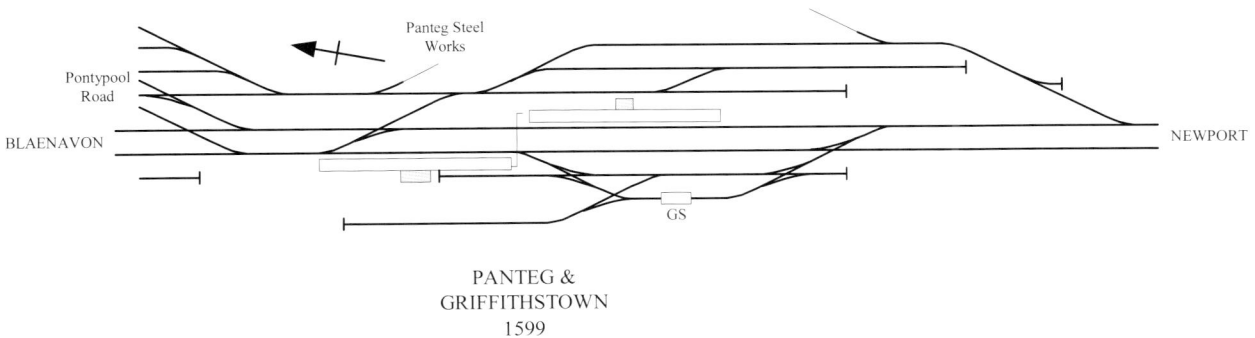

PANTEG &
GRIFFITHSTOWN
1599

1599   **PANTEG & GRIFFITHSTOWN**   **[MR&CC]**
OP: 01/08/1880   Photo: N. 1960
CP: 28/04/1962   R.M.Casserley

1599   **PANTEG & GRIFFITHSTOWN**   **[MR&CC]**
Photo: N. 1958
Stations U.K.

1600   **PONTYPOOL (BLAENDARE ROAD) HALT**   **[MR&CC]**
OP: 30/04/1928   Photo: E. c.1950
CP: 28/04/1962   LOSA

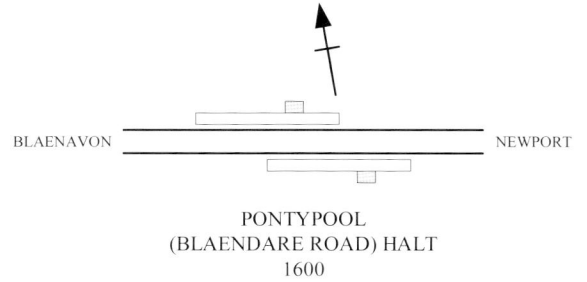

BLAENAVON   NEWPORT

PONTYPOOL
(BLAENDARE ROAD) HALT
1600

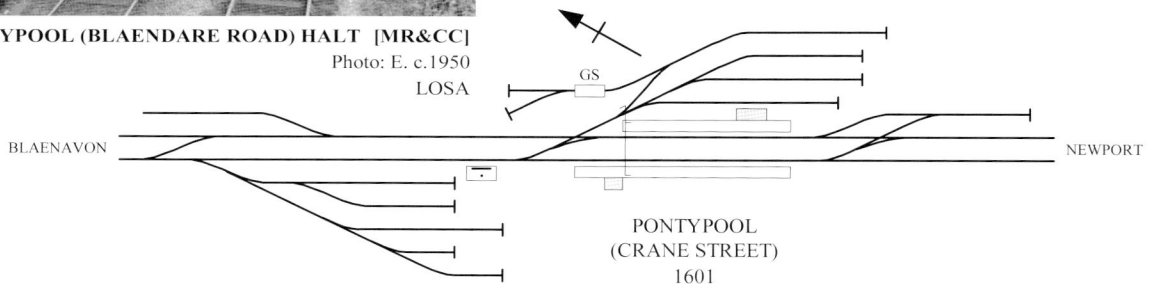

GS

BLAENAVON   NEWPORT

PONTYPOOL
(CRANE STREET)
1601

1601   **PONTYPOOL (CRANE STREET)**   **[MR&CC]**
OP: 01/07/1852   Photo: N. 1962
CP: 28/04/1962   Stations U.K.

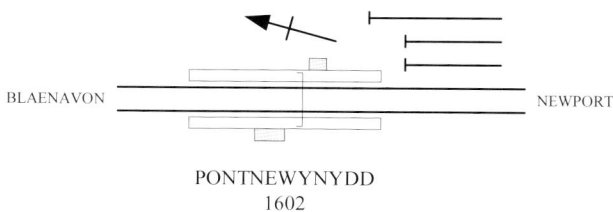

BLAENAVON   NEWPORT

PONTNEWYNYDD
1602

1602   **PONTNEWYNYDD**   **[MR&CC]**
OP: 02/10/1854   Photo: S. c.1939
CP: 28/04/1962   Stations U.K.

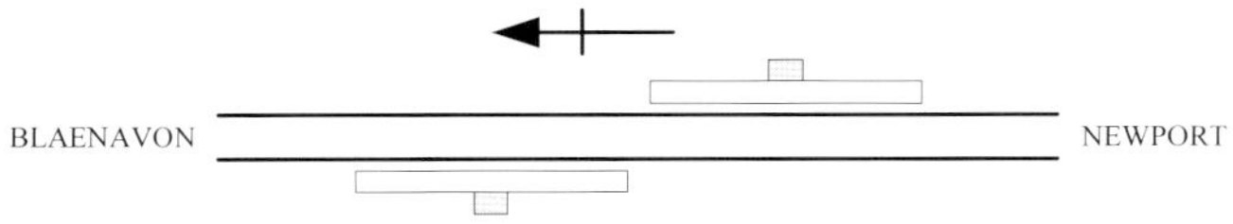

PHOTOGRAPH UNAVAILABLE

SNATCHWOOD HALT
1603

1603   **SNATCHWOOD HALT**   **[MR&CC]**
OP: 13/07/1912   Photo: None
CP: 05/10/1953   Available

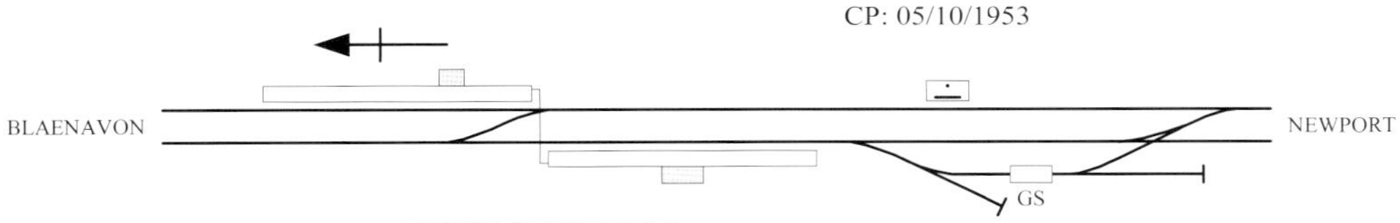

ABERSYCHAN (L.L.)
1604

1604   **ABERSYCHAN (L.L.)**   **[MR&CC]**
OP: 02/10/1854   Photo: N. 1961
CP: 28/04/1962   Stations U.K.

1604   **ABERSYCHAN (L.L.)**   **[MR&CC]**
    Photo: S. 1958
    H.C.Casserley

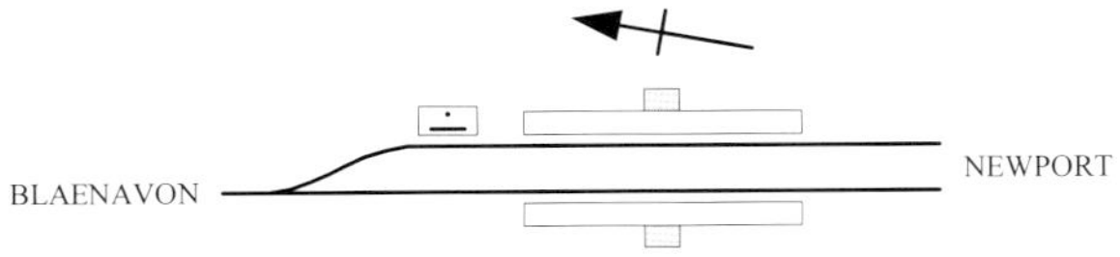

CWMFFRWD
HALT
1605

1605   **CWMFFRWD HALT**   **[MR&CC]**
OP: 13/07/1912   Photo: N. 1961
CP: 28/04/1962   Stations U.K.

1606   **CWMAVON (MON.)**   **[MR&CC]**
OP: 02/10/1854   Photo: N. 1961
CP: 28/04/1962   Stations U.K.

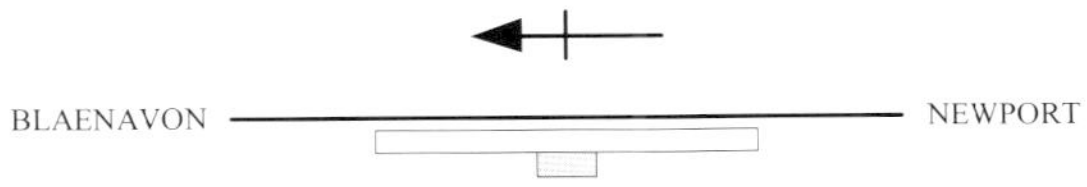

CWMAVON (MON.)
1606

1607   **BLAENAVON**   **[MR&CC]**
OP: 02/10/1854   Photo: N. 1958
CP: 28/04/1962   R.M.Casserley

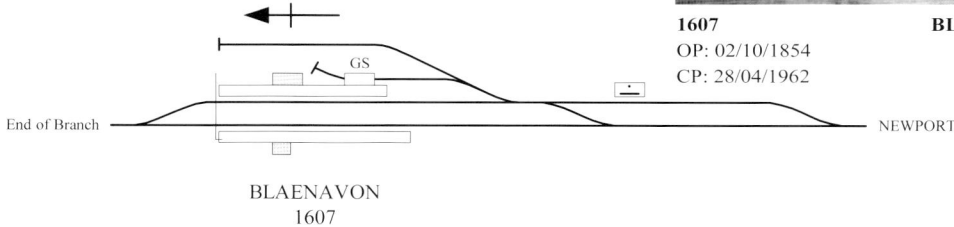

BLAENAVON
1607

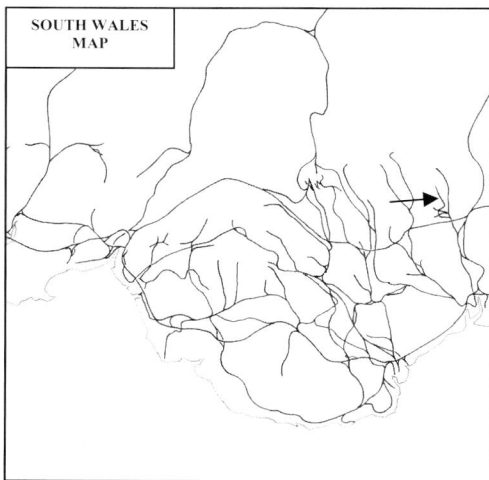

SOUTH WALES MAP

PONTYPOOL (CRANE STREET) (Exc) TO ABERSYCHAN & TALYWAIN TALYWAIN BRANCH, ABERSYCHAN STATION LINE

Monmouthshire Railway & Canal Company -
Great Western Railway (01/08/1880)
(Trevethin Junction to near Talywain Junction)
Monmouthshire Railway & Canal Company -
Monmouthshire Railway & Canal Company &
LNW Joint Railway (01/03/1875) -
Great Western & LNW Joint Railway (01/08/1880)
(Near Talywain Junction to 13 miles 12 chains)
ACT: 16/07/1874
OP: 01/05/1878 (LNWR Services)
OP: 13/07/1912 (GWR Services)
OG: 1879 (Trevethin Junction to Near Talywain Junction)
OG: 1877 (Abersychan Station Line via LNWR)
CP: 03/05/1941
CG: 23/08/1965 (Public Goods only)

1608   **WAINFELIN HALT**   **[MR&CC]**
NO INFORMATION AS CLOSED BY 1947
CP: 03/05/1941

1609   **CWMFFRWDOER HALT**   **[MR&CC]**
NO INFORMATION AS CLOSED BY 1947
CP: 03/05/1941

1610   **PENTREPIOD HALT**   **[MR&CC]**
NO INFORMATION AS CLOSED BY 1947
CP: 03/05/1941

1611   **PENTWYN HALT**   **[MR&CC]**
NO INFORMATION AS CLOSED BY 1947
CP: 03/05/1941

1612   **ABERSYCHAN & TALYWAIN**   **[MR&CC]**
OP: 13/07/1912   Photo: N. 1957
CP: 03/05/1941   W.A.Camwell

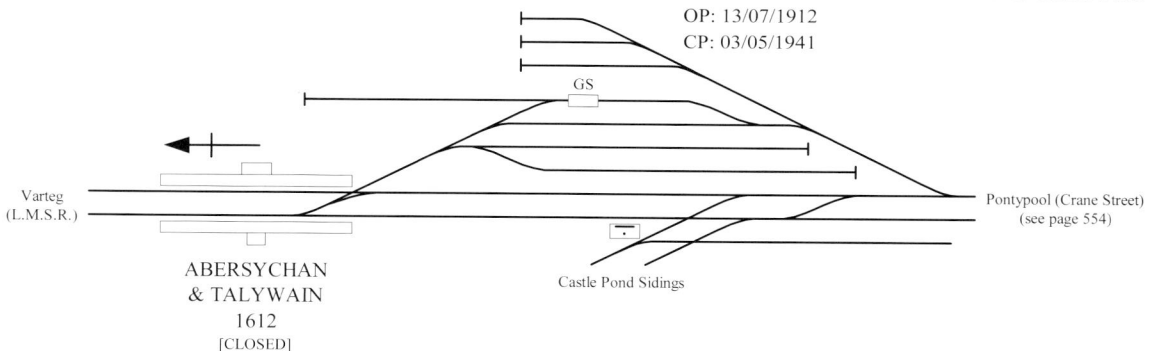

ABERSYCHAN
& TALYWAIN
1612
[CLOSED]

APPENDIX A
LIST OF NON STANDARD STATIONS
(ALPHABETICAL)

This list contains all stations in the survey which were not open to full passenger public services and shown in the timetables, at some time during 1947. Also shown are several stations which when first opened, were not open to the public until later.

No.	STATION NAME	RAILWAY	STATUS IN 1947
905	ABBEYDORE	[GVR]	STN OG
1069	ABERANGELL	[MR]	STN OG
1361	ABERCAMLAIS HALT	[N&BR]	STN OP Private
1365	ABERCRAVE	[SV&N&BJR]	STN OG
1612	ABERSYCHAN & TALYWAIN	[MR&CC]	STN OG
881	ALVELEY COLLIERY HALT	[SVR]	STN OP Workmen only (and throughout existence)
906	BACTON	[GVR]	STN OG
1025	BALA JUNCTION	[C&BR]	STN OP Not shown in Timetables
1024	BALA LAKE HALT	[B&DR]	STN OP Excursions only (from 24/09/1939)
1545	BARGOED COLLIERY HALT	[B&MR]	STN OP Workmen only (and throughout existence)
1426	BARRY PIER	[BR]	STN OP Excursion trains only (and throughout existence)
1450	CATHAYS (WOODVILLE ROAD) HALT	[TVR]	STN OP Served by Up trains only
1581	CELYNEN NORTH HALT	[MR&CC]	STN OP Workmen only (and throughout existence)
1068	CEMMAES	[MR]	STN OG
912	CLIFFORD	[GVR]	STN OG
778	COED POETH	[NWMR]	STN OG
985	COLEFORD	[S&WR]	STN OG
986	COLEFORD	[ColeRly]	STN OG
1343	CRUMLIN VALLEYS COLLIERY PLATFORM	[NA&HR]	STN OP Workmen only (and throughout existence)
1352	CRYNANT NEW COLLIERY HALT	[N&BR]	STN OP Workmen only (and throughout existence)
1383	CWMDU	[PTR&D]	STN OG
1547	CWMSYFIOG COLLIERY HALT	[B&MR]	STN OP Workmen only (from 06/12/1937)
1376	CYMMER CORRWG	[SWMR]	STN OP Workmen only
1371	CYNONVILLE HALT	[R&SB]	STN OP (When OP Workmen only. OP Public on ReOP 02/10/1912)
1352	DILLWYN & BRYNTEG PLATFORM	[N&BR]	STN OP Workmen only (and throughout existence)
1070	DINAS MAWDDWY	[MR]	STN OG
909	DORSTONE	[GVR]	STN OG
973	DRYBROOK ROAD	[S&WR]	STN OG
1372	DUFFFRYN RHONDDA HALT	[R&SB]	STN OP (When OP Workmen only. OP Public on ReOP 02/10/1912)
1022	FLAG STATION HALT	[B&DR]	STN OP (When OP Private. Not OP Public until 14/09/1931)
1488	GADLYS ROAD PLATFORM	[DVR]	STN OP Workmen only (and throughout existence)
1405	GILFACH GOCH	[EVER]	STN OG & OP Excursion trains only
964	GLASCOED FACTORY EAST ACCESS HALT	[CMU&PR]	STN OP Workmen only (and throughout existence)
965	GLASCOED FACTORY WEST ACCESS HALT	[CMU&PR]	STN OP Workmen only (and throughout existence)
1378	GLYNCORRWG	[SWMR]	STN OG & OP Workmen only
911	GREENS SIDING	[GVR]	STN OG
1551	GROESFAEN COLLIERY HALT	[RR]	STN OP Workmen only (and throughout existence)
1326	HIRWAUN POND HALT	[VNR]	STN OP Workmen only (and throughout existence)
1134	KERRY	[O&NR]	STN OG
1198	KIDWELLY FLATS HALT	[SWR]	STN OP Workmen only (and throughout existence)
1197	LANDO PLATFORM	[SWR]	STN OP Workmen only (and throughout existence)
782	LEGACY	[GWR]	STN OG
1220	LETTERSTON	[R&FR]	STN OG
1501	LLANBRADACH COLLIERY HALT	[RR]	STN OP Workmen only (and throughout existence)
1216	LLANYCEFN	[NR&MR]	STN OG
858	MADELEY (SALOP.)	[S&BR]	STN OG
1217	MAENCLOCHOG	[NR&MR]	STN OG
1382	MAESTEG (NEATH ROAD)	[PTR&D]	STN OG
1451	MAINDY (NORTH ROAD) HALT	[TVR]	STN OP Served by Up trains only
1590	MARINE COLLIERY PLATFORM	[MR&CC]	STN OP Workmen only (and throughout existence)
1477	NANTEWLAETH COLLIERY HALT	[SWMR]	STN OP Workmen only (and throughout existence)
1489	NANTMELYN PLATFORM	[DVR]	STN OP Workmen only (and throughout existence)
1316	NEATH ABBEY	[S&NR]	STN OG
1446	NINIAN PARK HALT	[PHD&R]	STN OP Matches only (from 10/09/1939)
1380	NORTH RHONDDA HALT	[SWMR]	STN OP Workmen only (and throughout existence)
1385	NOTTAGE HALT	[LVR]	STN OP Down trains to set down, Up trains to pick up only (When OP Golfers only. Not OP Public until 14/07/1924)
1554	OGILVIE COLLIERY HALT	[B&MR]	STN OP Workmen only (and throughout existence)
975	PARKEND	[S&WR]	STN OG
1362	PENPONT HALT	[N&BR]	STN OP Private
1534	PENYDARREN PLATFORM	[GW&RJR]	STN OP Workmen only (and throughout existence)
908	PETERCHURCH	[GVR]	STN OG
1308	PONT LLIW	[GWR]	STN OG
744	PORT SUNLIGHT	[C&BR]	STN OP (When OP Workmen only. Not OP Public until 09/05/1927)
1219	PUNCHESTON	[R&FR]	STN OG
782	RHOS	[SUR&CC]	STN OG
781	RHOSTYLLEN	[GWR]	STN OG
1218	ROSEBUSH	[NR&MR]	STN OG

No.	STATION NAME	RAILWAY	STATUS IN 1947
1087	SCAFELL	[L&NR]	STN OP Private station in public timetables, served by Up trains only
1379	SOUTH PIT HALT	[SWMR]	STN OP Workmen only (and throughout existence)
974	SPEECH HOUSE ROAD	[S&WR]	STN OG
1531	TAFF MERTHYR COLLIERY HALT	[GW&RJR]	STN OP Workmen only (and throughout existence)
1150	TIRCELYN HALT	[MWR]	STN OP Private
1182	TREMAINS HALT	[SWR]	STN OP Workmen only (and throughout existence)
1277	TYCOCH HALT	[BP&GVR]	STN OP Workmen only (and throughout existence)
983	UPPER LYDBROOK	[S&WR]	STN OG
907	VOWCHURCH	[GVR]	STN OG
910	WESTBROOK	[GVR]	STN OG
976	WHITECROFT	[S&WR]	STN OG
1524	WINDSOR COLLIERY HALT	[RR]	STN OP Workmen only (and throughout existence)
1366	YSTRADGYNLAIS	[SV&N&BJR]	STN OG

APPENDIX B
LIST OF STATIONS WITH PHOTOGRAPHIC VARIATION
OR TRACK DIAGRAM UNCERTAINTIES
TO THE STATION AS IT WAS IN 1947
(ALPHABETICAL)

This list contains all stations in the survey where there is a significant variation of the photograph shown, to the appearance of the station in 1947. This generally applies to the buildings, or re-location of the platforms. It does not apply to stations where the platform has been built in wood and replaced in concrete with no change to the form of the station structure. It should be noted that a number of stations had their footbridge canopy removed in the early 1950's. These are not included in the analysis.

Included here are several stations for which the photograph does not show, or show clearly, part of the station buildings. Some stations have no photograph available, although in some cases a sketch is provided.

In addition, there is analysis where it has not always been possible to ascertain the correct track diagram for 1947.

No.	STATION NAME	RAILWAY	VARIATION
1584	ABERBEEG	[MR&CC]	The headshunt in the goods yard had gone by 1921, even though it is still shown on the OS 1962 map along with the crossover which had moved by 1959.
1363	ABERBRAN	[N&BR]	There was a loop and short siding here, removed after 1959.
1529	ABERCANAID	[GW&RJR]	The track diagram for the north end is a best guess.
1064	ABERDOVEY	[A&WCR]	The siding arrangements around the shed (which is not a goods shed) are unclear. By 1955 the siding to this 'concrete store shed' and beyond, was out of use.
1527	ABERFAN	[GW&RJR]	The existence of the outer siding and the goods shed in 1947 is unclear. The up platform and building in the photograph had long been removed by 1947, on the singling of the line.
1089	ABERMULE	[O&NR]	Other photographs show two new sidings to the south, shown on the track diagram, but their date of installation is unknown. Access to the goods shed was via a trailing point to the down main, but this was changed to a facing point on the up main, at a date unknown, as shown.
1041	AFON WEN	[A&WCR]	The three sidings to the east and north are of unknown length. They are shown as ending as loops to the main line. But it is unknown if they still connected to the main line at the east end by 1947.
814	ALL STRETTON HALT	[S&HR]	Photograph of only the down platform, the up platform and shelter are similar, situated to the north, just beyond the road bridge. The remains of which can be seen in the second photograph.
923	ASHPERTON	[W&HR]	The main building does not show up well, but is similar to that at Withington on page 332.
1112	BANGOR-ON-DEE	[W&ER]	The outer westernmost siding may have been removed by 1947.
1428	BARRY	[BR]	At some time after 1935 but before 1956, the up bay platform line was connected to the up siding too, rather than just joining the up main line as shown.
1429	BARRY DOCKS	[BR]	The two slips in front of the signal box may have been removed by 1947.
1239	BEAVERS HILL HALT	[P&TR]	A photograph of the halt after removal of the shelter, its type is unknown.
1411	BEDDAU HALT	[L&TVJR]	No photograph currently available. A shelter is shown on the track diagram, as there is evidence one was provided in 1911, type and location unknown.
1532	BEDLINOG	[GW&RJR]	There was a workmen's platform on the down side just to the north west of the signal box by the crossover. Although on a 1952 signal box diagram it is believed to have been out of use by at least 1938.
1491	BIRCHGROVE HALT	[CardRly]	It is uncertain if the down (north side) siding was also accessed via a trailing crossover to the up line.
1398	BLAENGARW	[OVR]	The arrangement for the colliery sidings is a best guess.
1347	BLAENGWYNFI	[R&SB]	There is evidence to suggest the goods shed may have gone by 1947.
1270	BLAENPLWYF HALT	[LA&NQ]	A photograph of the closed halt, shelter type and location unknown.
1587	BOURNVILLE (MON.) HALT	[MR&CC]	It is unclear if there was a down shelter.
848	BREIDDEN	[S&WPoolJ]	The up platform shelter does not show well, but is a small wooden hut, with an apex roof at right angles to the railway line.
746	BROMBOROUGH	[C&BR]	The up platform building does not appear in the photographs, but is similar to that at Spital. Along the platform side, there is a door at each end and three sets of windows.
777	BRYMBO	[W&MR]	There is a pagoda on the down platform.
1093	BUTTINGTON	[O&NR]	The two down sidings by the junction may have been lifted by 1947, certainly some time before 1958.
1430	CADOXTON	[BR]	The main building is set back from the up platform and had been rebuilt with a modern structure closer to the platform, as shown in the photograph, by 1955.
1497	CEFN ON HALT	[RR]	Note the booking office pagoda at the top of the path, in the second photograph.
1166	CHEPSTOW	[SWR]	The diagram shows the racecourse platform, open only at race meetings.
752	CHESTER	[C&BR]	Track diagram is a best guess due to many crossover changes at various dates.
765	CHIRK	[SO&CJR]	Changes to the goods yard, not shown, involving the construction of a warehouse had taken place by 1960. Remains of the Glyn Valley Tramway platform can be seen behind the down shelter, with the goods shed just visible in the distance.
890	CLEOBURY MORTIMER	[T&BR]	The down platform has a typical Great Western pagoda, just visible.
1476	CLYDACH COURT HALT	[TVR]	The exact location of the shelter is uncertain. It is believed to be similar to that at Pontcynon Bridge Halt on page 516.
1319	CLYNE HALT	[VNR]	It is not known if the shelters survived up to 1947, the platforms had been cut back and the pagodas removed by 1961.

No.	STATION NAME	RAILWAY	VARIATION
811	CONDOVER	[S&HR]	The up shelter is barely visible, a slightly better view can be found on page vi. It is similar to that of Dorrington and Leebotwood on page 298.
1029	CORWEN	[C&BR]	Track diagram is a best guess in the turntable area. The engine shed is long gone despite being shown on a 1954 Ordnance Survey map.
819	CRAVEN ARMS & STOKESAY	[S&HR]	Photographs show no connection from the goods shed to the siding which goes behind the signal box, so this line is not shown.
1274	CROSSWAYS HALT	[LA&NQ]	A photograph of the closed halt, there was a pagoda on the platform.
1343	CRUMLIN VALLEYS COLLIERY PLATFORM	[NA&HR]	A sketch showing the halt in the 1950's, before rebuilding as an island platform in 1958. It is thought there were no shelters provided.
1352	CRYNANT NEW COLLIERY HALT	[N&BR]	A photograph of the remains of the halt. It is unknown if a shelter was provided.
1369	CWMAVON (GLAM.)	[R&SB]	The goods shed appears to have gone by 1947.
1371	CYNONVILLE HALT	[R&SB]	A photograph of the closed halt. There is evidence of a booking office up by the bridge, but shelters were probably not provided on the platform.
1295	DERWYDD ROAD	[LR]	Remains of the main down building can be seen, but the up shelter type and location are unknown. It is also not known if there was a footbridge.
1070	DINAS MAWDDWY	[MR]	Although the engine shed had closed it remained in situ until at least 1950.
1466	DINAS (RHONDDA)	[TVR]	It is unknown when the up shelter was replaced with the concrete one shown.
1372	DUFFRYN RHONDDA HALT	[R&SB]	There is no evidence of an up shelter, but as can be seen from the photograph there is a gap for the down shelter, its type is unknown.
726	DUNHAM HILL	[BL&CJR]	The up building does not show up well. Its sloping roof suggests it is not similar to the other shelters on the line.
1515	DYNEA HALT	[PC&NR]	A shelter is shown on the track diagram for the up platform. As can be seen this wooden shelter had gone by 1956 although the base where it stood is evident.
1176	ELY (MAIN LINE)	[SWR]	The down building does not show up well, the back of which can be seen in the second photograph, just beyond the footbridge.
1272	FELIN FACH	[LA&NQ]	A photograph after closure to passengers, so the up shelter type is unknown.
1309	FELIN FRAN HALT	[GWR]	A photograph of the closed halt, shelter type and locations unknown.
1008	FESTINIOG	[B&FR]	The down line loop has been cut back from joining the siding lines by 1948, as shown in the photograph. Also note the footbridge in the distance.
1215	FISHGUARD HARBOUR	[GWR]	There was a siding to the north west but this has been removed on the diagram, date unknown. A crossover on the westerly sidings, believed added later is also not shown. The straight lines on the diagram represent platforms, but these were not for passenger use, only two platforms were for passenger trains.
1488	GADLYS ROAD PLATFORM	[DVR]	A sketch showing the platform around 1950. It is believed there was no shelter.
1406	GILFACH GOCH COLLIERS PLATFORM	[EVER]	It is thought to have closed to Miners trains in 1930, but never appeared in the working timetable. Photographs exist of it in the late 1950's.
1121	GLANYRAFON	[TVLR]	A sketch showing the halt as it may have looked just prior to closure. The 75' wooden platform had a shelter similar to that at Llanyblodwell.
911	GREENS SIDING	[GVR]	It is possible that the shelter and platform had been removed by 1947.
1551	GROESFAEN COLLIERY HALT	[RR]	A photograph of the up platform for which there appears to have been no shelter. The down platform had a large shelter, its type unknown.
1513	GROESWEN HALT	[PC&NR]	A photograph of the closed halt, there appears to be remains of a shelter on the up platform. Note the down platform is set back as there used to be a siding here.
732	HADLOW ROAD	[GW&LNWJ]	The down shelter does not show up, but is similar to Thurstaston on page 273.
771	HAUGHTON HALT	[SO&CJR]	There appears to be a down loop visible in the photograph, but its date of installation is unknown.
1495	HEATH HALT (H.L.)	[RR]	The wooden platforms were rebuilt, presumably with the shelters at an unknown date. It is likely there were pagodas in 1947.
1116	HIGHTOWN HALT	[W&ER]	There is a suggestion there may have been a shelter.
728	INCE & ELTON	[BirkRly]	It is unclear if the outer siding was still in use by 1947.
1213	JORDANSTON HALT	[R&FR]	The photograph shows the up platform, it is thought the down platform was similar, unlike the situation at Welsh Hook Halt.
1198	KIDWELLY FLATS HALT	[SWR]	It appears from the photograph that there was no shelter on the down side.
895	KINGSLAND	[L&KR]	The siding behind the goods shed is shown joining the outer siding first as on the OS maps. There is a suggestion it joined the goods shed loop first.
1197	LANDO PLATFORM	[SWR]	It is unknown if there was a shelter on the up platform too.
924	LEDBURY	[W&HR]	There is a single slip on the siding near the goods shed. This may earlier have been a double slip.
859	LIGHTMOOR PLATFORM	[GWR]	There was a booking office at road level, its location has been estimated.
731	LITTLE SUTTON	[BirkRly]	The crossover from the up line to the down siding was removed by 1949.
1501	LLANBRADACH COLLIERY HALT	[RR]	No photograph currently available. This halt may have been at the beginning of the colliery sidings, with a short wooden platform, in the location shown.
1081	LLANBRYNMAIR	[N&MR]	It is assumed that the four sidings behind the goods shed still existed in 1947.
1310	LLANDARCY PLATFORM	[GWR]	A photograph of the closed platform, shelter type and locations unknown.
1026	LLANDDERFEL	[C&BR]	The inner siding does not appear to go to the signal box by the early 1950's, so is shown as shortened, joining the outer siding.
1027	LLANDRILLO	[C&BR]	There was a crossover to the east of the goods shed to the down loop line, but it is thought this had been removed by 1947, so is not shown.
1275	LLANERCH-AYRON HALT	[LA&NQ]	A photograph of the closed halt, shelter type and location unknown.
1221	LLANFALTEG	[W&TVR]	There is no evidence the goods shed survived to 1947, just an iron lock up.
1133	LLANFYLLIN	[O&NR]	The track diagram assumes the second goods shed was still there in 1947.
1395	LLANGEINOR	[OVR]	The photograph does not show the up (southbound) shelter. It was similar to that at Brynmenyn on the up (westbound) Nantymoel platform, see page 488.
1583	LLANHILLETH	[MR&CC]	At an unknown date, but by 1964, the goods shed line ended as a siding with the crossover to the down lines removed.
1496	LLANISHEN	[RR]	The line from Cherry Orchard siding, shown to the north joining the down line, had almost certainly been closed by 1947.

No.	STATION NAME	RAILWAY	VARIATION
1122	LLANSILIN ROAD	[TVLR]	The photograph shows the platform after removal of the shelter, which was similar to that at Llanyblodwell.
1172	LLANWERN	[SWR]	A photograph shows the old station, although the buildings were demolished around 1940, it appears that the platforms were still used. Note the goods shed in the distance. The main building from 1941 is shown, but not the platform shelters, they were probably similar to those at Magor, their location is unknown.
1097	LLANYMYNECH	[O&NR]	The headshunt at the north of the layout is assumed, it is also not clear if the goods shed covered the line as shown, or not. A more detailed photograph of the main building can be found on page iii.
1222	LOGIN	[W&TVR]	The headshunts at each end of the siding loop are not shown as these were believed to have been removed in 1928 at the same time as those at Kilgerran.
1237	LYDSTEP HALT	[P&TR]	A photograph of the closed halt, shelter type and location unknown.
1539	MACHEN	[B&MR]	There was a headshunt in the goods yard, parallel to the Caerphilly line. It is not shown, but was removed between 1920 and 1960.
1475	MAERDY	[TVR]	The existence of the goods shed is uncertain in 1947 as the siding was taken out of use in 1952.
1171	MAGOR	[SWR]	The inner up siding became a loop at the west end, probably in 1959, as can be seen in the photograph. The main building, at an angle to the line, is similar to that at Llanwern.
926	MALVERN WELLS	[W&HR]	Photographs show the southerly sidings join north of the crossover as shown.
928	MALVERN LINK	[W&HR]	It is not clear when the 4 westerly sidings were installed, nor how they join the up bay line, so may be incorrectly shown.
1590	MARINE COLLIERY PLATFORM	[MR&CC]	Photographs of only the up platform. The down platform had no shelter either.
1482	MATTHEWSTOWN HALT	[AberRly]	Note the canopy type shelter off the platform on the left.
1320	MELYNCOURT HALT	[VNR]	The platforms were originally opposite. It is assumed that the pagoda was moved when the platform was rebuilt in its staggered position. Whether the pagodas survived at 1947 is not known.
1463	MERTHYR	[VNR]	The track diagram is correct for 1919 and for 1947 in the station area. But the track diagram in the goods yard is fairly uncertain so is based around 1919.
1045	MINFFORDD	[A&WCR]	The siding arrangements with the Festiniog Railway are unclear, so only the first few sidings are shown as these are certainly correct.
1489	NANTMELYN PLATFORM	[DVR]	No photograph currently available. It is believed there was no shelter.
838	NANTYDERRY	[NA&HR]	For details of the down southbound shelter see page iii
939	NEWENT	[NR]	Note that a new signal box opened in June 1948, off the end of the up platform.
902	NEW RADNOR	[K&ER]	There is a suggestion that the goods shed siding was removed in 1945.
1088	NEWTOWN	[O&NR]	The second set of double slips (more northerly) in the sidings had become two single points by 1965. Date of the change unknown.
1550	NEW TREDEGAR	[B&MR]	There was a wooden shelter on the up platform, which was probably removed soon after 1930 when the line terminated here due to a landslip.
1208	NEYLAND	[SWR]	It is not thought that the departure platform had any kind of shelter.
1446	NINIAN PARK HALT	[PHD&R]	There does not appear to have been an up shelter until some time between 1940 and 1954.
774	OLDWOODS HALT	[SO&CJR]	There was probably a booking office. This would have been by the road at the end of the two sidings. The signal box was closed, open only when required.
1480	OLD YNYSYBWL HALT	[TVR]	A sketch showing the halt as it looked around 1947. Before the shelter was removed in 1949 and the platform edge moved about 3' west, as seen in the 1951 photograph.
820	ONIBURY	[S&HR]	The photograph does not show the up platform shelter, but it is similar to that of Leebotwood on page 298, with brickwork and sloping roof. A sketch on page vi gives an impression of a view around 1950, before the crossover to the goods yard was moved in 1954.
1110	OVERTON-ON-DEE	[W&ER]	The outer westernmost siding may have been removed by 1947.
1098	PANT (SALOP.)	[O&NR]	The two sidings shown behind the main building appear to have been removed long before 1961. The siding by the main line had gone too by 1961 even though closure to goods was in 1964.
1599	PANTEG & GRIFFITHSTOWN	[MR&CC]	The connection to the goods yard from the south was t.o.u. on 10/08/1947.
1556	PANTYWAUN HALT	[B&MR]	The shelter can just be observed through the middle of the railings.
1292	PARCYRHUN HALT	[LR]	No photograph currently available. Shelter type and location unknown.
734	PARKGATE	[GW&LNWJ]	The first siding by the running line may have been removed by 1947.
1279	PEMBREY HALT	[BP&GVR]	A photograph of the closed halt, remains of the shelter just visible.
1504	PENGAM (GLAM.)	[RR]	The crossover by the goods shed was removed by 1958.
1544	PENGAM (MON.)	[B&MR]	The down colliery siding connection may have been removed prior to 1947.
1315	PENTREFELIN (GLAM.) HALT	[GWR]	There probably was no up shelter.
1534	PENYDARREN PLATFORM	[GW&RJR]	It is not clear if the platforms were staggered or almost opposite one another.
1285	PONTHENRY	[BP&GVR]	A photograph of the closed station, remains of the building still evident.
1559	PONTSTICILL JUNCTION	[B&MR]	The was a crossover, not shown, in the Taf Fechan sidings to the north west of the platforms, removed at an unknown date, as was the turntable which was behind the signal box.
1285	PONTYBEREM	[BP&GVR]	The up shelter type and location is unknown, but is probably of corrugated iron.
1526	PONTYGWAITH HALT	[GW&RJR]	No photograph currently available. Shelter type and locations unknown.
1601	PONTYPOOL (CRANE STREET)	[MR&CC]	There is a smaller brick building beyond the footbridge for the up platform.
1044	PORTMADOC	[A&WCR]	The crossover to the west of the platforms had a single slip in 1928. Date of removal unknown. Also the crossover to the siding at the very west of the layout may not have been there in 1947. The footbridge is shown in its new position. It had been moved from a location by the signal box to that shown, some time between 1939 and 1948.

No.	STATION NAME	RAILWAY	VARIATION
744	PORT SUNLIGHT	[C&BR]	There is a roadside building at a lower level, not visible in the photograph. The up building can be seen in more detail on page iii.
770	REDNAL & WEST FELTON	[SO&CJR]	The track diagram of the goods yard is assumed from photographic evidence.
757	RHOSROBIN HALT	[NWMR]	A partial photograph of the closed halt, the shelter type is unknown.
1516	RHYDYFELIN HALT	[PC&NR]	A sketch showing the halt around 1948. There is a pagoda on the up platform with a similar one, out of view on the down platform.
1478	ROBERTSTOWN HALT	[TVR]	A sketch showing the halt as it looked around 1910, before the shelter, believed to be similar to that at Pontcynon Bridge Halt on page 516, was built. There is also a suggestion that a booking office was provided around 1918.
742	ROCK FERRY	[C&BR]	Buildings do not show up well in the photographs and may not all be shown.
755	ROSSETT	[NWMR]	The track diagram is based on an old diagram, but is probably correct.
761	RUABON	[NWMR]	Minor crossover changes which are not shown had taken place by 1960, these are to the south, from the bay line to the up main.
1141	ST. HARMONS	[MWR]	Just beyond the platform at ground level is a small wooden waiting room with sloping roof. Beyond which, is the level crossing.
1525	SENGHENYDD	[RR]	The extent to which the sidings in the goods yard had been removed is uncertain. The track diagram is based on a 1952 photograph.
776	SHREWSBURY	[SO&CJ,S&H]	Track diagram is correct for 1957, and may well be correct for 1947.
1269	SILIAN HALT	[LA&NQ]	A photograph of the closed halt, shelter type and location unknown.
1603	SNATCHWOOD HALT	[MR&CC]	No photograph currently available. I suspect the halt was similar to Cwmffrwd Halt with wooden platforms and pagodas, except that the platforms were staggered with the shelter location as shown.
1379	SOUTH PIT HALT	[SWMR]	A photograph of the relocated halt, moved 130 yards south in 1956.
729	STANLOW & THORNTON	[BirkRly]	There was a connection from the siding behind the down (north side) platform to the depot, but this was probably not installed until the 1950's.
922	STOKE EDITH	[W&HR]	The up platform building does not show well, but appears similar to that at Bransford Road on page 335.
887	STOURPORT	[SVR]	There is some uncertainty of where the short loop connection in the canal basin joins to form a loop. To the outer sidings, or to the canal shed siding as shown.
1035	SUN BANK HALT	[VLR]	No photograph currently available. Wooden platforms with corrugated iron shelters, their locations unknown.
1298	TALLEY ROAD HALT	[VTRJ]	A photograph of the closed halt, shelter type and location unknown.
1048	TALSARNAU	[A&WCR]	It is likely that the camping coach (inner) siding was disconnected by 1947.
1271	TALSARN HALT	[LA&NQ]	A photograph of the closed halt, shelter type and location unknown.
1387	TONDU	[LVR]	The down Porthcawl Bay joined the main line beyond the platform and was in the process of being changed to joining via the down siding. Both are shown as per signal box diagram of 1952.
1471	TREHERBERT	[TVR]	The 1954 photograph shows the southerly siding joining by a single point, not a single slip as shown on the track diagram (and 1956 signal box diagram).
766	TREHOWELL HALT	[SO&CJR]	No photograph currently available. Shelter type and location unknown.
1182	TREMAINS HALT	[SWR]	A sketch giving an impression of the halt around 1941. It appears that there were no shelters, just canopy protection along most of the platforms. Although the down platforms are of wooden construction, there is some evidence to suggest the up platforms were of more substantial material. At some point, the line to the far right, within the factory limits, had a little run around loop installed.
1340	TREOWEN HALT	[NA&HR]	A photograph showing that the down pagoda had gone by 1959, so its location is assumed.
1282	TRIMSARAN ROAD	[BP&GVR]	A photograph of the closed halt, shelter believed to be similar to that at Glyn Abbey Halt.
1389	TROEDYRHIEW GARTH	[LVR]	The siding is shown, CG:01/08/1947, but was probably out of use before then.
1528	TROEDYRHIW HALT	[GW&RJR]	No photograph currently available. Shelter type and location unknown.
1277	TYCOCH HALT	[BP&GVR]	A photograph of the closed halt, shelter type and location unknown.
1514	UPPER BOAT HALT	[PC&NR]	There is no evidence to suggest shelters were provided.
1592	VICTORIA	[MR&CC]	The up shelter is barely visible, but looks like a small wooden shelter with a rear sloping roof.
963	WERN HIR	[CMU&PR]	This has been removed from the survey as evidence suggests it was closed by 05/1941, the material being used to build Glascoed East Access Halt.
846	WESTBURY (SALOP.)	[S&WPoolJ]	The track diagram is a best guess.
766	WESTON RHYN	[SO&CJR]	Location of the siding connections at the north end may be incorrect.
864	WESTWOOD HALT	[MWCA&CR]	A photograph of the closed halt, the shelter believed to be similar to Farley Halt.
1203	WHITLAND	[SWR]	The goods shed was in the process of being demolished around 1947 and the old turntable is shown, as the relocated one was not opened until 1950.
769	WHITTINGTON (L.L.)	[SO&CJR]	There is evidence that at one time a second crossover from the main siding to the up line was in use. Not known if the private siding was still in use by 1947.
818	WISTANSTOW HALT	[S&HR]	Photograph of only the up platform, it is assumed the down platform was similar.
1164	WOOLASTON	[SWR]	The down platform building does not show up well in the photograph, its style is uncertain.
1472	YNYSHIR	[TVR]	The up shelter had been demolished by the time the photograph was taken, but was of similar construction to the down shelter, shown.
1477	YNYSYBWL (NEW ROAD) HALT	[TVR]	The exact location of the shelter is uncertain. It is believed to be similar to that at Pontcynon Bridge Halt on page 516.
845	YOCKLETON	[S&WPoolJ]	It is unclear when the short outer siding, shown, was removed.

APPENDIX C
ABBREVIATIONS & LOCATIONS OF RAILWAY COMPANIES
(ALPHABETICAL)

This list contains all lines referred to in the survey, for Part Two.
It should be noted that only the companies which absorbed other lines are referred to for those lines. Lines which were leased to other companies do not show under the leasing company in the list. For example, the Penarth Harbour Dock & Railway does not appear under the Taff Vale Railway.
Brackets are for the location of historical information for which there is no station attributable to that data. For example, the section from Brandy Bridge Junction to Mardy Junction was Great Western & Taff Vale Joint.

STATION OR LINE ABBREVIATION	RAILWAY COMPANY	PAGES WHERE THE COMPANIES HISTORY OR STATIONS ARE TO BE FOUND
AberRly	Aberdare Railway	516 – 518.
AVR	Aberdare Valley Railway	465.
A&WCR	Aberystwyth & Welsh Coast Railway	361, 370 – 378, 380 – 382.
	Alexandra (Newport & South Wales) Dock & Railway	526 – 527.
B&DR	Bala & Dolgelly Railway	362 – 365.
B&FR	Bala & Festiniog Railway	356 – 359.
BR	Barry Railway	496 – 500.
Birk Rly	Birkenhead Railway	270 – 271, 274 – 278.
BL&CJR	Birkenhead Lancashire & Cheshire Junction Railway	268 – 270, 274 – 278.
B&MR	Brecon & Merthyr Railway	528 – 529, 534 – 537, 538 – 544.
BM&LNWJ	Brecon & Merthyr & London & North Western Joint Rly.	544.
	Brynmawr & Western Valleys Railway	(545).
BP&GVR	Burry Port & Gwendraeth Valley Railway	448 – 451.
CAMRLY	Cambrian Railways	361, 370 – 392, 395 – 407.
CardRly	Cardiff Railway	519 – 520.
CP&BJR	Cardiff Penarth & Barry Junction Railway	500 – 501.
C&CR	Carmarthen & Cardigan Railway	438 – 440.
C&BR	Chester & Birkenhead Railway	274 – 278.
ColeRly	Coleford Railway	353.
CMU&PR	Coleford Monmouth Usk & Pontypool Railway	343 – 346, 353.
C&BR	Corwen & Bala Railway	365 – 367.
CR	Cowbridge Railway	492 – 493.
C&AR	Cowbridge & Aberthaw Railway	493.
DVR	Dare Valley Railway	518.
EVR	Ely Valley Railway	490 – 491.
EVER	Ely Valley Extension Railway	490.
F&BR	Festiniog & Blaenau Railway	360.
G&DFR	Gloucester & Dean Forest Railway	408.
GVR	Golden Valley Railway	327 – 329.
GWR	Great Western Railway (GWR lines from the beginning)	288, 296, 312 – 313, (347), 428 – 429, 440, 458 – 460, (491), 499, 503.
	Great Western and Bala & Festiniog Railway	360.
GW&LNWJ	Great Western & London & North Western Joint Railway	268 – 270, 272 – 278, 287, 293 – 294, 297 – 303, 308 – 310, 323, 455 – 456, (545), 556.
	Great Western & London Midland & Scottish Joint Railway	526, 544.
GW&MJ	Great Western & Midland Joint Railway	348 – 353.
GW&RJR	Great Western & Rhymney Joint Railway	530 – 533.
	Great Western & Taff Vale Joint Railway	(504).
	Gwendraeth Valleys Railway	(448).
HR&GR	Hereford Ross & Gloucester Railway	339 – 341.
K&ER	Kington & Eardisley Railway	325 – 326.
LA&NQ	Lampeter Aberayron & New Quay Light Railway	445 – 447.
L&BR	Leominster & Bromyard Railway	329 – 330.
L&KR	Leominster & Kington Railway	324 – 325, 326 – 327.
LR	Llanelly Railway	451 – 454, 456 – 458.
L&CR	Llangollen & Corwen Railway	367 – 368.
L&NR	Llanidloes & Newtown Railway	386, 401 – 402.
L&TVJR	Llantrisant & Taff Vale Junction Railway	491 – 492.
L&OR	Llynvi & Ogmore Railway	482 – 490.
LVR	Llynvi Valley Railway	482 – 485.
LNW&RJR	London & North Western & Rhymney Joint Railway	526.
M&MR	Manchester & Milford Railway	441 – 445.
MR	Mawddwy Railway	379.
MR	*Midland Railway*	351 – 352.
MWR	Mid Wales Railway	402 – 407.
MilRly	Milford Railway	427.
MR&CC	Monmouthshire Railway & Canal Company	545 – 552, 553 – 556.
	Monmouthshire Railway & Canal Company & LNW Jt. Rly.	556
MW&SJR	Much Wenlock & Severn Junction Railway	313 – 314.
MWCA&CR	Much Wenlock Craven Arms & Coalbrookdale Railway	313, 314 – 315.
N&MDR	Nantwich & Market Drayton Railway	291 – 292.
NR&MR	Narberth Road & Maenclochog Railway	430.
N&BR	Neath & Brecon Railway	471 – 476.
NR	Newent Railway	337 – 338.

STATION OR LINE ABBREVIATION	RAILWAY COMPANY	PAGES WHERE THE COMPANIES HISTORY OR STATIONS ARE TO BE FOUND
NA&HR	Newport Abergavenny & Hereford Railway	303 – 306, 466 – 470.
N&MR	Newtown & Machynlleth Railway	383 – 385.
	North Pembrokeshire & Fishguard Railway	429, 430 – 431.
NWMR	North Wales Mineral Railway	279 – 281, 287.
OVR	Ogmore Valley Railway	486 – 490.
O&NR	Oswestry & Newtown Railway	386 – 390, (395), 399 – 400.
OE&WR	Oswestry Ellesmere & Whitchurch Railway	390 – 392.
P&TR	Pembroke & Tenby Railway	434 – 437.
PER	Penarth Extension Railway	502.
PHD&R	Penarth Harbour Dock & Railway	503.
PC&NR	Pontypool Caerleon & Newport Railway	307, 552.
PC&NR	Pontypridd Caerphilly & Newport Railway	526 – 527, 528 – 529.
PTR&D	Port Talbot Railway & Docks	482.
R&SB	Rhondda & Swansea Bay Railway	477 – 480.
RR	Rhymney Railway	520 – 526, 529 – 530, 538.
R&FR	Rosebush & Fishguard Railway	429, 431.
R&LR	Ross & Ledbury Railway	337.
R&MR	Ross & Monmouth Railway	342 – 343.
	Rumney Railway	528, 534 – 537.
S&WR	Severn & Wye Railway	349 – 350, 352 – 353.
	Severn & Wye & Severn Bridge Railway	349 – 351, 352 – 353.
SBR	Severn Bridge Railway	350 – 351.
SVR	Severn Valley Railway	316 – 321.
S&BR	Shrewsbury & Birmingham Railway	293 – 296, 312.
S&CR	Shrewsbury & Chester Railway	279 – 286, 287, 289.
S&HR	Shrewsbury & Hereford Railway	297 – 303.
S&WPoolJ	Shrewsbury & Welshpool Railway	308 – 310.
SO&CJR	Shrewsbury Oswestry & Chester Junction Railway	282 – 286.
SO&CJR,S&HR	Shrewsbury Oswestry & Chester Junction Railway, Shrewsbury & Hereford Railway	286.
SUR&CC	Shropshire Union Railway & Canal Company	288.
SWR	South Wales Railway	347 – 348, 408 – 427.
SWMR	South Wales Mineral Railway	480 – 481.
S&NR	Swansea & Neath Railway	461.
SV&N&BJR	Swansea Vale & Neath & Brecon Junction Railway	476.
TVR	Taff Vale Railway	491 – 493, 500 – 501, 504 – 509, 510 – 518.
TVLR	Tanat Valley Light Railway	395 – 398.
TJ	Tenbury Railway	323.
T&BR	Tenbury & Bewdley Railway	322 – 323.
VofGR	Vale of Glamorgan Railway	494 – 496.
VLR	Vale of Llangollen Railway	369.
VNR	Vale of Neath Railway	461 – 465, 470, 509.
VTRJ	Vale of Towy Railway	455 – 456.
W&DR	Wellington & Drayton Railway	289 – 291.
W&SJR	Wellington & Severn Junction Railway	310 – 311.
WMR	West Midland Railway	303 – 306, 332 – 336, 466 – 470.
WMR,SVR	West Midland and Severn Valley Railways	321.
W&CR	Whitland & Cardigan Railway	431 – 434.
W&TVR	Whitland & Taf Vale Railway	431 – 433.
W&HR	Worcester & Hereford Railway	332 – 336.
WB&LR	Worcester Bromyard & Leominster Railway	330 – 331.
W&ER	Wrexham & Ellesmere Railway	393 – 395.
W&MR	Wrexham & Minera Railway	286 – 287.
WVR	Wye Valley Railway	354 – 355.

APPENDIX D
LIST OF STATIONS
(ALPHABETICAL)

The station names shown are those used on 6th October 1947, or the last name used, where stations closed before this date.
Those in italics do not have a photograph or track diagram as they were closed prior to 1947.
(Only included so there is a numerical sequence of 721 to 1612)

No.	STATION NAME	RAILWAY	PAGE	No.	STATION NAME	RAILWAY	PAGE
	[A]			941	BARBERS BRIDGE	[NR]	338
				1506	BARGOED	[RR]	524
905	ABBEYDORE	[GVR]	327	1545	BARGOED COLLIERY HALT	[B&MR]	536
1486	ABERAMAN	[AberRly]	517	1057	BARMOUTH	[A&WCR]	375
1069	ABERANGELL	[MR]	379	1058	BARMOUTH JUNCTION	[A&WCR]	376
1367	ABERAVON (SEASIDE)	[R&SB]	477		Barrs Court, see Hereford (Barrs Court)		
1368	ABERAVON (TOWN)	[R&SB]	477	1428	BARRY	[BR]	497
1276	ABERAYRON	[LA&NQ]	447	1429	BARRY DOCKS	[BR]	497
1546	ABERBARGOED	[B&MR]	536	1427	BARRY ISLAND	[BR]	496,7
1584	ABERBEEG	[MR&CC]	549	1426	BARRY PIER	[BR]	496
1363	ABERBRAN HALT	[N&BR]	475	773	BASCHURCH	[SO&CJR]	285
1361	ABERCAMLAIS HALT	[N&BR]	475	1536	BASSALEG	[B&MR]	534
1529	ABERCANAID	[GW&RJR]	531	1572	BASSALEG JUNCTION	[MR&CC]	545
1578	ABERCARN	[MR&CC]	547	1239	BEAVERS HILL HALT	[P&TR]	436
1365	ABERCRAVE	[SV&N&BJR]	476	743	BEBINGTON & NEW FERRY	[C&BR]	275
1485	ABERCWMBOI HALT	[AberRly]	517	1411	BEDDAU HALT	[L&TVJR]	491,2
1458	ABERCYNON	[TVR]	508	1532	BEDLINOG	[GW&RJR]	532
1329	ABERDARE (H.L.)	[VNR]	465	1541	BEDWAS	[B&MR]	535
1487	ABERDARE (L.L.)	[AberRly]	518	981	BERKELEY	[MR]	351
1064	ABERDOVEY	[A&WCR]	378	982	BERKELEY ROAD	[MR]	352
1318	ABERDYLAIS	[VNR]	462	870	BERRINGTON	[SVR]	316
1149	ABEREDW	[MWR]	405	824	BERRINGTON & EYE	[S&HR]	301
1039	ABERERCH	[A&WCR]	370	1033	BERWYN	[L&CR]	368
1527	ABERFAN	[GW&RJR]	530,1	1106	BETTISFIELD	[OE&WR]	392
836	ABERGAVENNY	[NA&HR]	305	885	BEWDLEY	[SVR]	320
835	ABERGAVENNY JUNCTION	[NA&HR]	305	809	BIRCHES & BILBROOK HALT	[S&BR]	296
1394	ABERGWYNFI	[L&OR]	486	1491	BIRCHGROVE HALT	[CardRly]	519
1499	ABER JUNCTION HALT	[RR]	521	*741*	*BIRKENHEAD TOWN*	*[C&BR]*	*274*
1089	ABERMULE	[O&NR]	386	740	BIRKENHEAD (WOODSIDE)	[GW&LNWJ]	274
1346	ABERNANT	[VNR]	470	1400	BLACKMILL	[OVR]	488
1612	ABERSYCHAN & TALYWAIN	[MR&CC]	556	1043	BLACK ROCK HALT	[A&WCR]	372
1604	ABERSYCHAN (L.L.)	[MR&CC]	555	1011	BLAENAU FESTINIOG	[F&BR]	360
1066	ABERTAFOL HALT	[A&WCR]	378	1607	BLAENAVON	[MR&CC]	556
1424	ABERTHAW	[VofGR]	495	1398	BLAENGARW	[OVR]	487
1586	ABERTILLERY	[MR&CC]	549	1374	BLAENGWYNFI	[R&SB]	479
1523	ABERTRIDWR	[RR]	529	1270	BLAENPLWYF HALT	[LA&NQ]	446
1071	ABERYSTWYTH	[A&WCR]	380,1	1375	BLAENRHONDDA	[R&SB]	480
1037	ACREFAIR	[VLR]	369	1588	BLAINA	[MR&CC]	550
795	ADDERLEY	[N&MDR]	292	950	BLAISDON HALT	[HR&GR]	341
801	ADMASTON	[S&BR]	293	1119	BLODWELL JUNCTION	[TVLR]	396
1041	AFONWEN	[A&WCR]	371	1228	BONCATH	[W&CR]	433
1441	ALBERTA PLACE HALT	[CP&BJR]	501	1016	BONTNEWYDD	[B&DR]	362
807	ALBRIGHTON	[S&BR]	295,6	1030	BONWM HALT	[L&CR]	367
814	ALL STRETTON HALT	[S&HR]	298	1074	BORTH	[A&WCR]	382
1262	ALLTDDU HALT	[M&MR]	444	1153	BOUGHROOD & LLYSWEN	[MWR]	406
881	ALVELEY COLLIERY HALT	[SVR]	319	932	BOUGHTON HALT	[W&HR]	336
1303	AMMANFORD	[LR]	456,7	1587	BOURNVILLE (MON.) HALT	[MR&CC]	550
1304	AMMANFORD COLLIERY HALT	[LR]	457	1072	BOW STREET	[A&WCR]	381
1095	ARDDLEEN	[O&NR]	388	930	BRANSFORD ROAD	[W&HR]	335
1001	ARENIG	[B&FR]	357	1566	BRECON	[B&MR]	542
883	ARLEY	[SVR]	320	848	BREIDDEN	[S&WPoolJ]	309
1012	ARTHOG	[A&WCR]	361	1183	BRIDGEND	[SWR]	417
923	ASHPERTON	[W&HR]	333	878	BRIDGNORTH	[SVR]	318
797	AUDLEM	[N&MDR]	292	1507	BRITHDIR	[RR]	524
1162	AWRE	[SWR]	409	1186	BRITON FERRY	[SWR]	418
				993	BROCKWEIR HALT	[WVR]	355
	[B]			746	BROMBOROUGH	[C&BR]	276
				821	BROMFIELD	[S&HR]	300
945	BACKNEY HALT	[HR&GR]	340	917	BROMYARD	[WB&LR]	330,1
906	BACTON	[GVR]	327	1244	BRONWYDD ARMS	[C&CR]	438
997	BALA	[B&FR]	356	777	BRYMBO	[W&MR]	286,7
1025	BALA JUNCTION	[C&BR]	365	1307	BRYNAMMAN	[LR]	458
1024	BALA LAKE HALT	[B&DR]	365	1003	BRYNCELYNOG HALT	[B&FR]	358
754	BALDERTON	[NWMR]	279	1132	BRYNGWYN	[O&NR]	400
943	BALLINGHAM	[HR&GR]	339	1399	BRYNMENYN	[OVR]	488
1112	BANGOR-ON-DEE	[W&ER]	394	1252	BRYN TEIFY	[M&MR]	441

No.	STATION NAME	RAILWAY	PAGE
	[E]		
879	EARDINGTON	[SVR]	319
	East Access Halt, see Glascoed Factory East Access Halt		
866	EASTHOPE HALT	[MWCA&CR]	314
894	EASTON COURT	[TJ]	323
1594	EBBW VALE	[MR&CC]	552
1433	EFAIL ISAF	[BR]	499
788	ELLERDINE HALT	[W&DR]	290
1104	ELLESMERE	[OE&WR]	391
730	ELLESMERE PORT	[BirkRly]	271
1549	ELLIOT PIT HALT	[B&MR]	537
958	ELMS BRIDGE HALT	[CMU&PR]	344
1108	ELSON HALT	[W&ER]	393
1176	ELY (MAIN LINE)	[SWR]	414
1151	ERWOOD	[MWR]	406
	[F]		
1059	FAIRBOURNE	[A&WCR]	376
862	FARLEY HALT	[MW&SJR]	313
944	FAWLEY	[HR&GR]	339
1266	FELINDYFFRYN HALT	[M&MR]	444
1272	FELIN FACH	[LA&NQ]	446
1309	FELIN FRAN HALT	[GWR]	458,9
915	FENCOTE	[L&BR]	330
1107	FENNS BANK	[OE&WR]	392
1474	FERNDALE	[TVR]	514
1200	FERRYSIDE	[SWR]	424
1008	FESTINIOG	[B&FR]	359
1296	FFAIRFACH	[LR]	454
779	FFRITH	[W&MR]	287
1214	FISHGUARD & GOODWICK	[R&FR]	429
1215	FISHGUARD HARBOUR	[GWR]	429
1022	FLAG STATION HALT	[B&DR]	364
1543	FLEUR-DE-LIS PLATFORM	[B&MR]	536
1555	FOCHRIW	[B&MR]	539
888	FOLEY PARK HALT	[WMR,SVR]	321
826	FORD BRIDGE	[S&HR]	302
1091	FORDEN	[O&NR]	387
	Foregate Street, see Worcester (Foregate Street)		
903	FORGE CROSSING HALT	[L&KR]	326
1521	FOUNTAIN BRIDGE HALT	[PC&NR]	529
1096	FOUR CROSSES	[O&NR]	389
938	FOUR OAKS HALT	[NR]	338
1103	FRANKTON	[OE&WR]	391
724	FRODSHAM	[BL&CJR]	269
998	FRONGOCH	[B&FR]	356
	[G]		
1488	GADLYS ROAD PLATFORM	[DVR]	518
1306	GARNANT	[LR]	457
1019	GARNEDDWEN HALT	[B&DR]	363
1423	GILESTON	[VofGR]	495
1505	GILFACH FARGOED HALT	[RR]	523
1405	GILFACH GOCH	[EVER]	490
1406	*GILFACH GOCH COLLIERS PLATFORM*	*[EVER]*	*490*
1305	GLANAMMAN	[LR]	457
1076	GLANDYFI	[A&WCR]	382
1299	GLANRHYD HALT	[VTRJ]	455
1121	GLANYRAFON	[TVLR]	396
1139	GLAN-YR-AFON HALT	[MWR]	402
964	GLASCOED FACTORY EAST ACCESS HALT	[CMU&PR]	346
965	GLASCOED FACTORY WEST ACCESS HALT	[CMU&PR]	346
966	GLASCOED HALT	[CMU&PR]	346
1226	GLOGUE	[W&TVR]	433
1283	GLYN ABBEY HALT	[BP&GVR]	449
1378	GLYNCORRWG	[SWMR]	481
1032	GLYNDYFRDWY	[L&CR]	368
1322	GLYN NEATH	[VNR]	463
768	GOBOWEN	[SO&CJR]	283
1067	GOGARTH HALT	[A&WCR]	378
1193	GOWERTON	[SWR]	421
1159	GRANGE COURT	[G&DFR]	408
1445	GRANGETOWN	[PHD&R]	503
	Great Malvern, see Malvern (Great)		
860	GREEN BANK HALT	[GWR]	313
911	GREENS SIDING	[GVR]	329
936	GREENWAY HALT	[R&LR]	337
756	GRESFORD	[NWMR]	280
1551	GROESFAEN COLLIERY HALT	[RR]	538
1565	GROESFFORDD HALT	[B&MR]	542
1513	GROESWEN HALT	[PC&NR]	526,7
1518	GWERNYDOMEN HALT	[B&MR]	528
	[H]		
732	HADLOW ROAD	[GW&LNWJ]	272
1342	HAFODYRYNYS PLATFORM	[NA&HR]	469
723	HALTON	[BL&CJR]	268
880	HAMPTON LOADE	[SVR]	319
844	HANWOOD	[S&WPoolJ]	308
1050	HARLECH	[A&WCR]	373
869	HARTON ROAD	[MWCA&CR]	315
771	HAUGHTON HALT	[SO&CJR]	284
1206	HAVERFORDWEST	[SWR]	426
1495	HEATH HALT (H.L.)	[RR]	520
1490	HEATH HALT (L.L.)	[CardRly]	519
725	HELSBY	[BL&CJR]	269
1337	HENGOED (H.L.)	[NA&HR]	468
1503	HENGOED (L.L.)	[RR]	523
1250	HENLLAN	[GWR]	440
933	HENWICK	[W&HR]	336
1571	HEOLGERRIG HALT	[BM&LNWJ]	544
829	HEREFORD (BARRS COURT)	[S&HR]	303
735	HESWALL	[GW&LNWJ]	272,3
882	HIGHLEY	[SVR]	319
1116	HIGHTOWN HALT	[W&ER]	394,5
1327	HIRWAUN	[VNR]	464
1326	HIRWAUN POND HALT	[VNR]	464
790	HODNET	[W&DR]	290
942	HOLME LACY	[HR&GR]	339
747	HOOTON	[C&BR]	276,7
856	HORSEHAY & DAWLEY	[W&SJR]	311
	[I]		
728	INCE & ELTON	[BirkRly]	270
874	IRONBRIDGE & BROSELEY	[SVR]	317
	[J]		
875	JACKFIELD HALT	[SVR]	318
1207	JOHNSTON (PEM.)	[SWR]	426
759	JOHNSTOWN & HAFOD	[NWMR]	281
1213	JORDANSTON HALT	[R&FR]	429
	[K]		
1386	KENFIG HILL	[LVR]	483
952	KERNE BRIDGE	[R&MR]	342
1134	KERRY	[O&NR]	400
852	KETLEY	[W&SJR]	310
853	KETLEY TOWN HALT	[W&SJR]	311
1199	KIDWELLY	[SWR]	423
1198	KIDWELLY FLATS HALT	[SWR]	423
1229	KILGERRAN	[W&CR]	433
1233	KILGETTY	[P&TR]	435
895	KINGSLAND	[L&KR]	324
899	KINGTON	[K&ER]	325
738	KIRBY PARK	[GW&LNWJ]	273
919	KNIGHTWICK	[WB&LR]	331
	[L]		
1256	LAMPETER	[M&MR]	442
1240	LAMPHEY	[P&TR]	437
1197	LANDO PLATFORM	[SWR]	423
1190	LANDORE	[SWR]	420

No.	STATION NAME	RAILWAY	PAGE

No.	STATION NAME	RAILWAY	PAGE

[N]

No.	STATION NAME	RAILWAY	PAGE
1377	NANTEWLAETH COLLIERY HALT	[SWMR]	480,1
1512	NANTGARW HALT	[PC&NR]	526
1489	NANTMELYN PLATFORM	[DVR]	518
838	NANTYDERRY	[NA&HR]	306
1391	NANTYFFYLLON	[LVR]	485
1589	NANTYGLO	[MR&CC]	550
1404	NANTYMOEL	[OVR]	489
1231	NARBERTH	[P&TR]	434
1316	NEATH ABBEY	[S&NR]	461
1187	NEATH (GENERAL)	[SWR]	419
1317	NEATH (RIVERSIDE)	[S&NR]	461
891	NEEN SOLLARS	[T&BR]	322,3
1336	NELSON & LLANCAIACH	[NA&HR]	467
733	NESTON	[GW&LNWJ]	272
995	NETHERHOPE HALT	[WVR]	355
1580	NEWBRIDGE	[MR&CC]	547
1145	NEWBRIDGE-ON-WYE	[WVR]	404
1251	NEWCASTLE EMLYN	[GWR]	440
854	NEW DALE HALT	[W&SJR]	311
939	NEWENT	[NR]	338
803	NEW HADLEY HALT	[S&BR]	294
929	NEWLAND HALT	[W&HR]	335
1161	NEWNHAM	[SWR]	409
892	NEWNHAM BRIDGE	[T&BR]	323
1173	NEWPORT (HIGH STREET)	[SWR]	413
902	NEW RADNOR	[K&ER]	326
1088	NEWTOWN	[O&NR]	386
1550	NEW TREDEGAR	[B&MR]	537
1208	NEYLAND	[SWR]	427
1446	NINIAN PARK HALT	[PHD&R]	503
1380	NORTH RHONDDA HALT	[SWMR]	481
884	NORTHWOOD HALT	[SVR]	320
722	NORTON (CHES.)	[BL&CJR]	268
1385	NOTTAGE HALT	[LVR]	483

[O]

No.	STATION NAME	RAILWAY	PAGE
804	OAKENGATES	[S&BR]	294
1158	OAKLE STREET	[G&DFR]	408
1554	OGILVIE COLLIERY HALT	[B&MR]	539
1553	OGILVIE VILLAGE HALT	[B&MR]	538
1402	OGMORE VALE	[OVR]	489
774	OLDWOODS HALT	[SO&CJR]	285
1480	OLD YNYSYBWL HALT	[TVR]	515
1259	OLMARCH HALT	[M&MR]	443
820	ONIBURY	[S&HR]	300
1356	ONLLWYN	[N&BR]	473
1100	OSWESTRY	[O&NR]	390
1110	OVERTON-ON-DEE	[W&ER]	393

[P]

No.	STATION NAME	RAILWAY	PAGE
833	PANDY	[NA&HR]	304
1558	PANT	[B&MR]	540
1098	PANT (SALOP.)	[O&NR]	389
1599	PANTEG & GRIFFITHSTOWN	[MR&CC]	553,4
1140	PANTYDWR	[MWR]	402
1355	PANTYFFORDD HALT	[N&BR]	473
1291	PANTYFFYNNON	[LR]	453
1567	PANTYSCALLOG HALT	[B&MR]	543
1556	PANTYWAUN HALT	[B&MR]	539
1292	PARCYRHUN HALT	[LR]	453
975	PARKEND	[S&WR]	349,50
734	PARKGATE	[GW&LNWJ]	272
784	PARK HALL HALT	[S&CR]	289
1126	PEDAIR FFORDD	[TVLR]	398
1196	PEMBREY & BURRY PORT	[SWR]	422,3
1279	PEMBREY HALT	[BP&GVR]	449
896	PEMBRIDGE	[L&KR]	324
1241	PEMBROKE	[P&TR]	437
1242	PEMBROKE DOCK	[P&TR]	437
989	PENALLT HALT	[WVR]	354
1236	PENALLY	[P&TR]	436
1442	PENARTH	[PER]	502
1444	PENARTH DOCK	[PER]	502

No.	STATION NAME	RAILWAY	PAGE
1247	PENCADER	[C&CR]	439
1255	PENCARREG HALT	[M&MR]	442
1181	PENCOED	[SWR]	416
1504	PENGAM (GLAM.)	[RR]	523
1544	PENGAM (MON.)	[B&MR]	536
1065	PENHELIG HALT	[A&WCR]	378
1013	PENMAENPOOL	[A&WCR]	361
837	PENPERGWM	[NA&HR]	306
1362	PENPONT HALT	[N&BR]	475
1332	PENRHIWCEIBER (H.L.)	[NA&HR]	466
1483	PENRHIWCEIBER (L.L.)	[AberRly]	516
1046	PENRHYNDEUDRAETH	[A&WCR]	372,3
1348	PENSCYNOR HALT	[N&BR]	471
1562	PENTIR RHIW	[B&MR]	541
1462	PENTREBACH	[TVR]	509
1249	PENTRECOURT PLATFORM	[GWR]	440
1124	PENTREFELIN	[TVLR]	397
1315	PENTREFELIN (GLAM.) HALT	[GWR]	460
1610	*PENTREPIOD HALT*	*[MR&CC]*	*556*
1611	*PENTWYN HALT*	*[MR&CC]*	*556*
1339	PENTWYNMAWR PLATFORM	[NA&HR]	468
1127	PENYBONTFAWR	[TVLR]	398
1040	PENYCHAIN	[A&WCR]	371
1534	PENYDARREN PLATFORM	[GW&RJR]	533
1409	PENYGRAIG	[EVR]	491
1522	PENYRHEOL	[RR]	529
789	PEPLOW	[W&DR]	290
908	PETERCHURCH	[GVR]	328
1178	PETERSTON	[SWR]	415
1113	PICKHILL HALT	[W&ER]	394
1281	PINGED HALT	[BP&GVR]	449
1312	PLAS MARL	[GWR]	460
847	PLAS-Y-COURT HALT	[S&WPoolJ]	309
849	PLEALEY ROAD	[S&WPoolJ]	309
1290	PONTARDULAIS	[LR]	452
1481	PONTCYNON BRIDGE HALT	[AberRly]	516
1084	PONTDOLGOCH	[N&MR]	385
850	PONTESBURY	[S&WPoolJ]	310
1285	PONTHENRY	[BP&GVR]	450
842	PONTHIR	[PC&NR]	307
1338	PONTLLANFRAITH	[NA&HR]	468
1260	PONT LLANIO	[M&MR]	443
1308	PONT LLIW	[GWR]	458
1509	PONTLOTTYN	[RR]	525
1602	PONTNEWYNYDD	[MR&CC]	554
1370	PONTRHYDYFEN	[R&SB]	478
1597	PONTRHYDYRUN HALT	[MR&CC]	553
832	PONTRILAS	[NA&HR]	304
1569	PONTSARN	[BM&LNWJ]	544
1559	PONTSTICILL JUNCTION	[B&MR]	540
1324	PONTWALBY HALT	[VNR]	464
1284	PONTYATES	[BP&GVR]	450
1286	PONTYBEREM	[BP&GVR]	450
1397	PONTYCYMMER	[OVR]	487
1526	PONTYGWAITH HALT	[GW&RJR]	530
1600	PONTYPOOL (BLAENDARE ROAD) HALT	[MR&CC]	554
1344	PONTYPOOL (CLARENCE STREET)	[NA&HR]	470
1601	PONTYPOOL (CRANE STREET)	[MR&CC]	554
839	PONTYPOOL ROAD	[NA&HR]	306
1457	PONTYPRIDD	[TVR]	507
1396	PONTYRHYLL	[OVR]	486,7
1094	POOL QUAY	[O&NR]	388
1465	PORTH	[TVR]	510
1384	PORTHCAWL	[LVR]	482,3
1118	PORTHYWAEN	[TVLR]	395
1044	PORTMADOC	[A&WCR]	372
1167	PORTSKEWETT	[SWR]	411
744	PORT SUNLIGHT	[C&BR]	275
1381	*PORT TALBOT (CENTRAL)*	*[PTR&D]*	*482*
1185	PORT TALBOT (GENERAL)	[SWR]	418
904	PRESTEIGN	[L&KR]	326,7
865	PRESTHOPE	[MWCA&CR]	314
1219	PUNCHESTON	[R&FR]	431
1038	PWLLHELI	[CAMRLY]	370
1184	PYLE	[SWR]	417,8

No.	STATION NAME	RAILWAY	PAGE	No.	STATION NAME	RAILWAY	PAGE
				913	STOKE PRIOR HALT	[L&BR]	329
				887	STOURPORT-ON-SEVERN	[SVR]	321
	[Q]			1263	STRATA FLORIDA	[M&MR]	444
1333	QUAKERS YARD (H.L.)	[NA&HR]	466	918	SUCKLEY	[WB&LR]	331
1459	QUAKERS YARD (L.L.)	[TVR]	508	1437	SULLY	[CP&BJR]	500.1
	Queen Street, see Cardiff (Queen Street)			1035	SUN BANK HALT	[VLR]	369
				1438	SWANBRIDGE HALT	[CP&BJR]	501
	[R]			1191	SWANSEA (HIGH STREET)	[SWR]	420
1453	RADYR	[TVR]	506	954	SYMONDS YAT	[R&MR]	343
959	RAGLAN	[CMU&PR]	344				
960	RAGLAN ROAD CROSSING HALT	[CMU&PR]	345		**[T]**		
988	REDBROOK-ON-WYE	[WVR]	354				
770	REDNAL & WEST FELTON	[SO&CJR]	284	1531	TAFF MERTHYR COLLIERY HALT	[GW&RJR]	532
1321	RESOLVEN	[VNR]	463	1454	TAFFS WELL	[TVR]	506
1143	RHAYADER	[MWR]	403	1082	TALERDDIG	[N&MR]	384
1325	RHIGOS HALT	[VNR]	464	1155	TALGARTH	[MWR]	407
1492	RHIWBINA HALT	[CardRly]	519	1298	TALLEY ROAD HALT	[VTRJ]	455
1537	RHIWDERIN	[B&MR]	534	1048	TALSARNAU	[A&WCR]	373
1425	RHOOSE	[VofGR]	496	1271	TALSARN HALT	[LA&NQ]	446
783	RHOS	[SUR&CC]	288	1053	TALWRN BACH HALT	[A&WCR]	374
757	RHOSROBIN HALT	[NWMR]	280	1055	TALYBONT HALT	[A&WCR]	375
781	RHOSTYLLEN	[GWR]	288	1563	TALYBONT-ON-USK	[B&MR]	541
762	RHOSYMEDRE HALT	[SO&CJR]	282	1564	TALYLLYN JUNCTION	[B&MR]	542
1224	RHYDOWEN	[W&TVR]	432	1009	TEIGL HALT	[F&BR]	360
1516	RHYDYFELIN HALT	[PC&NR]	527	1232	TEMPLETON	[P&TR]	435
1510	RHYMNEY	[RR]	525	893	TENBURY WELLS	[TJ]	323
1511	RHYMNEY BRIDGE	[LNW&RJR]	526	1235	TENBY	[P&TR]	435
1575	RISCA	[MR&CC]	546	792	TERN HILL	[W&DR]	291
1478	ROBERTSTOWN HALT	[TVR]	515	1154	THREE COCKS JUNCTION	[MWR]	406,7
742	ROCK FERRY	[C&BR]	275	736	THURSTASTON	[GW&LNWJ]	273
1573	ROGERSTONE	[MR&CC]	545	996	TIDENHAM	[WVR]	355
1218	ROSEBUSH	[NR&MR]	430	1101	TINKERS GREEN HALT	[OE&WR]	390
755	ROSSETT	[NWMR]	279	994	TINTERN	[WVR]	355
946	ROSS-ON-WYE	[HR&GR]	340	1150	TIRCELYN HALT	[MWR]	405
916	ROWDEN MILL	[L&BR]	330	1508	TIR PHIL	[RR]	524
787	ROWTON HALT	[W&DR]	290	1293	TIRYDAIL	[LR]	453
761	RUABON	[NWMR]	281	898	TITLEY	[L&KR]	325
868	RUSHBURY	[MWCA&CR]	315	1387	TONDU	[LVR]	483,4
931	RUSHWICK HALT	[W&HR]	335	1062	TONFANAU	[A&WCR]	377
971	RUSPIDGE HALT	[SWR]	348	1434	TONTEG HALT	[BR],[GWR]	499
				1467	TONYPANDY & TREALAW	[TVR]	511
	[S]			1408	TONYREFAIL	[EVR]	490,1
				1561	TORPANTAU	[B&MR]	541
1422	ST. ATHAN	[VofGR]	495	1063	TOWYN	[A&WCR]	377
991	ST. BRIAVELS	[WVR]	354	830	TRAM INN	[NA&HR]	303
1202	ST. CLEARS	[SWR]	424	1265	TRAWSCOED	[M&MR]	444
831	ST. DEVEREUX	[NA&HR]	304	1005	TRAWSFYNYDD	[B&FR]	358
1177	ST. FAGANS	[SWR]	415	1006	TRAWSFYNYDD LAKE HALT	[B&FR]	359
1141	ST. HARMONS	[MWR]	403	1328	TRECYNON HALT	[VNR]	465
753	SALTNEY	[NWMR]	279	1156	TREFEINON	[MWR]	407
1201	SARNAU	[SWR]	424	1456	TREFOREST	[TVR]	507
1234	SAUNDERSFOOT	[P&TR]	435	1455	TREFOREST ESTATE	[TVR]	506
1087	SCAFELL	[L&NR]	386	1517	TREFOREST HALT	[PC&NR]	527
1598	SEBASTOPOL	[MR&CC]	553	1261	TREGARON	[M&MR]	443
1525	SENGHENYDD	[RR]	530	1464	TREHAFOD	[TVR]	510
1114	SESSWICK HALT	[W&ER]	394	1334	TREHARRIS	[NA&HR]	467
1354	SEVEN SISTERS	[N&BR]	473	1471	TREHERBERT	[TVR]	512
979	SEVERN BRIDGE	[SBR]	351	766	TREHOWELL HALT	[SO&CJR]	283
1169	SEVERN TUNNEL JUNCTION	[SWR]	411	1335	TRELEWIS HALT	[NA&HR]	467
980	SHARPNESS	[SBR]	351	1530	TRELEWIS PLATFORM	[GW&RJR]	531
805	SHIFNAL	[S&BR]	295	1182	TREMAINS HALT	[SWR]	416
776	SHREWSBURY	[SO&CJR, S&HR]	286	1109	TRENCH HALT	[W&ER]	393
				1470	TREORCHY	[TVR]	512
1269	SILIAN HALT	[LA&NQ]	445	1340	TREOWEN HALT	[NA&HR]	469
1585	SIX BELLS HALT	[MR&CC]	549	1416	TRERHYNGYLL & MAENDY	[CR]	493
1188	SKEWEN	[SWR]	419	1540	TRETHOMAS	[B&MR]	535
1603	SNATCHWOOD HALT	[MR&CC]	555	1036	TREVOR	[VLR]	369
1418	SOUTHERNDOWN ROAD	[VofGR]	494	1282	TRIMSARAN ROAD	[BP&GVR]	449
1379	SOUTH PIT HALT	[SWMR]	481	1389	TROEDYRHIEW GARTH	[LVR]	484
974	SPEECH HOUSE ROAD	[S&WR]	349	1461	TROEDYRHIW	[TVR]	509
745	SPITAL	[C&BR]	276	1528	TROEDYRHIW HALT	[GW&RJR]	531
729	STANLOW & THORNTON	[BirkRly]	271	1165	TUTSHILL HALT	[SWR]	410
900	STANNER HALT	[K&ER]	325	1277	TYCOCH HALT	[BP&GVR]	448
772	STANWARDINE HALT	[SO&CJR]	284	999	TYDDYN BRIDGE HALT	[B&FR]	356,7
970	STAPLE EDGE HALT	[SWR]	348	1049	TYGWYN HALT	[A&WCR]	373
914	STEENS BRIDGE	[L&BR]	330	1593	TYLLWYN HALT	[MR&CC]	552
922	STOKE EDITH	[W&HR]	332	1473	TYLORSTOWN	[TVR]	513

No.	STATION NAME	RAILWAY	PAGE
1138	TYLWCH	[MWR]	402
1574	TYNYCWM HALT	[MR&CC]	546

[U]

1170	UNDY HALT	[SWR]	412
1514	UPPER BOAT HALT	[PC&NR]	527
983	UPPER LYDBROOK	[S&WR]	352
1596	UPPER PONTNEWYDD	[MR&CC]	553
969	UPPER SOUDLEY HALT	[SWR]	347
751	UPTON-BY-CHESTER HALT	[C&BR]	278
799	UPTON MAGNA	[S&BR]	293
962	USK	[CMU&PR]	345

[V]

1592	VICTORIA	[MR&CC]	551
907	VOWCHURCH	[GVR]	328

[W]

1608	*WAINFELIN HALT*	*[MR&CC]*	*556*
800	WALCOT	[S&BR]	293
951	WALFORD HALT	[R&MR]	342
1519	WATERLOO HALT	[B&MR]	528
802	WELLINGTON (SALOP.)	[S&BR]	294
1105	WELSHAMPTON	[OE&WR]	392
1211	WELSH HOOK HALT	[GWR]	428
1092	WELSHPOOL	[O&NR]	387
1431	WENVOE	[BR]	498
963	*WERH HIR*	*[CMU&PR]*	*345*
	West Access Halt, see Glascoed Factory		
	West Access Halt		
910	WESTBROOK	[GVR]	328
846	WESTBURY (SALOP.)	[S&WPoolJ]	308
1160	WESTBURY-ON-SEVERN HALT	[SWR]	408
739	WEST KIRBY	[GW&LNWJ]	274
767	WESTON RHYN	[SO&CJR]	283
947	WESTON-UNDER-PENYARD HALT	[HR&GR]	340
864	WESTWOOD HALT	[MWCA&CR]	314
1493	WHITCHURCH (GLAM.)	[CardRly]	519
990	WHITEBROOK HALT	[WVR]	354
976	WHITECROFT	[S&WR]	350
1520	WHITE HART HALT	[B&MR], [PC&NR]	528
764	WHITEHURST	[SO&CJR]	282
1203	WHITLAND	[SWR]	425
1102	WHITTINGTON (H.L.)	[OE&WR]	391
769	WHITTINGTON (L.L.)	[SO&CJR]	284
1524	WINDSOR COLLIERY HALT	[RR]	530
818	WISTANSTOW HALT	[S&HR]	299
921	WITHINGTON	[W&HR]	332
1017	WNION HALT	[B&DR]	363
1210	WOLFS CASTLE HALT	[GWR]	428
791	WOLLERTON HALT	[W&DR]	291
823	WOOFFERTON	[S&HR]	300,1
1164	WOOLASTON	[SWR]	410
934	WORCESTER (FOREGATE STREET)	[W&HR]	336
758	WREXHAM	[NWMR]	280,1
1117	WREXHAM CENTRAL	[W&ER]	395
987	WYESHAM HALT	[CMU&PR]	353
1403	WYNDHAM HALT	[OVR]	489
760	WYNNVILLE HALT	[NWMR]	281
889	WYRE FOREST	[T&BR]	322

[Y]

1472	YNYSHIR	[TVR]	513
1075	YNYSLAS	[A&WCR]	382
1479	YNYSYBWL	[TVR]	515
1477	YNYSYBWL (NEW ROAD) HALT	[TVR]	515
845	YOCKLETON	[S&WPoolJ]	308
1366	YSTRADGYNLAIS	[SV&N&BJR]	476
1502	YSTRAD MYNACH	[RR]	522,3
1415	YSTRADOWEN	[CR]	493
1469	YSTRAD (RHONDDA)	[TVR]	512

APPENDIX E
LIST OF PHOTOGRAPHERS
(ALPHABETICAL)

CAPTION	DISTRIBUTOR / PHOTOGRAPHER
A.Attewell	Austin Attewell
Audie Baker	Kidderminster Railway Museum
J.Beardsmore	John Beardsmore, Tony Jones Collection
J.M.Bentley	Mike Bentley
F.A.Blencowe	R. K. Blencowe
R.K.Blencowe	R. K. Blencowe
S.V.Blencowe	Stewart Blencowe Collection
W.A.Brown	Jeremy Suter
C.L.Caddy	Colin Caddy
W.A.Camwell	The Stephenson Locomotive Society Collection
R.Carpenter	Roger Carpenter
H.C.Casserley	R. M. Casserley
R.M.Casserley	R. M. Casserley
T.C.Cole	Terry Cole Collection
P.Coutanche	Phil Coutanche
J.D.Darby	Jeremy Suter
Hugh Davies	Hugh Davies, Photos from the Fifties
R.Dyer	Mike Bentley
N.Forrest	The Transport Treasury (www.transporttreasury.co.uk)
John Gale	John Gale
P.Garland	Roger Carpenter
E.T.Gill	R. K. Blencowe
R.Grant	Kidderminster Railway Museum
M.Hale	The Great Western Trust
HMRS (reference)	The Historical Model Railway Society
B.Johnson	Roger Carpenter
D.K.Jones	D. K. Jones
P.Kingston	Patrick Kingston
D.Lawrence	Hugh Davies, Photos from the Fifties
LOSA	Lens of Sutton Association (Terry Walsh)
R.J.Leonard	Kidderminster Railway Museum
M.J.Lewis	M. J. Lewis, Don Powell Collection, Kidderminster Railway Museum
L&GRP	Locomotive & General Railway Photographs
A.W.Mace	Milepost 92½
J.Maden Collection	Jon Maden
J.Marshall	Kidderminster Railway Museum
M.M.Lloyd	Mike Morton Lloyd, Welsh Railways Research Circle
Joe Moss	Roger Carpenter
C.Mowat	Brunel University Mowat Collection, (W.R.Burton, 3 Fairway, Clifton, York, YO30 5QA)
R.G.Nelson	Roger Carpenter
J.E.Norris	The Transport Treasury (www.transporttreasury.co.uk)
G.Parker	Kidderminster Railway Museum
S.C.Philips	D. K. Jones
W.Potter	Kidderminster Railway Museum
H.B.Priestley	Milepost 92½
R.C.Riley	The Transport Treasury (www.transporttreasury.co.uk)
P.Rutherford	
R.G.Simmonds	R. G. Simmonds Collection
N.C.Simmons	Hugh Davies, Photos from the Fifties
Bill Smith	Bill Smith Collection, Kidderminster Railway Museum
R.J.Smith	Robin Smith
Stations U.K.	Stations U.K.
SLS Collection	The Stephenson Locomotive Society Collection
R.Stewartson	The Stephenson Locomotive Society Collection
J.Tarrant	Kidderminster Railway Museum
G.H.Tilt	Garth Tilt
C.H.Townley	C. H. Townley Collection, Industrial Railway Society
I.Travers	Jeremy Suter
unknown	Unknown photographer or distributor
V.R.Webster	Kidderminster Railway Museum
WRRC Collection	Welsh Railways Research Circle
P.B.Whitehouse	M. Whitehouse
D.Wittamore	Kidderminster Railway Museum
S.Wolstenholme	S. Wolstenholme
F.G.Wood	Kidderminster Railway Museum
F.A.Wycherley	Alan Wycherley